SANDMAN MYSTERY THEATRE

BOOK TWO

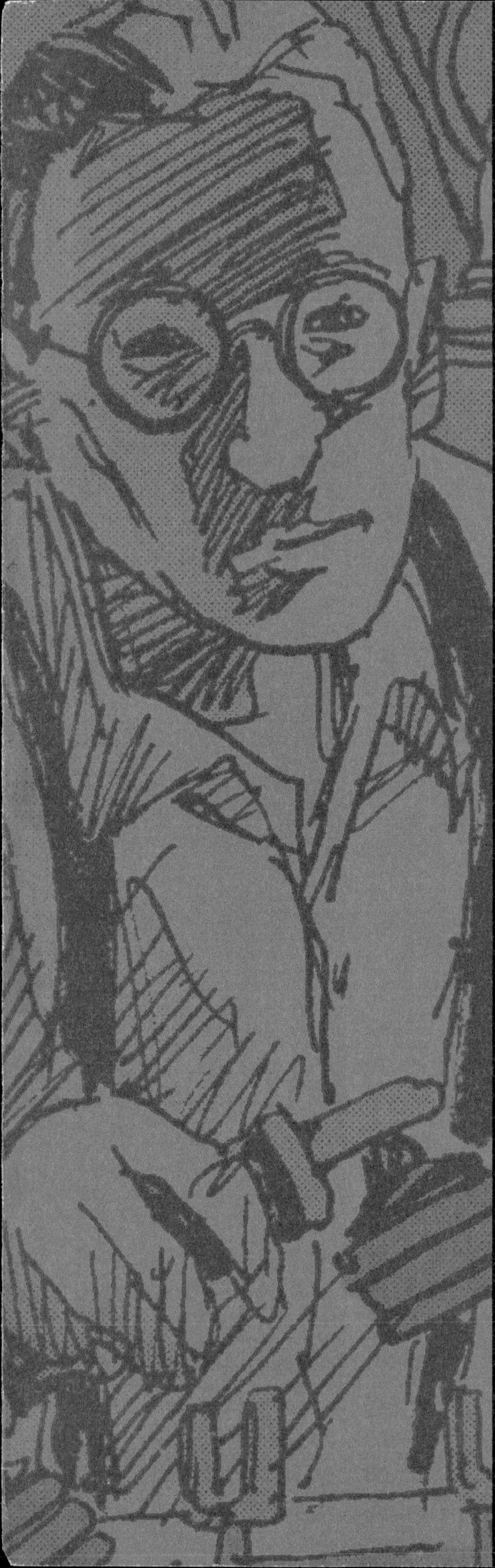

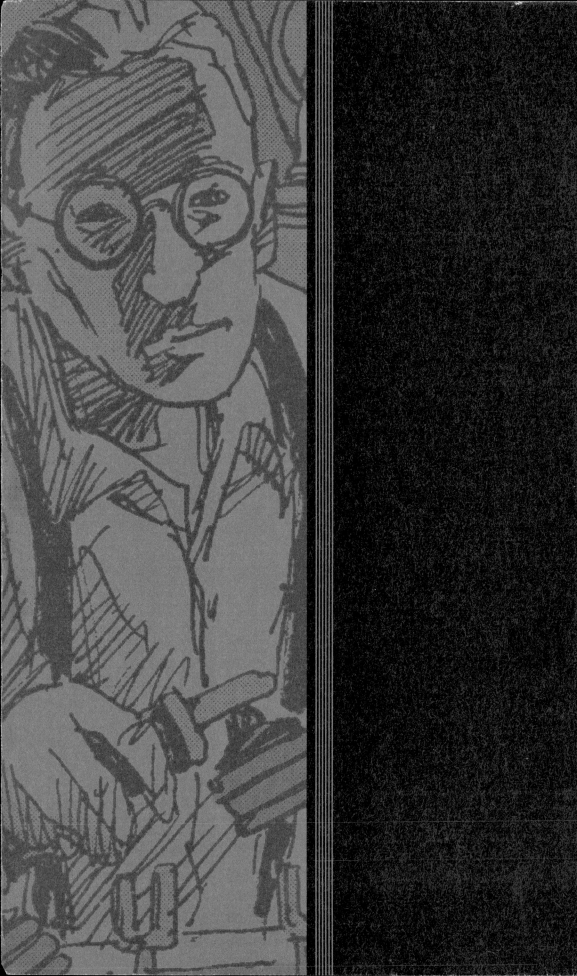

SANDMAN MYSTERY THEATRE

BOOK TWO

MATT WAGNER
STEVEN T. SEAGLE
WRITERS

GUY DAVIS
VINCE LOCKE
DAVID LLOYD
JOHN BOLTON
STEFANO GAUDIANO
GEORGE PRATT
ALEX ROSS
PETER SNEJBJERG
DEAN ORMSTON
ARTISTS

DAVID HORNUNG
DAVID LLOYD
MIKE DANZA
COLORISTS

JOHN COSTANZA
CLEM ROBINS
GASPAR SALADINO
LETTERERS

GAVIN WILSON
AND RICHARD BRUNING
COVER ART AND
ORIGINAL SERIES COVERS

THE SANDMAN/WESLEY DODDS
CREATED BY
GARDNER FOX

SANDMAN MYSTERY THEATRE BOOK TWO

Published by DC Comics. Compilation and all new material Copyright
© 2016 DC Comics. All Rights Reserved.

Originally published in single magazine form as SANDMAN MYSTERY
THEATRE 13-24 and SANDMAN MYSTERY THEATRE ANNUAL 1.
Copyright © 1994, 1995 DC Comics. All Rights Reserved. All characters,
their distinctive likenesses and related elements featured in this publication
are trademarks of DC Comics. VERTIGO is a trademark of DC Comics.
The stories, characters and incidents featured in this publication are entirely
fictional. DC Comics does not read or accept unsolicited submissions of
ideas, stories or artwork.

DC Comics, 2900 West Alameda Avenue, Burbank, CA 91505
Printed in the USA. First Printing. ISBN: 978-1-4012-6569-4

Library of Congress Cataloging-in-Publication Data is available.

Table of Contents

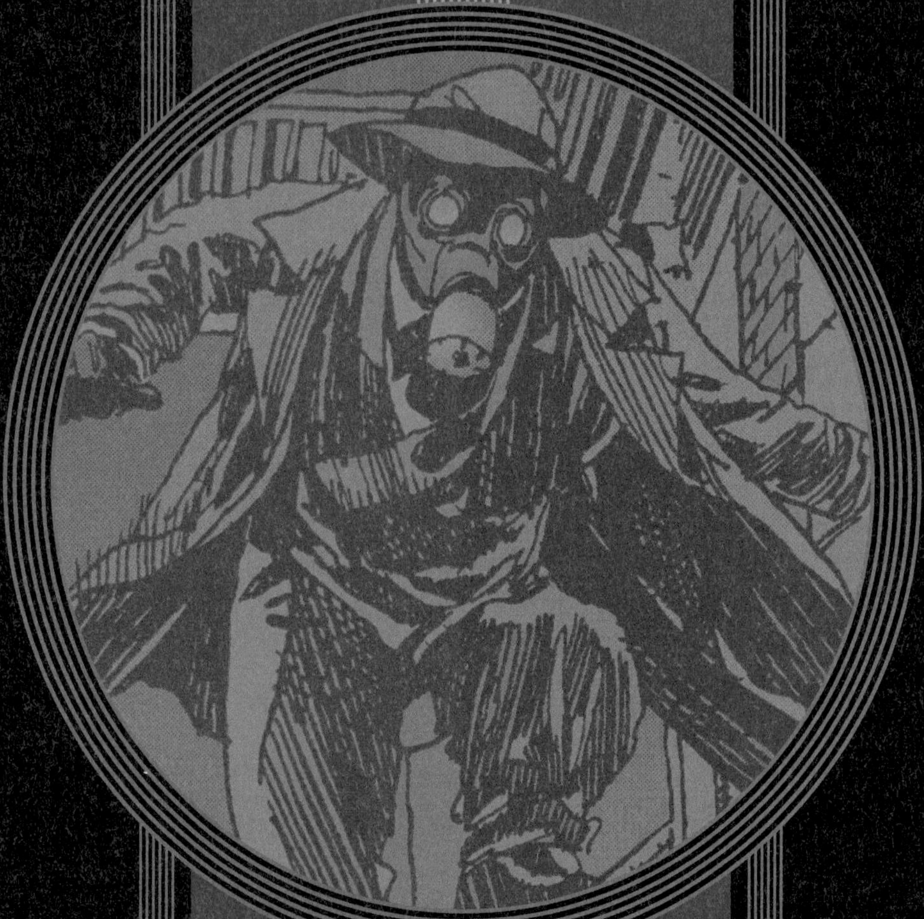

SANDMAN MYSTERY THEATRE

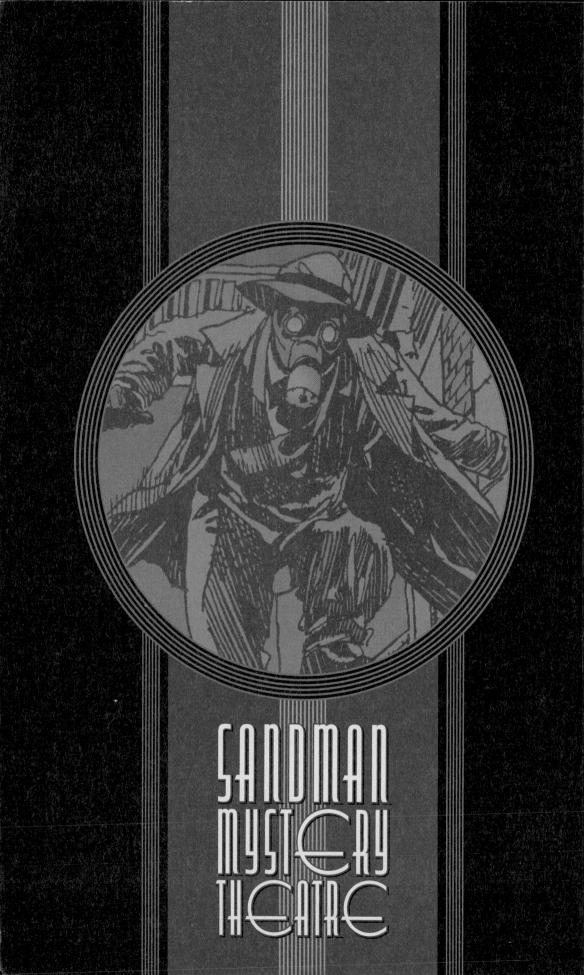

RTIGO

13
94
5 US
CAN
UK
ESTED
MATURE
ERS

matt wagner
steven t. seagle
guy davis

SANDMAN MYSTERY THEATRE

one of four

the vamp

GAVIN WILSON
RICHARD BRUNING

"You'd be so easy to kiss,
so easy to press my lips to,
so close to perfect bliss..."

THE VAMP

♪--you made me fall for you although I didn't want you to--♪

MMMM--

MMMMM--

MMM-OW

YOU'RE... YOU'RE REALLY--

I KNOW. TAKE OFF YOUR CLOTHES, BLONDIE.

I MUST SAY, I LIKE A FORWARD WOMAN. OF COURSE, I DON'T USUALLY--

I DO.

YOU KNOW, YOU HAVE BEAUTIFUL BREAS--

YES, NOW WHY DON'T YOU STOP *LOOKING* AND TRY THEM?

MY PLEASUR--

UHH UH. ME ON TOP. I LIKE TO SEE WHAT I'M WORKING ON.

MMMMMMMM...

OH? DOES THIS FEEL GOOD?

OH YEAH, I REALLY LIKE A WOMAN WHO CAN HOLD ME DOWN LIKE--

HOW FUNNY YOU SHOULD SAY THAT.

WHAT DO YOU MEA--

HEY! WHAT THE HELL IS THIS? I--

IT'S THE *END*, PRETTY BOY.

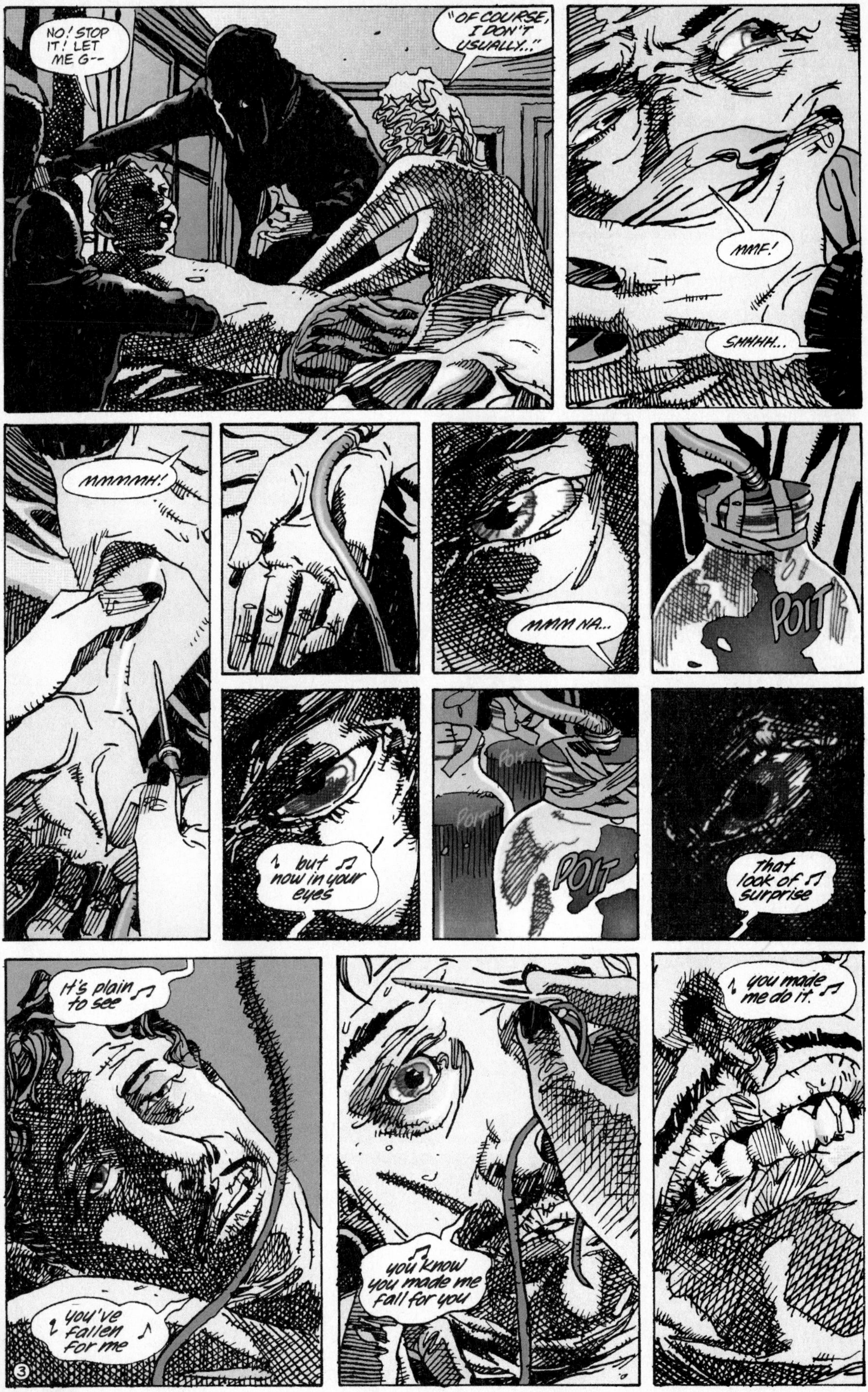
NO! STOP IT! LET ME G--
"OF COURSE, I DON'T USUALLY..."
MMF!
SHHHH...
MMMMMH!
MMM NA...
POIT
♪ but ♫ now in your eyes
POIT
POIT
POIT
that look of ♫ surprise
It's plain to see ♫
♪ you've fallen for me ♪
♫ you know you made me fall for you
♪ you made me do it. ♫

THE VAMP
ACT ONE

MATT WAGNER   **STEVEN T. SEAGLE**
WRITERS

GUY DAVIS   **DAVID HORNUNG**
ARTIST   COLORIST

JOHN COSTANZA   **ANDROID IMAGES**
LETTERER   SEPARATOR

SHELLY ROEBERG   **KAREN BERGER**
ASST. EDITOR   EDITOR

Mother used to tell me, "WHAT DADDY DOESN'T KNOW WON'T HURT HIM!"

AND MO'S OUT THERE, RIGHT?

YEAH.

It especially comes to mind on the nights when I sneak out to the HARLEM clubs with my old college friends.

--SO I SAID, "I DON'T WANT YA TO MOVE THAT HAND OFF, I WANT THE OTHER ONE-- WELL, WELL! LOOK WHO'S HERE!"

DIAN! HI!

HI, TRUDIE! CAROL. BETSY.

WE DIDN'T EXPECT TO SEE YOU HERE TONIGHT.

LAST WE HEARD YOU WERE INSEPARABLE FROM THAT CHARLIE CHAN BOYFRIEND OF YOURS.

YEAH, WHERE IS YOUR LITTLE "FORTUNE COOKIE"?

④

12

YEAH, NO, IT'S *WAY* UPTOWN--

CLUB VOO DOO

While I don't remember everything mother said, it seems that as I get older, I remember this particular phrase much more often than I ought to.

ACTUALLY, WE'RE NOT ONLY SEPARABLE, WE'RE COMPLETELY SEPARATED FOR NOW. AND...THERE'S SOMEONE *NEW* IN MY SOCIAL REGISTER.

AND WE THOUGHT *JIMMY* WAS AN OPERATOR!

EXCUSE ME, GALS. BACK IN A FLASH.

AND WHO IS THIS NEW CASANOVA? DO WE KNOW HIM? IS IT DENNIS HAMPTON?

DON'T BE *SILLY!* OF *COURSE* IT'S NOT DENNIS, AND NO, YOU *DON'T* KNOW HIM. AND NO, I WON'T TELL YOU ANYTH--

SORRY TO INTERRUPT, GIRLS, BUT HOW WOULD MY THREE CLOSE FRIENDS LIKE TO TRY SOMETHING A LITTLE--

"DARING?"

13

RIGHT THIS WAY, LADIES.

SHOULD WE EVEN BE OUT HERE--

OH, SHUT UP, TRUDIE.

HIYA, BERNIE!

I'M TELLIN' YA, BERNIE, HE WAS HITTIN' NOTES THAT AIN'T EVEN ON THE DAMN HORN!

WHOZZAT?

DON'T WORRY, FELLAS. I KNOW THESE BIRDS.

WE WERE GETTING A LITTLE HOT IN THE CLUB AND CAME OUT FOR A COOL-DOWN!

MIND IF WE TRY A LITTLE OF YOUR MUGGLE? WE REALLY LOVED YOUR JAZZ, BERNIE!

HIS JAZZ?

D'WHITE PART AT LEAST--

UH-HUH.

NOW TAKE IT EASY ON THAT REEFER, LADIES, IT'S MIGHTY STRONG--

DON'T WORRY, BERNIE. WE CAN HANDLE IT. WE CAN HANDLE ANYTHING! WHO'S FIRST...DIAN?

OKAY!

HOW IS IT?

DIFFERENT. IT'S... THICKER.

AH-HUCKK HUCKK HUCKK!

AH HUCKK HUCKK HUCKK!

HAHAHA! WHAT'S THE MATTER? NEVER SMOKED BEFORE? WATCH A PRO--

AH HUCKK HUCKK, HUCKK!

6

14

HIS--HIZ--HIZZIPPER! HA!

HEE HEE HEE!

HA HA HA HA!

HEE HEE!

HA HA!

OOOHHHH... ARE WE DOPEY?

WE ARE DOPED, HA!

HEY!

HUH?

WHERE THE HELL DID BETSY GO?

UHHH, SHE--

OH MY GOD! THERE SHE IS!

LOOK AT HER. SHE'S JITTERBUGGING!

WHEN DID SHE GET SO DARK?

CAROL! THAT'S A VERY RUDE THING TO SAY.

WHAT? IT'S TRUE, ISN'T IT?

WELL, NO, BUT IT'S...IT'S--

WHAT?

I DON'T REMEMBER. WHAT WERE WE TALKING ABOUT?

7

WHO KNOWS? WHO CARES?

I FEEL SO DIZZY! THIS IS A LOT DIFFERENT FROM JIMMY'S OPIUM PIPES.

HMMMM...

OKAY.

OH, LET'S NOT RUIN THIS EVENING BY BRINGING HIM UP AGAIN.

I LIKE YOU, DIAN. I'VE ALWAYS LIKED YOU.

OH WELL, TIME TO HIT THE SACK. SHARE A CAB?

UH... NO THANKS. I'M GOING TO... WIND DOWN A LITTLE.

Alone.

OH, DIAN-- YOU'RE HOME. GOOD. IT'S AWFULLY LATE. WHERE WERE YOU?

Funny, a little bit of reefer hours ago and I'm still dizzy and confused. Sure hope Daddy isn't waiting up.

I WAS JUST OUT WITH SOME--

LISTEN, THERE'S BEEN A MURDER. I'VE GOT TO GET DOWN TO THE STATION.

UH-HUH.

ARE YOU OKAY? YOU LOOK--

I'M FINE.

WELL, ANYWAY, LOCK THE DOOR AFTER I LEAVE.

THIS KILLER, WHOEVER IT IS, IS BRUTAL. DID TERRIBLE THINGS TO SOME BOY I THINK YOU KNEW IN COLLEGE... UH... TREVOR... BARNES?

DID--DID YOU SAY TREVOR BARNES IS... DEAD?

DEAD AS DIRT. OH, THAT REMINDS ME. WESLEY DODDS CALLED FOR YOU EARLIER. GOT TO RUN. LOCK THE DOOR, SWEETHEART.

Wesley called? Why, that's so--

9

17

SO...SO...

SEWN?

SEWN SHUT.

HIS MOUTH WAS SEWN SHUT?

NOT *JUST* HIS MOUTH, LARRY. KEEP READING.

"MOUTH, NOSE, AND...URETHRA ALL SEWN..."

SEWED HIS DICK SHUT. KINDA MAKES YA FLINCH A LITTLE, HUH, BELMONT?

"VICTIM HAD LESS THAN 10% OF NATURAL BLOOD SUPPLY. MULTIPLE PUNCTURE WOUNDS SUGGEST CATHETER-STYLE DRAINING AIDED BY POSSIBLE SUCTIONING--"

AND IT GETS BETTER, TOO. TRACES FROM THE KID'S PENIS INDICATE THAT HE WAS HAVING A LITTLE HOOTCHIE AROUND THE TIME HE WAS KILLED.

CRIME OF PASSION?

PASSION? SOUNDS TO ME LIKE SOMEBODY REALLY *HATED* THIS POOR BASTARD. I WOULDN'T CALL IT PASSION.

"LET'S START RUNNING DOWN SOME OF THE FRIENDS OF TREVOR BARNES."

"SEE WHERE THAT TAKES US."

10

I can't believe I slept so late this morning. Must be a hangover from the smoking we did. Still might make it to Carol's in time, though, if I can just get out the door.

DONG DONG DONG

DIAN!

WESLEY! HELLO!

MWAH!

I'M JUST HEADING OUT.

I WAS JUST IN THE NEIGHBORHOOD AND THOUGHT--

SO SORRY I DIDN'T CALL YOU BACK, I GOT IN RATHER-- UH, LATE.

THAT'S ALL RIGHT. I WAS JUST IN THE NEIGHBORHOOD AND THOUGHT I'D OFFER YOU A LUNCH IF YOU'RE FREE.

OH, YOU'RE SO SWEET, REALLY, BUT I HAVE A FORMER ENGAGEMENT. I'M ACTUALLY RUNNING LATE BECAUSE I WAS OUT AT CLUB VOODOO LAST NIGHT.

CLUB VOODOO? ISN'T THAT NEIGHBORHOOD A BIT ROUGH?

IT WAS FINE. IN FACT, IT WAS A WILD NIGHT.

REALLY? HOW SO?

WELL...I'M NOT SURE I SHOULD EVEN TELL YOU THIS, BUT I AND THE OTHER GIRLS EXPERIMENTED WITH A MARIJUANA CIGARETTE!

OH YES, TRIED IT MYSELF SEVERAL TIMES IN MY YOUNGER DAYS.

YOU? BUT YOU DON'T EVEN LIKE ALCOHOL.

TRUE, BUT THE FACT THAT I DON'T LIKE IT DOESN'T MEAN I HAVEN'T TRIED IT.

OH! I'M LATER THAN I THOUGHT. I'VE GOT TO GET ALONG. SORRY ABOUT THE LUNCH OFFER.

WHY BE SORRY? LET'S JUST MAKE IT A DINNER OFFER. AROUND EIGHT?

sigh

TERRIFIC! 'BYE!

11

BONG BONG

OH, DIAN...

CAROL, HI!

WHAT BRINGS YOU UPTOWN?

Last night with Carol was a little... strange. Still, I hope I didn't do anything to discourage her from working with me on the United Way.

WELL...WE *HAD* AGREED LAST NIGHT TO MEET AND DISCUSS THE UNITED WAY FUND DRIVE TODAY.

AT LEAST, I *THINK* I REMEMBER US DOING THAT. IT'S ALL A LITTLE SMOKY, BUT--

CAROL? I DIDN'T KNOW YOU WERE EXPECTING SOME-ONE.

PLEASE... COME IN.

IF YOU HAVE COMPANY I COULD COME BACK ANOTHER TIME--

NO, REALLY.

DO YOU REMEMBER--

MADELINE? MADELINE GILES? I'M DIAN BELMONT. DO YOU REMEMBER ME FROM VASSAR? I WAS ONLY A SOPHOMORE BUT I--

OF COURSE I REMEMBER YOU, DIAN. HOW COULD I FORGET SUCH A PRETTY FACE?

12

PLEASE, HAVE A SEAT, DIAN.

THANKS.

MADELINE? YOU'RE WELCOME TO JOIN--

NO, I HATE TO INTERRUPT THINGS. I'LL KEEP MYSELF BUSY.

SO ANYWAY, CAROL, IT FINALLY HIT ME -- WHAT WE CAN DO AS THE UNITED WAY FUND-RAISING ACTIVITY. WE'LL HOLD A BAZAAR! WE CAN CALL IT THE SPRING FLI--

THEY CAN REALLY BE A CRUSHING BORE. MY MOTHER USED TO ORGANIZE THEM BACK IN NORFOLK. TEDIOUS.

OH...WELL...IT SEEMED LIKE IT MIGHT WORK, UH...

ANYWAY, CAROL, I'VE ALREADY LINED UP THE ELKS HALL FOR--

BUNCH OF PATHETIC DRUNKS, THAT CROWD.

I'VE GOT TO GO, CAROL. WILL YOU SEE ME OUT?

OH, UH, CERTAINLY. EXCUSE ME, DIAN.

WITH PLEASURE.

GOOD LUCK WITH YOUR CHARITY CASE, DIAN.

13

--YOU AGAIN LATER TONIGHT, BUT ALONE. I HAVE--

--SOME THINGS TO DISCUSS WITH YOU THAT ARE *VERY* IMPORTANT, BUT PRIVATE.

I'LL SEE YOU TONIGHT, CAROL.

SORRY ABOUT HER RUDENESS. MADELINE'S A DEAR, JUST A LITTLE HIGH-STRUNG. WOULD YOU CARE FOR A DRINK?

WELL, IT'S A LITTLE EARLY, BUT YES... A *DOUBLE* I THINK.

14

NO, *SERIOUSLY,* IT WAS HIS FATHER'S CAR! CAN YOU BELIEVE THAT?

EVENING, GENTLEMEN. LT. BURKE *N.Y.P.D.*

AND I SAID, "*I'M A WENTWORTH, I'LL PUT MY HAND WHERE I LIKE.*"

HOW CAN WE HELP YOU?

I NEED TO ASK YOU SOME QUESTIONS ABOUT A FORMER MEMBER, TREVOR BARNES.

POOR BASTARD, UNFORTU- NATE, REALLY.

WHAT DO YOU KNOW ABOUT HIM? WAS HE WELL-LIKED HERE IN THE CLUB?

WELL -LIKED? HARDLY. HE WAS LIKED, BUT HIS FATHER BOUGHT HIS WAY IN HERE. MEMBERS DON'T REALLY RESPECT THAT. BUT HE WASN'T *HATED,* AT LEAST, NOT ENOUGH TO BE DONE IN BY SOME BIRD LIKE THAT.

WHO SAID ANYTHING ABOUT A WOMAN?

OH, COME ON, LIEUTENANT. IT'S ALL OVER TOWN THAT HIS WOMANIZING FINALLY CAUGHT UP WITH HIM.

NO WOMAN COULD HAVE DONE WHAT WAS DONE TO BARNES. AT LEAST NOT ALONE. HE WAS--

UH--

15

...LIEUTENANT?

SAY, WHAT'S THAT WAITER'S PROBLEM? HE KEEPS STARING AT ME.

OH, HE'S PROBABLY JUST SURPRISED TO SEE YOU HERE. WE DON'T HAVE ANY ITALIANS IN THE CLUB.

I'M SICILIAN.

WELL, WHATEVER YOU ARE, WE DON'T HAVE ANY OF *THOSE* EITHER, AT LEAST I DON'T *THINK* WE DO.

EXCUSE ME.

SAY, FREDDIE! I'VE BEEN LOOKING ALL OVER FOR YOU, DID YOU HEAR ABOUT THE NEW DUESENBERG?

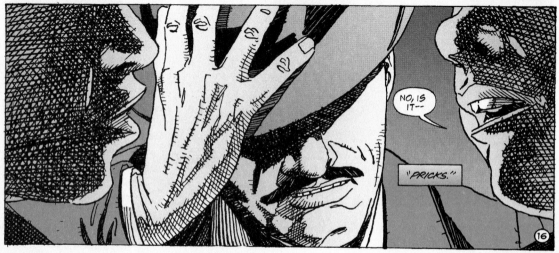

NO, IS IT--

"PRICKS."

16

NOW, I'VE HAD JUST ABOUT ENOUGH BULLSHIT AND ATTITUDE FOR ONE AFTERNOON, AND I SURE DON'T NEED ANY MORE FROM A LOW-LIFE LIKE YOU!

YOU SEE WHO COMES AND GOES IN THIS SHITHOLE.

SO YOU EITHER LOOSEN YOUR LIPS, OR I'LL LOOSEN 'EM FOR YOU.

BUT--BUT MR. BARNES, THE BOY'S FATHER, WILL KILL ME IF HE FINDS OUT I TALKED--

AND I'LL MAKE YOU WISH YOU WERE DEAD IF YOU DON'T TALK.

ALL RIGHT! ALL RIGHT! TREVOR CAME IN ALL THE TIME. EVERY WEEK ON THE SAME DAY.

USUALLY A DIFFERENT WOMAN EACH TIME--

BUT ALWAYS THAT SAME ROOM.

SO, YOU'RE SAYIN' PEOPLE MIGHT HAVE KNOWN TO EXPECT HIM?

SURE, BUT I DIDN'T LET ANYONE IN THERE! I SWEAR IT!

WE'LL SEE. I WANT THE NAMES OF ANY OF THESE WOMEN THAT YOU KNOW.

DORIS, YOU BETTER BE GLAD YOU DON' HAVE T' CLEAN THAT ONE UP, YESSSIREEE.

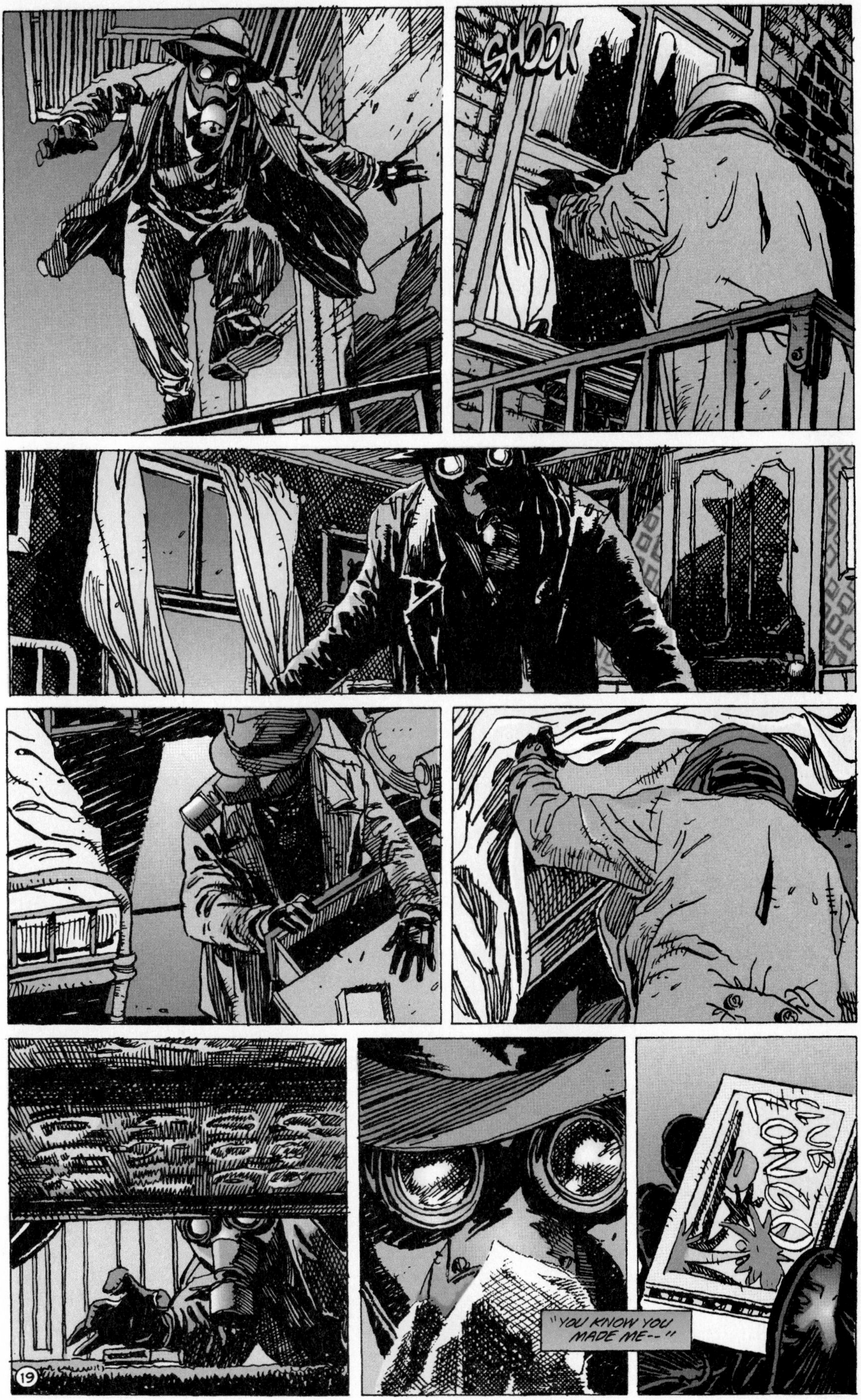
SHOOK
19
"YOU KNOW YOU MADE ME--"

"LOVE YOU."

"THANK YOU."

"AND LET'S HAVE A BIG ROUND OF APPLAUSE FOR THE SONG STYLINGS OF MISS MARGO FRANKLIN."

HERE YOU GO, MISS. THE HOUSE SPECIALT--

I DIDN'T ORDER THIS.

'S FROM THE GENNELMAN AT THE END OF TH' BAR.

THE "GENNELMAN" THAT FINDS YOU TO BE QUITE A LADY.

OH? TELL ME MORE, STRANGER. GOT ANYTHING BIGGER THAN A LINE TO OFFER A LADY?

THAT DEPENDS. WHAT WOULD YOU LIKE TO HEAR?

THE SOUND OF BEDSPRINGS NEEDING OIL.

20

TAP TAP
TAP TAP
TAP

WHAT? WHO THE HELL 'RE YOU?

LT. BURKE, POLICE. CAN I COME IN?

C'N DO WHAT-EVER TH' HELL YA *WANNA* DO. WHAT'M I GONNA DO? STOP TH' *GODDAMN* POLICE?

I WAS GIVEN YOUR NAME BY A HOTEL OWNER WHO SAID YOU KNEW TREVOR BARNES.

SURE I KNEW 'IM.

HOW WELL?

I BANGED HIM A COUPLE A' TIMES. THAT WHAT YA WANNA HEAR?

ONLY IF MY WEEK WAS *REALLY* BAD. DID YOU *KILL* TREVOR BARNES?

KILL 'IM? YOU-- YOU!

THANKS FOR YOUR TIME, MISS. I THINK I'VE SEEN ALL I NEED HERE. AIM LIKE THAT COUPLED WITH A WEEK-LONG DRUNK LIKE THAT -- YOU COULDN'T KILL A COCKROACH.

21

HERE YOU ARE, A WONDERFUL VIEW OF THE CONGO DANCERS.

Wesley can be so stiff sometimes, and then, out of the blue he'll choose an exotic place like Club Congo for no real reason. He's so alluring.

OUR SPECIAL TONIGHT IS THE--

WE'LL HAVE THE SPECIAL. THAT'S FINE. THANK YOU.

WES, YOU'RE SO--SO IMPETUOUS TONIGHT.

DOES THAT BOTHER YOU?

NO, IT'S JUST SO UNLIKE YOU.

PERHAPS IT'S THE COMPANY I KEEP. BRINGS OUT THE "WILD" SIDE IN ME.

I'M LEARNING SO MUCH ABOUT YOU THAT I NEVER KNEW. IT'S... INTRIGUING.

WELL, I AM FULL OF SECRETS.

YOUR WATERS.

22

FULL OF SECRETS?

YOU BET.

TELL ME ONE, THEN.

WELL...UH, LET'S SEE. I DON'T KNOW QUITE HOW TO TELL YOU THIS, BUT... SOMETIMES AT NIGHT, I DRESS UP IN--IN--

IN NOTHING BUT MY UNDERGARMENTS AND I DANCE AROUND MY APARTMENT PRETENDING TO BE LOUIS ARMSTRONG.

YOU KNOW, YOU CAN BE SO CHARMING SOMETIMES. IT'S QUITE... DREAMY.

REALLY?

YES, KEEP IT UP AND I'LL HAVE TO FIND OUT ALL OF YOUR SECRETS.

23

DIAN!

HUH?

SOMEONE YOU KNOW?

UNFORTUNATELY.

WHAT A *DELIGHT* TO RUN INTO YOU AGAIN, DIAN, DARLING.

UH...YES, WELL--

AREN'T YOU GOING TO INTRODUCE ME TO YOUR DASHING COMPANION?

WESLEY DODDS, MISS...?

GILES, MADELINE. BUT YOU CAN CALL ME MADDY.

SO LONG AS YOU *DO* CALL ME, MR. DODDS.

PARDON MY RUDENESS, BUT YOU SEEM TO HAVE A SMALL SPOT OF PAINT -- OR... BLOOD, ON YOUR --

SO I HAVE. MUST BE A PAPER CUT. NAPKINS SHARP AS STEEL HERE AT THE CONGO.

WES.

MMM. ALL BETTER NOW, MR. DODDS?

matt wagner

steven t. seagle

guy davis

SANDMAN
MYSTERY
THEATRE

two of four

the
tramp

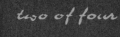

GAVIN WILSON
RICHARD BRUNING

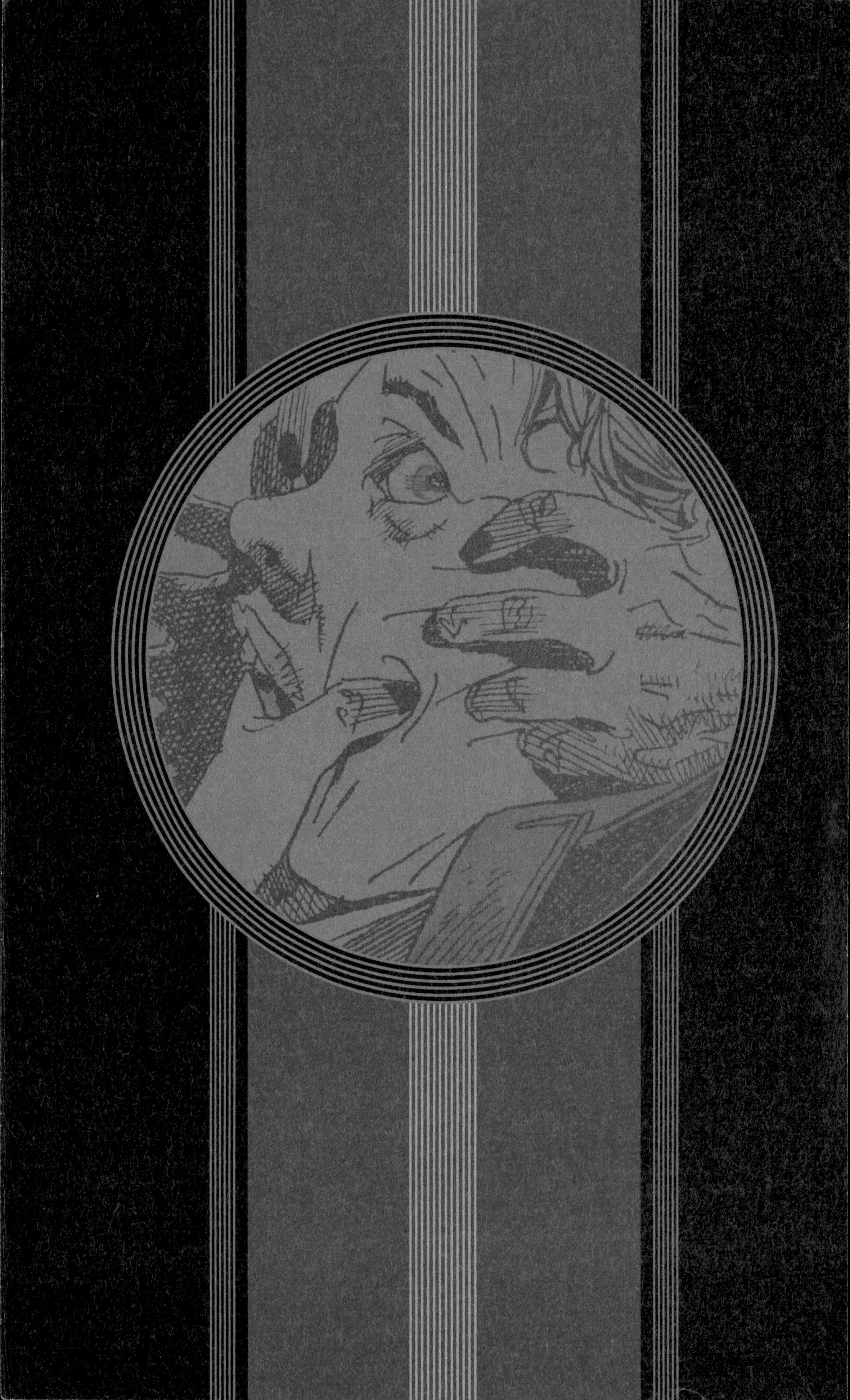

WELL... IT WAS CERTAINLY A PLEASURE TO MAKE YOUR ACQUAINTANCE, WESSY.

ACTUALLY, HE *PREFERS* "WESLEY," DON'T YOU, WESLEY?

HIM? OH... WESLEY, WES, WHATEVER YOU--

YES... WHATEVER INDEED. I'VE *GOT* TO BE RUNNING. AND A REAL PLEASURE SEEING *YOU* AGAIN, DIAN.

I'M SORRY ABOUT THAT, WESLEY. REALLY, I BARELY KNOW HER.

SORRY? I THOUGHT SHE WAS RATHER ENGAGING.

Engaging?!

PARDON ME FOR A MOMENT. I HAVE TO FIND THE WASHROOM.

Engaging! I can't believe he--such a beautiful evening ruined by that--that-- OOOOOH!

THE VAMP
ACT·TWO

MATT WAGNER **STEVEN T. SEAGLE**
WRITERS

GUY DAVIS **DAVID HORNUNG**
ARTIST COLORIST

JOHN COSTANZA **ANDROID IMAGES**
LETTERER SEPARATOR

SHELLY ROEBERG **KAREN BERGER**
ASST. EDITOR EDITOR

--UP TO ROOM 324, AND DON'T DROP THEM THIS TIME--

--*THERE* YOU ARE! I WAS BANGING ON YOUR DOOR FOR THE LAST--

-- THE MANAGER OF THE CONGO IS A *HER.* SALLY STARR.

OH? OH! OF COURSE... UH...

WHAT MESSAGE DID YOU WANT TO LEAVE HER?

OH, UH... TELL HER I... SEND MY REGARDS.

HM. CERTAINLY, MISTER...?

BILL. JUST BILL. SHE'LL KNOW.

MR. SAMUELS!

FRANKIE! I'VE TOLD YOU NOT TO INTER-RUPT WHEN I'M WITH A CUSTOMER.

THAT'S ALL RIGHT, I'M DONE. THANK YOU.

ALL RIGHT, THEN, WHAT IS IT?

SOMETHING REALLY BAD--

-- THERE'S A *DEAD* GUY UPSTAIRS.

EXCUSE ME?

YES? HOW CAN I HELP YOU?

I NEED TO LEAVE A MESSAGE FOR THE MANAGER OF THE CONGO. THE, *UH*, BARTENDER SAID THAT THE MANAGER PICKS UP HIS MESSAGES *HERE*.

YOU CAN LEAVE A MESSAGE, BUT NOT FOR *HIM*--

THERE YOU ARE! I'D BEGUN TO THINK YOU'D LEFT ME FOR "*ENGAGING MADDY.*"

DON'T BE SILLY, DIAN. I HARDLY NOTICED HER. SHE--WELL, THE REST ROOMS ARE QUITE A WALK FROM HERE, THAT'S ALL.

NO, THEY'RE NOT. I CAN SEE THE SIGN RIGHT OVER BY THE KITCHEN.

UH... WHY DON'T WE ORDER?

WE ALREADY DID.

OH, RIGHT. I MEANT... DRINKS.

Why would Wesley deliberately not tell me the truth? What is he trying to hide?

37

--NO. NOT *KNIFE* WOUNDS. MORE LIKE CATHETER PIERCINGS. BUT A WHOLE LOT OF THEM.

FOOSH

RUN THAT BY ME AGAIN, HUBERT.

OH, LIEUTENANT BURKE. YOU'RE HERE, GOOD. I THINK WE MAY HAVE ANOTHER ONE.

WHAT'S THE RUN-DOWN?

PUNCTURE WOUNDS LIKE THE BARNES BOY BUT A LOT MORE OF THEM.

AND THIS TIME, THEY LEFT HIS BLOOD IN THE SHEETS.

THE PENIS WAS *"ENGAGED"* JUST BEFORE DEATH ONCE AGAIN, BUT THERE IS NO THREAD, THOUGH THERE ARE MULTI-PLE PUNCTURES ON THE UPPER HALF.

ONLY *HALF,* HUH? LUCKY STIFF.

PLOIP

JUDGING FROM THE DEPTHS OF THESE PUNCTURE WOUNDS--

--I'D SAY THAT THEY WERE MADE WITH EXTREME FORCE.

UH, THANKS. ANY IDEA WHERE THE NEAREST PISSER IS?

DOWN THE HALL TO THE LEFT.

38

JESUS, THAT LITTLE GODDAMN KIKE GHOUL--

LIEUTENANT? BEFORE YOU HEAD OUT, WE FOUND *THESE* IN THE BATHROOM.

BLOODY TOWELS, HUH?

YES, SIR. SHOWER WAS RUN, TOO.

CLEANED THEMSELVES UP AND LEFT THE MESS FOR US. GREAT. I'M HEADIN' BACK TO THE STATION. KEEP ME POSTED AND KEEP THIS ROOM SEALED.

WELL!

'SCUSE ME, LADY.

OH! LIEUTENANT BURKE! LIEUTENANT BURKE!

C'MON, WES! *HE* CAN TELL US WHAT'S HAPPENED!

OH, MISS BELMONT. SORRY, I DON'T HAVE TIME TO TALK--

THIS IS WESLEY DODDS. WESLEY, LIEUTENANT BURKE WORKS WITH MY FATHER.

PLEASURE TO--

WHAT'S HAPPENED? WHY ARE THERE SO MANY POLICE OFFICERS?

MURDER.

YOU'LL HAVE TO EXCUSE ME, I WANNA TALK TO THE BARTENDER NEXT DOOR.

IS THE BARTENDER A SUSPECT?

NAH, THE VICTIM SMELLED LIKE A CHEAP GIN THE BAR SELLS. PLUS, HE APPEARED TO HAVE BEEN SCR-- UH-- IN THE *COMPANY* OF A LADY. EXCUSE ME.

HAVE A GOOD EVENING, LIEUTENANT... WELL.... I MEAN--

HM...

Who would think something like this would happen so close? I'm glad I have Wes to hang on to--

UM, DIAN? I HAVE TO BE GETTING HOME.

HOME? IT'S ONLY--

I KNOW. I HAVE AN EARLY APPOINTMENT TOMORROW AND SOME WORK TO FINISH UP.

TAXI!

OH... ALL RIGHT, I GUESS I--

GOODNIGHT, DIAN. I HAD A WONDERFUL TIME. REALLY, LET'S DO IT AGAIN AS SOON AS POSSIBLE.

AREN'T YOU RIDING WITH ME?

OH NO, MY PLACE IS OUT OF THE WAY. I'LL CATCH ANOTHER. GOODNIGHT, DIAN.

OKAY, DRIVER!

...NIGHT...

Well, don't think I can't tell what's going on here, Mr. Dodds. One look at "Maddy" and you want nothing more to do with plain old Dian. Fine. Have it your way. Men!

They only have one thing in mind.

Just like that damn Jimmy. Nothing but a bunch of lying, secretive--

--sneaks.

6

-- SORRY, OFFICER, BUT YER ASKIN' ME DID I SEE A GUY? SURE I SEEN A GUY. I SEE 'EM ALL THE TIME. I'M A *BARTENDER.* I SEE ALL SORTS. I DON'T REMEMBER ALL OF 'EM, THOUGH.

LOOK, I'M NOT ASKIN' YOU TO REMEMBER *ALL* OF 'EM. I'M ASKIN' ABOUT *ONE* BETWEEN ONE AND THREE HOURS AGO.

I JUS' DO MY JOB, OFFICER BURKE. YA KNOW? 'S NOT THAT I DON'T WANNA HELP YA OUT, 'S JUS' THAT I DON'T--

WAITTAMINUTE! YEAH, SURE! I DO REMEMBER THAT GUY YER TALKIN' ABOUT.

HE WAS IN ABOUT TWO HOURS AGO. HE WAS BUYIN' DRINKS FOR TH' VAMP.

THE WHO? WHO IS THE VAMP?

AH, SHE'S HARMLESS. A LITTLE LOOSE, MAYBE, BUT HARMLESS. COMES IN NOW AN' AGAIN. SOAKS FREE DRINKS OUTTA TH' REGULARS. WE JUS' CALL HER THE VAMP.

YOU KNOW HER REAL NAME?

NOPE.

WHAT'S SHE LOOK LIKE?

OH, YOU KNOW, LONGISH HAIR, AVERAGE HEIGHT, NICE LOOKS, WHAT YA CAN SEE OF 'EM--

GREAT. YOU'VE NARROWED IT DOWN TO ABOUT THREE-FOURTHS OF THE WOMEN ON THE ISLAND. WHAT ELSE?

YA KNOW... IT'S KINDA STRANGE, BUT SHE'S GOT THIS SMILE...

A SMILE?

YEAH, THIS SMILE THAT KINDA--

7

--KINDA--

--KINDA SUCKS YOU IN.

WHAT ARE YOU TALKIN' ABOUT?

HEY! HEY, YOU THERE! WHAT ARE YOU DOING THERE?

--A LITTLE LIKE LOUISE BROOKS, Y'KNOW--

HUH?

YOU GET AWAY FROM THERE!

CLAC CLAC CLAC

YOU'RE NOT SUPPOSED TO BE BACK HERE!

CONGO PROPERTY! YOU-- HUFF-- YOU COME BACK HERE-- PUFF--

YOU-- HUFF-- YOU BETTER NOT-- HUFF-- YOU-- AH--SHIT.

8

42

HOW WOULD MEN LIKE IT IF WOMEN WERE ALWAYS KEEPING TO THEMSELVES? HMH. THEY'D PROBABLY LOVE IT.

DIAN? WHY ARE YOU HOME SO EARLY? WEREN'T YOU OUT WITH WESLEY DODDS TONI--

WESLEY DODDS BE DAMNED!

DIAN?

I'M SORRY, DADDY. IT'S JUST THAT WE WERE HAVING SUCH A WONDERFUL EVENING, AND THEN WESLEY SAW THIS... ACQUAINTANCE OF MINE AND COMPLETELY FORGOT THAT I EXISTED.

WHY CAN'T MEN JUST PAY SOME ATTENTION TO THE WOMAN THEY'RE WITH AND NOT--

OOP! GOTTA GET THAT!

RRING RRING

IT'S PROBABLY POLICE HEADQUARTERS. THERE WAS ANOTHER KILLING DOWNTOWN.

ANOTHER? MY GOD. HOW DO YOU KNOW ABOUT THAT?

JUST BEFORE WESLEY SHOVED ME INTO A CAB WE RAN INTO THE LIEUTENANT BURKE. HE TOLD ME. I JUST DON'T KNOW WHY WESLEY RUSHED OFF SO SUDDENLY, HE--

WELL, HE'S A RESPONSIBLE FELLOW, BUT HE'S ALWAYS BEEN A TRIFLE STRANGE.

YES... A TRIFLE.

At least.

9

--UNITED WAY IS IMPORTANT. HAVE YOU READ ABOUT POLAND? IT SOUNDS ABSOLUTELY TERRIBLE.

--LIKE TO SEE THE RED ONE, PLEASE--

POLAND? WHO HAS TIME TO READ WHEN THERE'S SUCH A TERRIFIC SALE HERE AT BLOOMIES.

I MEAN LOOK AT THE PRICE ON THIS! AND IT'S CASHMERE.

CAROL, I'M SERIOUS!

SO AM I. THIS IS CHEAPER.

CAROL!

HUH?

WHAT HO, SISTER? YOU'VE BEEN IN HIDING.

UH...OH, I NO...NO. I HAVEN'T.

DIAN? THESE ARE TWO OF MY OLD SORORITY SISTERS, SALLY AND DEBBIE.

SURE. I THINK I REMEMBER SEEING YOU AT THE COLLEGE.

A PLEASURE, DIAN. BUT WE'RE NOT *THAT* "OLD."

I'M SORRY, SALLY, I DIDN'T MEAN--

DON'T SWEAT IT. LISTEN, WE'RE ON OUR WAY TO THE CONGO FOR A DRINK. JOIN US?

WE WON'T TAKE "*NO*" FOR AN ANSWER.

10

44

OH, YOU KNOW ABOUT THE CONGO? I WAS JUST THERE LAST NIGHT.

KNOW ABOUT IT? SALLY MANAGES IT.

OH REALLY? WELL THEN, I SUPPOSE YOU HEARD ABOUT THE MURDER AT THE HOTEL ABOVE IT. GRISLY.

YEAH, I HEARD. LOOKS LIKE SOME YOUNG WOLF PICKED UP ON THE WRONG BIRD.

WHY DON'T WE GO FOR LUNCH INSTEAD OF DRINKS?

U/H, THAT'S OKAY, I THINK DIAN--

NO, DON'T BE SILLY! I'D LOVE TO. I'M FAMISHED.

3^{48}

CAFE

YOU KNOW, I SAW MADELINE RECENTLY.

J LARGE PORK CHOPS SOUP 30

COFFEE TEA OR BUTTERMILK 75¢ VEAL CUTLET

BEEF STEW 15¢

HONK

EEEEE

SURE, WE'VE SEEN HER A LOT IN THE PAST FEW MONTHS WE'D BEEN WANTING TO INVITE YOU OUT ON OUR ROMPS, BUT YOU'D MOVED AND DIDN'T GIVE ANYONE A FORWARDING ADDRESS.

MADELINE SAID SHE WAS WORKING ON IT. AND MADELINE USUALLY GETS WHAT SHE'S AFTER.

I'll bet.

11

WELL, SHE FOUND ME. YOU'VE BEEN SEEING HER FOR *MONTHS*? I COULD HAVE SWORN SHE SAID SHE'D ONLY BEEN BACK IN NEW YORK FOR A FEW WEEKS.

WELL, TIME *DOES* FLY WHEN YOU'RE HAVING FUN.

WHERE THE HELL ARE THOSE DRINKS? DIDN'T WE ORDER AGES AGO?

SO WHAT *WAS* MADELINE DOING IN EUROPE? SHE NEVER DID SAY.

SORRY FOR THE DELAY, LADIES.

WHO KNOWS? I'M SURE SHE MADE A KILLING OVER THERE, THOUGH. LET'S DO THE OLD HOUSE TOAST, SHALL WE?

OVER THE LIPS, DOWN THE THROAT, GIRLS OF K-HOUSE, FLOAT THE BOAT!

CAROL? REMEMBER THAT TIME WE ALL GOT RIP-ROARING DRUNK AND BROUGHT THAT TEENAGE BOY BACK TO THE HOUSE?

BOY, I SURE DO! YOUNG AND HUNG!

SALLY! STOP IT!

Yes, please. Why do sorority girls have to be so cliquish? It's so rude. It seems like everyone I know has their own private world that I'm not in.

I heard my mother tell my aunt once that women have to try to work themselves into this society.

Well, today, Dian Belmont starts working, starting with Wesley.

MISS BELMONT TO SEE YOU, SIR.

THANK YOU, HUMPHRIES. DIAN! WHAT A LOVELY SURPRISE! AND I DO MEAN LOVELY.

NO NEED TO GET UP, WESLEY.

I JUST DROPPED BY TO THANK YOU FOR A DELIGHTFUL, THOUGH BRIEF, EVENING.

YOU KNOW, DIAN, I'M REALLY SORRY ABOUT MY CLUMSY EXIT. I HAD A SUDDEN THOUGHT ABOUT MY WORK AND HAD TO GET RIGHT TO IT.

NO NEED TO APOLOGIZE.

SO WHAT BRINGS YOU OUT THIS FAR?

OH, I WAS OUT WITH CAROL, AND THEN WE RAN INTO SOME OF HER OLD SORORITY SISTERS.

THEY WERE AN ODD BUNCH. ONE OF THEM WAS A WOMAN NAMED SALLY, WHO APPARENTLY MANAGES THE CONGO.

ISN'T THAT A STRANGE COINCIDENCE? ANYWAY, THEY MADE ME NERVOUS. THEY--

WESLEY? WHAT IN THE WORLD IS THIS LITTLE STRAW MAN?

13

47

IT'S KIND OF CUTE! IT LOOKS LIKE-- OH SHOOT, I CAN'T QUITE PLACE IT--

UH, BE CAREFUL, DIAN, THAT'S A VERY RARE PIECE OF... OF AMISH FOLK ART. IT'S FRAGILE, HERE--

--LET ME HELP YOU WITH THAT.

HM?

TELL ME MORE ABOUT THESE SORORITY SISTERS, WHY DID THEY MAKE YOU NERVOUS?

OH, I DON'T KNOW. THEY SEEM TO HAVE THEIR OWN SECRET WAYS OF DOING EVERYTHING THAT I DON'T KNOW.

AND CAROL IS ALWAYS ACTING SO TIMIDLY WHEN SHE'S AROUND THEM... LIKE SHE'S AFRAID OF THEM OR SOMETHING.

AND YOU REMEMBER THAT--THAT MADELINE CREATURE WE MET AT THE CONGO?

CREATURE? I THOUGHT SHE WAS--

"ENGAGING." I KNOW. BUT, I SAW HER AND CAROL KISSING EACH OTHER THE OTHER DAY. PASSIONATELY.

IF THEY MAKE YOU UNCOMFORTABLE, PERHAPS YOU SHOULD JUST STAY AWAY FROM THEM.

OH, I DON'T KNOW. THEY ARE FUN, IT'S JUST... WELL...

ENOUGH! I DIDN'T MEAN TO INTERRUPT YOUR WORK. I'LL CALL SOON. MWAH! I'VE GOT TO GET BACK AND MEET MY DAD AT THE OFFICE! 'BYE!

GOODBYE, DIAN.

14

-- OF COURSE I'LL HAVE TO GET THE REPORT TO REMEMBER ALL THE DETAILS, LIEUTENANT, BUT I *CAN* TELL YOU THAT THIS KILLER AND THE KILLER OF TREVOR BARNES ARE ONE AND THE SAME.

YOU'RE POSITIVE?

I'M QUITE CERTAIN.

THE BLOOD SAMPLES AND SALIVA SAMPLES MATCH. LET ME JUST GET THE LIGHT AND I'LL FIND THAT REPOR--

-CLIK-

WHAT THE HELL?

YOU AGAIN! HOLD IT RIGHT THERE, YOU TRICKY BASTARD!

CHINKLE

I SAID FREEZE!

15

WHAT
SHOULD I--

GET OUTTA
HERE, HUBERT! I'LL
HANDLE THIS! BUT
GET SOME BACKUP
FOR ME!

SLAM

CLIC-

WHOOOSH

PANG
PANG

FOOOOSH

UNH!

16

CHUFFLE

UNH!

BLAM
BLAM.

HUH?

UH?

(17)

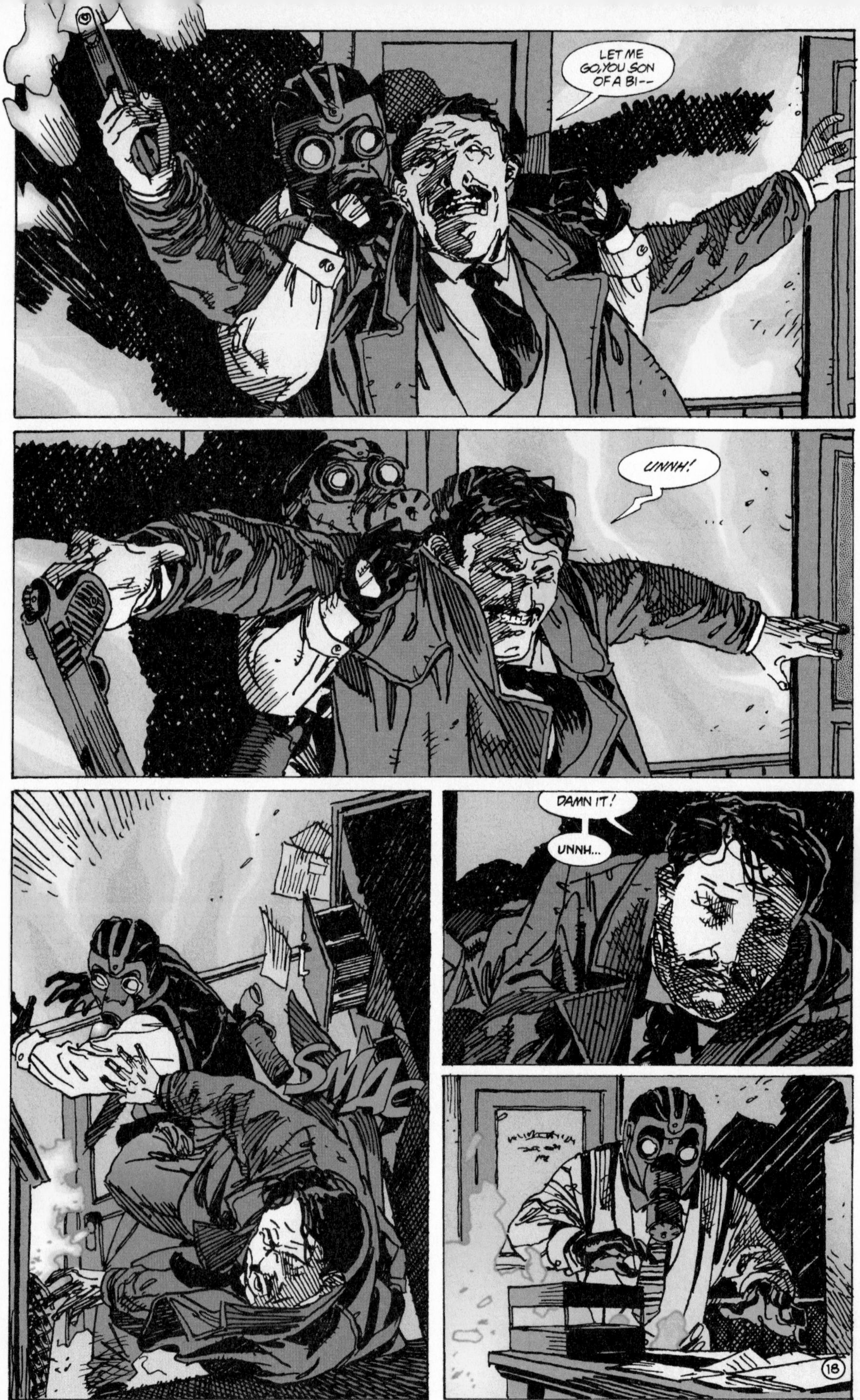
LET ME GO, YOU SON OF A BI--
UNNH!
DAMN IT!
UNNH...
18

YOU--
YOU CAN'T--

--SMOKE--

UH
HOUGH
HACK
HACK!

SSSSSSHHHHH

BASTARD...

19

53

HMM HM HMMMM HM HM HMMMM--

"YOU'D--♪ BE--SO EAS-Y ♪ TO KISS--"

MADELINE? YOU STARTLED ME.

♪ "SO EAS-Y TO ♪ PRESS MY LIPS TO--

I UH, SAW... UH, SALLY AND DEBBIE, THEY--

♪ "SO-- ♪ CLOSE--TO PER-FECT BLISS--

KISS ME, CAROL.

MMMMM.

MM-HM.

'SCUZE ME, UH...

LOOK AT THIS! I LOVE A MAN IN UNIFORM!

YOU'LL HAVE TO INVITE ME UP MORE OFTEN, CAROL, DARLING.

SIXTH FLOOR, CUTIE.

YES, MA'AM.

20

Well, that could have been worse. "Engaging." Hmph. What on earth could he have been thinking?

DADDY? I'M HERE...

TAP TAP TAP

Shoot. Not here. I hope I don't have to wait too long.

What's this...?

Hmm, the murder report... my goodness! Punctures in his--

MISS BELMONT!

NOTHING! I--I MEAN, I'M WAITING FOR--FOR MY--

THAT REPORT IS OFFICIAL POLICE BUSINESS.

AND YOU DON'T LOOK LIKE OFFICIAL POLICE TO ME. HAVE YOU EVER HEARD OF THE WAITING ROOM?

DON'T YOU YELL AT ME. I REALIZE YOU HAVE SOME VERY DISTURBING CASES AFOOT, LIEUTENANT, BUT I'M STILL A LADY AND EXPECT TO BE TREATED LIKE ONE!

IF THAT'S THE CASE, A WORD OF ADVICE. "LADIES" DON'T GO POKIN' THEIR NOSES INTO MEN'S BUSINESS AFFAIRS.

Why, that pompous snot! How dare he get--

21

--on my back!

I HAVE TO TELL YOU, MADELINE, I WAS AFRAID TO START SOMETHING LIKE THIS WITH YOU AGAIN, BUT THAT WAS...EXQUISITE. WHEN YOU TOUCH ME I--

I'M GLAD YOU LIKED IT, CAROL, AND I'M SURE WE'LL DO THIS AGAIN, BUT I'VE GOT TO GET GOING.

YOU'RE NOT... STAYING?

NO. I HAVE WORK TO DO.

WORK? WHAT KIND OF WORK GETS DONE AT THIS TIME OF THE NIGHT?

NOT THE KIND OF WORK YOU'RE THINKING.

NO... I'M JUST DOING A LITTLE CHARITY WORK, LIKE YOUR TIGHT LITTLE FRIEND, DIAN.

INCIDENTALLY, CAROL, WE'RE HAVING A LITTLE SORORITY MEETING THURSDAY.

I WILL SEE YOU THERE.

YES?

22

WHAT DID YOU SAY YOUR NAME W--

I DIDN'T.

CLOP CLOP CLOP

YOU DON'T REALLY CARE, DO YOU?

I GUESS NOT.

YOU'LL HAVE TO CATCH ME IF YOU WANT ANY MORE--

HEY! WAIT!

HERE YOU GO, DRIVER!

GOOD LUCK, SONNY.

THANKS!

HEY! HELLO? WHERE'D YOU GET T--

IF I WAS A SNAKE, I'D HAVE BIT YOU.

I MIGHT ANYWAY.

HEY, WHATEVER YOU WANT, I'M--

YES, WHATEVER I WANT, AND I KNOW WHAT I WANT. AND I WANT IT NOW.

23

MMMMMMM...

GOD, YOU ARE SOMETHING ELSE--

LET ME SHOW YOU WHAT I AM.

OH WOW--

OOOH, LOOK AT HOW PRETTY IT IS. MMMM.

HERE? YOU CAN'T GIVE ME--CHRIST, YOU ARE CRAZY, YOU--

SHHH.

MMMM--

MMHMM--

MMM...UHH... MMM...UHH--

HUH!? UH-UH!! UH!!!

58

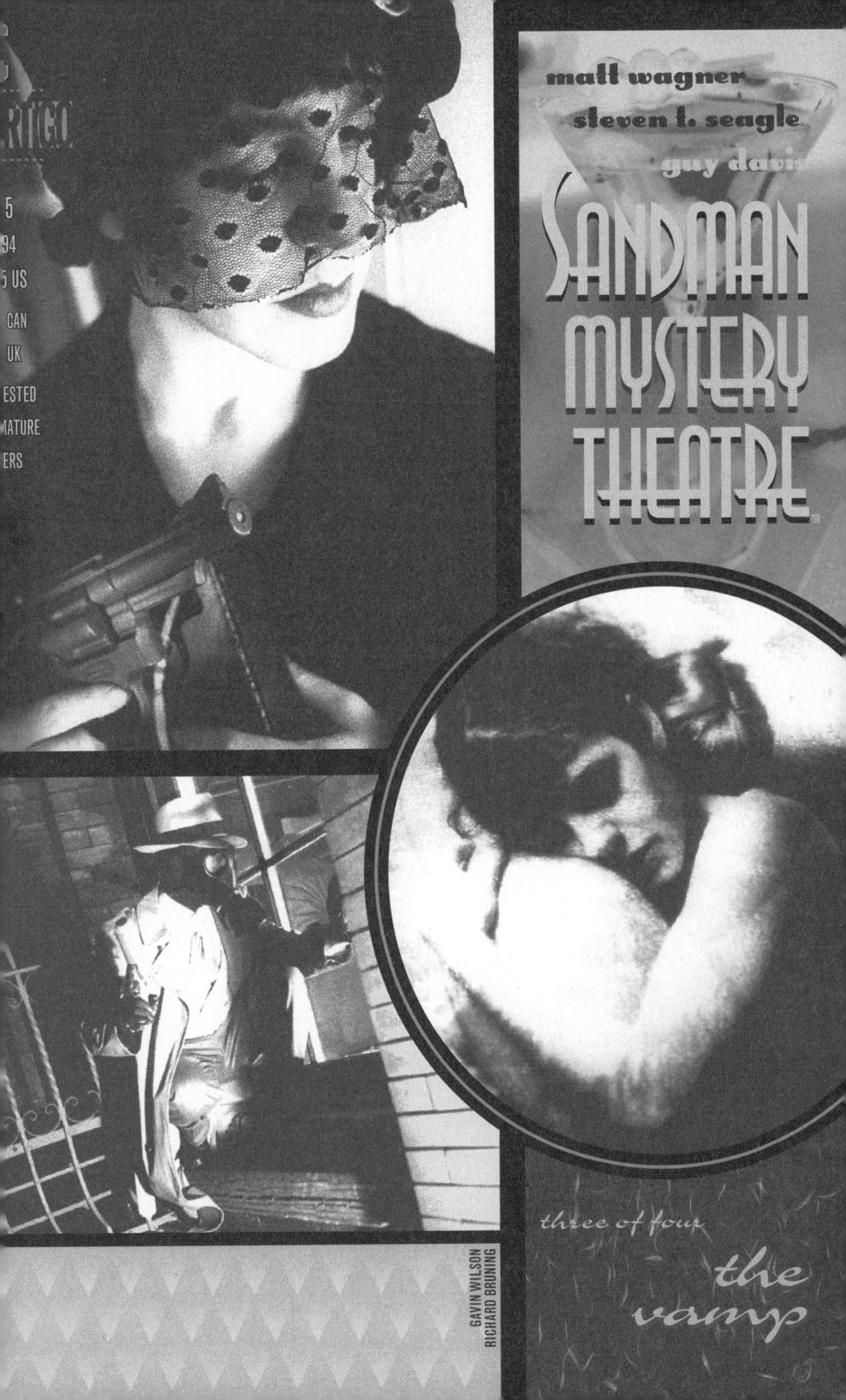

VERTIGO

5
94
5 US
CAN
UK
ESTED
MATURE
ERS

matt wagner

steven t. seagle

guy davis

SANDMAN MYSTERY THEATRE

GAVIN WILSON
RICHARD BRUNING

three of four

the vamp

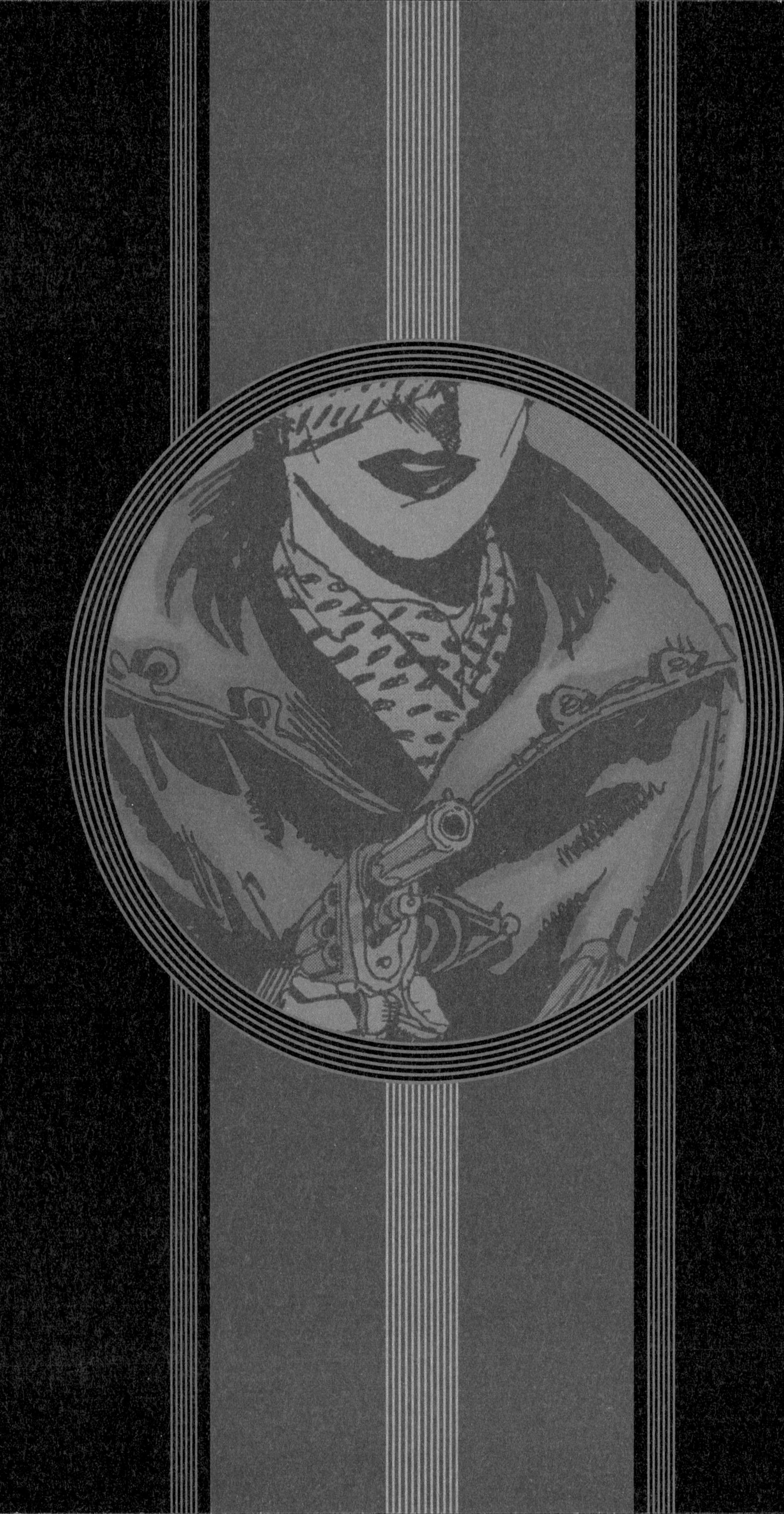

I've got to stop sleeping so late. The world rushes by each morning while I just doze.

GOOD MORNING, MARTHA.

GOOD MORNING, MISS BELMONT. YOU SURE LOOK LIKE YOU COULD USE A CUPPA.

I CERTAINLY COULD. THANK YOU.

Like Martha...she's been up for hours. I'll bet she does more most mornings than I get done all day.

HERE YOU GO, THEN, DRINK HER DOWN AND YOU'LL FEEL MUCH BETTER.

I can't help but think that the world needs more action and less dreaming.

GOOD MORNING, EVERYONE! COFFEE, MARTHA? THANKS!

DADDY? IS SOMETHING WRONG?

NEW YORK CITY, DIAN. SOMETHING'S ALWAYS WRONG. ANOTHER MURDER. SOMEBODY'S REALLY GOT IT IN FOR THOSE CLUB BOYS.

ANOTHER? ARE YOU SURE?

YEAH, UH--

SAMUEL SILBERT. BE BACK LATE, I'M SURE, DON'T WAIT UP.

Another friend of Trevor's? That's strange. Hmm.

Three murders in one week, and all of them club members and old fraternity brothers.

I'm starting to think there's more to this than mere coincidence. Maybe Carol can help me think through this.

...COME ON, CAROL...PICK UP...

That's odd. Carol's never the sort to get an early start either. She must be having a bath. I think I'll just drop by. Someone has to get to the bottom of this.

Maybe Dian Belmont will become the Big Apple's newest sleuth!

--"JUST DON'T KNOW IF WE SHOULD CONTINUE"...NO, THAT'S NOT RIGHT...UM..."MADELINE? I'VE BEEN THINKING ABOUT US AND WE'RE JUST TOO DIFFERENT"...NO, TOO CLICHÉ.

OH HELL, HERE IT IS. GUESS I'LL JUST WING IT--

WELL, HI THERE, STRANGER. WE'VE BEEN WAITING FOR YOU.

OH, HI SALLY.

SORRY, I HAD A ROUGH NIGHT.

OH REALLY?

LOOK WHO DECIDED TO SHOW.

HI, CAROL, I THOUGHT YOU WERE GOING TO CALL ME LAST NIGHT.

OH, SORRY, DEBBIE, I WAS... BUSY.

YES, SO WE'VE *HEARD*, DARLING. HOW WAS--

CAROL! I'VE BEEN WAITING FOR YOU, SO GLAD YOU COULD MAKE IT.

HERE, CAROL, YOU LOOK A LITTLE PEAKED. DRINK THIS DOWN, IT'LL MAKE YOU FEEL BETTER.

OH, THANK YOU. I WAS A BIT--*UH*--AM A BIT SICK THIS MORNING.

THAT'S WHY I WAS LATE, I HOPE YOU WEREN'T ALL WAITING FOR ME FOR THE LUNCHEON... *UH*... WELL, YOU ALL LOOK LOVELY THIS--

YOU'RE SO CUTE WHEN YOU'RE NERVOUS AND TRYING TO BE POLITE, CAROL. IT GOES AGAINST YOUR NATURAL TENDENCIES.

③

THE VAMP
ACT·THREE

MATT WAGNER   **STEVEN T. SEAGLE**
WRITERS

GUY DAVIS   **DAVID HORNUNG**
ARTIST   COLORIST

JOHN COSTANZA   **ANDROID IMAGES**
LETTERER   SEPARATOR

SHELLY ROEBERG   **KAREN BERGER**
ASST. EDITOR   EDITOR

WE DO IN FACT HAVE SOME *BUSINESS* TO DISCUSS. WHAT AN INTERESTING WORD. *"BUSINESS."* YES, CAROL, I THINK THIS WILL SUIT YOU QUITE WELL.

WHAT I AM ABOUT TO TELL YOU WILL GO NO FARTHER THAN THIS ROOM. IS THAT CLEAR TO--

DON'T INTERRUPT, CAROL. THAT'S RULE NUMBER--

OF COURSE, MADELINE. I'D NEVER TELL ANY--

I'LL LAY DOWN THE LAWS AROUND HERE, DEBBIE, IF YOU DON'T MIND.

NOW, ABOUT *OUR BUSINESS.* WE *"SISTERS"* ARE IN THE PROCESS OF PURCHASING A SMALL PARCEL OF LAND IN THE UPSTATE REGION. A *RETREAT,* IF YOU WILL.

YEAH, A PLACE WE CAN REALLY CALL OUR OWN. YOU KNOW, AWAY FROM ALL THE NOISE...AND *MEN--*

WELL SPOKEN.

④

AND IT'S YOUR TENDENCIES WE'RE HERE TO DISCUSS TODAY. *YOURS* AND *OURS.*

YES, YOU HAD SAID YOU WANTED TO TALK TO ME ABOUT SOMETHING. SOME *BUSINESS* PERHAPS, OR--?

CAROL. I THINK IT'S TIME *YOU* JOINED US IN THIS GRAND VISION. WOMEN *NEED* A PLACE TO GO TO FEEL PROTECTED FROM MEN'S SOCIETY.

OH?

WELL, IT SOUNDS VERY NICE, BUT I'M NOT REALLY SURE I COULD GIVE YOU MUCH FINANCIAL SUPPORT. TIMES ARE SORT OF TIGHT--

I'VE GOT MONEY, CAROL, I WANT YOU TO BE WITH US IN *SPIRIT...* AND IN PURPOSE. TO WORK TOWARD A COMMON GOAL, LIKE WE ALL USED TO DO IN COLLEGE.

LAST NIGHT, CAROL, I THINK WE *CAME* TO A CERTAIN UNDER-STANDING ABOUT ONE ANOTHER. WOULDN'T YOU SAY SO?

UH... THIS ISN'T REALLY THE PLACE TO TALK ABOUT THAT, MAD--

NOW, THERE'S NO NEED TO BE EMBARRASSED. I HAVE THE SAME UNDERSTANDING WITH *ALL* OF THE SISTERS. AND I THINK YOU'RE ONE OF US.

AREN'T YOU, CAROL?

5

NOW, THE LAST TIME I WAS HERE I GOT NOTHING BUT A BUNCH OF WIND FROM YOU SELF-RIGHTEOUS SHITHEADS. THAT'S GOING TO CHANGE RIGHT NOW.

BASED ON LAST NIGHT'S MURDER, IT'S PRETTY CLEAR THAT SOMEBODY'S PUNCHIN' YOUR IVY LEAGUE TIMECARDS ONE BY ONE. MAYBE IT'S EVEN ONE OF YOU. WHO KNOWS?

COME ON, LIEUTENANT. WE'RE JUST YOUNG MEN ENJOYING OUR PRIMES. SURELY YOU REMEMBER WHAT THAT WAS LIKE. WHO WOULD POSSIBLY WANT TO KILL US?

ANY MORE STATEMENTS LIKE THAT AND YOU CAN PUT MY NAME ON THE SHORT LIST, PUNK.

LT. BURKE? I'VE BEEN THINKING.

DID IT HURT?

MAYBE THIS IS SOMEONE WITH A VENDETTA AGAINST US--

I'VE HEARD THE SUSPECT IS A WOMAN. PERHAPS IT'S SOMEONE FROM OUR FRATERNITY DAYS. WE HAD A FEW--

LISTEN, LIEUTENANT, WE PAY YOUR SALARY TO PROTECT US, YOU SHOULD BE OUT LOOKING FOR SUSPECTS OR SOMETHING.

NO YOU LISTEN, ASSHOLE, I'M IN NO MOOD FOR GAMES. SO I'LL JUST GO OUT "LOOKING FOR SUSPECTS OR SOMETHING."

AND TO "PROTECT YOU," I'LL LEAVE ONE OF MY MEN HERE. I HOPE HE'S ENOUGH TO KEEP AN EYE ON ALL SIX OF YOU RICH SNOTS. I DOUBT IT, BUT YOU NEVER KNOW.

SLEEP WELL, BOYS.

6

WELL, *THAT* WAS A GRAND SHOW. I DIDN'T THINK THE OLD WINDBAG HAD IT IN HIM.

THIS IS NO LAUGHING MATTER, FREDDIE. WHAT IF IT *DOES* HAVE SOMETHING TO DO WITH HELL NIGHT?

OH, PLEASE. MAKE HIM STOP.

SSSHHH!

YEAH. SHUT UP, BARRY. BURKE MIGHT STILL BE OUTSIDE.

HELL NIGHT? THAT WAS *YEARS* AGO.

IT DOESN'T MATTER. I THINK IT'S CONNECTED TO HELL NIGHT.

EVEN IF IT IS, WE CAN'T *TELL* ANYONE-- ESPECIALLY THE POLICE. IT'S A TRADITION SACRED TO THE FRATERNITY.

ANYONE TALKS ABOUT HELL NIGHT OR WHAT HAPPENED AND THEY'RE *OUT.* UNDERSTOOD? I'M NOT GOING TO JAIL FOR SOMETHING THAT HAPPENED SO LONG AGO.

SOMEONE *IS* AFTER US. ANYBODY WHO FEELS HE IS IN IMMINENT DANGER SHOULD SIMPLY MAKE HIS WAY TO THE CABIN OUTSIDE OF ALBANY. AGREED?

ALBANY.

AGREED.

AGREED.

IT'S SAFE, AND NO ONE WILL KNOW YOU'RE THERE, YOU CAN LIE LOW UNTIL THE MURDERER IS CAUGHT. UNTIL THEN, KEEP A LOW PROFILE, GENTLEMEN, AND KEEP AN EYE OUT FOR STRANGERS.

7

CAROL?

MADELINE?!

MADELINE? NO, IT'S *ME*, DIAN.

OF COURSE, I'M SORRY, IT'S JUST BEEN A KILLER OF A DAY.

"*KILLER*" IS THE WORD FOR IT. ANOTHER ONE OF YOUR OLD FRATERNITY FRIENDS HAS TURNED UP DEAD... SAM SILBERT?

SAM SILBERT? THAT CAN'T BE. ARE YOU *SURE*?

QUITE, DID YOU KNOW HIM?

WELL, OF COURSE I KNEW HIM. BUT NOT *WELL*.

THE ... THE DELTA PHI'S WERE OUR BROTHER HOUSE.

HAD YOU SEEN HIM RECENTLY?

HAD I...? DIAN! I'M *NOT* INVOLVED IN THIS IF *THAT'S* WHAT YOU'RE THINKING.

LOOK, I'VE HAD AN AWFUL DAY OF IT. I'LL CALL YOU TOMORROW. ALL RIGHT?

SURE... I GUESS.

What are you keeping locked inside, Carol? What about this situation is making you so nervous?

8

68

Let's see if it's *just* you or if *all* of your sorority sisters are jittery.

MISS STARR? THIS YOUNG LADY PUSHED HERSELF BACK HERE CLAIMIN' SHE KNEW YA--?

IT'S ALL RIGHT, BRUNO. LET HER IN.

WELL WELL WELL, DIAN. LOOKING SWELL SWELL SWELL. WHAT BRINGS YOU DOWN TO THE CONGO?

THIS MAY SOUND STRANGE, SALLY, BUT IT'S ABOUT THE MURDERS... THE DELTA PHI MEMBERS?

WELL, HONEY, I WOULDN'T KNOW *ANYTHING* ABOUT THEM. WHY DO YOU WANT TO TALK TO ME?

I'M TRYING TO HELP MY FATHER OUT. THERE MUST BE SOME CONNECTION INVOLVING THE FRATERNITY ITSELF. I JUST WONDERED IF YOU REMEMBERED ANYTHING--

DIAN... I THINK IT'S VERY... *SWEET* THAT YOU'RE TRYING TO PLAY DETECTIVE, BUT *REALLY*, IT WAS SEVERAL YEARS AGO. I'M SURE THAT STUCK-UP BUNCH HAS MANAGED TO BUILD UP PLENTY OF NEW ENEMIES SINCE COLLEGE.

BESIDES, TWO MURDERS IS HARDLY ENOUGH TO DRAW A CONCLU--

TWO? NO, IT'S THREE. SAM SILBERT WAS KILLED LAST NIGHT. IN THE PARK--

AND THE POLICE ARE *CERTAIN* THE KILLING NEXT DOOR AT THE EXCELSIOR WAS COMMITTED BY THE SAME PERSON.

THE EXCELSIOR--? UH... DIAN, I HAVE TO GET THE BOOKS IN TO THE... UH... ACCOUNTANT BEFORE FOUR. COULD WE CONTINUE THIS LATER?

I SUPPOSE, BUT IF YOU THINK OF ANYTHING, PLEASE CALL.

OH, YOU'LL BE THE FIRST TO KNOW.

9

I can't believe this. Nothing. After a whole morning's work! I feel like everyone is deliberately keeping things from me.

HMM...

And yet I can't help but feel like the answer to all of this is somehow right under my nose...

OH! UH... HELLO, MISS, WHAT--

I THINK I'LL DO THE USUAL.

PSSSST! 'SHER--

'SCUSE ME--

I, UH, COULDN'T HELP NOTICING YOU FROM ACROSS THE--

I LIKE A MAN WHO NOTICES ME. EVEN MORE SO IF HE'S DOING IT IN PRIVATE. SHALL WE?

YOU LEAD. I'LL FOLLOW.

10

SORRY I DON'T HAVE AN UMBRELLA, I WASN'T EXPECTING THE RAIN TO--

OH, THAT'S ALL RIGHT. A LITTLE *WETNESS* NEVER HURT ANYONE.

WHY DON'T WE WAIT IT OUT IN THIS ALLEY? IT'S NOT AS--

THE ALLEY I DON'T MIND, THE WAITING I *DO.*

UFFH!

MMMM. THAT'S QUITE AN IMPRESSIVE BUNDLE YOU'RE CARRYING THERE.

I THINK WE SHOULD GO SOMEWHERE AND MAKE BETTER USE OF IT.

WE'LL "GO SOMEWHERE" ALL RIGHT. DOWN-TOWN. FOR QUESTIONING.

YOU BASTARD!

NOT SO FAST, SISTER. NOBODY GRABS MY PACKAGE AND GETS AWAY WITH IT. YOU--

AH! FUHHH--

YOU BITCH!

CRAC-

WIG, HUH? THAT JUST CONFIRMS MY SUSPICIONS. YOU'RE IN SOME BIG TROUBLE, LADY. YOU BETTER--

OOOOOFFF!

PLINT

OOOH... COME... COME--

NO, NOT TONIGHT, SWEETIE, BUT MAYBE WE'LL MEET AGAIN...

12

Wesley always seems to have a keen mind. He's not really the crime solver type with his head in his books all day, but who knows? Maybe he can help me make sense of this.

I hope that he's not asleep already. Besides, he could use the company.

DIAN?

HI, WES... WHERE'S HUMPHRIES?

WELL HE'S ALREADY IN BED, ACTUALLY. I WAS HEADING THERE MYSELF. IT IS RATHER LATE--

I'M SORRY, WES, BUT MY FATHER'S NOT AT HOME AND I SIMPLY, HAVE TO TALK TO SOMEONE.

I TAKE IT SOMETHING'S BOTHERING YOU, DIAN?

AND HOW.

IT'S THESE FRATERNITY MURDERS. I'VE BEEN FOLLOWING LEADS ALL DAY AND--

SHOULDN'T YOU BE LEAVING THAT TO YOUR FATHER?

WESLEY... THIS IS DIFFICULT TO SAY, BUT I THINK MY FRIEND CAROL MIGHT KNOW SOMETHING ABOUT THESE KILLINGS. I'VE TRIED TALKING TO HER ABOUT THEM AND SHE JUST CLAMS UP.

HAVE YOUR FATHER PUT A MAN ON HER. REALLY, DIAN, IT'S DANGEROUS TO GO POKING AROUND IN THESE MATTERS ALONE.

⑬

OH, WESLEY, I JUST WANT TO--TO--

I KNOW, DIAN. I KNOW HOW EXCITING IT CAN BE TO TAKE THE INITIATIVE IN SOMETHING.

TO GRAB THE BULL BY THE HORNS CAN SOMETIMES BE QUITE EXHILARATING.

TO BE THE TREASURE HUNTER WHO FINDS THE PRIZE--

HMUPH--

FWUMP

I'M SORRY, WES, I JUST COULDN'T HELP MYSEL--

NO NO! YOU JUST TOOK ME BY SURPRISE IS ALL.

GOOD...

...WESLEY? ARE YOU... STILL HEADING TO BED SOON?

WE NEVER DID FINISH OUR EVENING TOGETHER...

OH! UH... I CAN'T... I MEAN I REALLY HAVE TO-- HAVE TO, UH...

WESLEY? WHAT'S WRONG?

NO, I MEAN, *NOTHING.* IT'S TEMPTING-- GOOD LORD, IT'S TEMPTING --BUT I *HAVE* TO...UH--

IT'S JUST-- I ...HAVE A MEETING EARLY TOMORROW THAT I *MUST* GET READY FOR, I MEAN I'D *LIKE* TO, BUT THIS REALLY ISN'T THE RIGHT TIME, I'M--

I'M REALLY EXHAUSTED, AND I WANT IT TO BE... TO BE... JUST RIGHT.

YOU UNDERSTAND, DON'T YOU?

WELL, N--

GOOD NIGHT. TAKE CARE.

No I don't understand. I practically threw myself at you and you-you-- oh! I never!

And you may never *either,* Wesley Dodds.

CLAC

"*Exhausted*"? Well, you get your rest mister. And plenty of it!

In fact, I don't care if you never-- oh shoot! My purse!

BONG BONG BONG BONG

Why won't you answer the door? Are you sleeping already? Come on, come on.

CAN I *HELP* YOU, MISS BELMONT?

HUMPHRIES? I LEFT MY PURSE. WHERE'S *WES*? I WOULD HAVE THOUGHT HE'D HEAR ME RINGING.

YES, QUITE. HE MUST NOT BE AT HOME THIS EVENING.

DON'T BE *SILLY!* I JUST LEFT A FEW MINUTES AGO AND HE WAS HERE. HONEST, I SWEAR.

BE THAT AS IT MAY, HE DOES *NOT* APPEAR TO BE IN *NOW*, MISS BELMONT.

BUT THAT'S...

⁓ *YAWN* ⁓

NEVER MIND, HUMPHRIES, I'M SORRY TO HAVE BOTHERED YOU. GOODNIGHT.

GOODNIGHT.

Where could you have gone so quickly, Wesley?

And why would you go when we were getting so... intimate?

Did you have somewhere else to go? Someone else to see tonight... like that... that... Vamp, Madeline Giles?

Well, I'm tired of questions. Starting tomorrow morning I'm getting up early, and I'm getting some answers.

⑯

Daddy says there are three things that a good detective always does, "start early, keep your hat low," and...oh shoot! What was the third thing?

I hate to test his method on you, Carol, but I have to know--

--what you do all day, and--My God! Carol--you're not a natural blond?

--oh! "stick with it." That was the third thing. stick with it--

SHOE SHINE PARLOR

--because you never know when the big break will come--

TAXI!

And you've got to be there when it does.

Well, now, this isn't your normal neck of the woods, Carol.

--NO, NO NEED TO WAIT. THANKS. HERE. KEEP THE CHANGE.

THANK YOU, MA'AM.

In fact, for a woman who hasn't been too interested in anything but the latest sales at Bloomingdale's, I'd call a trip to the lower east side--

Downright suspicious. What could possibly bring you here, Carol?

TAP TAP TAP

WHO IS IT?

IT'S CAROL.

I'VE BEEN WAITING FOR YOU.

That woman, can't quite make her out, but it must be Madeline--

That's not Madeline. Sally maybe? No...

Shoot! Who was that? I can't believe Carol is involved with more than one woman.

18

78

I'm certainly not going to see any more from the hallway--

SHOOK

And while I'm not one for heights, I'm not leaving here until I find out who that woman is.

that looked to be *more* than a friendly kiss in the hallway--

And given Carol's confession to me in Club Voodoo as well as her goodbye kiss with Madeline the other day, I'm starting to wonder if she isn't very interested in the... company... of women.

SNAP!

Shoot! My heel! Well, I guess that officially makes me a flat foot.

Think this is the window to the room they went in--

So let's just have a look at what they-- oh--

Oh--

Ohhhhh--

Oh... wow...

ALL RIGHT, ROSS, I'M HERE--

7TH PRECIN...

NOW, WHAT'S SO GODDAMN IMPORTANT YOU HAD TO WAKE ME UP?

IT'S ABOUT THE TAILS YOU HAD US PUT ON THE FRAT BOYS-- SAY! WHAT HAPPENED TO YOUR FACE? ROUGH NIGHT?

YOU COULD SAY THAT. NOW WHAT GIVES?

SEEMS LIKE ONE OF THE YOUNG TURKS GOT WISE TO HIS TAIL AND SLIPPED HIM.

AH, SHIT! I THOUGHT TELLIN' 'EM I ONLY HAD ONE GUY ON 'EM WOULD-- SHIT! SHIT! SHIT!

GREAT! NOW WE GOTTA FIGURE OUT WHERE THE HELL THAT IDIOT WENT.

20

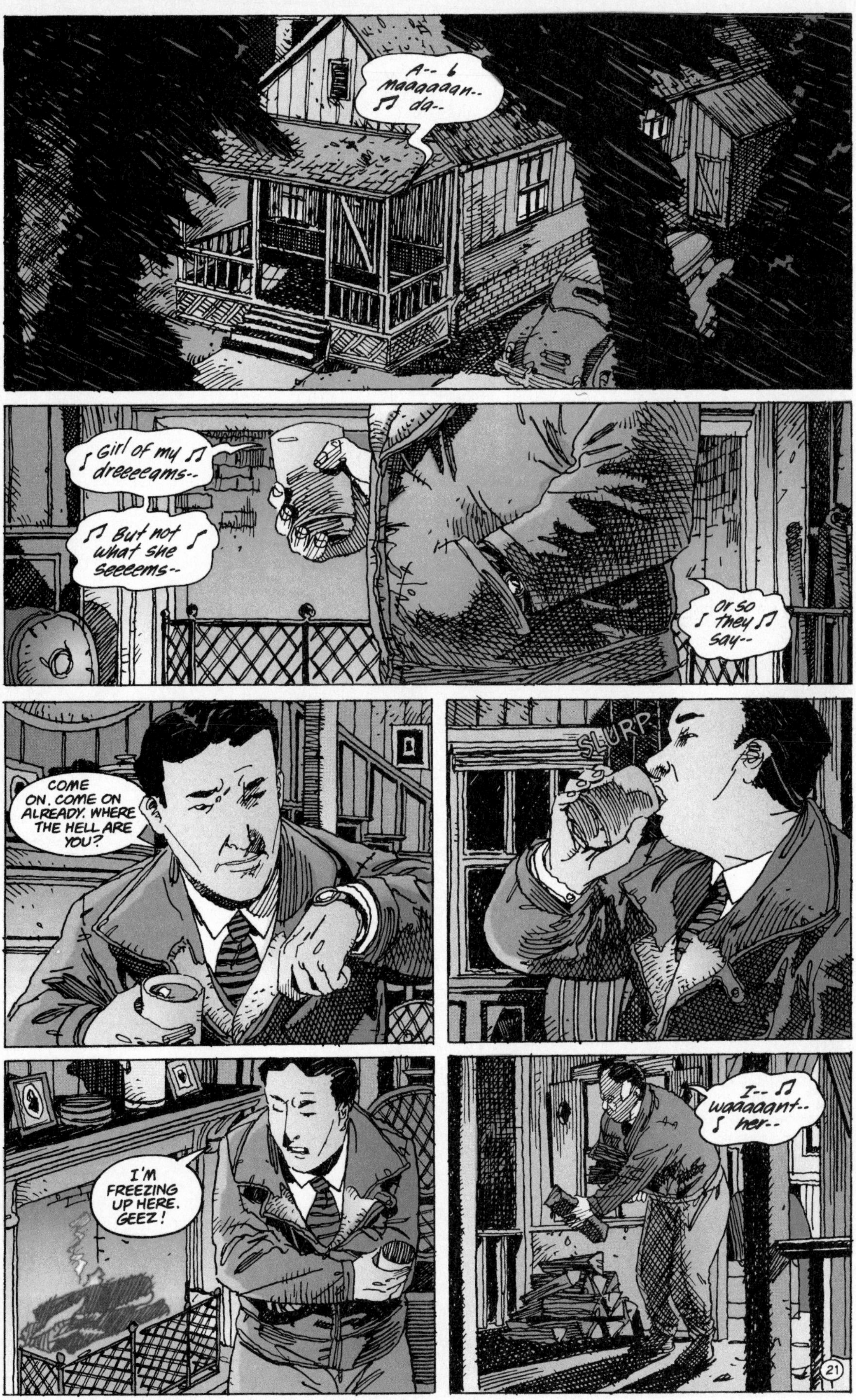
A-- b maaaaaan-- ♫ da--
♪ Girl of my ♫ dreeeeams--
♫ But not what she ♪ seeeems--
Or so ♪ they ♫ say--
COME ON. COME ON ALREADY. WHERE THE HELL ARE YOU?
SLURP
I'M FREEZING UP HERE. GEEZ!
I-- ♫ waaaaant-- ♪ her--
21

In ever-y way-- ♪

About time you got here--

RELEASE THE WOOD AND MEET YOUR DARKEST NIGHTMARE, BARRY SMITHERS.

TELL ME WHAT IS "HELL NIGHT"?

I--I--

YOU WILL ANSWER MY QUESTIONS OR YOU WILL FACE A LIFETIME OF HELL NIGHTS IN YOUR DREAMS.

SURE, BUDDY, SURE, DON'T SHOOT, I--

WHAT IS "HELL NIGHT"?

UH, LISTEN, I'M ABOUT TO PISS MYSELF HERE. I'M A LITTLE NERVOUS. MIND IF I HAVE A CIGARETTE BEFORE I SPILL IT?

UH...YEAH.

INHALE YOUR FOUL MISTS.

THANKS.

NOW UH, "HELL NIGHT," YOU SAY?

CAN'T SAY I'VE EVER--

22

PAF

--HEARD OF IT!

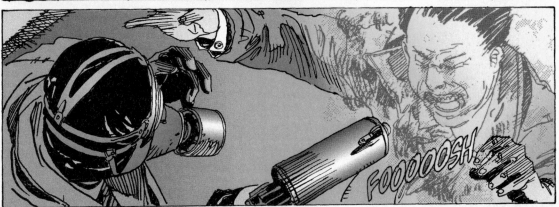

FOOOOOSH!

NIGHTS OF TROUBLED SLEEP AWAIT YOU, BARRY SMITHERS.

YOU WOULD HAVE DONE WELL TO TELL ME WHAT I--

WHAT--

BREATHE?!

23

WELL WELL--

YOU REALLY SHOULDN'T HAVE. REALLY.

I DON'T KNOW WHO YOU ARE, BUT IT APPEARS HALF MY JOB'S BEEN DONE ALREADY.

BY THE WAY, HANDSOME--

"-- I LIKE THE MASK."

BLAM

VERTIGO

matt wagner

steven t. seagle

guy davis

SANDMAN
MYSTERY
THEATRE.

the vamp

four of four

GAVIN WILSON
RICHARD BRUNING

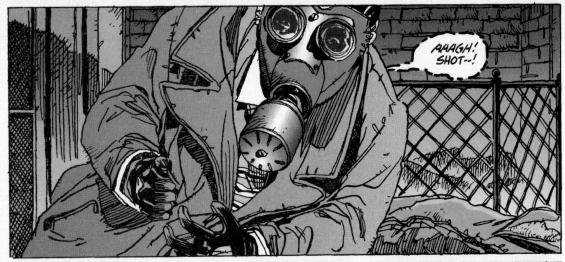

AAAGH! SHOT--!

HOW VERY PERCEPTIVE,

LOOKS AND BRAINS. I LIKE YOU MORE AND MORE.

THUD

♫ Don't-- keep-- ♫ hangin' on--

THUD

THUD

♫ When love is ♫ gone--

♫ When love is ♫ gone--

THUD

♫ And-- ♫ don't-- keep--

THUD

♫ "Hangin' ♫ on--"

SKIRT

♫ When-- ♫

SSKKIT.

♫ Huh? ♫

TO SING SO SWEETLY AND YET BE SO EVIL.

HOW--NNN--UNFORTUNATE. IT'S TIME FOR YOU TO SLEEP--

FOOOSH

THE ONLY ONE OF US SLEEPING AROUND HERE TONIGHT IS YOU, YOU--

≶ Cough Cough Cough ≶

YOU--COUGH-- YOU BASTARD-- COUGH--

YOU'LL GET YOURS-- COUGH-- MISTER!

≶ cough ≶

AH! JESUS! LOOKS LIKE I ALREADY HAVE--NNNN!

GOT TO STOP THE BLEEDING --NNN!

2

THE VAMP
FINAL · ACT

MATT WAGNER **STEVEN T. SEAGLE**
WRITERS

GUY DAVIS **DAVID HORNUNG**
ARTIST COLORIST

JOHN COSTANZA **ANDROID IMAGES**
LETTERER SEPARATOR

SHELLY ROEBERG **KAREN BERGER**
ASST. EDITOR EDITOR

SSSSSS

OKAY, WESLEY. YOU CAN DO THIS...

--OH SHIT--

NNN-- OHHH SIIIIIT--

SSSSSSS

GNNF FAAAK UNHHH!

OH! OH! UNNH! SHIT!

3

Boring boring *boring*. Detective work is nothing but waiting and *more* waiting.

Who would have thought that tracking down the most vicious killer in the city would be so *tedious*?

Oh well, at least I know that wherever *Wes* is right now, he's bound to be having more fun than I am.

It's about *time* you left, Carol. *Now's* my chance. I hope you won't *hate* me when all is said and done, but *really*, this is for your own good.

I have to know what you know about all of this, and I can't help but think that your new mystery woman will be able to shed some light on things.

TAP TAP TAP

WELL, WHAT'D YOU FORGET *THIS* TIME? OH! I'M SORRY. I THOUGHT YOU WERE SOMEONE ELSE.

OH, THAT'S ALL RIGHT. I'M A... *FRIEND* OF CAROL'S ACTUALLY. DIAN BELMONT. COULD I COME IN FOR A MOMENT? I REALLY NEED TO TALK TO YOU.

UH...WELL, YOU LOOK HARMLESS ENOUGH. COME ON IN AND LET'S GET THIS OVER WITH. ACTUALLY, I'VE BEEN EXPECTING YOU TO FOLLOW HER HERE.

YOU HAVE?

SURE. I KNEW CAROL WAS SEEING SOMEONE ELSE.

FIGURED IT WAS ONLY A MATTER OF TIME BEFORE THE SHOWDOWN.

THOUGH YOU DON'T REALLY STRIKE ME AS HER *TYPE*--

OH, NO! I'M NOT CAROL'S... I MEAN... WE'RE JUST FRIENDS.

COFFEE?

THANKS. SO I'M NOT MISTAKEN? YOU AND CAROL ARE...

WELL, I GUESS I'VE ALREADY LET THAT CAT OUT. IT'S NOT THAT I HATE MEN OR ANYTHING. I JUST FEEL VERY *CLOSE* TO CAROL. ALWAYS HAVE.

WE GREW UP ON THE WRONG SIDE OF TOWN TOGETHER. CAROL'S MANAGING TO GET OUT OF IT BUT I'M STILL HERE. SO WHY'RE *YOU* ON HER TAIL?

I'M *WORRIED* ABOUT HER. HAS CAROL, WELL, THIS IS A LITTLE *INDELICATE*, BUT HAS CAROL MENTIONED ANYTHING TO YOU ABOUT THE MURDERS THAT HAVE BEEN IN THE PAPERS?

MURDERS? CAROL? MISS BELMONT. CAROL MAY SNEAK OUT MY WAY FOR A LITTLE SECRET ROMANCE NOW AND THEN, BUT THAT DOESN'T MAKE HER A *CRIMINAL*.

NO. OF COURSE NOT. I DIDN'T MEAN TO *SUGGEST* THAT, BUT--

THE ONLY THING CAROL'S GUILTY OF IS TRYING TO HOOK UP WITH SOME UNSUSPECTING *SCHMOE* WHO LIVES UP ON THE WEST SIDE. SHE THINKS SHE CAN *MARRY* HER WAY INTO HAPPILY EVER AFTER.

SO WHY DO YOU PUT UP WITH THAT?

I ALLOW IT BECAUSE I *HAVE* TO. *FIRST*, CAROL'S A BEAUTIFUL WOMAN AND I KNOW SHE LOVES ME IN HER OWN WAY.

SECOND. WE *BOTH* KNOW THERE'S NO WAY WE COULD LIVE TOGETHER AS A COUPLE. NOT WITH *OUR* FAMILIES, AND NOT IN THIS COUNTRY, SO--

I'M SORRY, BUT I *SHOULD* GET GOING. I DIDN'T MEAN TO *PRY*, BUT YOU'VE CERTAINLY PUT MY MIND TO REST ABOUT CAROL.

SHE'S A GOOD WOMAN.

JUST CONFUSED.

SPEAKING OF WHICH, IF YOU COULD JUST KEEP THIS CON-VERSATION BETWEEN US? I'D *HATE* FOR CAROL TO THINK--

DON'T WORRY, SWEETIE. I'M USED TO KEEPING *SECRETS* WHEN I WANT TO.

How sad. How utterly sad. To have to live one's life awash in secrecy must surely be--

--the most painful thing possible.

WHOOOOO. THAT'S GOING TO HURT TOMORROW. HELL, HURTS *NOW*...

WELL, LET'S SEE ABOUT BARRY--

AAAH! PULSE IS STILL--*NNN*--THERE-- HAVE TO FIND OUT WHA--*HNNN*--KNOWS.

WAKE NOW, BARRY SMITHERS, THE TIME HAS COME TO TELL THE TRUTH.

YESS... *MUST* TELL... TRUTH...

SPEAK IT-- *NNN*--FREELY

--MUST TELL... WHAT WE... DID... WHAT WE...

IF YOU HOPE TO WAKE FROM THIS DREAM, YOU WILL TELL ME WHAT YOU'VE DONE.

WHAT IS HELL NIGHT?

--PARTY GIRL... HELL NIGHT AT THE FRATERNITY...

CONTINUE.

FRATERNITY TRADITION... ALWAYS GET A GIRL TO DANCE... STRIP HERE AT THE CABIN--

PLAY WITH THE GRADUATING BROTHERS A LITTLE... THAT WOULD BE THAT--

SENIOR YEAR... THINGS GOT A LITTLE OUT OF HAND... GOT THE GIRL... BUT SHE WAS LATE... WE'D ALL BEEN DRINKING A BIT TOO MUCH AND WE--WE--

YOU WHAT? WHAT DID YOU DO?

FORCED HER INTO THE BACK ROOM... TIED HER HANDS TOGETHER... TOOK OUR TURNS WITH HER...

NNNN!! NOW-- HOW--HOW MANY OF YOU?

DON'T KNOW... CERTAIN... ALL OF US... TWENTY... MAYBE THIRTY... DON'T REMEM--

WE SENIORS WENT FIRST, OF COURSE--

THIS PARTY GIRL, WHO WAS SHE?

VASSAR GIRL--

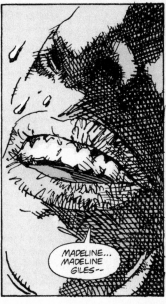

MADELINE... MADELINE GILES--

"I THOUGHT SHE ENJOYED IT."

RING RING RING RING RING

JUST A MINUTE. JUST A MINUTE.

I may not be any closer to the answer, but at least I know it probably doesn't involve Carol--

BELMONT RESIDENCE, THIS IS DIAN SPEAKING--

WES! UM... HELLO, WESLEY. WELL, I'VE BEEN... OUT...UH HUH--

ARE YOU ALL RIGHT? YOU SOUND LIKE YOU'RE IN PAIN OR... OH...I SEE--

EXCUSE ME? NO, I DON'T KNOW HOW YOU CAN GET HOLD OF MADELINE GILES!

YES, I DO HAVE ONE IDEA. GO LOOK FOR HER AT CAROL'S!

AND IF MADELINE ISN'T THERE. MAYBE YOU CAN BIRDDOG ANOTHER OF MY FRIENDS. GOOD BYE!

Madeline Giles. Really!

CLAC

Is there anyone I know who isn't attracted to her?

MMM?

KLIK

I WAS STARTING TO THINK YOU WEREN'T COMING, MADELI--

8

OH MY GOD! WHO ARE YOU? GET OUT OF HERE! GET--

DO NOT FEAR ME. I MEAN YOU NO HARM. I SEEK AN ASSOCIATE OF YOURS.

WH--WHO DO YOU MEAN? WHO ARE YOU TALKING ABOUT?

MADELINE GILES.

UH... I--I DON'T KNOW A MADELINE... GILES DID YOU SAY?

UNNH! THERE IS NO TIME FOR GAMES. YOU MUST TELL ME WHERE SHE IS.

ALL RIGHT! ALL RIGHT! DON'T COME ANY CLOSER. I DON'T KNOW WHERE SHE IS, BUT SHE AND SOME FRIENDS OF HERS OWN SOME LAND, UP NORTH, NEAR STUYVESANT. ARE... ARE YOU ALL RIGHT?

SLEEP WELL CAROL SWANSON. I WILL SEE YOU IN YOUR-- IN YOUR-- NNNH! DAMN...

OH MY GOD...

"JESUS! FEEL LIKE SOMEONE KICKED ME WITH POINTY SHOES--"

NECK FEELS LIKE A *TRUCK* RAN OVER IT--

AND WHY DO I FEEL LIKE I HAVE A HANGOV--?

KNOCK KNOCK

OPEN THE DOOR, SMITHERS! I KNOW YOU DRAGGED YOUR STUPID ASS BACK IN THERE! OPEN UP!

AH, LIEUTENANT BURKE. WHAT AN UNEXPECTED PL--

STUFF IT UP YER ASS. YOU REALLY PISSED ME OFF SNEAKING OUTTA HERE. WHERE THE HELL *WERE* YOU?

I WAS-- I WAS WITH A WOMAN. A RATHER *ROUGH* WOMAN. YOU WOULDN'T *BELIEVE* WHAT HAPPENED.

UH-HUH. YOU LOOK LIKE YOU WENT TEN ROUNDS WITH A BARE-KNUCKLER AND *LOST.* WHO WAS SHE?

JUST A WOMAN. I MET HER SEVERAL WEEKS AGO. JONES I THINK HER NAME WAS... *CARMILLA* JONES.

YOU'D BETTER *HOPE* YOU'RE RIGHT, ASSHOLE 'CAUSE--

FUNNY... I JUST HAD THE STRONGEST FEELING OF DEJA VU. AS IF YOU'D ALREADY ASKED ME THESE QUESTIONS.

I'm just going to ask you flat out, Wesley Dodds--

10

96

What can that social dragon Madeline do for you that *I* can't?

RING! RING!

If you ever answer your phone.

Oh well—you won't escape me that easily.

BAM BAM BAM

Here's hopin' the electric company records are actually *right* for a change.

Carmilla Jones! Open up. Police! Open--

Just hold your horses! I'm coming.

Enough already. What do -- *YOU!*

Hey! You're--

UNNH!

SLAM!

Open this door!

You open it or I do, bitch!

SMAC

11

97

HAVE IT *YOUR* WAY--

CRAC

TURNIN' OFF THE LIGHTS AIN'T GONNA HELP YA! NOW YOU'D BETTER JUST COME OUT WITH YOUR HANDS--

UP YOURS, BASTARD!

THWIP

DAMN! WHAT THE HELL--?

DAMN IT! DAMN IT! GOD *DAMN* IT!

EH--WHAT HAVE WE HERE? YOU MAY'VE GOTTEN OUT THE DOOR, BUT YOU DIDN'T GET AWAY YET--

--'CAUSE I KNOW *YOU*, LADY--

SALLY STAR...YOU MANAGE THE CONGO.

AND I'M BETTIN' YOU KNOW A WHOLE LOT MORE THAN THE SAMBA.

12

HUMPHRIES? WHAT'S ALL THAT RACKET OUT THERE? SOUNDS LIKE A HURRICANE.

I'M SORRY, SIR, BUT SHE ABSOLUTELY *OVERPOWERED* ME--

OH, IS *THAT* WHAT I SOUND LIKE TO YOU?

THAT'S ALL RIGHT, HUMPHRIES... MISS BELMONT AND I HAVE SOME *PRIVATE* MATTERS TO ATTEND TO.

I'LL MAKE *CERTAIN* YOU'RE NOT DISTURBED.

ENOUGH SMALL TALK. SO WHAT *IS* YOUR MORBID FASCINATION WITH MADELINE GILES?

AND WHY DO YOU SEEM TO HAVE *NO* INTEREST IN *ME* ASIDE FROM SEEING HOW QUICKLY YOU CAN ESCAPE MY COMPANY?

DIAN, IT IS *NOTHING* LIKE THAT, REALLY. YOU'RE OVERREACTING.

WELL, THEN, WHY DON'T YOU TELL ME WHAT IT *IS* LIKE?

VERY WELL... *UH*, WELL, IT'S A LITTLE *EMBARRASSING* TO ADMIT, BUT IN MY SPARE TIME, I LIKE TO PERFORM A LITTLE... *AMATEUR* SLEUTHING.

IS THAT SUPPOSED TO *IMPRESS* ME?

13

NO, NO, IT ISN'T. *NNNH*-- NOT AT ALL.

WELL THEN--

ACTUALLY, IT'S NOTHING DRAMATIC. JUST A *MENTAL* EXERCISE.

I'VE BEEN LOOKING INTO THE CLUB MURDERS AND I'VE LINKED THEM ALL BACK TO A SINGLE *FRATERNITY*. I'VE *SINCE* DECIDED THAT MADELINE MAY HOLD IMPORTANT INFORMATION ABOUT THE CRIMES.

THAT'S *ALL* YOU WANT HER FOR?

OF COURSE. WHAT ELSE *COULD* IT BE?

WELL, IT'S JUST... I THOUGHT--

OH, WESLEY. YOU MUST THINK ME A TERRIBLE FOOL!

OF COURSE NOT, DIAN. I THINK YOU'RE *MARVELOUS,* TRULY *UNIQUE* AND BEAUTIFUL.

YOUR REACTIONS WERE *MORE* THAN UNDERSTANDABLE, THEY WERE...THEY WERE *FLATTERING.* AND I FEEL THE SAME ABOUT *YOU!*

IF ONLY THERE WERE SOME WAY TO--

THERE IS.

MMM...

MM-- *NNH!* MMMMM...

14

BAM BAM BAM BAM

WHO IS IT--

OPEN THE GODDAMN DOOR!

OH, *MADELINE*.

WHAT IS IT? YOU LOOK LIKE--

SHUT UP!

AND CLOSE THE DOOR, FOR CHRISSAKES!

MADELINE? WHAT'S THE MATTER?

NOTHING'S THE MATTER! PACK A CHANGE OF CLOTHES, *NOW*. I'VE GOT TO CALL SALLY AND THEN WE'RE OUT OF--

SALLY! MADELINE... STOP *TALKING* AND LISTEN! I'M *BLOWN*. GET A CAR AND I'LL MEET YOU BEHIND THE CLUB. WE'RE HEADING TO THE RETREAT... JUST DO IT!

UM, MADELINE? I *HEARD* YOU TALKING, AND I--

-- I DON'T THINK I *WANT* TO GO WITH YOU. I JUST DON'T--

OH, QUIT BEING SO *PATHETIC* AND SPIT IT OUT.

I'M NOT *LIKE* YOU, MADELINE. I DON'T *WANT* TO GET INTO ANY TROUBLE. I WON'T TELL ANYONE. I SWEAR BUT I--

DAMN *RIGHT* YOU WON'T, *DARLING*.

15

"Love is not a thing--"

"Love is not a place--"

"Love is not a ring--"

"For love is but a dream--"

"And love is not a face--"

"In your true love's soft embrace--"

HNNH!

WESLEY? IS SOMETHING THE MATTER?

NO, DIAN. EVERYTHING IS WONDERFUL.

I DON'T WANT YOU TO FEEL LIKE YOU-- FEEL--OOOOH!!

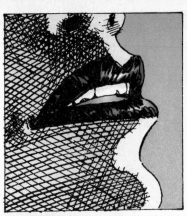

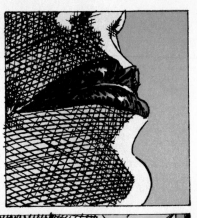

My mother wrote that poem as a young woman. I always thought it trite--

Until tonight.

WHEEEW... SOMEDAY, MISS DIAN BELMONT, I PROMISE YOU WE'LL HAVE SOMETHING *MORE*. BUT FOR TONIGHT--

--SLEEP WELL, MY LOVE.

PLEASANT DREA--UH... SLEEP WELL...

17

...YOU CAME BACK FOR ME?...

MADELINE?

...DIDN'T MEAN TO MAKE YOU ANGRY...

...DON'T BE MAD...I'LL GO... PLEASE... JUST DON'T HURT ME ANYMORE...

I WILL PHONE HELP FOR YOU; DON'T TRY TO SP--

--I'LL MEET SALLY AT THE CONGO WITH YOU... PLEASE... JUST DON'T...

REST FREE FROM WORRY, CAROL SWANSON. I WON'T LEAVE YOU ALONE IN THE DARKNESS.

18

104

WESLEY?

Where could he have gone? Maybe it was all just a dream--

Or maybe not.

What an experience. I never... felt that way before.

And yet, if it was so special, where is...

WESLEY?

WESLEY?

Madeline? He wouldn't--

Oh my gosh! Carol!

I hope that she's all right--

CAROL? YOUR DOOR WAS OPEN SO I--

MY GOD! WHAT HAVE YOU DONE TO HER? WHAT--

MISS BELMONT, TEND TO YOUR FRIEND.

CALL TO HER AND KEEP HER IN IN THE WORLD OF THE LIVING.

AN AMBULANCE IS ON ITS WAY, BUT YOU MAY BE HER ONLY HOPE FOR HOLDING ON.

WAIT, I...DON'T KNOW WHAT TO DO--

I HAVE FAITH IN YOU, DIAN.

WAIT, YOU CAN'T JUST LEAVE! THIS IS A CRIME SCENE!

DIAN? LET HIM GO...

HE'S GOING TO STOP HER...

SALLY!

ARE YOU OUT OF YOUR *MIND?*

WHY ARE YOU JUST *STANDING* HERE? WHY AREN'T YOU IN THE CAR?

FIGURE IT OUT, MADELINE.

WHA--?

END OF THE LINE, SISTER. YOU *ALMOST* GOT AWAY WITH IT, BUT THEN YOU GOT SLOPPY. DON'T FEEL BAD. YOUR KIND *ALWAYS* DOES.

REALLY, *OFFICER,* I'M NOT WHO YOU THINK I--

SHUT UP AND DROP THE GUN.

CL-CHIK

YOU NEED TO LEARN HOW TO TREAT A LADY, MISTER.

I DON'T DOUBT THAT, BUT YOU ARE WHO I'M--

WHO THE--

SHE'S NO--

I SAID SHUT UP AND DROP THE GUN OR I'LL MAKE YOU A NEW MOUTH.

CLAC

EXCELLENT, DEBRA.

SHOULD'VE BROUGHT SOME HELP, LIEUTENANT.

JUST LIKE A MAN--

ENOUGH OF YOUR HATRED, MADELINE GILES. ENOUGH OF YOUR BLOODLUST.

MADDY?!

SHIT!

NOT AGAIN!

≋COUGH! COUGH!≋

≋COUGH! COUGH!≋

22

BLAM! BLAM! BLAM!

GET IN THE CAR, SALLY.

:COUGH:

DEBBIE?

WHERE ARE Y--

CLOSER THAN YOU THINK.

DR--DROP THE GUN, SISTER.

YOU ASKED FOR IT.

BLAM!

UNHHHH!

I'VE BEEN--I'VE BEEN--

MADELINE!

THEY DESERVED IT... EVERY LAST ONE OF... TAKE IT... TAKE THE BLOOD... CONSECRATE... OUR HOME--

23

≈COUGH COUGH.≈

I WILL... THEY DID... YES.

YES, MADELINE... YES THEY DID...

WHERE THE HELL DID THAT LUNATIC GO?

YES THEY DID...

"DIAN? SORRY TO WAKE YOU, SWEETIE--"

BUT I HEARD ABOUT CAROL. I WANTED TO BE SURE SHE WAS ALL RIGHT.

HM? OH, YEAH, YES, THEY THINK SHE'LL PULL THROUGH. I'M GOING TO SEE HER LATER.

WELL THAT'S FINE, JUST FINE. YOU KNOW, IF YOU SLEEP ALL DAY, YOU WON'T HAVE TIME TO RETURN WESLEY'S CALL. HE PHONED A LITTLE WHILE AGO.

THANKS, DADDY.

"For love is but a dream--"

"In your true love's embrace--"

HELLO, WES?

I WAS JUST THINKING ABOUT LAST NIGHT...

T H E · E N D

Matt Wagner Steven T Seagle Guy Davis
SANDMAN MYSTERY THEATRE
"...a sudden blur of coiled leather and the flesh opened up like a rose."
THE SCORPION 1 of 4

"People starving on the
streets and we sit here
like kings of the world,
throwing around
imaginary money
like it was newsprint."

THE
SCORPION

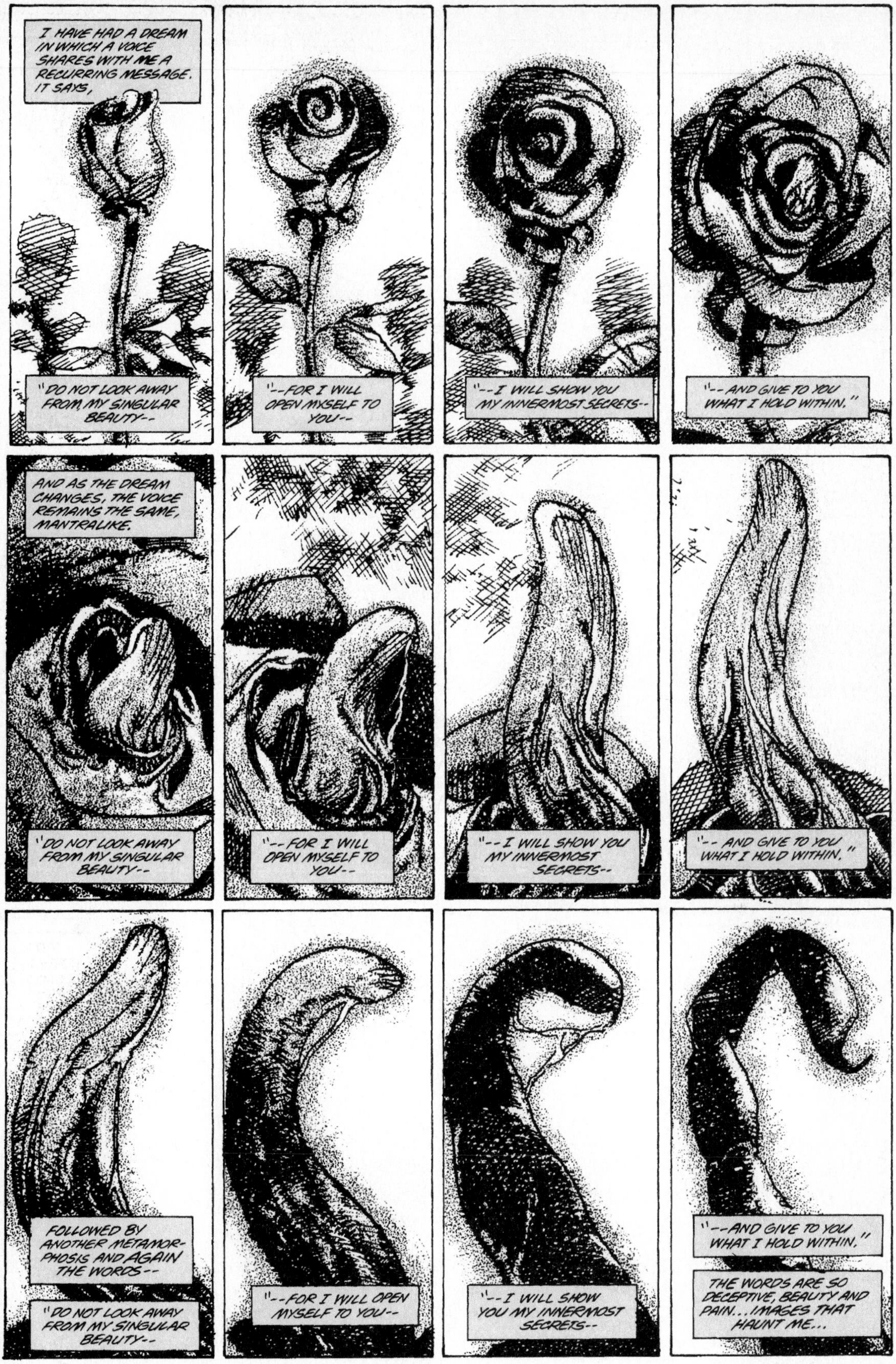

I HAVE HAD A DREAM IN WHICH A VOICE SHARES WITH ME A RECURRING MESSAGE. IT SAYS,
"DO NOT LOOK AWAY FROM MY SINGULAR BEAUTY--
"--FOR I WILL OPEN MYSELF TO YOU--
"--I WILL SHOW YOU MY INNERMOST SECRETS--
"--AND GIVE TO YOU WHAT I HOLD WITHIN."
AND AS THE DREAM CHANGES, THE VOICE REMAINS THE SAME, MANTRALIKE.
"DO NOT LOOK AWAY FROM MY SINGULAR BEAUTY--
"--FOR I WILL OPEN MYSELF TO YOU--
"--I WILL SHOW YOU MY INNERMOST SECRETS--
"--AND GIVE TO YOU WHAT I HOLD WITHIN."
FOLLOWED BY ANOTHER METAMORPHOSIS AND AGAIN THE WORDS--
"DO NOT LOOK AWAY FROM MY SINGULAR BEAUTY--
"--FOR I WILL OPEN MYSELF TO YOU--
"--I WILL SHOW YOU MY INNERMOST SECRETS--
"--AND GIVE TO YOU WHAT I HOLD WITHIN."
THE WORDS ARE SO DECEPTIVE, BEAUTY AND PAIN...IMAGES THAT HAUNT ME...

THE SCORPION

ACT ONE

MATT WAGNER / STEVEN T. SEAGLE
WRITERS

GUY DAVIS
ARTIST

DAVID HORNUNG
COLORIST

JOHN COSTANZA
LETTERER

ANDROID IMAGES
SEPARATOR

SHELLY ROEBERG
ASSOCIATE EDITOR

KAREN BERGER
EDITOR

...EVEN IN MY WAKING WORLD.

A WORLD WITH THE RUMOR OF WAR ON ITS LIPS. A NATION OF RAMPANT MOBSTER ACTIVITY AND REEKING STREET PEOPLE. A CITY IN WHICH BEAUTY SHOULD BE SNUFFED OUT THE INSTANT IT ARISES. AND YET--

--A PLACE WHERE BEAUTY...INEXPLICABLY... FLOURISHES.

UH--HERE'S YOUR--UH-- COFFEE, MA'AM. SIR? WE WERE *OUT* OF THE RHUBARB, SO I BROUGHT YOU--UH--A SLICE OF THE *PUMPKIN*, BUT IF IT'S NOT UH--TO YOUR *LIKING*, I CAN--

I MUST TELL YOU, DIAN, I *REALLY* ENJOYED OUR EVENING TOGETHER THE OTHER NIGHT.

YOU ENJOYED YOURSELF? BUT *I* WAS THE ONE-- WELL...I MEAN... YOU RAN AWAY SO QUICKLY.

IT WAS *ALL* VERY SPECIAL FOR ME, DIAN, BUT I *DO* HAVE TO APOLOGIZE...FOR NOT BEING THERE WHEN YOU WOKE.

AFTER *YOU* WENT TO SLEEP, I FELT I SHOULD ADJOURN TO MY STUDY. I-- I WAS AFRAID THAT YOU MIGHT HAVE BEEN... *OFFENDED.*

OH MY, *NO.* QUITE THE *OPPOSITE.* I THINK I WAS JUST A BIT... DRAINED, WHAT WITH CAROL AND ALL. I JUST COULDN'T PUT THE PIECES IN PLACE--

--UNLIKE *YOU* WHO FIGURED IT OUT QUITE *EASILY* IT SEEMS. SOME "AMATEUR" DETECTIVE YOU TURNED OUT TO BE.

2

NO, I'M SURE IT'S PERFECTLY FINE, THANK YOU VERY MUCH.

AN AWKWARD BREAKFAST IS A FITTING CAP TO A *TROUBLED* NIGHT.

THERE IS A NEWFOUND INTIMACY BETWEEN DIAN AND ME NOW.

AND THOUGH IT LONGS TO FIND A *VOICE,* IT IS A DIFFICULT BREACH TO CROSS. BUT I BOTH *NEED* AND *WANT* TO MAKE THAT CROSSING.

OH, I WOULDN'T SAY I HAD THE *WHOLE* SOLUTION. IT NEVER CROSSED MY MIND THAT MADELINE--

LET'S NOT TALK ABOUT HER ANYMORE, WES. THAT'S AN UGLY CHAPTER THAT'S BEST LEFT CLOSED NOW.

I'M SORRY. I SUPPOSE IT *IS* ALL A LITTLE FRESH STILL.

SPEAKING OF FRESH, I WAS WONDERING WHEN WE COULD BE TOGETHER AGAIN--

--I'D LIKE TO GET YOU *ALONE* FOR A LITTLE WHILE SO I CAN...

...RETURN YOUR FAVOR...

WELL, YOU'VE CERTAINLY GOT MY *ATTENTION,* DIAN--

③

115

--BUT I HAVE AN *IMPOSSIBLY* BUSY WEEK AHEAD, SO BUSY IN FACT, THAT I DON'T EVEN THINK I'M GOING TO MAKE IT TO THE BUSTER CALHOUN CHARITY CONCERT THIS EVENING--

BUSTER CALHOUN? THE WESTERN FILM STAR? OH, DADDY *LOVES* HIM!

REALLY? THEN IT'S *PERFECT.* YOU'LL HAVE MY TICKETS, TWO SEATS, FRONT ROW CENTER.

OH NO, WESLEY, WE *COULDN'T.*

I *INSIST.*

THE CHARITY FUNCTION IS MERELY A RUSE FOR THE SPONSORS TO CONTACT INVESTORS FOR AN OIL DEAL THEY HAVE GOING. I'M NOT THE *LEAST* BIT INTERESTED SO TAKE THEM.

OTHERWISE, THEY'LL JUST GO TO WASTE

WHY ARE YOU THE SWEETEST MAN IN NEW YORK CITY? DADDY WILL BE *SO* THRILLED.

ACTUALLY, THE TICKETS ARE FOR YOU *AND* YOUR FATHER, BUT THIS... IS JUST FOR YOU.

DIAN IS SO CARING. YET, FOR ALL HER CHARITY WORK, SHE DOESN'T SEEM TO REALIZE HOW LUDICROUS A HIGH-TICKET GALA IS IN THE EBBING TIDES OF THE DEPRESSION.

AN ORIGAMI ROSE? IT'S LOVELY...

BUT NEXT TO YOU IT'S ONLY PAPER.

--AT TIMES WHEN FATHERS DIG DINNER FROM GARBAGE CONTAINERS WE DRESS UP IN OUR SUNDAY'S FINEST AND PAY LUDICROUS AMOUNTS OF MONEY TO HEAR THE NASAL MEWLINGS OF A WESTERN SIMPLETON. BEAUTY AND PAIN.

4

♪--and thaaat--♪ was the ennnd--of Black Heart Bart!

THANK YEW, LADIES AN' GENTS! I'M BUSTER CALHOUN AND THAT'S THE SHOW FER THIS EVENING! YEEEEE-HA!

OH, THAT WAS TERRIFIC, HE WAS JUST TERRIFIC! DON'T YOU THINK, DIAN?

HE WAS DEFINITELY--

IT WAS SUPER, JUST SUPER!

OH! THERE'S THE MAYOR. WE SHOULD SAY HELLO.

MR. MAYOR? MR. MAYOR?

LARRY! HOW ARE YOU DOING? I MUST BE PAYING YOU TOO MUCH IF YOU CAN AFFORD TICKETS TO AN EVENT LIKE THIS.

OH, NO, MR. MAYOR. YOU'RE NOT OVERPAYING ME AT ALL. WESLEY DODDS GAVE ME HIS TICKETS AS A GIFT. I LOVE THAT COWBOY MUSIC, AND ESPECIALLY BUSTER CALHOUN!

OH, YES, I WAS WONDERING WHY DODDS WASN'T HERE.. THAT MAN SEEMS TO MISS EVERY-THING THESE DAYS.

I WAS HOPING TO INTRODUCE HIM TO THE MEN WHO PUT ON TONIGHT'S SHOW, BUT I GUESS--

IF IT'S NOT AN IMPOSITION, SIR, I'D BE HONORED TO MEET THEM, AND TO BE ABLE TO THANK THEM PERSONALLY.

WELL, SINCE YOU *ARE* HERE IN WESLEY'S *PLACE*--AHURUMPH--GENTLEMEN, I'D LIKE TO INTRODUCE YOU TO DISTRICT ATTORNEY LAWRENCE BELMONT. LAWRENCE--THE ENTREPRENEURS BEHIND TONIGHT'S EVENT--

MR. EMMANUEL LANE--

HELLO.

--MR. HELMET RUMMEL--

A PLEASURE.

--AND MR. KARL DECHERT.

EH? WHO IS DIS?

WELL, IT'S CERTAINLY A PLEASURE TO MEET YOU, BUT WE WERE JUST LEAVING. I'M AFRAID WE ALL FIND CROWDS MORE THAN A LITTLE...TAXING.

WELL SPOKEN, LET'S DO BE ON OUR WAY.

DON'T WORRY ABOUT IT, GENTLEMEN, THEY'RE *ALWAYS* LIKE THAT.

UH...I JUST WANTED TO EXPRESS MY THANKS FOR YOUR ARRANGING TO GET BUSTER IN HERE, HE WAS *GREAT*.

YEAH, TANKS. GOODNIGHT.

DID I SAY SOMETHING TO *OFFEND* THEM?

AH, MR. CUTLER. I HOPE WE DIDN'T INSULT YOUR SENIOR PARTNERS.

INSULT THEM? GENTLEMEN OF *THEIR* STATURE OFTEN FORGET THE INTRICACIES OF COURTESY.

AND WHO IS THIS *RADIANT* YOUNG WOMAN IN YOUR COMPANY, GENTLEMEN?

OH, THIS IS MY DAUGHTER... MISS DIAN BELMONT.

A *PLEASURE*, MR. CUTLER. I'VE HEARD A LOT ABOUT YOU.

I'LL DO MY BEST TO DISPEL IT, AND PLEASE, CALL ME *STEPHEN.*

ALLOW ME TO INTRODUCE MY DAUGHTER, AND RIGHT-HAND GAL, CASSANDRA, AND THE GATECRASHER *NEXT* TO HER IS OUR ADVERTISING MAN, TERRY STETSON.

HELLO.

A PLEASURE TO MEET YOU, SIR.

YOU KNOW, I'VE BEEN THINKING ABOUT A CAMPAIGN FOR THE CITY HERE. NEW IDEA, ADVERTISING A WHOLE CITY TO THE--

UH--

YOU WORK FOR YOUR FATHER, CASSANDRA?

WITH HIM, ACTUALLY. I'M IN CHARGE OF OUR EUROPEAN DISTRIBU- TION. OF COURSE, WITH THE OIL SITUATION BEING WHAT IT IS OVER *THERE* THESE DAYS, IT'S ALMOST TOO MUCH FOR EVEN *ME* TO KEEP TRACK OF.

LARRY, TELL ME, WHAT BRINGS OUR DISTRICT ATTORNEY TO A HIGHBROW AFFAIR LIKE THIS?

I'M STANDING IN FOR WESLEY DODDS, ACTUALLY.

REALLY? AND WHERE *IS* DODDS TONIGHT? I HAD HOPED TO DISCUSS SOME INVESTMENT POSSIBILITIES WITH HIM. NOW I'M GOING TO HAVE TO TRACK HIM DOWN.

OH, UM...HE HAD SOME WORK TO FINISH. THAT'S *WESLEY* FOR YOU. SOMETIMES, HE'S JUST ALL WORK AND NO PLAY.

SOLITUDE...

⑦

--I SEEK A PERFECT QUIETNESS--

--THOUGH IT IS IMPOSSIBLE TO SHUT OFF THE WORLD I SEE COLLAPSING AROUND ME--

--A WORLD THAT HAS BEEN KNOCKED OUT OF BALANCE.

EUROPE IS DESTROYING ITSELF AND THE ASIAN ECONOMIES ARE CRUMBLING --EVEN AS AMERICA CONTINUES TO DREAM.

I SEE THE VALUES OF DECENCY AND HONESTY BEING SLOWLY EATEN AWAY BY SOME PARASITIC COMPULSION --

AND ALL THE WHILE THE PEOPLE IN MY LIFE PRETEND THAT ALL IS AS IT WAS IN THE GOOD OLD DAYS.

AND SOLITUDE? SOLITUDE IS MERELY AN IMAGINARY CONSTRUCT TOPPLED BY THESE INTRUSIVE TRUTHS.

TRUTHS WHICH WILL ELUDE ME AS WELL WHEN I TRY TO EXPLAIN THIS SCAR TO DIAN. HOW WILL I EXPLAIN IT? ANY WAY I CAN, I'M SURE.

8

SO MUCH OF MY TIME SEEMS TO BE DEVOTED TO TRYING TO EXPLAIN AWAY WHAT I REALLY AM.

PARK IT, PROBST. MISS BONBA UND I VILL NOT BE GOINK BACK OUT.

YES, MR. DECHERT.

TSK TSK TSK TSK--

--TSK TSK TSK.

YOU KNOW... YOU HAFF BEEN A NAUGHTY LITTLE GIRL TONIGHT, SABINA.

121

OH, *REALLY,* MR. DECHERT?

YA, YOU HAFF. I ZAW YOU MAKINK EYES AT YOUNG HERR SHTAMPER.

VAS HE MAKINK EYES AT *YOU?*

DID HE TRY TO--

NUH--

--TRY TO PUT HIZ HANDS ON YOUR *TITTIES?* ON YOUR *BOTTOM?*

SPLOP

DID HE, SABINA?

TELL ME.

I SUPPOSE HE *DID,* MR. DECHERT.

YA. PLEASE, I HAFF *TOLD* YOU... CALL ME *POPPY.*

10

ALL RIGHT, *POPPY*. I *DID* LOOK AT HIM, AND I *DID* LET HIM *TOUCH* ME.

DOES THAT MAKE ME A BAD GIRL?

OH JA JA. UND YOU VILL HAFF TO BE *PUNISHED*.

OH, POPPY! *PLEASE!* YOU'RE NOT GOING TO *SPANK* LITTLE SABINA'S BOTTOM... *ARE YOU?*

I AM *ZORRY,* BUT YOU *LEAF* POPPY NO *CHOICE.*

EIN!--ZWEI!-- DREI!--

OH...! POPPY! STOP! MMMMM...

IS POPPY'S HAND TOO FIRM?

YES, POPPY. IT'S VERY FIRM.

POPPY DOESN'T MEAN TO BE ZO *ZTRICT,* LITTLE SABINA...

...BUT YOU *KNOW* ZAT NO VUN OTHER THAN POPPY IS ALLOWED TO TOUCH ON THOSE MAR-VELOUS TITTIES. TO *SUCK* ON THEM...

RUSTLE

11

123

POPPY? I DIDN'T LET HIM TOUCH *EVERY* PART. I SAVED A SPECIAL PART JUST-- FOR-- YOU.

HMMMM... VELL ZEN, POPPY FORGIVES YOU, LITTLE SABINA, POPPY--

NNH! POPPY FOR-- UNH! GIVES YOU--

POPPY-- NNH!-- FOR--

SWK-

UNH!-- GIVES--

CRAC-

UNNGH!

OCK! CHEESUS!

POPPY?

POPPY?

UNGAAFF--

FUNGH! URK--

POPPY? POPPY? EEEEEE!

DON'T TOUCH HIM YET, EDDIE, I WANT TO GET A SHOT OF HIS *BACK*--

LISTEN, HONEY. NO POINT IN CLAMMIN' UP. WHY DON'T YOU JUST TELL ME WHAT YOU DID TO MR. DECHERT THERE?

I DIDN'T DO *ANYTHING* TO HIM.

LOOK, SISTER, JUST *LOOKIN'* AT THE GUY I KNOW YOU WAS DOIN' *SOMETHIN'* WITH HIM.

HONEST, I WASN'T--

TOOTS, IT'S NO BIG MYSTERY THAT YOU'RE DECHERT'S *TWIST*, SO IF *THAT'S* WHAT YOU'RE TRYIN' TO HIDE, JUST *SAVE* IT.

I'M *TELLING* YOU, I DIDN'T HAVE ANYTHING TO *DO* WITH THIS.

THEN YOU'D BETTER RAT AND *QUICK.* HM...

HE WAS SPANKING ME, HE WAS *ON* ME, THEN HE FELL OVER. I JUST FIGURED HE HAD A HEART ATTACK. THAT'S ALL.

GOT YOUR KILLER THERE, BURKE?

NAH. NO MOTIVE, AND BESIDES--

--I CHECKED UNDER HER NAILS... NO BLOOD.

WHATEVER MADE THIS MARK, IT *WASN'T* A STREET GIRL GETTING TOO WILD WITH AN OLD MAN.

13

I TELL YA, ROSS, THIS DAMN TOWN IS GETTING WEIRDER BY THE DAY.

I KNOW WHAT YOU MEAN, BURKE. ANY NEW NEWS ON THAT DECHERT KILLING?

YEAH, WORD'S IN FROM THE CORONER. POISON. FAST-ACTING, LETHAL SHIT TOO... KICKED IN ALMOST INSTANTLY.

SAYS HERE THE POISON GOT IN THROUGH THE WOUND ON HIS BACK? SO THAT *MUST* MEAN IT WAS THE GIRL.

NAH, SHE ISN'T OUR FINGER. WHOEVER PUT THE CUT IN DECHERT'S BACK IS WHO WE'RE LOOKIN' FOR. AND GET *THIS*--

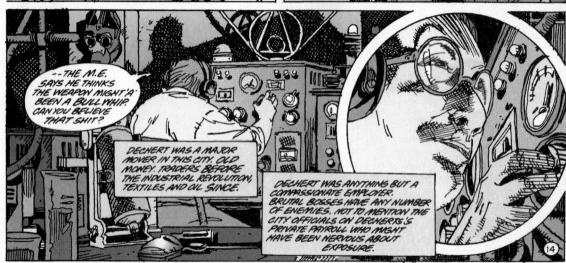

--THE M.E. SAYS HE THINKS THE WEAPON MIGHT'A BEEN A *BULLWHIP.* CAN YOU BELIEVE THAT SHIT?

DECHERT WAS A MAJOR MOVER IN THIS CITY. OLD MONEY. TRADERS BEFORE THE INDUSTRIAL REVOLUTION, TEXTILES AND OIL SINCE.

DECHERT WAS ANYTHING BUT A COMPASSIONATE EMPLOYER. BRUTAL BOSSES HAVE ANY NUMBER OF ENEMIES. NOT TO MENTION THE CITY OFFICIALS ON DECHERT'S PRIVATE PAYROLL WHO MIGHT HAVE BEEN NERVOUS ABOUT EXPOSURE.

14

REGARDLESS OF *WHO* DID HIM IN, IT ISN'T OFTEN THAT SOMEBODY SO *HIGH UP* IN THIS CITY--

GENTLEMEN, CASSANDRA, BEFORE WE START THIS MEETING, I THINK I SHOULD SAY A FEW WORDS ABOUT OUR LONGTIME COLLEAGUE NOW DEPARTED.

--TAKES THAT KIND OF FALL.

HARRY WAS A *PIVOTAL* FORCE IN THIS COMPANY, AND HIS PASSING SHOULD SERVE TO REMIND US ALL THAT LIFE IS A FLEETING, DELICATE THING.

HIS STRONG SENSE OF DISCIPLINE SHALL ALWAYS REMAIN A FOUNDATION FOR THIS COMPANY IN EVERY ENDEAVOR.

A MOMENT OF SILENCE, PLEASE.

GOOD.

THAT SAID, I THINK IT'S TIME WE GOT BACK TO BUSINESS AND TURNED THE MEETING OVER TO TERRY.

THANKS, MR. CUTLER. MR. DECHERT'S PASSING *WAS* A SHOCK, BUT IT CAN'T STOP THE WHEELS OF HIGH FINANCE, SO ON THE BRIGHTER SIDE OF THINGS-- THE BUSTER CALHOUN SHOW WAS A *HUGE* SUCCESS.

⑮

COMPASSIONATE LITTLE SON OF A BITCH, ISN'T HE?

DID THIS LITTLE COWBOY STUNT BRING US ANY CLOSER TO OUR REAL GOAL, STETSON?

YESSIR. NOT ONLY ARE WE BACK IN THE PUBLIC EYE IN A POSITIVE WAY, SIR, BUT WE LINED UP OVER 30 NEW CONTRIBUTORS FOR THE FOREIGN OIL REFINERY DEPOSITORY PROJECT, OR THE F.O.R.D. AS I'M NOW CALLING IT-- HEH HEH, LITTLE JOKE THERE--

YES, VERY LITTLE. WHERE DOES THAT LEAVE US IN TERMS OF FUNDING?

IT IS MY OPINION THAT WE ARE SHORT ONLY ONE MAJOR INVESTOR. WESLEY DODDS SEEMS TO BE THE MOST LIKELY TO BE ABLE TO FORWARD THE BALANCE OF THE START-UP CAPITAL.

I'VE HEARD HE'S A TOUGH NUT TO CRACK WHEN IT COMES TO GETTING MONEY AWAY FROM HIS HOLDINGS.

TRUE ENOUGH, AND THAT'S WHY I'M RECOMMENDING THAT YOU AND I, MR. CUTLER, PURSUE AN AGGRESSIVE COURT-SHIP FOR...

I DON'T WANT TO APPEAR TOO VORACIOUS FOLLOWING THE COMPANY'S RECENT TRAGEDY. I SUGGEST THAT CASSANDRA TAKE MY PLACE.

CASS-- WITH ALL DUE RESPECT, MR. CUTLER, THIS IS A MAN'S GAME. WE CAN'T BE PLAYIN' AROUND WHILE THE WINDOW'S OPEN.

WHERE THERE'S AN OPEN WINDOW, THERE'S USUALLY A DRAFT, MR. STETSON. YOU AND ME. TAKE IT OR LEAVE IT.

HEH. OKAY... YOU WIN, MISS CUTLER. LET'S HOPE YOU'RE AS LUCKY WITH WESLEY DODDS.

16

ONE OF THE PROBLEMS WITH HAVING INHERITED MY FATHER'S INTERESTS IS THAT I INHERITED THE SOCIAL RESPONSIBILITIES ATTACHED TO THEM AS WELL.

IT'S NOT THAT I HATE BEING WEALTHY. ONLY A FOOL WOULD DENY THE OBVIOUS ADVANTAGES. STILL, MY FORTUNE DOES OFTEN BECOME A PUBLIC ALBATROSS. ONE I WOULD JUST AS SOON REMOVE FOREVER.

WELL, AT LEAST THE RIDE OVER HERE WAS NICE.

WES...IT'S FINE. REALLY. YOU'VE GOTTEN ALL WORKED UP OVER THIS DINNER AND I DON'T UNDERSTAND WHY. I DIDN'T THINK WE'D EVEN SEE EACH OTHER TONIGHT, AND NOW WE'LL BE HAVING A FULL EVENING TOGETHER.

YES... JUST YOU AND ME... AND THE CUTLER CUTTHROATS. I WISH IT COULD HAVE BEEN JUST US, BUT I REALLY COULDN'T THINK OF ANOTHER DELICATE WAY TO BACK OUT OF THIS.

BETTER TO JUST HEAR THEM OUT, DECLINE, AND HOPEFULLY BE DONE WITH THEM FOR ANOTHER YEAR OR SO. I JUST HOPE IT ISN'T TOO DREADFUL FOR YOU--

IT'S ALL RIGHT, WES. ANY TIME SPENT WITH YOU WILL BE EXCITING, I'M SURE.

DID I MENTION THIS WAS A MEETING TO DISCUSS AN OIL IMPORTING DEAL?

OH...DO YOU THINK OUR CAB HAS ALREADY LEFT?

HEH. OKAY, OKAY... I'LL STOP.

RIGHT THIS WAY, PLEASE.

WESLEY, GLAD YOU COULD MAKE IT. WE MISSED YOU AT THE BUSTER CALHOUN SHOW.

DON'T TAKE IT PERSONALLY, I ALWAYS HAVE TROUBLE MAKING IT TO FUNDRAISERS.

SHARP! VERY SHARP! I LIKE A MAN WITH WIT.

ALLOW ME TO INTRODUCE MY... FRIEND, MISS DIAN BELMONT, DIAN THIS IS--

WE'VE ALREADY MET.

129

THAT WE HAVE, LAST EVENING.

I MUST SAY THAT I'M *SURPRISED* TO SEE *YOU* HERE, MISS CUTLER. I WOULD HAVE THOUGHT THAT STEPHEN WOULD ATTEND.

HAHAHA! WELL, YOU KNOW HOW *WOMEN* ARE THESE DAYS... CAN'T KEEP THEM DOWN LONG ENOUGH TO *TAME* 'EM.

TERRY'S USED TO *HORSES*, AS YOU CAN SEE, MR. DODDS. FORTUNATELY FOR US ALL HE'S LEFT HIS SPURS AT HOME TONIGHT.

MR. DODDS, I ASSURE YOU, I'M FULLY QUALIFIED TO REPRESENT MY FATHER'S INTERESTS HERE, SO LET'S CUT TO THE CHASE, *SHALL* WE? WHAT WOULD IT TAKE TO SEE YOU AS A PRINCIPAL BACKER OF COAST TO COAST OIL?

WELL, I'M ACTUALLY NOT HERE TO OFFER *MY* VIEWS, I'M MUCH MORE INTERESTED IN HAVING YOU EXPLAIN *YOUR* POSITION, AND THEN CONVINCE ME MY INVOLVEMENT IS BENEFICIAL TO MORE THAN JUST ONE SIDE OF THIS TRIANGLE.

TERRY'S HYPERBOLE ASIDE, WE HAVE A COM-PREHENSIVE PLAN THAT IS GOING TO NET *YOU* THE MAXI-MUM PROFIT ON THE BUSINESS WHILE HELPING *US* EXPAND OUR TRADE CORRIDORS.

BENEFICIAL? WHY IT'S THE BEST THING T'COME DOWN THE LINE IN A *LONG* TIME.

NOT TO MENTION THE POTENTIAL FOR FUTURE GROWTH THROUGH THE--

PEOPLE STARVING ON THE STREETS AND WE SIT HERE LIKE KINGS OF THE WORLD, THROW-ING AROUND IMAGIN-ARY MONEY LIKE IT WAS NEWSPRINT.

I'LL NOT BE PART OF IT.

⑱

THE EVENING WAS LONG AND UNPRODUCTIVE. I FOUND MY MIND LESS AND LESS ON NUMBERS AND MORE AND MORE ON DIAN--

--AND ON THE MENTION OF DECHERT'S UNTIMELY DEMISE, WHICH CASSANDRA SLIPPED IN SOMEWHERE BETWEEN "DUTIES" AND "EUROPEAN WARTIME SURPLUS."

WELL, THAT WAS CERTAINLY AN INTERESTING EVENING. NOT AT ALL WHAT I HAD EXPECTED.

YES, A LITTLE DRY... AND THAT WAS JUST THE PRIME RIB.

OH I DON'T KNOW. I FIND THAT WHOLE WORLD OF CORPORATE MACHIN- ATIONS QUITE COMPELLING--

--THOUGH I FIND YOU MUCH MORE SO.

OH, WESLEY! AH DO BELIEVE AH FEEL FAINT! THERE'S SOMETHIN' ABOUT YOUR TOUCH THAT--

WELL WHAT IF I TOUCH YOU LIKE... THIS?

AND THIS!

YOU STARTED THIS!

NO--HAHA-- STOP IT! I'M TICKL--HA-- ISH!

OW... MY SIDES HURT! ARE YOU... COMING UP?

SORRY, ANOTHER EARLY MORNING TOMORROW. SOON THOUGH, SOON.

OH POOH. GOODNIGHT, YOU ARTFUL DODGER!

THOUGH I DON'T FOR THE LIFE OF ME KNOW WHY, DECHERT WINS OUT OVER DIAN.

17139

19

THIS TIME IT'S MY *PRIVATE* RESPONSIBILITIES THAT TAKE *PRECEDENCE* OVER MY *IMMEDIATE DESIRES.*

WELL, HERE WE ARE THEN.

THANKS FOR THE LIFT HOME, TERRY.

IT WAS MY *PLEASURE,* CASSIE.

CASSANDRA?

I WANT YOU TO KNOW THAT I *MEAN* THAT, *REALLY,* I DO.

TERRY... I *UH...*

YEAH?

I THINK WE... WORKED WELL TOGETHER TONIGHT. DODDS WILL ALMOST CERTAINLY GO FOR THE DEAL NOW.

YEAH... YEAH, I'M *SURE* HE WILL TOO.

YES... WELL, GOODNIGHT.

YOU'RE A *SLICK* ONE, TERRY. I'LL GIVE YOU THAT. A LITTLE *PRIMITIVE* PERHAPS, BUT SLICK.

I'LL TAKE THAT AS A COMPLIMENT.

YOU CAN TAKE THAT *ANY* WAY YOU WANT TO TAKE IT. GOODNIGHT.

20

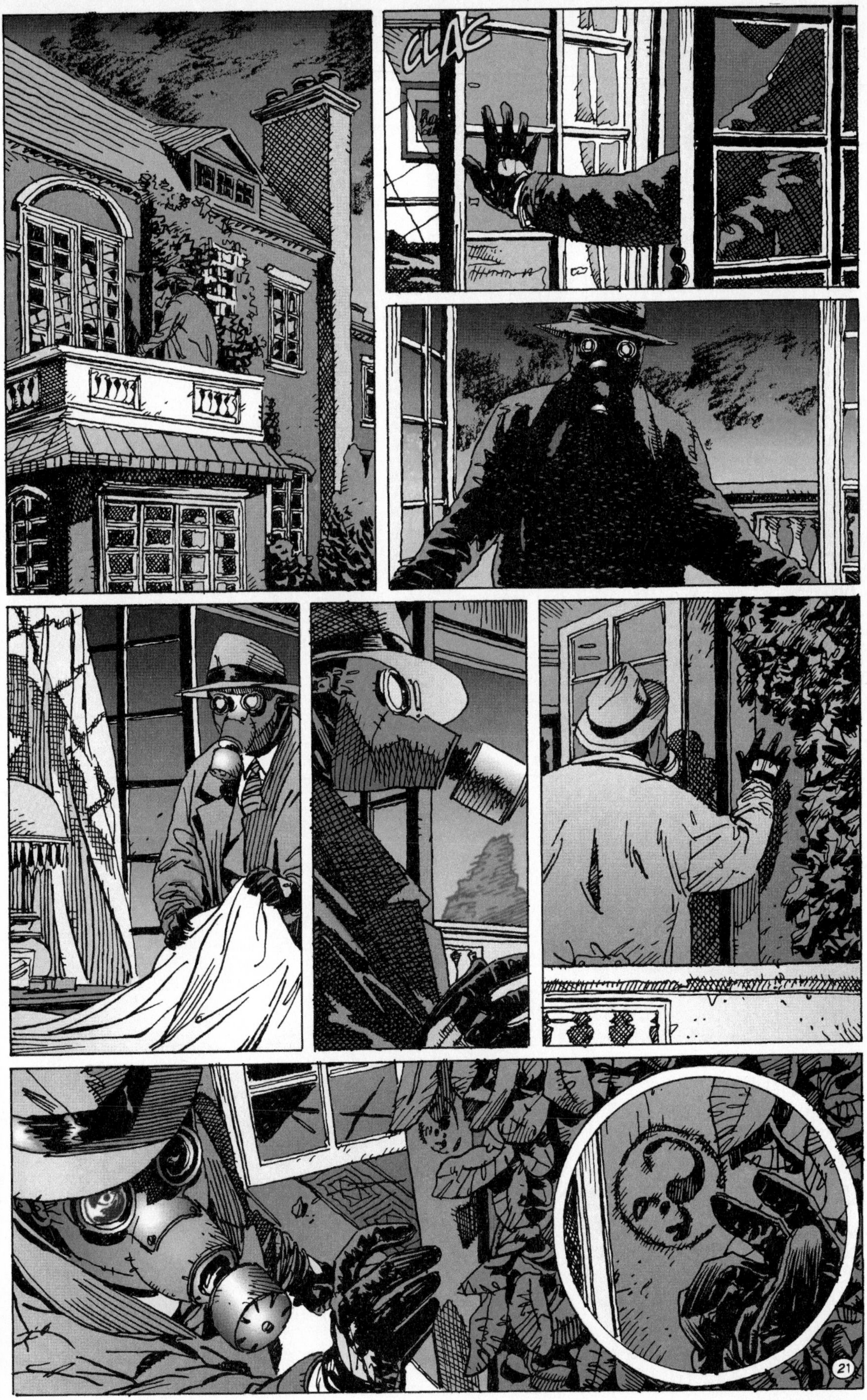
CLAC
21

DOMINICK! WHERE IN HELL ARE YOU?

I'M SO SORRY, MR. RUMMEL. I DIDN'T HEAR YOU COME IN--

NO, OBVIOUSLY YOU DIDN'T. I'M GOING TO MY STUDY. I'LL HAVE COFFEE AND BRANDY THERE, IN TEN MINUTES.

YES, SIR--

AND I WANT MY BATH DRAWN BY ELEVEN THIRTY. NOW BE OFF.

YES, SIR.

I SHOULD HAVE KNOWN A SPIC WOULD NEVER AMOUNT TO A MINUTE'S WORTH OF USE AROUND HERE.

...NOT AROUND WHEN YOU NEED HIM...

TOK

...UNDERFOOT WHEN YOU DON'T...

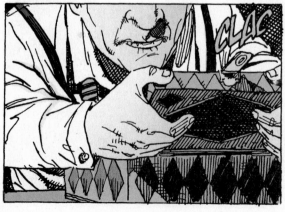

CLAC

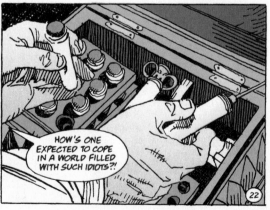

HOW'S ONE EXPECTED TO COPE IN A WORLD FILLED WITH SUCH IDIOTS?!

22

IDIOTS AND...

IDIOTS AND FOOLSSS...

TAP TAP

EH?

I THOUGHT I TOLD YOU *NOT* TO BOTHER ME.

BUT... YOU SAID YOU WANTED COFFEE AND...?

DON'T TELL ME WHAT *I* WANT! LIKE A FINE STEED, YOUR RESPONSES SHOULD BE... IMMEDIATE! FLUID! PRECISE!

DON'T TELL *ME* WHAT I WANT!

NO, SIR, I *WOULDN'T*--

DID I *ASK* YOU TO ANSWER ME, DOMINICK? YOU ARE A *SERVANT!* DON'T SPEAK UNLESS YOU'RE *SPOKEN TO!*

YES, SIR

WOULD YOU LIKE ME TO PUT AWAY YOUR--

KEEP YOUR HANDS *OFF* OF THAT. JUST SERVE THE DAMNED COFFEE! MOVE!

YES, SIR!

23

I WANT MY HASSOCK! OH GOOD, YOU'VE GOT IT. GOOD.

DID YOU KNOW, DOMINICK, THAT MY PARTNER, MR. DECHERT, WAS *KILLED* IN HIS HOME LAST NIGHT? GO AHEAD, YOU MAY ANSWER ME.

NO, I DID *NOT* KNOW THAT, SIR. WAS IT NATURAL CAUSES?

YES...IT WAS NATURAL. HE *DIED*. RUB MY FEET.

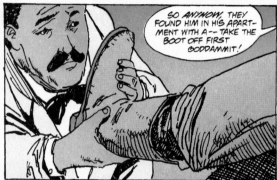

SO *ANYHOW*, THEY FOUND HIM IN HIS APARTMENT WITH A -- TAKE THE BOOT OFF FIRST GODDAMMIT!

I'M TRYING TO --

TRY HARDER!

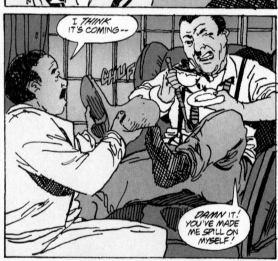

I *THINK* IT'S COMING --

CHUF

DAMN IT! YOU'VE MADE ME SPILL ON MYSELF!

WHAC WHAC WHAC WHAC WHACK!

YOU -- STUPID -- IGNORANT -- BASTARD

(24)

CRAC-

AH!

SHIT! WHAT DID YOU DO TO ME?

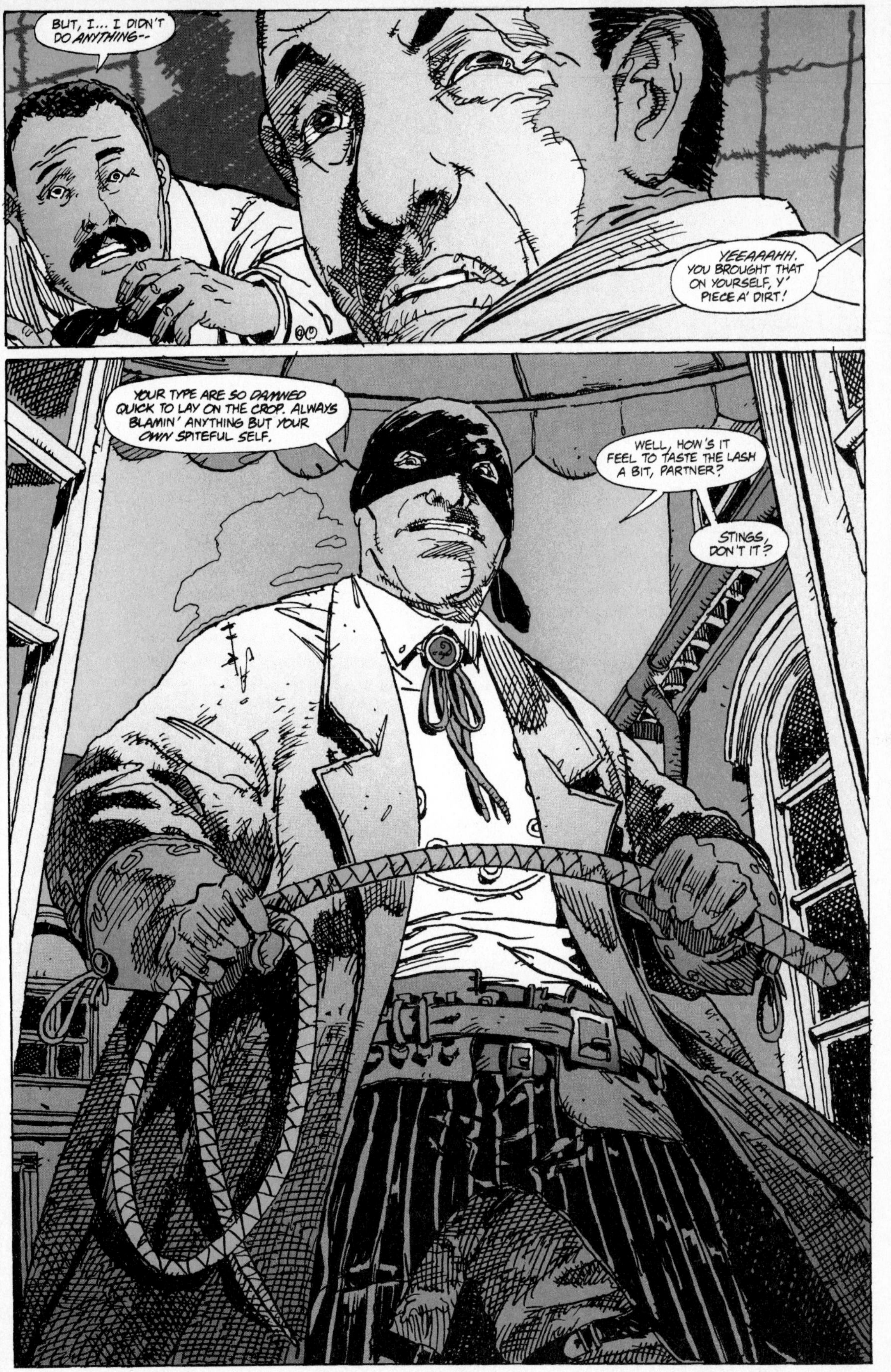
BUT, I... I DIDN'T DO ANYTHING--
YEEAAAHH. YOU BROUGHT THAT ON YOURSELF, Y' PIECE A' DIRT!
YOUR TYPE ARE SO DAMNED QUICK TO LAY ON THE CROP. ALWAYS BLAMIN' ANYTHING BUT YOUR OWN SPITEFUL SELF.
WELL, HOW'S IT FEEL TO TASTE THE LASH A BIT, PARTNER?
STINGS, DON'T IT?

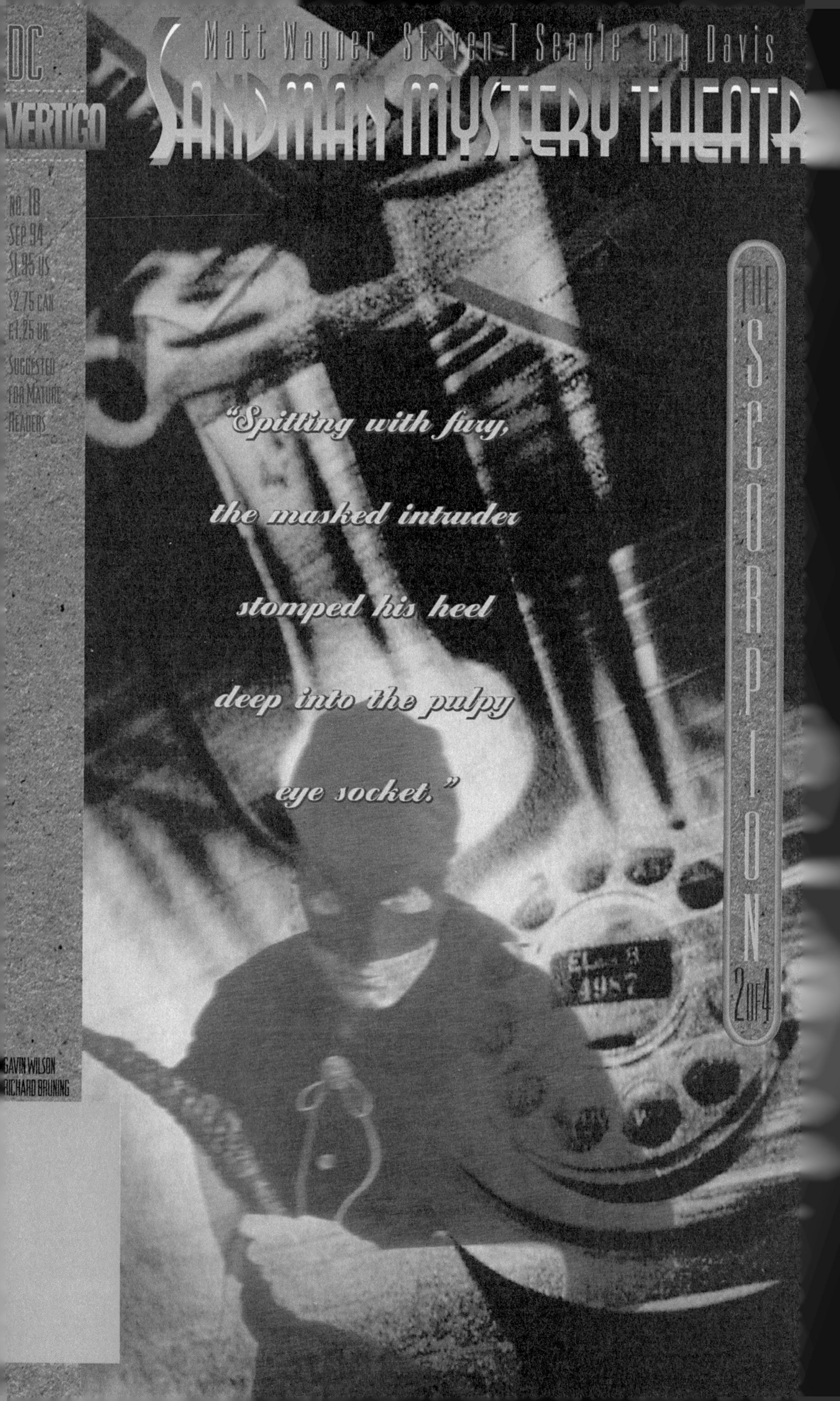

DC VERTIGO

Matt Wagner · Steven T Seagle · Guy Davis

SANDMAN MYSTERY THEATRE

no. 18
Sep 94
$1.95 US
$2.75 CAN
£1.25 UK

Suggested
for Mature
Readers

GAVIN WILSON
RICHARD BRUNING

THE SCORPION

2 of 4

"Spitting with fury,

the masked intruder

stomped his heel

deep into the pulpy

eye socket."

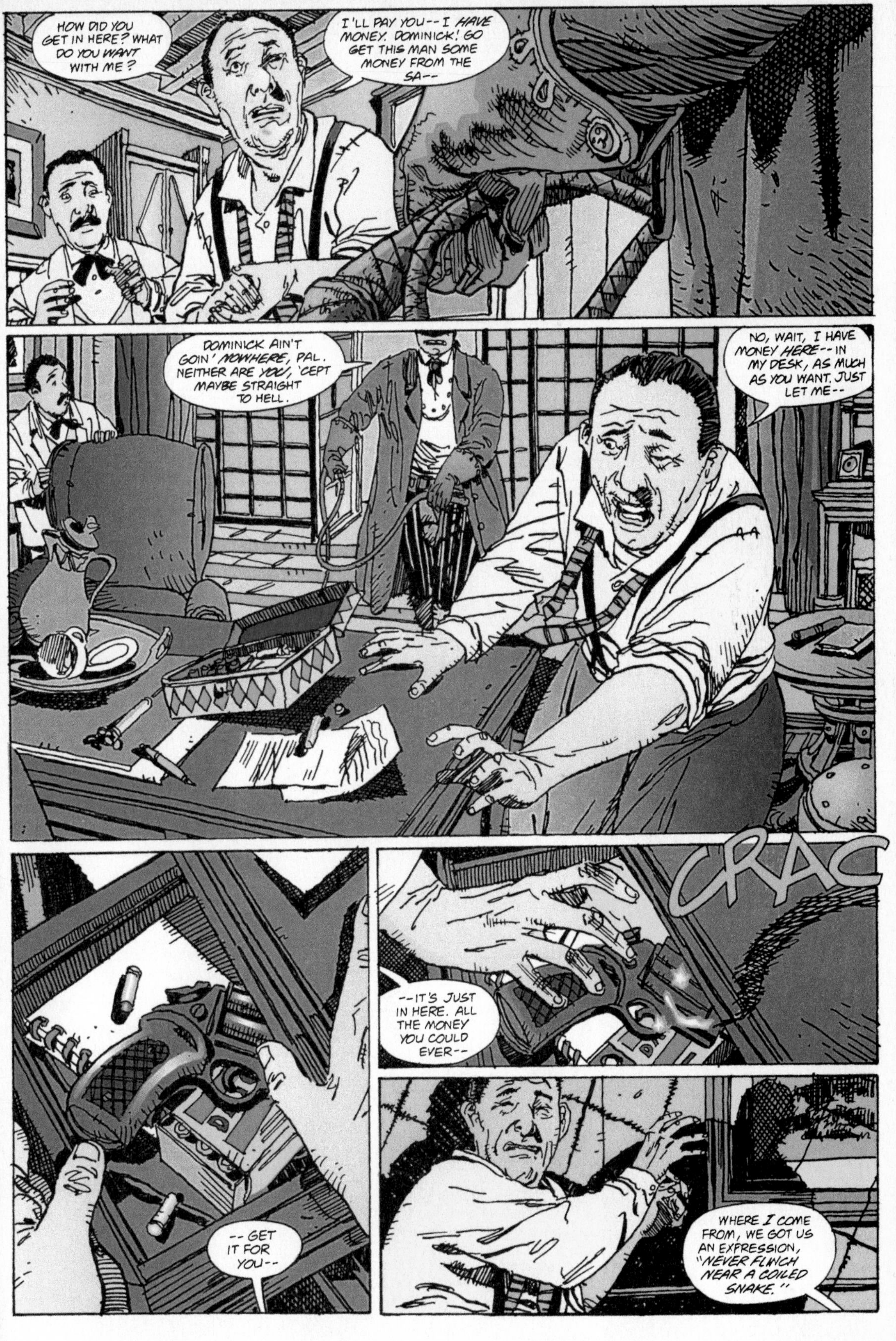
HOW DID YOU GET IN HERE? WHAT DO YOU WANT WITH ME?
I'LL PAY YOU-- I HAVE MONEY. DOMINICK! GO GET THIS MAN SOME MONEY FROM THE SA--
DOMINICK AIN'T GOIN' NOWHERE, PAL. NEITHER ARE YOU, 'CEPT MAYBE STRAIGHT TO HELL.
NO, WAIT, I HAVE MONEY HERE-- IN MY DESK, AS MUCH AS YOU WANT. JUST LET ME--
-- GET IT FOR YOU--
CRAC
--IT'S JUST IN HERE. ALL THE MONEY YOU COULD EVER--
WHERE I COME FROM, WE GOT US AN EXPRESSION, "NEVER FLINCH NEAR A COILED SNAKE."

YOU *HEARD* THAT ONE BEFORE?

NO! PLEASE, I *WASN'T*-- I DIDN'T *REMEMBER* THAT GUN BEING IN THE DRAWER--

DON'T CARE MUCH FOR *LIARS* EITHER, OLD MAN.

WHERE I'M FROM, WE *HANG* LIARS.

STOP! PLEASE, I'LL DO *ANYTHING* YOU WANT. GIVE YOU ANYTHING YOU WANT, JUST--

WHAT I *WANT* IS TO SEE YOU *FALL*.

THUD

UNH!

HOW'S IT FEEL T'BE ON THE GROUND WHERE YOU TRY TO KEEP THE REST OF THE WORLD, RUMMEL?

UNNH...

HOW'S IT FEEL TO BEND YOUR BACK IN PAIN FOR A CHANGE? HUH?

WHUMP

AAAAF!

WHAT'S IT LIKE T'BE *UNDER* SOMEONE'S *BOOTS* AND KNOW THAT *NOTHIN'* YOU CAN DO IS GONNA GET YOU *OVER* THOSE BOOTS?

STOP IT! ST--

②

--AAAAAH!

THUD THUD THUD

IT DOESN'T STOP, RUMMEL. THAT'S THE PROBLEM.

THE PEOPLE WITH THE POWER-- *BORN* WITH IT, MIND YOU-- THEY *START* ON TOP, AND THEY *END* ON TOP.

...DOMINICK-- NUCK-- H--HELP ME...

YOU SON OF A BITCH! WHY ARE YOU *HURTING* ME? WHAT DO YOU WANT?

WHAT DO I WANT? TELL YA WHAT I *DON'T* WANT. I DON'T WANT YOUR *MONEY*. NOSIREE BOB, DON'T *WANT* IT,... DON'T *NEED* IT, GOT ENOUGH MONEY.

WHAT I WANT IS *YOU* AND EVERY OTHER RICH BASTARD *LIKE* YOU ON YOUR *KNEES.*

AND IF I HAVE T' KILL EVERY LAST ONE O' YOU T' PUT YOU THERE--

CRAG

-- THEN, BY GOD, I'LL DO IT.

AAAAAAAAAA!

-- I'M SORRY, MR. RUMMEL-- SORRY-- SO SORRY--

HE WOULDN'T 'A BEEN SORRY IF YOUR PLACES WERE SWITCHED, BET ON IT.

3

THE SCORPION
ACT TWO

MATT WAGNER **STEVEN T. SEAGLE**
WRITERS

GUY DAVIS **DAVID HORNUNG**
ARTIST COLORIST

JOHN COSTANZA **ANDROID IMAGES**
LETTERER SEPARATOR

SHELLY ROEBERG **KAREN BERGER**
ASSOCIATE EDITOR EDITOR

CHRIST! BAD ENOUGH WE GOT THIS FREAK STORM, NOW WE GOTTA START RUNNIN' DOWN *SUSPECTS* IN IT--

OKAY, KLEIN, I'M *HERE*. WHAT'S TH' RUNDOWN? SAME AS THE LAST ONE?

NOT QUITE, LT. BURKE. THERE ARE SIMILARITIES, BUT THERE ARE *ALSO* SOME MAJOR DIFFERENCES.

GIMME TH' DIFFERENCES FIRST.

...THIS GUY PART OF THAT SAME COMPANY?

OH YEAH, SAME COMPANY ALL RIGHT. EVEN THE SAME...

WELL, AS YOU CAN TELL BY THE SKIN DISCOLORATION MR. RUMMEL WAS SEVERELY TRAUMATIZED. FROM THE SHAPE AND DEPTH OF THE CONTUSIONS, I'D SAY HE WAS MOST LIKELY KICKED.

HOW MUCH DOES THE CITY PAY YOU TO STATE THE *OBVIOUS*, KLEIN!

I'M SORRY, LIEUTENANT, BUT YOU ASKED ME-- WELL, ANYHOW--

--WE HAVE A SET OF IMPACT MARKS VERY SIMILAR TO THOSE FOUND IN THE DECHERT CASE.

4

THE GOOD THING ABOUT THIS SITUATION IS THAT IT GETS ME OUTTA HAVIN' T'SEE THAT STUPID ASS CLARE BOOTH LUCE PLAY WITH THE MISSUS. "THE WOMEN"? JESUS --

-- CAN YOU IMAGINE A COUPLE O' HOURS IN A THEATER LISTENIN' T' BROADS BITCH ABOUT BEIN' BROADS?

SHUT UP, MATTHEWS, I'M TRYIN' T'THINK HERE.

WELL, I WAS JUST--

GO CHECK THE PERIMETER, MATTHEWS.

SURE, LIEUTENANT. SURE.

AGAIN, I'D HAVE TO SAY A WHIP IS MOST LIKELY THE CAUSE.

ANOTHER MULTIPLE HOMICIDE IN THE MAKING, HUH? WHAT THE HELL'S GOING ON? DOESN'T ANYBODY IN NEW YORK EVER JUST KILL ONE PERSON AND THEN MOVE ON ANYMORE?

JESUS, LOOK AT HIS FACE.

LIEUTENANT BURKE?

WHY THE HELL ARE YOU ACTIN' LIKE SUCH A LIMP ROD TODAY, MATTHEWS? JUST TELL ME WHAT YOU WANT.

YES, SIR, SORRY SIR. SOME REPORTERS OUT FRONT. I THOUGHT YOU OUGHTA HANDLE 'EM.

YEAH YEAH...

TAYLOR? DID YOU SEE THESE?

SEEMS TO BE A TRAIL OF BLOODY SPLOTCHES... HMM...

LET'S MAKE SURE WE GET SOME PHOTOS OF THESE.

YOU GOT IT... HUBERT.

5

AS A CHILD I HELD AN EXTREME AND UNWAVERING FEAR OF INSECTS.

THE FACT THAT MY FATHER'S HOUSE STOOD IN AN UPPER-CLASS NEIGHBOR-HOOD--

--DID NOT PREVENT THE OCCASIONAL UN-INVITED SPIDER FROM DROPPING TO MY BED ON A SINGLE LUMINES-CENT STRAND JUST BEFORE I DRIFTED OFF TO SLEEP.

THE APPEARANCE OF SUCH A CREATURE WOULD DEPRIVE ME OF ANY REST.

I WOULD SIT UP, AWAKE, THE COVERS BUNCHED BENEATH MY COWERING CHIN UNTIL LONG AFTER THE BREAK OF THE SUN.

IT WAS LATER, IN COLLEGE, THAT I LEARNED THE SPIDERS WERE NOT INSECTS AT ALL, BUT RATHER, ARTHROPODS--

--THE SAME ORDER TO WHICH SCORPIONS BELONG.

--IT IS SCORPIONS THAT HAVE KEPT ME AWAKE THIS NIGHT.

THE VOICE IN MY DREAMS IS UNCHANGED, THOUGH ITS WORDS ARE NOW FAR FROM MEDITATIVE...

"LONG HAD I STOOD IN THIS UNMOVING PLACE OF HEAT AND DRY DEATH--"

"--THE BLACK BIRDS SOARING ABOVE ME JUST AS I WISHED TO SOAR."

"TO SLAKE MY THIRST AND BREAK FREE OF MY COARSE SKIN--"

"--I DRANK DEEPLY OF THE LIQUID OF REBIRTH."

"AND YET, THOUGH I BECAME MORE LIKE YOU-- JUST LIKE YOU--"

"--YOU DESCEND UPON ME CRYING--"

"--YOU ARE NOT ONE OF US YOU ARE NOT ONE OF US YOU ARE NOT ONE OF US!"

"I DIED THAT DAY AS I DIE EACH DAY."

7

THERE'S A SAYING MAKING ITS WAY AROUND THE ISLAND LATELY-- "EVERY FLOOR OF A SKYSCRAPER SITS FIRMLY ON THE BACKS OF 1000 AMERICANS."

I CAN'T HELP BUT THINK OF THIS AS I RIDE THE FORTY FLOORS UP TO STEPHEN CUTLER'S OFFICE FOR YET ANOTHER INVESTMENT MEETING.

THOUGH I HAVE NO INTEREST IN HIS BUSINESS, IT DOES SEEM THE BEST WAY TO STAY CLOSE TO THE CRIMES INFLICTED ON HIS PARTNERS.

PLEASE COME RIGHT IN, MR. DODDS. WE'VE BEEN EXPECTING YOU.

I CERTAINLY HOPE SO. AFTER ALL, YOU DID CALL ME THIS MORNING AND ASK THAT I BE HERE, AS I RECALL.

NOW, WESLEY, DON'T GO GETTING YOUR FLANNELS IN A BUNCH!

WE JUST CAN'T STAND THE THOUGHT OF LETTING YOU LOSE OUT ON THE BEST INVESTMENT OF THE DECADE.

WHILE I APPRECIATE YOUR PERSISTENCE, THE MURDER OF TWO TOP OFFICIALS IN A COMPANY IS ENOUGH TO MAKE ANY POTENTIAL INVESTOR ANXIOUS, DON'T YOU THINK?

WES, YOU'RE A STRAIGHT SHOOTER, AND I LIKE THAT, BUT HEAR ME OUT.

THIS SITUATION HAS BEEN VERY DIFFICULT FOR US, BUT WE CAN'T JUST LET THIS OPPORTUNITY SLIP OUT OF OUR HANDS.

AND TO BE PERFECTLY FRANK, WITHOUT YOU WE MAY NOT BE ABLE TO SECURE THE DEAL BEFORE OTHER BACKERS SNATCH IT OUT FROM UNDER US.

SO WHAT TERRY AND I WORKED UP IS A NEW PROFIT SHARING PLAN UNDER WHICH YOU WOULD BE COMPENSATED AN EXTRA 11% ABOVE AND BEYOND WHAT YOU DISCUSSED WITH TERRY AND CASSANDRA LAST NIGHT, PLUS THE--

STEPHEN, PLEASE, I'M FLATTERED THAT YOU'D GO TO THIS MUCH TROUBLE, BUT AS I'VE ALREADY EXPLAINED, I DON'T THINK THAT EXPLOITING THE EUROPEAN WAR SITUATION TO MAKE A FAST PROFIT OFF THE OIL INDUSTRY IS ACCEPTABLE--

8

146

NOW, MR DODDS, DON'T *TELL* ME THAT I HAVE T'BE THE ONE T'POINT OUT T'YOU THAT IN BUSINESS IT'S NOT QUALITY THAT MATTERS, IT'S *QUANTITY.*

WE MAY HAVE OUR ROUGH EDGES HERE AND THERE, BUT THE BOTTOM LINE IS THAT NO OTHER INVESTMENT OPPORTUNITY IN THE CURRENT MARKETPLACE IS GOING TO BE ABLE TO PROVIDE YOU WITH THIS LEVEL OF POTENTIAL.

OH *COME* NOW, MR. STETSON, WE *BOTH* KNOW THAT QUALITY IS FAR MORE IMPORTANT A FACTOR. IT'S QUALITY THAT LASTS. AND WHAT LASTS PAYS OFF IN THE LONG-RUN AS *WELL* AS THE SHORT.

THIS IS 1938, MR. DODDS. THE *LONG TERM* WON'T BE VISIBLE AGAIN UNTIL THE FORTIES, *IF* THEN. AND WE'RE ONLY LOOKING FOR YOU TO INVEST FOR THE FIRST YEAR. AFTER THAT IF YOU'RE NOT HAPPY, WE'LL BUY YOU RIGHT BACK OUT.

WHAT TERRY IS TRYING TO SAY IS THAT WE ARE *SO* CONFIDENT THAT THIS INVESTMENT IS GOING TO PRODUCE A HIGH YIELD THAT AFTER A YEAR'S TIME YOU'LL BE BEGGING US TO LET YOU INCREASE YOUR SHARE.

CASSANDRA'S RIGHT ON IT, MR. DODDS. YOU DON'T NEED ME TO TELL YOU THAT THIS WAR'S ON ITS WAY TO AMERICA.

ANYBODY LOOKIN' AT THE WORLD KNOWS *THAT.* AND WHEN THE WAR *HITS* OUR SHORES, WHOEVER'S GOT THE OIL IS GONNA HAVE THE GOLD.

YOU... WELL, YOU *DO* HAVE A POINT THERE. I HATE THE IDEA OF MAKING MONEY OFF THE WORLD'S DILEMMAS, BUT I MUST ADMIT... YOU'VE GOT ME THINKING.

YOU'RE A SHARP ARGUER, MR. STETSON. I'M *STILL* NOT SOLD, BUT... I'LL THINK THIS OVER A LITTLE MORE.

I'LL BE IN TOUCH.

NCHK!

NICELY DONE, TERRY.

NICELY DONE.

9

BING BONG

HELLO? HUMPHRIES? ARE YOU HOME?

YES, MISS BELMONT. I'M *SORRY* I COULDN'T GET TO THE DOOR FASTER. IT IS A VERY LARGE HOUSE, AS YOU WELL KNOW.

NO, *I'M* SORRY, HUMPHRIES. I'M JUST VERY EXCITED TO GIVE WESLEY THIS GIFT I GOT HIM.

CERTAINLY. ALLOW ME TO HELP YOU WITH IT. MR. DODDS IS--

I KNOW HE'S NOT HERE, HE TOLD ME HE HAD A LUNCH MEETING THIS AFTERNOON, BUT I WAS HOPING TO LEAVE THIS FOR HIM AS A SURPRISE.

DOES THIS ITEM REQUIRE ANY PARTICULAR ROOM?

ACTUALLY, I WAS THINKING THE *STUDY.*

WES ALWAYS SEEMS SO RESOLUTE IN HERE. THIS MIGHT JUST BE THE THING TO LIVEN HIM UP A LITTLE.

IS THERE ANYTHING YOU WOULD LIKE ME TO TELL MR. DODDS ABOUT THE GIFT?

ALREADY TAKEN CARE OF. I HAVE A NOTE HERE IN MY CLUTCH.

AND... THE PERFECT MESSENGER.

UH, MISS BELMONT, PLEASE. THAT IS--

I KNOW, WES LOVES THIS THING. DON'T WORRY, I'LL BE *CAREFUL.*

I JUST WANT TO MAKE *SURE* HE NOTICES MY NOTE--

--AND I THINK *THIS* WILL BE *JUST* THE WAY TO ENSURE IT.

YES, QUITE.

HUMPHRIES, YOU'VE BEEN A GEM. THANK YOU EVER SO MUCH.

MY PLEASURE, MISS BELMONT, AS ALWAYS.

TA!

--AND I WANT PAUL AND ISABEL INVITED AS WELL. WE *STILL* DON'T HAVE ANY SOLID CONNECTIONS INTO FRANCE, AND THEY MIGHT JUST BE OUR GATE-WAY.

YES, MISS CUTLER. WILL THERE BE ANYTHING *ELSE?*

OH, THERE *ALWAYS* IS, BUT YOU CAN JUST CHECK BACK WITH ME AFTER YOU'VE GOTTEN THOSE INVITATIONS OUT.

VERY GOOD, MISS CUTLER.

WHAT'S *THIS...?*

DINNER TONIGHT?

--T.

I SHOULD HAVE KNOWN... T AS IN *TEXAS.*

IN THE FLESH.

THE CACTUS IS VERY NICE, TERRY. WHAT A UNIQUE GIFT.

TOUGH EXTERIOR PROTECTIN' A BEAUTIFUL AND FRAGILE BLOOM SEEMED APPROPRIATE.

I DON'T KNOW WHAT TO SAY...

WELL THEN SAY YES.

YOU REALLY *ARE* A CONSTANT SURPRISE, BUT I SIMPLY DON'T LIKE TO GET INVOLVED WITH PEOPLE IN THE WORKPLACE.

IF WE'RE OUT AT DINNER, WE WON'T *BE* IN THE WORK-PLACE.

11

YOU *KNOW* WHAT I MEAN, TERRY.

CASSANDRA, YOU ARE A *BEAUTIFUL* WOMAN. AND THOUGH I ADMIRE YOUR WORK ETHIC, YOU STAY *HERE* EVERY NIGHT WHEN YOU *SHOULD* BE OUT ON THE TOWN *SHARING* THAT BEAUTY WITH THE REST OF MANHATTAN... OR CUTTING A RUG UP IN HARLEM.

HOW MANY WOMEN DO YOU KNOW WHO ARE IN THE POSITION *I'M* IN? I *HAVE* TO WORK TWICE AS HARD TO PROVE THAT I'M NOT JUST HERE BECAUSE I'M MY FATHER'S DAUGHTER.

THAT MAY BE TRUE, BUT YOU CERTAINLY *DON'T* HAVE TO PROVE THAT TO *ME*.

I-- OHHH... *ONE* DINNER.

BUT *ABOVE* THAT I CAN'T PROMISE YOU ANYTHING MORE. SHALL WE MAKE RESERVATIONS?

ALREADY MADE. A TABLE FOR TWO AT THE PERSIAN ROOM. EDDIE DUCHIN'S THERE TONIGHT. I'LL PICK YOU UP AT YOUR PLACE AT EIGHT.

"ALREADY MADE THEM"... WHAT A PUSHOVER I TURNED OUT TO BE, *HUH?*

"TOUGH EXTERIOR"... RIGHT. ALL LOOKS AND NO--

OW!

HUMPHRIES?

SOMEONE APPEARS TO HAVE BEEN IN MY STUDY--

YES, SIR. THAT WAS MISS BELMONT. I BELIEVE SHE LEFT YOU A NOTE...?

"MY DEAREST WES, FOR THE MAN WHO HAS EVERYTHING... SOMETHING NEW. I WANTED TO BE THE ONE TO BRINGS A LITTLE MUSIC INTO YOUR LIFE. HARMONIOUSLY YOURS, DIAN."

AH, GOOD, YOU FOUND IT. I TRIED TO TELL MISS BELMONT NOT TO--

IT'S ALL RIGHT, HUMPHRIES. YOU NEEDN'T TELL ME ABOUT DIAN'S PERSISTENCE. LET'S JUST SEE WHAT SHE'S BROUGHT US.

WELL, I'LL BE. IT'S A NEW PHONO-GRAPH PLAYER. ALONG WITH A PHONOGRAPH.

WOW! IT'S LOUIS ARMSTRONG! ISN'T IT TERRIFIC?

RCA VICTOR

TIK-- SSSHHHCRKSHHSSS

WHY YES, SIR. YOUR TEA, SIR?

I ONLY WISH I HAD THE TIME TO TAKE HER OUT AND THANK HER PROPERLY THIS EVENING.

I SEE. I TAKE IT THEN THAT YOU WILL BE HEADING OUT, HOWEVER?

YES... I'M AFRAID SO.

I CAN ONLY HOPE THAT DIAN WILL UNDERSTAND--

(13)

151

-- AND THAT SOMEDAY THERE WILL BE NO NEED TO HAVE THIS FAÇADE SEPARATING US.

THAT SHE WILL COME TO KNOW THE IMPORTANCE OF MY SECRETS.

AND WHY SOMETIMES MY OTHER LIFE MUST TAKE PRECEDENCE OVER OUR TIME TOGETHER.

OF COURSE THE WAY THAT TECHNOLOGY IS ADVANCING, I MAY SOON BE ABLE TO DO BOTH.

--LAMBERT? THIS IS BURKE... ANY NEW LEADS ON THE WHIP KILLER AT YOUR END?

...NO, NOTHIN' CONCRETE, HERE EITHER.

KLEIN JUST SHOWED ME SOME PICS HE TOOK OF SOME MARKS ON THE FLOOR. HE'S GOT SOME THEORIES, BUT NOTHIN' WORTH REPEATIN'...

...YEAH, UH-HUH... TELL YA WHAT, MEET ME TONIGHT AROUND SIX. I THINK WE'D BETTER STAKE OUT LANG'S PLACE, IF SOMEONE'S NEXT, IT'S HIM.

TCHK

14

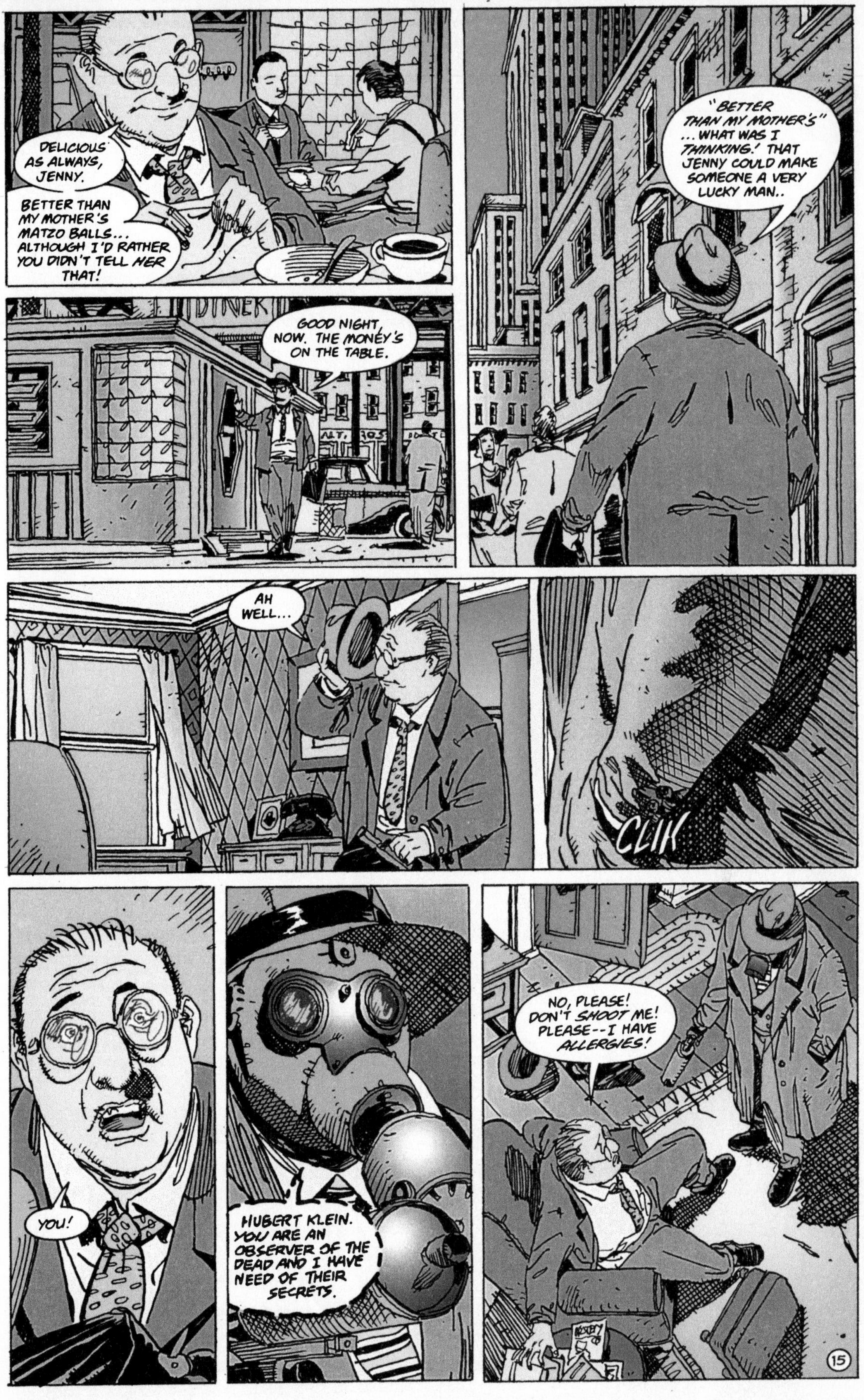
DELICIOUS AS ALWAYS, JENNY.
BETTER THAN MY MOTHER'S MATZO BALLS... ALTHOUGH I'D RATHER YOU DIDN'T TELL HER THAT!
"BETTER THAN MY MOTHER'S" ... WHAT WAS I THINKING! THAT JENNY COULD MAKE SOMEONE A VERY LUCKY MAN..
DINER
GOOD NIGHT, NOW. THE MONEY'S ON THE TABLE.
AH WELL...
CLIK
YOU!
HUBERT KLEIN. YOU ARE AN OBSERVER OF THE DEAD AND I HAVE NEED OF THEIR SECRETS.
NO, PLEASE! DON'T SHOOT ME! PLEASE--I HAVE ALLERGIES!
15

PLEASE NO--!

THE MISTS WILL NOT *HARM* YOU--

NO, PROBABLY *NOT* UNLESS YOU'VE GOT A *HEART CONDITION,* BUT MY *SINUSES* WOULD NEVER RECOVER.

I'LL TELL YOU WHAT YOU WANT TO KNOW... IF I *CAN*... BUT DON'T SHOOT ME WITH THAT CONTRAPTION.

YOU HAVE MY WORD. I SEEK KNOWLEDGE CONCERNING THE RECENT BULLWHIP MURDERS.

YOU'RE AFTER THIS GUY TOO, HUH? WELL... TWO VICTIMS TO DATE. BOTH WERE SUBJECTED TO *VARIOUS* PHYSICAL TRAUMA, BUT I'VE ESTABLISHED THAT THAT WASN'T THE *CAUSE* OF EITHER DEATH. BOTH MEN WERE KILLED BY *POISON,* EXCEPTIONALLY *STRONG* POISON.

AS STRANGE AS IT MAY SOUND, THE POISON SEEMS TO HAVE BEEN EXTRACTED FROM *SCORPION* VENOM. OH! AND THE MOST RECENT VICTIM'S INJURIES SUGGEST THAT THE KILLER WAS WEARING *COWBOY-STYLE* BOOTS.

HOW DID YOU COME TO THIS DETERMINATION?

THE SHAPE OF THE IMPRINTS LEFT ON THE BODY INDICATED IT, BUT THERE WERE ALSO BLOODY PRINTS ON THE FLOOR.

SHAPE OF THEM WAS A LITTLE CONFUSING, BUT THEN I REALIZED THEY WERE THE EXTREME ENDS OF THESE COWBOY BOOTS.

QUITE A STRIDE ON THIS GUY AS WELL. I'D GUESS OVER SIX FEET. THESE THINGS CONSIDERED, I'D SAY THAT OUR KILLER IS EITHER FROM THE SOUTHWEST ... OR WANTS US TO *THINK* HE IS,

AT THE SCENE OF THE FIRST KILLING, THERE WAS A BRAND INSCRIBED IN THE SHAPE OF A SCORPION. HAVE LIEUTENANT BURKE LOOK FOR A SIMILAR MARK AT THIS NEW SCENE.

WHY DON'T *YOU* TELL HIM YOURSELF? YOU ARE BOTH WORKING ON THE SAME CASE AFTER ALL.

16

THOUGH OUR GOALS ARE *INDEED* SIMILAR, LIEUTENANT BURKE AND I DO NOT SEE THE WORLD THROUGH THE SAME EYES.

SO... LET ME GET THIS STRAIGHT. YOU'RE SOME SORT OF REAL-LIFE VIGILANTE DETECTIVE? LIKE DICKIE BONES, BUT IN A GAS MASK?

WHO?

YOU KNOW... DICKIE BONES, THE PULP HERO. WAIT A MINUTE... I THINK I HAVE ONE AROUND--

--HERE--DICKIE BONES. HE'S A CHARACTER IN THESE SHOOT-EM-UP CRIME THRILLERS. IS THAT WHAT *YOU'RE* SUPPOSED TO BE? HEH!

YSTERY THEATRE MAGAZINE MAY 11 10¢

DICKIE BONE "THE DANSE MAC BY ALEX BURTO

I SCATTER THE DARK SANDS OF OBLIVION OVER BRUTALITY AND HATE.

I PROTECT THE SLEEP OF THE JUST BY DELIVERING THE NIGHTMARES OF THE DAMNED.

DO NOT MAKE LIGHT OF MY PURPOSE, HUBERT KLEIN, FOR NONE CAN ESCAPE THE SANDMAN'S DARK DREAM.

NO! MY ALLERGIES! YOU FORGOT ABOUT MY ALLERGIES! DON'T--

SHOOT--?

"SANDMAN," HUH? OH WELL... COULDN'T *HURT.*

⑰

HELLO, HUMPHRIES, IT'S DIAN BELMONT CALLING. IS WES THERE?... OH... SO I TAKE IT HE HASN'T COME *BACK* YET, THEN?

OH HE *DID?*... WELL, UH, DID HE HAPPEN TO SEE MY... HE *DID?*... NO, I JUST THOUGHT THAT HE WOULD CALL TO... *UH HUH*...

WELL THAT'S VERY NICE OF *YOU*, HUMPHRIES... OF COURSE IT WOULD HAVE BEEN *NICER* COMING FROM WESLEY HIMSELF, BUT THANK *YOU* AT LEAST.

OH, NO... THERE'S *NO* NEED TO TELL HIM I CALLED.

NO NEED AT ALL...

POP

CHAMPAGNE?

OF COURSE. ONLY THE BEST FOR *YOU.*

TERRY, I'M SORRY I WAS SO STAND-OFFISH EARLIER. I'VE JUST ALWAYS HAD DIFFICULTY BEING TAKEN SERIOUSLY AT WORK AND-- WELL, *YOU* KNOW HOW IT IS.

ABSOLUTELY. BUT EVEN THOUGH YOU'RE WILLING T'BE SEEN IN PUBLIC WITH A GUY LIKE ME, MY OPINION OF YOU WON'T DROP AT ALL! A TOAST--

TO?

TO POSSIBILITIES.

I'LL DRINK TO *THAT.*

DAMN BUBBLES. NEVER *HAVE* GOTTEN USED TO THIS STUFF.

18

I TAKE IT YOU WEREN'T BROUGHT UP ON CHAMPAGNE LUNCHEONS?

ME? NAH. MEN DRINK BEER OR WHISKEY IN TEXAS, NOT THIS FIZZY STUFF.

WHAT *WAS* IT LIKE GROWING UP IN THE WEST? I IMAGINE IT WAS QUITE DIFFERENT THAN MANHATTAN.

ONE MAJOR DIFFERENCE IS THAT THERE AREN'T ANY FILLIES LIKE YOURSELF DOWN SOUTH.

I'M *SERIOUS*, TERRY.

WELL, MY FATHER WAS A RAILROAD WORKER, BUT HE CAME UP WITH A NEW TYPE OF LOCKING CLAMP AND *MADE* A BUNDLE, SO I GOT TO BE THE FIRST STETSON TO MAKE IT TO COLLEGE, TEXAS A&M--

--GET THE HELL OUTTA M'WAY! ⚡ HIC ⚡

MY GOODNESS, WHAT WAS *THAT?*

MY APOLOGIES, SIR, BUT WE *DO* HAVE A DRESS CODE HERE AND YOU--

I--AM BUSTER CALHOUN, YOU CONPILE! I'M A STAR! I DRESS--DRESS LIKE THIS *WHEREVER* I GO! *INCLUDING* THIS LITTLE--POISON PIT OF YOURS.

SIR? I'M GOING TO HAVE TO ASK YOU TO--

YOU AIN'T GONNA ASK ME *NOTHIN'.* I'LL LEAVE THIS SWILL SHACK WHEN I'M ⚡ HIC ⚡ DARN GOOD AN' READY TO! NOW YOU BETTER GET YER HANDS OFFA ME OR I'M GONNA KICK THE SHIT OUTTA *YOU!*

WHASSA MATTER? I'M NOT GOOD ENOUGH FOR YOUR--

THAT WAS CERTAINLY... COLORFUL. I'M GLAD HE DIDN'T SHOW UP TO *OUR* FUNCTION DRUNK. *IS* THAT A *TYPICAL* TEXAS DISPOSITION?

NO. I'M SORRY YOU HAD TO BE SUBJECTED TO THAT, CASSANDRA--

WHILE I AM PROUD OF MY HOMESTATE, THERE ARE SOME THINGS ABOUT IT THAT I'D RATHER FORGET ALTOGETHER.

19

157

--SO ANYHOW, WE CAME TO BE PRETTY WELL KNOWN AROUND TEXAS AND I THOUGHT THE TIME HAD COME TO TRY MY HAND AT A *REAL* CITY. THE REST, AS THEY SAY, IS HISTORY.

WHAT A *FASCINATING* STORY. IT MUST HAVE BEEN QUITE EXHILARATING COMING TO A NEW CITY, ALONE, AND HAVING TO START AT THE BOTTOM OF THE SOCIAL STRATA ALL OVER AGAIN. I ADMIRE THAT.

IT'S BEEN A MIGHT DIFFICULT TO MAKE THE ADJUSTMENT...BUT I *LOVE* A GOOD CHALLENGE.

I HAD A *WONDERFUL* EVENING, TERRY. WOULD YOU LIKE TO COME IN FOR A NIGHTCAP?

I'D LIKE THAT VERY MUCH.

OH-- THERE YOU TWO ARE-- WELL-- 'BOUT TIME-- S'ALMOS' *MIDNIGHT*.

FATHER? WHAT'S THE MATTER. WHY ARE YOU SITTING ALONE IN THE DARK? HAVE YOU BEEN DRINKING?

OH JUSSA BIT, NOTHIN' MAJOR--YET.

WHAT IS IT? WHAT'S THE MATTER?

DEAD IN TH' WATER, CASSIE. DODDS CALLED AN' DECLINED TH' INVESTMENT. PULLED OUT. NOT EVEN A *MAYBE*.

WHAT? WHY, FOR GOD'S SAKE?

DON'T KNOW--

DON'T WORRY, FATHER. I'M SURE THERE'S SOMEONE ELSE WE CAN FIND TO--

FUCK THAT LITTLE FOUR-EYED MULE SUCKER!

TERRY!

NOW CALM DOWN THERE, SON. NO REASON T'FLY OFF THE HANDLE--

CASSANDRA? MR. CUTLER? I'M SORRY, BUT I'LL BE *DAMNED* IF I'M GONNA LET THIS FALL APART *NOW*. IF YOU'LL EXCUSE ME.

20

Baah da duh duh duh--

Daah da duh duh duh--

Baaaaaa duh!

THANK YOU! THANK YOU...

THIS CONCLUDES OUR BROADCAST OF "BELSHAZZAR'S FEAST," THE NEW WORK BY BRITISH COMPOSER WILLIAM WALTON. TONIGHT'S NEW YORK PHILHARMONIC ORCHESTRA WAS UNDER THE DIRECTION OF THE INIMITABLE TOSCANINI--

--COMING UP NEXT... THE JUPITER PLAYHOUSE AND THEIR PRODUCTION OF *DEVIL MAY CARE*--

MISTER LANE? YOUR WATER IS DRAWN, SIR.

AH, RUDY, DID YOU HEAR THE SYMPHONY? IT WAS QUITE *CARNAL*. VERY PAGAN IN ITS RHYTHMS.

QUITE UNCHARACTERISTIC FOR A *WALTON* PIECE. IT HAS *STIRRED* ME.

YES SIR?

OH, YES... QUITE.

I FOUND IT AROUSING, BUT STILL A TRIFLE... *UNSATISFYING.* IT LACKED A FINAL... RELEASE. I *NEED* THAT RELEASE, RUDY.

YOU REALLY *ARE* A VERY PRETTY BOY. ARE THERE ANY *MORE* OF YOU AT HOME?

JUST MY BROTHER, MAURICE, MR. LANE.

21

159

MMMMMMM...

MAURICE, HM? WE MAY HAVE TO SEE ABOUT SECURING *HIS* SERVICES HERE AS WELL.

YEE-YIKES!

WHAT *IS* IT, LAMBERT?

ENOUGH TO MAKE A GUY SICK. HERE. LOOK FOR YOURSELF.

UH HUH. SO LANG LIKES TO GET HIS WHISTLE POLISHED BY HIS HOUSEBOY, HUH?

IT'S DOWNRIGHT SICK.

SO HE'S A PERVERT. SO WHAT? WE AIN'T OUT LOOKIN' TO ARREST A DEGENERATE. WE'RE HOLDIN' OUT FOR A *KILLER*.

STILL, IT'S PRETTY APPALLIN'. HIM... YEP.. SICK AS ALL GET OUT...

WELL, JUST KEEP WATCHIN'. DOESN'T LOOK LIKE IT'S GONNA GO DOWN TONIGHT, BUT WE'LL STAY UP A LITTLE LONGER.

YEAH, WELL, LANG WON'T... IF YOU CATCH MY DRIFT--

22

THESE NIGHTS SEEM TO GET LONGER AND LONGER.

BUT THE DREAMS, IF ANYTHING, DRIVE ME TO INCREASE MY ACTIVITIES.

CLAC

HOW LONG CAN THIS LAST?

HOW MUCH HORROR AND CRIME AND MORAL TRANSGRESSION CAN ONE CITY FIND WITHIN ITSELF?

I WONDER IF THE PULP SLEUTHS HAVE ACHING JOINTS-- NEEDLING PAINS IN THE SMALL OF THE BACK--

--VOICES IN THE BACK OF THEIR HEADS.

23

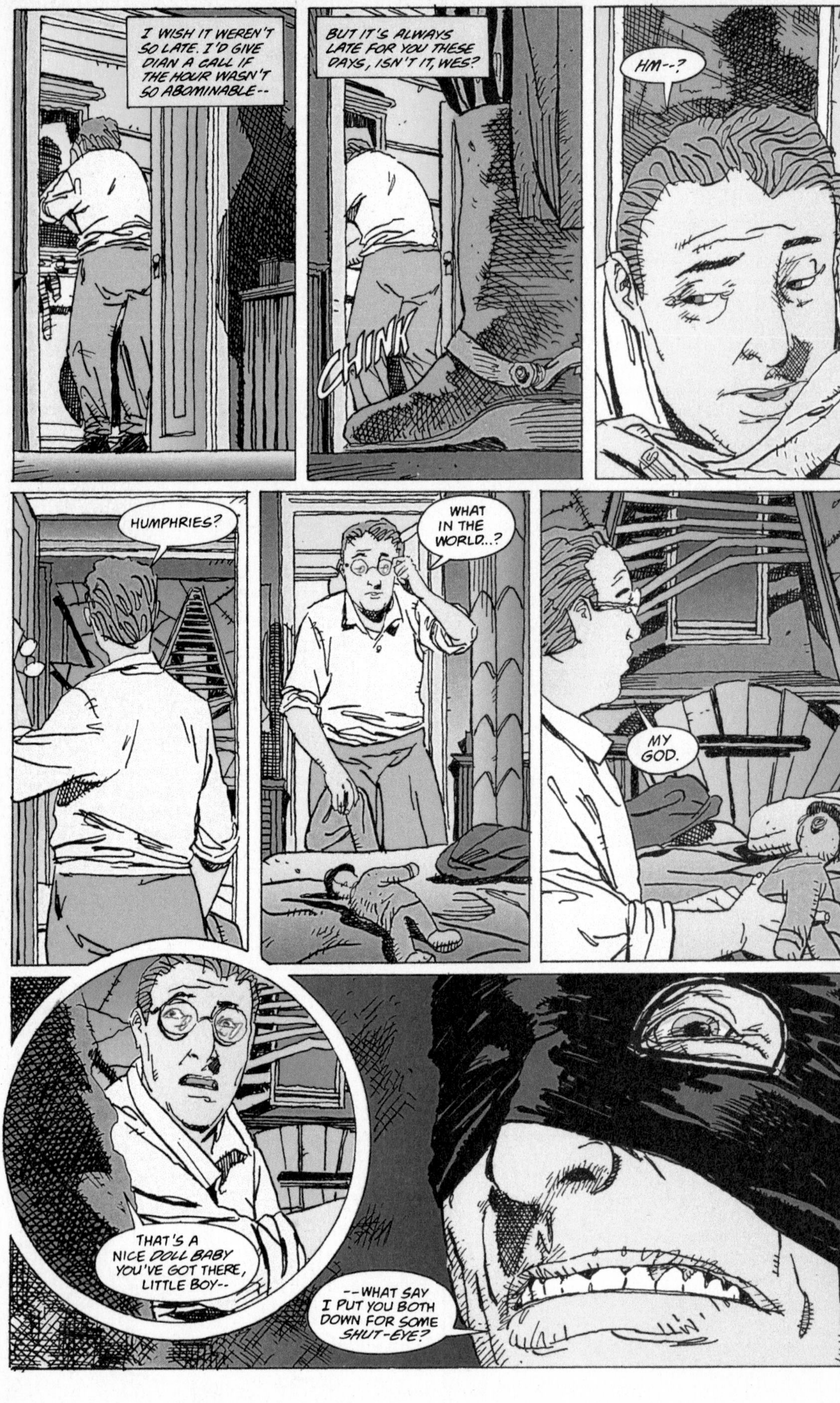

I WISH IT WEREN'T SO LATE. I'D GIVE DIAN A CALL IF THE HOUR WASN'T SO ABOMINABLE--
BUT IT'S ALWAYS LATE FOR YOU THESE DAYS, ISN'T IT, WES?
CHINK
HM--?
HUMPHRIES?
WHAT IN THE WORLD..?
MY GOD.
THAT'S A NICE DOLL BABY YOU'VE GOT THERE, LITTLE BOY--
--WHAT SAY I PUT YOU BOTH DOWN FOR SOME SHUT-EYE?

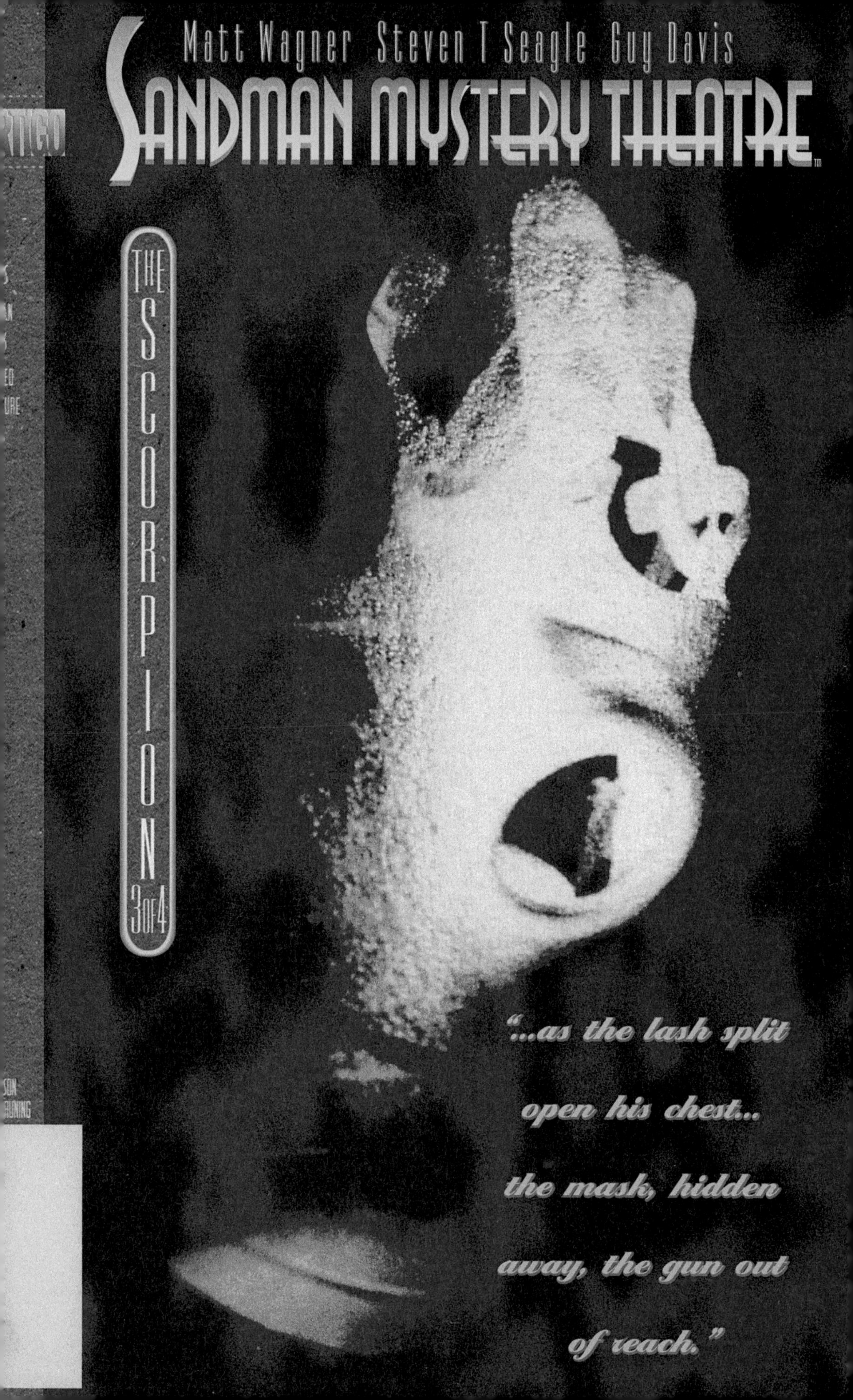
Matt Wagner Steven T Seagle Guy Davis
SANDMAN MYSTERY THEATRE
THE SCORPION
3 OF 4
"...as the lash split open his chest... the mask, hidden away, the gun out of reach."

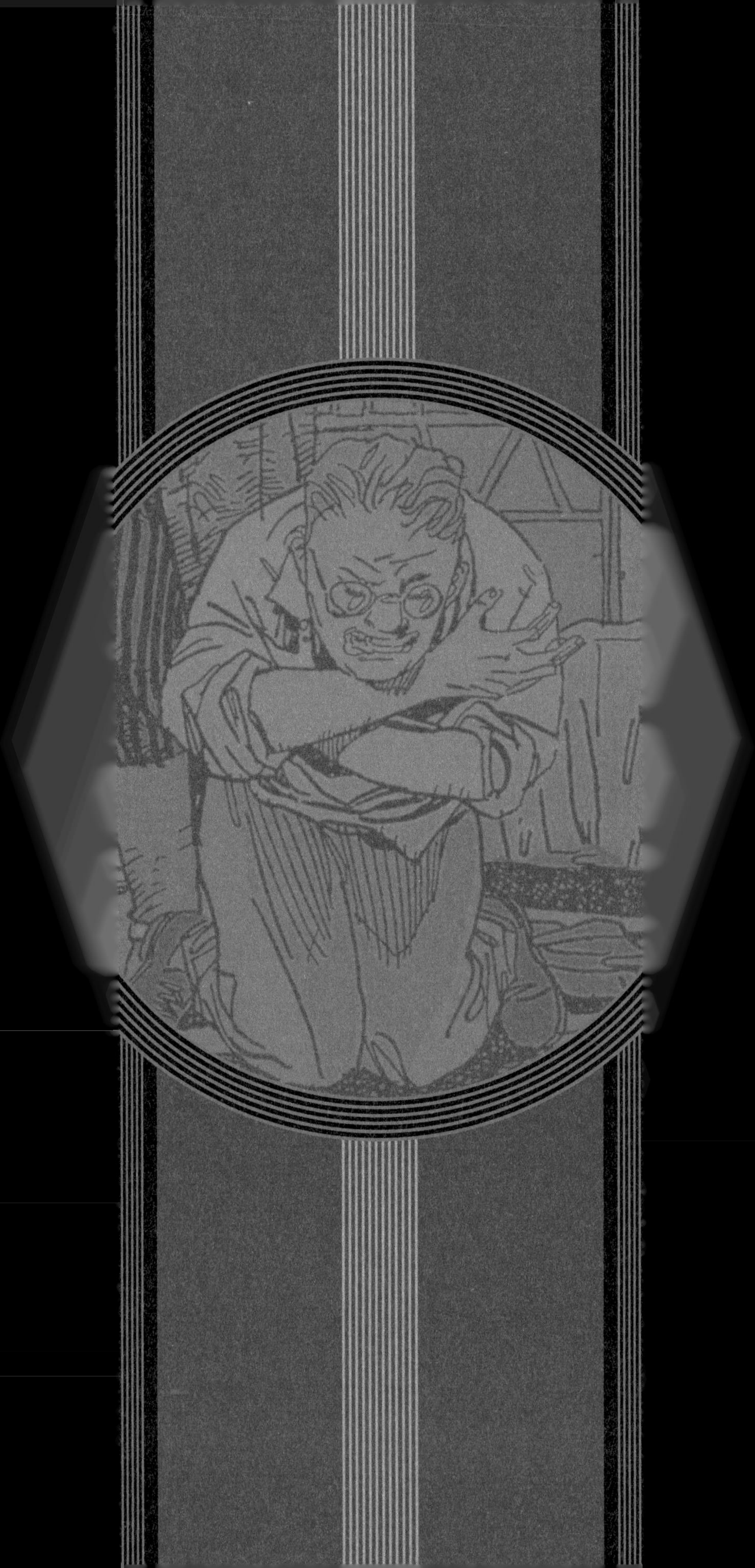

...AT THE *W.P.A.* ART SHOW, AND HE SAID HE COULDN'T AFFORD IT.

COULDN'T *AFFORD* IT? HOW DROLL...

OH! HELLO, JUDGE SCHAEFFER.

GOOD AFTERNOON, DIAN. I WAS HOPING TO HAVE A WORD WITH *YOUR* FATHER. IS HE IN?

ACTUALLY, HE *ISN'T*, BUT I EXPECT HIM BACK AT ANY TIME. IN FACT I THOUGHT *YOU* MIGHT BE HIM. PLEASE, COME IN AND WE'LL HAVE SOME COFFEE AND SEE IF HE TURNS UP.

WELL, NOW, I DON'T WANT TO *TROUBLE* YOU--

IT'S NO TROUBLE. I WAS JUST READING, BUT IT'S *CHAUCER*, SO I COULD *USE* A BREAK.

CHAUCER, *EH?* I HAVEN'T HEARD OF HIM SINCE MY UNIVERSITY DAYS.

YES, WELL, MY--*FRIEND*-- WESLEY DODDS LENT IT TO ME, SO I--

YOU AND WESLEY, *EH?* I NEVER WOULD HAVE THOUGHT. OF COURSE I CAN SEE WHY HE'S ATTRACTED TO A LOVELY YOUNG WOMAN LIKE *YOURSELF*, BUT HE SEEMS A LITTLE... WELL, OVERWORKED.

I KNOW HE CAN BE A BIT DISTANT AT TIMES, BUT ACTUALLY, WES IS *VERY* FUN AND COMPASSIONATE IN HIS OWN FASHION.

IN *CERTAIN* WAYS, HE'S THE MOST *NORMAL* MAN I EVER DATED.

THE SCORPION
ACT THREE

MATT WAGNER   STEVEN T. SEAGLE
WRITERS

GUY DAVIS   DAVID HORNUNG
ARTIST   COLORIST

JOHN COSTANZA   ANDROID IMAGES
LETTERER   SEPARATOR

SHELLY ROEBERG   KAREN BERGER
ASSOCIATE EDITOR   EDITOR

JUST CALM DOWN. IF YOU LEAVE NOW, THERE'LL BE NO TROUBLE FROM ME--

A MAN IS ENTITLED TO WHAT HE'S EARNED--

EARNED? DON'T THINK I DON'T KNOW WHERE YOUR MONEY CAME FROM.

ONLY DAY YOU WORKED IN YOUR MISERABLE LIFE WAS THE DAY YOU SIGNED THE ACCEPTANCE AGREEMENT TAKIN' OVER YOUR DADDY'S MONEY WHEN HE KICKED THE BUCKET.

YOU BE SURE AN' TELL HIM "HOWDY" FROM ME WHEN YOU MEET HIM IN HELL!

②

YOU'RE TYPICAL, DODDS.

TYPICAL OF TH' WHOLE CONSPIRACY OF WEALTH THAT'S GOT A STRANGLEHOLD ON THIS COUNTRY.

TYPICAL OF EVERY RICH BASTARD WHO'S GOT MORE THAN HE COULD EVER USE BUT PLANS ON *KEEPIN'* EVERY PLUG NICKEL OF IT ANYWAY.

VERY *TRICKY.* YOU CRAFTY LITTLE BASTARD--

--BUT IT AIN'T GONNA DO YA--HUH--?

HNH!

--WAAAAA--

--GUHFF!

YOU GODDAMN MONKEY! FIGHT LIKE A MAN, WHY DON'TCHA!

YOU MEAN LIKE ATTACKING AN UNARMED OPPONENT?

3

OH, YOU'RE ARMED. YOU'RE ARMED WITH BANK ACCOUNTS, AND TRUST FUNDS, AND DIVIDENDS--

--BUT I THINK IT'S TIME YOU GOT SOMETHING YOU CAN TRULY CALL YOUR OWN--

-- THE ONLY THING A MAN CAN EVER CALL HIS OWN--

CRAC

UNNNH!

--HIS DEATH.

NO!

NNH!

YA KNOW, DODDS, I AM KINDA SORRY ABOUT THIS--

ANNNNH! S-SORRY?

SORRY THE POISON WORKS SO FAST--

I'D A LIKED TA SEE YOU SUFFER MORE.

HUFF!

4

YA CAN'T HAVE EVERYTHING YA WANT IN LIFE.

BUT YA LEARNED AN IMPORTANT LESSON HERE T'DAY, PARTNER.

EVEN IF YA GOT ALL THE MONEY IN THE WORLD--

--SOMETIMES IT *STILL* AIN'T ENOUGH.

HAPPY TRAILS.

SECONDS LEFT--

--SHOULD HAVE TOLD DIAN--

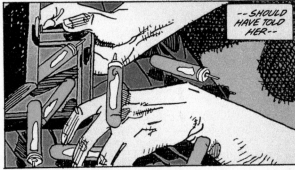

--SHOULD HAVE TOLD HER--

MASTER DODDS?

--EVERY-THING...

STP

I WAS IN THE KITCHEN AND SAW A MAN RUNNING FROM THE GROUNDS AND--

GOOD LORD!

MASTER DODDS! MASTER DODDS! OH DEAR...

5

169

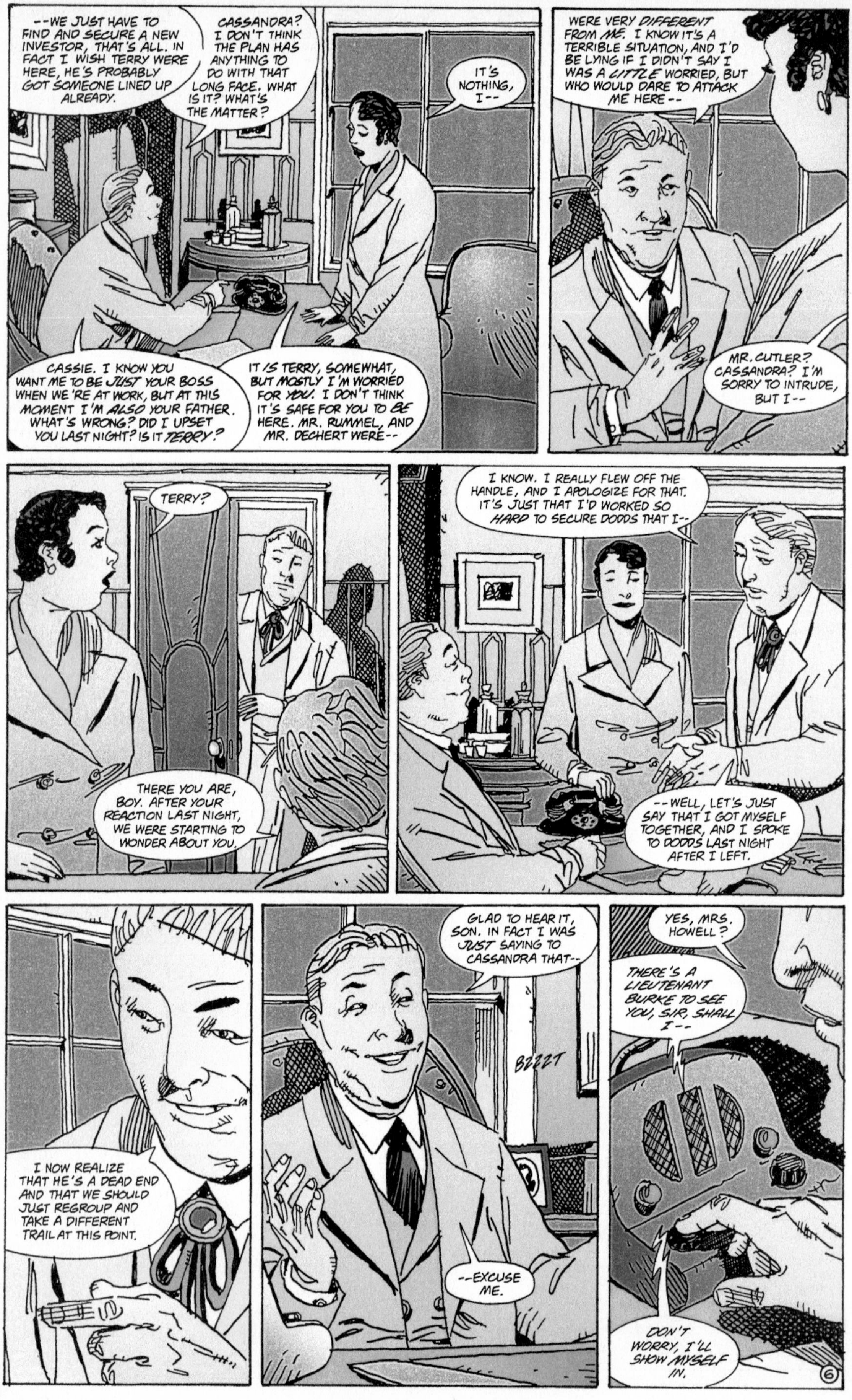
--WE JUST HAVE TO FIND AND SECURE A NEW INVESTOR, THAT'S ALL. IN FACT I WISH TERRY WERE HERE, HE'S PROBABLY GOT SOMEONE LINED UP ALREADY.
CASSANDRA? I DON'T THINK THE PLAN HAS ANYTHING TO DO WITH THAT LONG FACE. WHAT IS IT? WHAT'S THE MATTER?
IT'S NOTHING, I--
CASSIE. I KNOW YOU WANT ME TO BE JUST YOUR BOSS WHEN WE'RE AT WORK, BUT AT THIS MOMENT I'M ALSO YOUR FATHER. WHAT'S WRONG? DID I UPSET YOU LAST NIGHT? IS IT TERRY?
IT IS TERRY, SOMEWHAT, BUT MOSTLY I'M WORRIED FOR YOU. I DON'T THINK IT'S SAFE FOR YOU TO BE HERE. MR. RUMMEL, AND MR. DECHERT WERE--
WERE VERY DIFFERENT FROM ME. I KNOW IT'S A TERRIBLE SITUATION, AND I'D BE LYING IF I DIDN'T SAY I WAS A LITTLE WORRIED, BUT WHO WOULD DARE TO ATTACK ME HERE--
MR. CUTLER? CASSANDRA? I'M SORRY TO INTRUDE, BUT I--
TERRY?
THERE YOU ARE, BOY. AFTER YOUR REACTION LAST NIGHT, WE WERE STARTING TO WONDER ABOUT YOU.
I KNOW. I REALLY FLEW OFF THE HANDLE, AND I APOLOGIZE FOR THAT. IT'S JUST THAT I'D WORKED SO HARD TO SECURE DODDS THAT I--
--WELL, LET'S JUST SAY THAT I GOT MYSELF TOGETHER, AND I SPOKE TO DODDS LAST NIGHT AFTER I LEFT.
I NOW REALIZE THAT HE'S A DEAD END AND THAT WE SHOULD JUST REGROUP AND TAKE A DIFFERENT TRAIL AT THIS POINT.
GLAD TO HEAR IT, SON. IN FACT I WAS JUST SAYING TO CASSANDRA THAT--
BZZZT
--EXCUSE ME.
YES, MRS. HOWELL?
THERE'S A LIEUTENANT BURKE TO SEE YOU, SIR, SHALL I--
DON'T WORRY, I'LL SHOW MYSELF IN.
6

AFTERNOON. YOU STEPHEN CUTLER?

UH...YES, LIEUTENANT... *BURKE* WAS IT?

YEAH, LOOK, SORRY TO BUST RIGHT IN BUT THIS DAY'S BEEN A REAL BALL BUSTER, IF YOU CATCH MY DRIFT--

HAVE I INTRODUCED MY *DAUGHTER*, CASSANDRA?

OH. *SORRY.* PLEASURE.

LISTEN, I'M ON THE MURDER CASE INVOLVIN' YOUR PARTNERS, AND I'VE GOT A FEW QUESTIONS. CAN WE TALK PRIVATE SOME-WHERE?

NO NEED FOR PRIVACY. CASSANDRA AND YOUNG TERRY HERE ARE FULLY AWARE OF THE SITUATION. MAYBE THEY CAN *HELP* SHED SOME LIGHT ON THESE TRAGIC EVENTS.

FINE. THE KILLER SEEMS TO BE SOME KIND OF WESTERN CHARACTER. NOW, THE WAY I UNDERSTAND IT, YOUR COMPANY HAS CONNECTIONS WITH A FEW TEXAS OIL FIELDS.

CAN YOU THINK OF ANYONE WHO MIGHT BE TICKED OFF WITH YOU IN THAT PART OF THE COUNTRY?

YOU MEAN ASIDE FROM THE INDIANS?

YEAH. FUNNY. *THANKS.*

WE'VE BEEN IN THE TEXAS OIL GAME FOR ALMOST *TWENTY YEARS* NOW, LIEUTENANT. IN FACT, TERRY HERE CAME TO US FROM ONE OF OUR *ABERDEEN* AFFILIATES.

I CAN'T REMEMBER A SINGLE INCIDENT THAT WOULD WARRANT THIS SORT OF VICIOUS ATTACK.

WELL, IF YOU *DO* REMEMBER SOMETHING, MAKE SURE YOU GET HOLD OF ME. NOW THE OTHER THING IS--

--WE FOUND THIS *MARK* AT THE SCENE OF THE CRIME.

MEAN ANYTHING TO ANYONE HERE?

CAN'T SAY *I'VE* EVER SEEN THAT MARK BEFORE. HOW STRANGE.

WHAT ABOUT YOU? GOT ANY JOKES ABOUT THIS?

IT'S A DEADLY CREATURE, MR. BURKE. NOTHING TO JOKE ABOUT.

GOT THAT RIGHT. I DON'T MEAN TO SCARE YOU FOLKS, BUT I'D KEEP A LOW PROFILE UNTIL WE CATCH THIS CREEP.

THANKS FOR YOUR TIME. I'VE GOT A FEW MORE LEADS TO FOLLOW UP, SO I'M GONNA GET GOING. YOU THINK OF ANYTHING, CONTACT THE STATION.

WE WILL, LIEUTENANT.

AFTERNOON, MR. CUTLER, MISS CUTLER--

SEE YA' ROUND, TEX.

WHAT A CHARAC- TER! WOULDN'T YOU SAY SO, TERRY?

TERRY?

FOR THE FIRST TIME IN AGES I AWAKE FROM A SOUND SLEEP.

OF COURSE, A POISON INDUCED COMA IS NOT THE BEST WAY TO ARRIVE AT SUCH REST--

THANKFULLY, MY ANTIDOTE MADE IT A TEMPORARY SLUMBER.

I DON'T THINK HE'S--

WESLEY? WHAT ON EARTH HAPPENED TO YOU?

OH, DIAN. HI. YOU LOOK NICE. IT'S NOTHING--

NOTHING? LOOK AT YOU! WHAT HAPPENED?

WELL, IT'S A BIT EMBARRASSING, ACTUALLY--

172

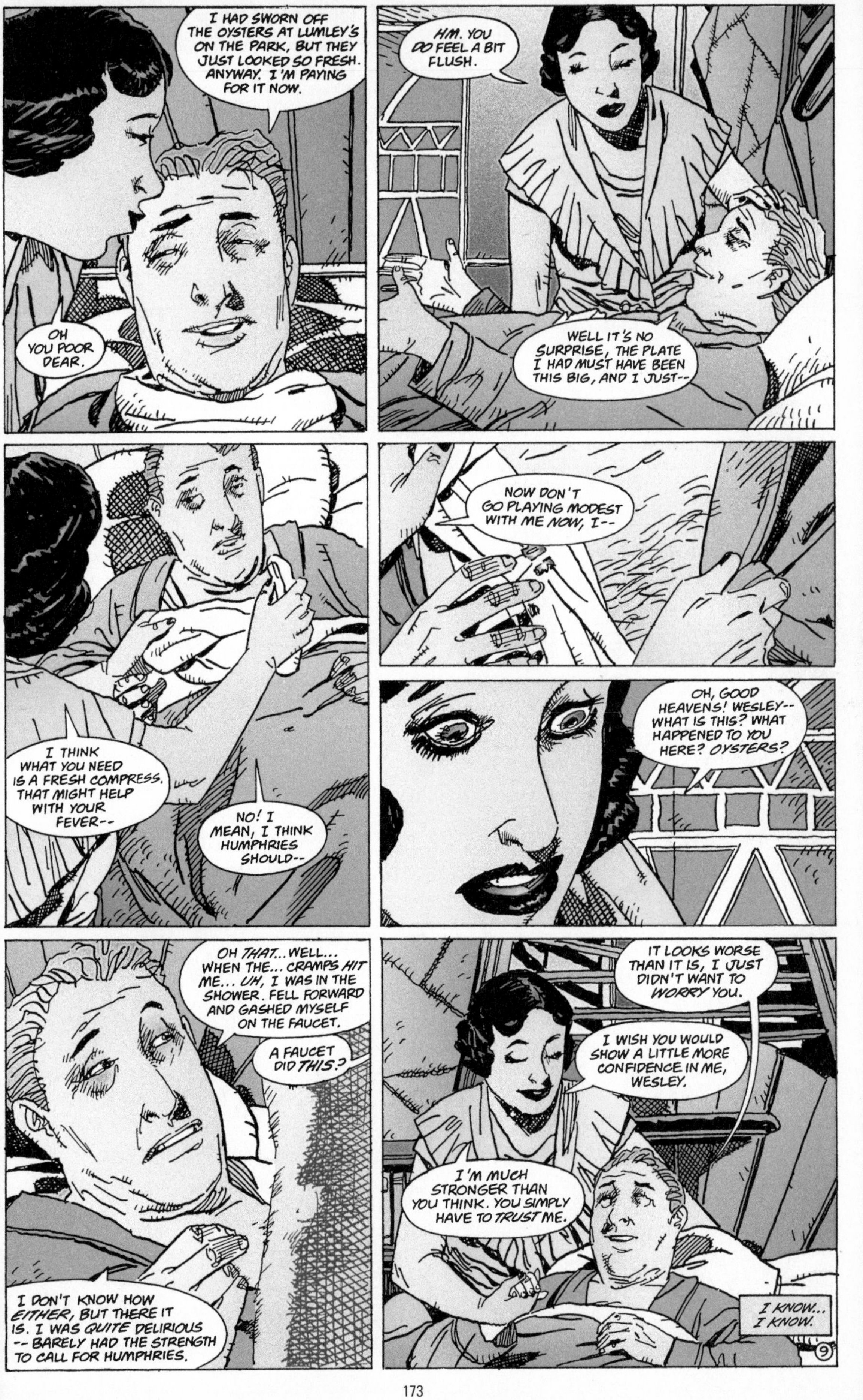
I HAD SWORN OFF THE OYSTERS AT LUMLEY'S ON THE PARK, BUT THEY JUST LOOKED SO FRESH. ANYWAY. I'M PAYING FOR IT NOW.
OH YOU POOR DEAR.
HM. YOU DO FEEL A BIT FLUSH.
WELL IT'S NO SURPRISE, THE PLATE I HAD MUST HAVE BEEN THIS BIG, AND I JUST--
I THINK WHAT YOU NEED IS A FRESH COMPRESS. THAT MIGHT HELP WITH YOUR FEVER--
NO! I MEAN, I THINK HUMPHRIES SHOULD--
NOW DON'T GO PLAYING MODEST WITH ME NOW, I--
OH, GOOD HEAVENS! WESLEY-- WHAT IS THIS? WHAT HAPPENED TO YOU HERE? OYSTERS?
OH THAT... WELL... WHEN THE... CRAMPS HIT ME... UH, I WAS IN THE SHOWER. FELL FORWARD AND GASHED MYSELF ON THE FAUCET.
A FAUCET DID THIS?
I DON'T KNOW HOW EITHER, BUT THERE IT IS. I WAS QUITE DELIRIOUS -- BARELY HAD THE STRENGTH TO CALL FOR HUMPHRIES.
IT LOOKS WORSE THAN IT IS, I JUST DIDN'T WANT TO WORRY YOU.
I WISH YOU WOULD SHOW A LITTLE MORE CONFIDENCE IN ME, WESLEY.
I'M MUCH STRONGER THAN YOU THINK. YOU SIMPLY HAVE TO TRUST ME.
I KNOW... I KNOW.
9

WHAT YOU NEED IS SOME FRESH AIR IN HERE. IT'S A BEAUTIFUL DAY OUT, AND THIS PLACE IS AS CLOSE AS A TOMB. MAY I?

YES, CERTAINLY.

HMMM. WES? WHO OWNED THIS HOUSE *BEFORE* YOU?

UH...A BANKER. MENDELBAUM WAS THE NAME. WHY?

I THINK HE HAD SOME STRANGE TASTES. HE APPEARS TO HAVE *BRANDED* THE WINDOW.

YES...WELL, I DID DO A LOT OF REDECORATING. MUST HAVE *MISSED* THAT.

LISTEN, I HAVE A LIBRARY VOLUNTEERS MEETING TO GET TO SO I'M GOING TO LEAVE YOU TO YOUR REST. I'LL CALL LATER TO SEE HOW YOU'RE DOING.

IN THE MEANTIME, STAY AWAY FROM THE OYSTERS.

I HAD ALWAYS HEARD THEY HAD A TOTALLY *DIFFERENT* EFFECT ON A MAN.

YOU JUST GET BETTER... AND WE WON'T *NEED* ANY OYSTERS.

OH, REALLY?

SWEET DREAMS!

I ENJOY DIAN'S BOLDNESS MORE AND MORE--

⑩

-- YOU LOOK LIKE YOU'RE OFF TO THE RACES.

NO, I'M JUST *BUSY.* WE STILL HAVE A BUSINESS TO ATTEND TO EVEN IN THE FACE OF THESE TERRIBLE EVENTS.

HER ABILITY TO BE PLAYFUL WITHOUT BEING VULGAR IS ENOUGH TO LIFT ANY MAN'S... SPIRITS.

WELL, I CAN *APPRECIATE* THE INITIATIVE, BUT A LADY'S GOT TO EAT, DON'T YOU THINK?

NO, I REALLY *CAN'T* RIGHT NOW, I--

YES, MILLIE?

BZZT

I FORGOT TO TELL YOU, MISS CUTLER, MR. WESLEY DODDS ALSO CALLED FOR YOU WHILE YOU WERE IN WITH YOUR FATHER.

THANKS, MILLIE.

DODDS? THAT'S... UNEXPECTED.

TRUE, BUT MAYBE HE'S HAD A CHANGE OF HEART.

I'D BETTER PHONE HIM RIGHT AWAY.

YES... THAT *WOULD* BE A GOOD IDEA. STRIKE WHILE THE IRON'S HOT... SO TO SPEAK.

EXACTLY.

HELLO? IS MR. DODDS THERE?... IT IS? HELLO, THIS IS CASSANDRA CUTLER RETURNING YOUR CALL...?

11

...UH HUH... I SEE... NO, NO, I UNDERSTAND. THESE DEALINGS *CAN* BE VERY TOUCH AND GO, I'M JUST DELIGHTED TO HEAR THAT...

...YES... I'M *SURE* HE'LL BE AGREEABLE TO THAT... YES, I WILL... YOU TOO. GOOD-BYE.

GOOD NEWS, TERRY, *REMARKABLE* ACTUALLY. DODDS HAS RECONSIDERED.

OH... REALLY?

YES, HE WANTS TO MEET WITH MY FATHER, ALONE, TO TALK ABOUT IT.

I DON'T KNOW IF THAT'S SUCH A GOOD IDEA.

DODDS HAS ALREADY PROVED HIMSELF UNRELIABLE. I'M NOT SURE WE SHOULD *TRUST* HIM NOW.

WELL, THAT'S A DECISION MY FATHER WILL HAVE TO MAKE, ISN'T IT.

OF COURSE, I DIDN'T MEAN TO -- DODDS IS COMING HERE THEN?

HE DIDN'T SAY, ONLY THAT HE WAS GOING TO BE IN PHILADELPHIA AND WOULD CALL WHEN HE RETURNED.

PHILADELPHIA? HM... I--I CAN TELL YOU'RE BUSY. I'LL SEE YOU LATER.

DADDY? IT'S CASSANDRA... GREAT NEWS--

12

176

HI, DADDY. SORRY I'M LATE, BUT I JUST STOPPED BY WESLEY'S.

THEN I HAD TO RETURN THE OUTFIT I BORROWED FROM LILY--

OOP.

ZZZZ-- SNORK-- ZZZZ

HMINUHMEN...

POOR MAN'S EXHAUSTED...

WONDER WHAT'S GOT HIM SO--

--WORN OUT?

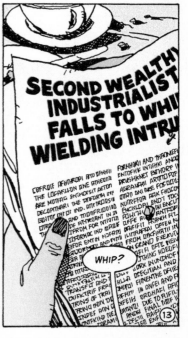

SECOND WEALTHY INDUSTRIALIST FALLS TO WHIP WIELDING INTRU

WHIP?

13

177

"...BOTH VICTIMS HAD LONG LASH MARKS BELIEVED TO BE CAUSED BY A BULL WHIP...

...RUMMEL AND DECHERT BOTH CONSIDERED AMONG MANHATTAN'S WEALTHIEST MEN..."

WHIEEEE!!!

TEA TIME, SWEETHEART?

SORRY, DADDY, I SHOULD HAVE CAUGHT IT SOONER. I DIDN'T MEAN TO WAKE YOU--

'S OKAY. I WASN'T SLEEPING, I WAS JUST... RESTING MY EYES.

ACTUALLY, I WASN'T PAYING ATTENTION BECAUSE I WAS ENGROSSED IN THIS NEWSPAPER STORY.

I HAD NO IDEA THOSE MEN WE MET AT THE BUSTER CALHOUN SHOW HAD BEEN KILLED.

WHEN DID THIS ALL START?

THIS'S THE FIRST YOU'VE HEARD OF THAT? I'M SURPRISED.

YES, WELL, I HAVE HAD MY HEAD UP IN THE CLOUDS LATELY.

YAAAAWN... UHN. THAT'S WHAT'S BEEN KEEPING ME UP NIGHTS LATELY. RUMMEL AND DECHERT WERE BIG MEN IN THIS CITY.

PRESSURE'S REALLY ON TO CATCH THEIR KILLER.

CALHOUN...HIM, HADN'T THOUGHT OF THAT

ANY IDEAS YET?

OH, A FEW. HOMICIDE'S HANDLING THE FOOTWORK, OF COURSE. LOOKS TO BE A VENDETTA OF SOME SORT. STRANGE ONE TOO.

KILLER LASHES THE VICTIMS WITH A POISON-TIPPED WHIP AND THEN BRANDS A SYMBOL SOMEWHERE AT THE SCENE. THE BOYS'VE TAKEN TO CALLING HIM THE SCORPION.

DID YOU SAY... "SCORPION"?

14

...POISON-TIPPED WHIP. JESUS H. CHRIST. HASN'T THIS LUNATIC EVER HEARD OF A GUN?

TUNK TUNK

ROOM SERVICE.

WHAT'S SHAKIN', SHEPARD? THE KING OF THE LUSH LIFE SPILLED IT YET?

UH, NOTHIN' SO FAH, LOOTENANT--

ACTUALLY, I MAY HAVE SOMETHIN' FOR YOU HERE, SIR.

YEAH? WHAT IS IT, CARLSON?

BUSTER CALHOUN JUST CALLED LANE AT HOME. HE'S DRUNK AS A SKUNK AND--WELL, JUST LISTEN--

I WILL IF YOU GIVE ME THE DAMNED HEADSET.

...STILL OWE ME FOR MAH SHOW! NOW, YOU'RE GONNA PAY ME TODAY OR I'M GONNA MAKE YOU WISH YOU HAD, YOU SHIT-LICKIN'--

MAN'S A REGULAR SHAKESPEARE.

LOOKS LIKE WE'VE GOT OUR TEXAN, HUH, LIEUTENANT?

WE'LL SEE. KEEP LISTENIN' AND CALL O'DONALD. TELL 'IM I'M GONNA PUT A TAIL ON CALHOUN FOR A BIT. MAYBE WE'LL GET LUCKY.

15

INDEED I WILL. A GOOD EVENING TO YOU.

OH, I KNOW THIS MAY SOUND STRANGE, BUT I'M VERY WORRIED ABOUT HIM. COULD YOU LOOK IN ON HIM FAIRLY REGULARLY THIS EVENING?

OYSTERS AND FAUCETS INDEED.

HUMPHRIES? THIS IS DIAN BELMONT CALLING. IS WESLEY AWAKE BY CHANCE?

I'M SORRY, MISS BELMONT, HE'S NOT. HE TOOK A SEDATIVE AND IS FAST ASLEEP.

--JUST VERY IMPORTANT THAT WE LET *HIM* WALK INTO THIS. I THINK TERRY HAD GOOD *INTENTIONS*, BUT HE SIMPLY PUSHED TOO HARD.

I SUPPOSE WE MIGHT *HAVE* SOUNDED A LITTLE DESPERATE TO DODDS.

I'LL CERTAINLY REMAIN SENSITIVE TO THAT APPEARANCE, CASSIE, BUT I STILL WANT ALL OF THE REPORTS AND ESTIMATES DELIVERED TO WHEREVER WE END UP MEET-ING JUST IN CASE.

I'LL PUT MILLIE ON THAT.

OH, BY THE BY, TERRY ASKED ME WHERE THE MEETING WAS GOING TO *BE*. HE'S THINKING OF STOPPING BY, I GUESS, SO WHEN WE FIND OUT, WE NEED TO MAKE SURE HE KNOWS.

THAT'S FUNNY. TERRY WAS IN MY OFFICE WHEN I SPOKE WITH DODDS AND HE *KNOWS* THAT DODDS REQUESTED A *PRIVATE* MEETING, JUST YOU AND HE.

THAT'S WHY I HIRED HIM! WHAT A FIREBALL THAT BOY IS.

I SUPPOSE...

16

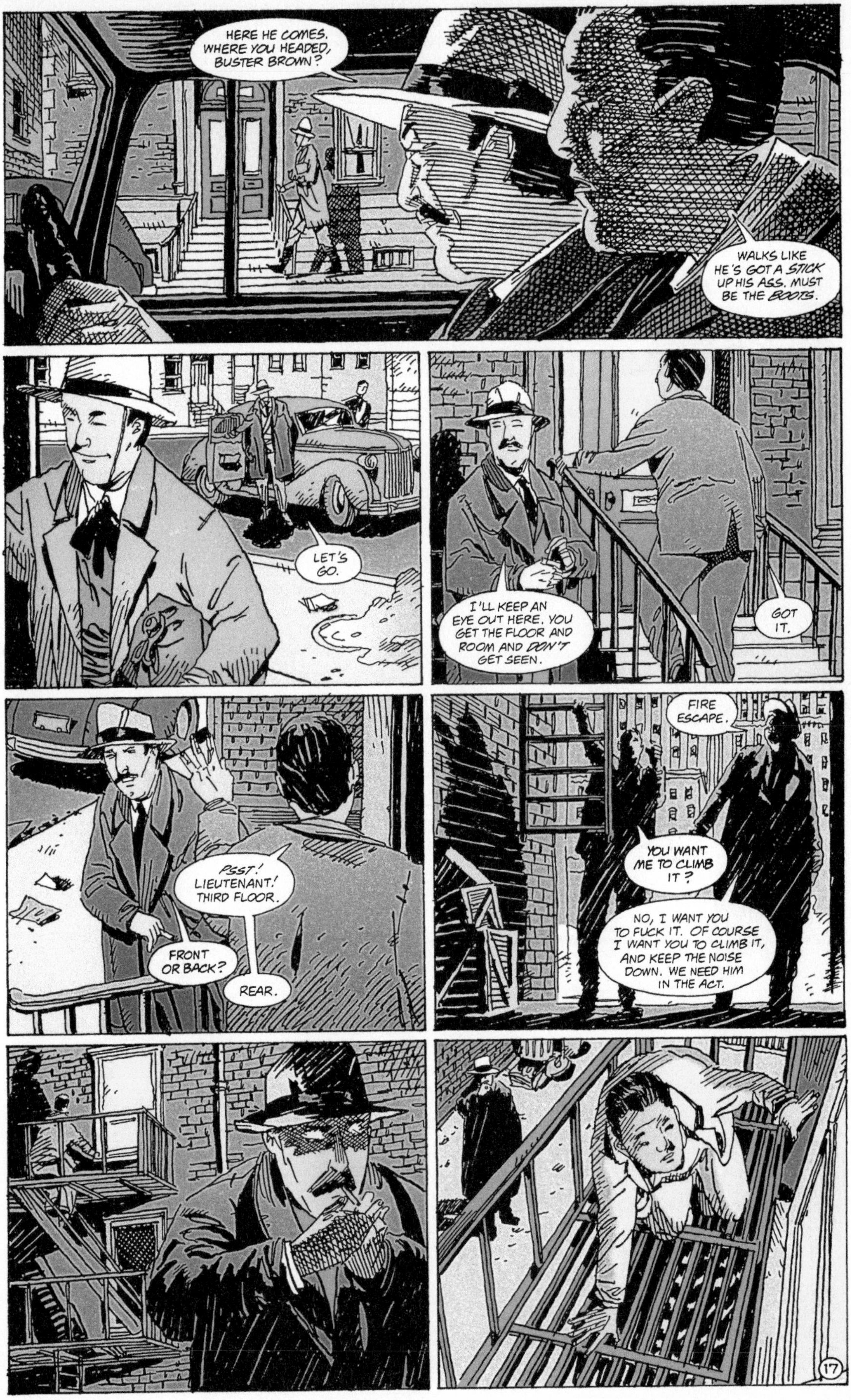
HERE HE COMES. WHERE YOU HEADED, BUSTER BROWN?
WALKS LIKE HE'S GOT A STICK UP HIS ASS. MUST BE THE BOOTS.
LET'S GO.
I'LL KEEP AN EYE OUT HERE. YOU GET THE FLOOR AND ROOM AND DON'T GET SEEN.
GOT IT.
PSST! LIEUTENANT! THIRD FLOOR.
FRONT OR BACK?
REAR.
FIRE ESCAPE.
YOU WANT ME TO CLIMB IT?
NO, I WANT YOU TO FUCK IT. OF COURSE I WANT YOU TO CLIMB IT, AND KEEP THE NOISE DOWN. WE NEED HIM IN THE ACT.
17

YOU READY TO TAKE YOUR LASHES? HUH?

EEEEEEEK!

CRAG

OMIGOD--

WE GOT 'IM! IT'S HIM! HE'S DOIN' IT!

LET ME GET TO THE FRONT, THEN WE GO IN!

SLAM

SLAM

THIRD FLOOR--HUFF-- REAR--HUFF--

CAN'T--HUFF-- WAIT FOR MY GODDAM-- HUFF--RETIREMENT--

WHAM

HUNH!

⑱

FREEZE, ASSHOLE! HANDS UP AND DON'T EVEN *THINK* ABOUT--

--MOVIN'--?

WHOA THERE, BUDDY! I--I--

HE AIN'T EVEN *PAID* ME FOR THIS ONE YET, SO DON'T YOU GO 'BOUT RUNNIN' ME IN.

DONE *BEEN* IN TWICE THIS WEEK AS IS.

WHAT THE HELL IS GOING ON *HERE?*

LIKE TO RIDE YOUR WHORES LIKE YOUR HORSES, HUH, BUSTER?

NOW, I RESENT THAT REMARK AND I--I--

BURKE!

WHERE THE HELL WERE *YOU?*

THE WINDOW WAS STUCK--

WHY THE HELL DIDN'T YA *BREAK* IT?

I DIDN'T WANNA *CUT* MYSELF.

OH *CHRIST.*

19

183

NO LUCK? I THOUGHT YOU HAD HIM.

YEAH, SO DID I. BUT HE AIN'T THE SCORPION. HE'S GOT SOME *VICES*, BUT IT DOESN'T LOOK LIKE MURDER'S ONE OF 'EM--

MY INTENTIONAL CONTACT WITH CUTLER WILL, I'M SURE, TRIGGER SUSPICION IN THE SCORPION WHO NO DOUBT BELIEVES ME DEAD.

NOW, ABOUT THIS DOE-EYED DOUCHE BAG OF A DETECTIVE YOU SENT WITH ME--

I ALLOW MYSELF TO GET LOST IN THE SWIRL OF INFORMATION AND POSSIBLE LEADS.

ALWAYS CAREFUL NOT TO PERMIT MYSELF TOO MUCH TIME TO THINK OF WHY I LOOKED DIAN STRAIGHT IN THE FACE--

--AND CONCOCTED YET ANOTHER FANTASTIC LIE TO KEEP MY TRUE SELF FROM HER.

I AM DISGUSTED IN MANY WAYS THAT I COULD MAINTAIN SUCH SECRECY.

WHY AM I SO COMFORTABLE BEING INTIMATE WITH DIAN IN EVERY WAY BUT ONE... HONESTY.

THIS CONFLICT IS TEARING AT ME, AND I KNOW I MUST SOON RESOLVE IT--

--EVEN IF IT MEANS THAT I MUST ALSO RISK LOSING HER FOREVER.

20

GOOD MORNING, TERRY.

CASSANDRA. YOU'RE MAKING AN EARLY DAY OF IT.

I JUST WANTED TO MAKE SURE I HAD A CHANCE TO TOUCH BASE WITH MY FATHER BEFORE HE--

SORRY TO SAY IT, BUT YOU'RE TOO LATE. HE STEPPED OUT A WHILE AGO TO MEET WITH LANG. PROBABLY TO DISCUSS DODDS, I'D IMAGINE.

REALLY? THEN WHAT WERE YOU DOING IN HIS OFFICE?

OH, I WAS JUST... DROPPING OFF A BUDGET REDRAFT. WANT US TO BE READY TO MOVE WHEN DODDS RECONSIDERS AT THAT MEETING TONIGHT.

YOU KNOW, TERRY, IT JUST SO HAPPENS THAT I'M FREE TONIGHT...GIVE YOU ANY IDEAS?

WELL NOW, YOU ARE A HEART-BREAKER. TURNS OUT I'M ALREADY COMMITTED FOR TONIGHT, BUT MAYBE TOMORROW--

I'D SAY THAT MAKES YOU THE HEARTBREAKER, BUT TOMORROW IT IS. I'LL BE LOOKING FORWARD TO IT--

--TEX.

21

185

MILLIE, I WANT YOU TO--

--I'M SORRY, I THOUGHT YOU WERE MY SECRETARY, MISS--?

DIAN. DIAN BELMONT. SORRY TO LET MYSELF IN, MISS CUTLER, BUT WE *HAVE* MET. THE BUSTER CALHOUN SHOW?

OH YES, OF COURSE. AND OUR *DINNER* THE OTHER EVENING. I'M SORRY I DIDN'T PLACE YOU SOONER. AND YOU'RE HERE TODAY IN REGARD TO...?

WELL, AS YOU KNOW, MY FATHER IS THE DISTRICT ATTORNEY, AND I'M HERE IN CON-JUNCTION WITH HIS INVESTIGATION INTO... WELL--

THE MURDERS.

YES, EXACTLY. IT SEEMS THE DEATHS ARE ALL CENTRAL TO THE COMPANY.

CAN YOU THINK OF ANY EMPLOYEES THAT MIGHT--UM, THAT MY FATHER MIGHT QUESTION IN THIS CASE?

MISS BELMONT, I DON'T MEAN TO BE *RUDE*, BUT ISN'T THIS A BIT UNORTHODOX? THE DISTRICT ATTORNEY SENDING HIS DAUGHTER OUT TO ROUND UP SUSPECTS?

I SIMPLY HAVE TO ASK YOU, ARE YOU HERE IN AN OFFICIAL CAPACITY?

WELL... I UNDER-STAND YOUR TREPIDA-TION, BUT YOU DON'T THINK I'D BE HERE IF IT *WASN'T*, DO YOU? I MEAN, EVEN *I* KNOW THAT'S *HARDLY* MY PLACE.

I...SUPPOSE. LOOK I'M SORRY I *SNAPPED* AT YOU. IT'S JUST THAT THINGS HAVE BEEN TROUBLING ME TODAY-- I MEAN-- *LATELY.*

IF YOU'D LIKE TO TALK ABOUT IT, I'M ALWAYS WILLING TO--

MISS BELMONT, I REALLY CAN'T JEOPARDIZE MY POSI-TION HERE BY SPREADING SPECULATION, BUT I WILL SAY *THIS*, I DO *THINK* THERE IS ENOUGH CAUSE TO INVESTI-GATE OUR EMPLOYEES IN THIS MATTER.

THAT'S REALLY ALL I CAN SAY.

I UNDER-STAND. THANK YOU FOR YOUR TIME, AND IF YOU EVER JUST WANT TO TALK, CALL ME.

GOOD AFTERNOON, MISS BELMONT.

22

I'M SUPPOSED TO MEET A DRIVER NAMED HUMPHRIES. THAT YOU?

INDEED IT IS, MR. CUTLER. RIGHT THIS WAY, SIR.

UH, NOT THAT I DON'T *TRUST* YOU, MR. HUMPHRIES, BUT WHERE *IS* DODDS?

MR. DODDS HAD PLANNED TO RIDE ALONG WITH YOU, BUT HAS HAD A LAST-MINUTE CHANGE OF PLANS. HE'LL BE *MEETING* YOU AT THE HOTEL.

I ASSURE YOU THERE IS NO CAUSE FOR *ALARM.*

I'M THAT OBVIOUS, HUH? WELL, NO OFFENSE INTENDED, BUT WITH ALL OF THESE KILLINGS, ANYTHING EVEN SLIGHTLY OUTSIDE THE USUAL CAN MAKE A MAN NERVOUS.

I MEAN, FOR ALL *I* KNOW, *DODDS* COULD BE THE KILLER.

OH, I ASSURE YOU, MR. CUTLER. THERE IS *NO* POSSIBILITY OF *THAT.*

IN FACT, SECURITY IS THE PRIME REASON HE SUGGESTED HOLDING THIS MEETING SOME-WHERE OTHER THAN EXPECTED.

WELL, THAT MAKES SENSE, I SUPPOSE.

SLATE.

MR. DODDS ASKED ME TO GIVE YOU THIS KEY. IT IS FOR THE *LARGO* SUITE, WHERE HE WILL EITHER BE WAITING FOR YOU, OR WILL MEET YOU SHORTLY. GOOD DAY, SIR.

I CERTAINLY *HOPE* IT'S A "GOOD DAY."

HELLO?

FWUP

23

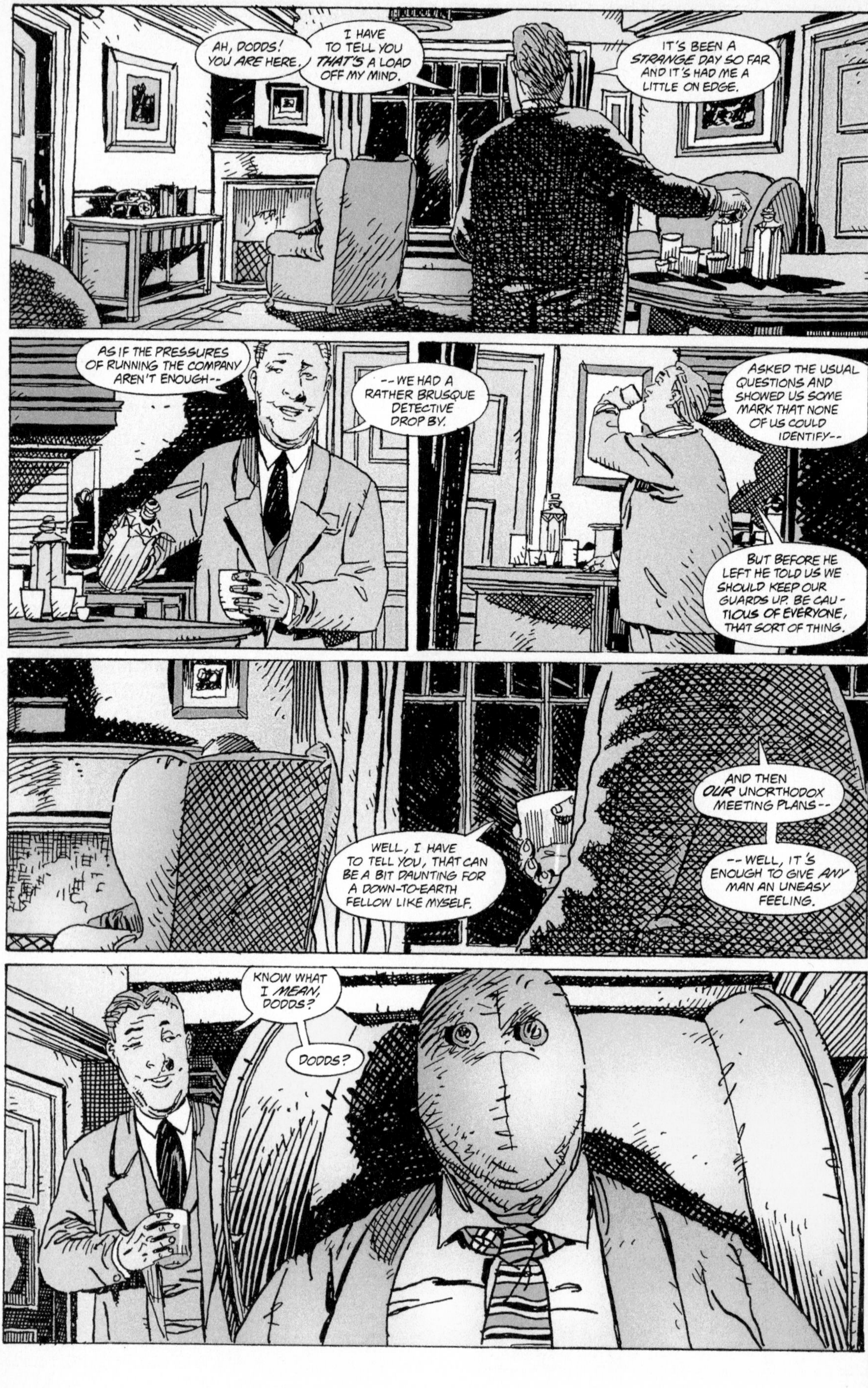
AH, DODDS! YOU ARE HERE.
I HAVE TO TELL YOU THAT'S A LOAD OFF MY MIND.
IT'S BEEN A STRANGE DAY SO FAR AND IT'S HAD ME A LITTLE ON EDGE.
AS IF THE PRESSURES OF RUNNING THE COMPANY AREN'T ENOUGH--
--WE HAD A RATHER BRUSQUE DETECTIVE DROP BY.
ASKED THE USUAL QUESTIONS AND SHOWED US SOME MARK THAT NONE OF US COULD IDENTIFY--
BUT BEFORE HE LEFT HE TOLD US WE SHOULD KEEP OUR GUARDS UP. BE CAU-TIOUS OF EVERYONE, THAT SORT OF THING.
AND THEN OUR UNORTHODOX MEETING PLANS--
--WELL, IT'S ENOUGH TO GIVE ANY MAN AN UNEASY FEELING.
WELL, I HAVE TO TELL YOU, THAT CAN BE A BIT DAUNTING FOR A DOWN-TO-EARTH FELLOW LIKE MYSELF.
KNOW WHAT I MEAN, DODDS?
DODDS?

Matt Wagner Steven T Seagle Guy Davis
SANDMAN MYSTERY THEATRE
"..the sudden smell of sulphur
as her eyes shot steely,
cold death.."
THE SCORPION
4 OF 4

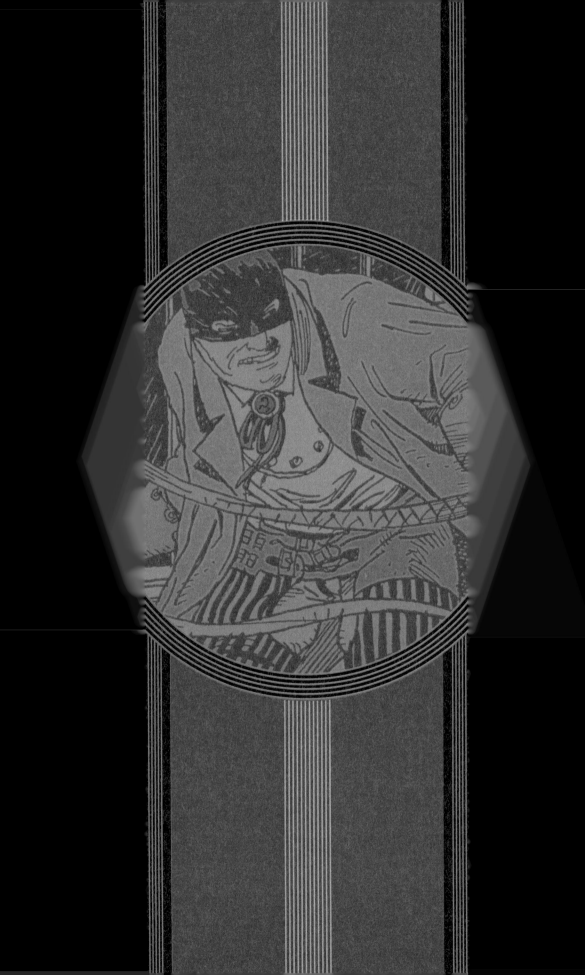

--CAN'T TELL YOU WHAT A RELIEF IT IS TO HAVE *YOU* WORKIN' WITH ME, MAX.

YEAH, BURKE? WHY SO?

HAD SOME REAL LIMP DICKS WITH ME THE PAST COUPLE OF DAYS.

MORE LIKELY TA *PISS* THEMSELVES THAN TO CATCH A KILLER. AT LEAST I KNOW *YOU* WON'T ACCIDENTALLY SHOOT YOURSELF IN THE FOOT OR SOMETHIN'.

YEAH, WELL, IT'S *ALWAYS* A *PLEASURE* TO WORK WITH *YOU*, BURKE.

YEAH, YOU CAN KISS *MY* SWEET ASS *TOO*, MAX.

LIEUTENANTS BURKE AND COLLINS, N.Y.P.D.

G-GOODNESS, LIEUTENANT, HAVE I DONE SOME-THING--

WE GOT A TIP THAT YOU'VE GOT A ROOM REGISTERED TO WESLEY DODDS.

Y-YES, SIR. THE LARGO SUITE, FIFTH FLOOR--

KEEP EVERYBODY AWAY FROM THAT FLOOR AND KEEP YER YAP SHUT ABOUT THIS 'TIL YOU HEAR FROM ME OTHER-WISE. UNDERSTOOD?

Y-YES. ABSOLUTELY.

YOU *HAVE* TO BE THAT ROUGH ON HIM, BURKE?

NAH, BUT HE WAS A SQUIRMER. NERVOUS. I HATE THAT IN PEOPLE, BRINGS OUT THE WORST IN ME. WHAT CAN I SAY?

GOING UP?

YEP, BUT *ALONE.* POLICE BUSINESS. TAKE THE NEXT CAR, TOOTS.

GOOD HEAVENS!

191

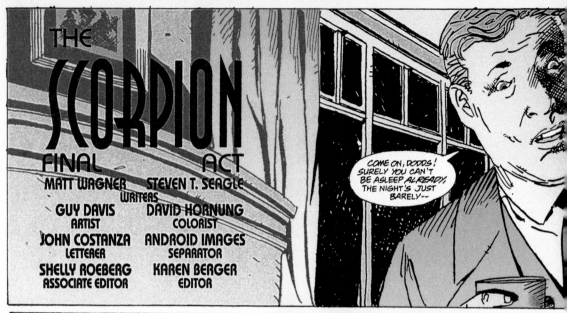

THE SCORPION
FINAL ACT

MATT WAGNER   **STEVEN T. SEAGLE**
WRITERS

GUY DAVIS   **DAVID HORNUNG**
ARTIST   COLORIST

JOHN COSTANZA   **ANDROID IMAGES**
LETTERER   SEPARATOR

SHELLY ROEBERG   **KAREN BERGER**
ASSOCIATE EDITOR   EDITOR

COME ON, DODDS! SURELY YOU CAN'T BE ASLEEP *ALREADY!* THE NIGHT'S JUST BARELY--

OH GOD... OH DEAR GOD...

DODDS?! IF YOU'RE IN HERE, AND THIS IS SOME SORT OF *PRANK* ON YOUR PART--

I CAN ASSURE YOU IT'S *NOT* FUNNY.

YOU WANT SOMETHIN' *FUNNY,* CUTLER? I GOT A *JOKE* FOR YOU.

HOW *MANY* WEALTHY BUSINESSMEN DOES IT TAKE T'FILL A GRAVE?

AS MANY AS YOU CAN *STUFF* IN IT.

BAM

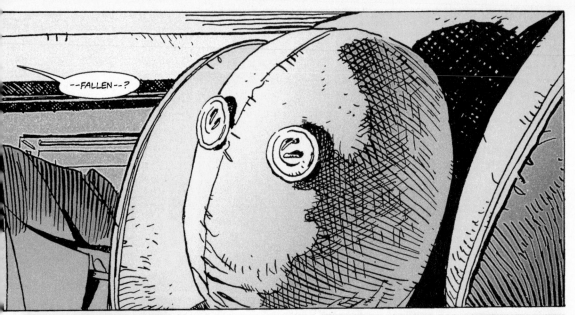

--FALLEN--?

LOOKS LIKE I'LL BE FILLIN' ONE WITH *TWO* OF YOU TONIGHT.

NOW LOOK HERE, WHATEVER YOU AND DODDS HAVE GOING ON HAS GONE FAR ENOUGH, MR.--

YOU CAN MAKE THAT SCORPION, PAL.

SCOR--? OH *NO*...

AND THE *ONLY* THING I'VE GOT GOING ON WITH THE QUIET "MR. *DODDS*" HERE--

--IS THAT HE'S GIVIN' ME THE PLEASURE OF KILLIN' A MAN *TWICE.*

AIN'T THAT RIGHT, "*DOLL BABY*"--?

③

WHAT THE HELL?

YES...YOU WILL BE. LAY DOWN YOUR WEAPON, SCORPION--

I'LL BE DAMNED--

--AND PREPARE YOURSELF FOR THE NIGHTMARES THAT RIGHTFULLY AWAIT YOU.

THE HELL I WILL.

I WILL NOT ASK AGAIN. LAY DOWN YOUR WHIP.

I GOT NO COMPLAINT WITH YOU, PARTNER, WHOEVER YOU ARE, SO WHY DON'T YOU JUST TROT YOUR BUTT RIGHT BACK OUTTA HERE AND LEAVE ME T'MY WORK?

YOU HAVE KILLED MANY IMPORTANT MEN, SCORPION. YOU WILL NOT--

POLICE!

HANDS UP AND STAND VERY STILL.

WHAT--?

WELL, HELL'S BELLS. MY TWO FAVORITE NUTCASES IN ONE ROOM TOGETHER.

MUST BE YOUR LUCKY DAY, BURKE.

MUST BE.

④

DIAN? THAT YOU? LISTEN, I WON'T BE ABLE TO--TO--

DAMN IT! WHERE IS THAT *PAPER?* HERE! GOOD--*UH*--I WON'T BE ABLE TO --

DADDY? YOU SOUND ABSOLUTELY *HAGGARD.* WHAT'S WRONG?

SEEMS LIKE I CAN'T GET HOME THESE DAYS BEFORE I'M CALLED RIGHT BACK OUT. THE STATION JUST GOT AN UNEX-PECTED BREAK ON THIS SCORPION CASE.

ANONYMOUS TIP, UH...

DADDY...YOU'RE KEEPING SOMETHING FROM ME. WHAT *IS* IT?

WELL, I SUPPOSE YOU'D FIND OUT *ANYHOW.* THE TIP WAS THAT THE SCORPION IS GOING AFTER STEPHEN CUTLER TONIGHT--

--AND WHEN THEY CONTACTED HIS OFFICE TO *WARN* HIM, HIS DAUGHTER--

CASSANDRA?

YES, CASSANDRA. SHE TOLD US THAT HER FATHER HAD GONE OFF TO A PRIVATE MEETING ...WITH *WESLEY.*

CLAC

WESLEY? BUT HE'S TOO ILL TO-- DO YOU MEAN THAT HE--?

NOW, DIAN, DON'T GO GETTING ALL EXCITED, EVERYTHING WILL BE JUST FINE--

DAMN RIGHT IT WILL, AND I INTEND TO *BE* THERE WHEN IT DOES.

CLAC

DIAN--?

I'M GOING *WITH* YOU.

NOW DIAN--

LET'S GO, DADDY.

ALL RIGHT, YA HALLOWEEN REJECTS, DROP THE WEAPONS AND GET YOUR HANDS UP HIGH.

DON'T EVEN *THINK* IT, BOYS. YOU'RE GOING NOWHERE BUT TO THE STATION.

THE *HELL* I AM.

CRAC

DAMN IT! YOU ASKED FOR THIS, BUB!

BLAM BLAM

AAGH!

WATCH IT!

DON'T WORRY, CUTLER. YOU'RE A DEAD MAN REGARDLESS--

ONE MORE PEEP OUT OF YOU, SCORPION, AND I'LL--

--BURKE--!

MAX?

SHIT.

'M DYING-- UNNK--

196

GOTCHA, LAWMAN!

BASTARD!

HARDLY. I *KNEW* WHO MY DADDY WAS.

CHRIST!

NOPE, NOWHERE *NEAR*. THOUGH CUTLER AN' MEN LIKE 'IM WENT AHEAD AN' HUNG 'IM UP ANYHOW. I'D STAY DOWN IF I WERE YOU.

YOU KISS MY ASS. IF I--

--I-- HUH?

NOT BAD ENOUGH I GOTTA GO *DOWN*, I GOTTA GO SUCKIN' UP YOUR GAS--

AAAHHH! INSIDES EATIN' ME UP!

197

YOU GOT IN MY WAY, BURKE. ;COUGH; NEVER STEP ON A SCORPION.

AND AS FER YOU ;COUGH; CUTLER. THERE'S STILL A STING WAITIN'. COUNT ON IT.

;COUGH COUGH;

YOU'LL BE ALONE AGAIN SOMETIME IN THE FUTURE, BUT NOT AS ALONE AS YOU THINK.

DO NOT SURRENDER TO THE SCORPION'S STING.

HOFF! DON'T LET HIM--AWAY--

--JESUS-- BURNIN' UP--

DON'T TRY TO MOVE. THIS WILL STOP THE POISON'S EFFECTS.

AND DON'T WORRY... THE SCORPION WILL NOT ELUDE ME.

;COUGH;

HUNNH!

HE WILL LEAVE A TRAIL--

NNNNN...

WHICH I WILL FOLLOW TO HIS BITTER END.

8

NNNH! SHIT!

EH?

DAMN IT!

THE EMBERS OF THE SCORPION'S ESCAPE ROPE FALL AWAY AS QUICKLY AND CLEANLY AS MAX'S LIFE.

THE NIGHT AIR HITS THE BACK OF MY NECK WITH A CHILL THAT IS AMPLIFIED BY THE REALIZATION THAT I HAVE PLAYED MY SURPRISE CARD, AND HAVE STILL COME UP EMPTY-HANDED.

⑨

THE DIFFICULTIES OF THIS NIGHT HAVE ONLY JUST BEGUN.

NO, NO... I'LL STOP BY MAX'S PLACE AND TELL HER... MAGGIE'D *WANT* TO HEAR IT FROM A FRIEND. UH-HUH. RIGHT.

SOMETHING HAPPEN, ROSS?

I'LL SAY SO, LARRY. THAT WAS OUR BACKUP MAN AT THE SCENE. THE TIP WAS DEAD ON, BUT THE WHOLE THING WENT UP IN THEIR FACES.

THE SCORPION *WAS* THERE, BUT MANAGED TO GET AWAY *AFTER* KILLING COLLINS. BURKE TOOK A LASHING TOO, BUT PULLED THROUGH IT SOMEHOW--

COLLINS? OH GEEZ, THAT'S--

WHAT ABOUT WESLEY DODDS? IS HE ALL RIGHT? OH... AND MR. CUTLER, OF COURSE.

CUTLER'S KNOCKED OUT, BUT OTHERWISE FINE. DODDS WASN'T EVEN THERE, THOUGH.

LOOKS LIKE *THAT* WAS JUST A SETUP TO DRAW CUTLER OUT.

THAT CAN'T *BE.* WHY WOULDN'T HE JUST GO AFTER MR. CUTLER IN HIS HOME, LIKE HE DID WITH THE OTHERS?

NOT TO MENTION THE ANONYMOUS TIP-- WHY WOULD HE GIVE HIMSELF UP?

I JUST CAN'T GET OVER POOR MAX.

YOU KNOW, THAT'S TRUE, YOUR DAUGHTER'S QUITE A LITTLE DETECTIVE, LARRY.

YEAH, WELL, NOT *TOO* SURPRISING, I GUESS, GIVEN THAT THAT *SANDMAN* CHARACTER WAS INVOLVED IN THE WHOLE BLOWUP.

THE SANDMAN, HUH?

THE SANDMAN... HM.

10

200

--SORRY, DAD, 'M SORRY--

--I'LL GET 'EM FOR YA--

--I'LL STILL GET 'EM--

--I'M NOT INCOMPETENT, I JUST--

--JUST-- DAMN IT!

WELL ISN'T THIS LUCKY?

--NO, NOTHING. I JUST WANT TO... FRESHEN UP A BIT. I'LL BE RIGHT BACK.

HELLO, HUMPHRIES, I KNOW HE'S STILL *AILING*, BUT COULD YOU PROP WESLEY UP TO THE PHONE? I PROMISE I WON'T BE A MOMENT AND THEN HE CAN GET BACK TO REST.

I WOULD BE HAPPY TO, EXCEPT THAT MR. DODDS LEFT *JUST* THIS MORNING FOR PHILADEL-PHIA ON BUSINESS.

PHILADELPHIA? THAT CAN'T BE. HE WAS PAINFULLY ILL JUST *YESTERDAY*.

YES, WELL, HE *DOES* HAVE REMARKABLE RESTORATIVE ABILITIES, AND THE BUSINESS SEEMED *QUITE* URGENT--

FINE THEN, I'LL CALL HIM *THERE*. COULD YOU GIVE ME THE HOTEL NAME, PLEASE?

I AM ASHAMED TO ADMIT IT, BUT I NEGLECTED TO ASK MR. DODDS WHERE HE WOULD BE LODGING. IF YOU'D CARE TO CALL BACK *TOMORROW*, I MIGHT--

NO NO NO. THAT'S FINE. JUST TELL WESLEY TO CALL ME AS SOON AS YOU *SEE* HIM. GOOD-BYE.

OH, *WESLEY*...

PING

WELL ISN'T *THIS* LUCKY?

CASSANDRA!

I *KNOW* IT WAS IMPULSIVE OF ME TO DROP BY, BUT I REALLY WANTED TO SEE YOU.

UH, I TELL YOU, CASSANDRA --I'VE BEEN *OUT* ALL DAY AN' I SMELL LIKE THE BACK END OF A PACK MULE. WHY DON'T WE MEET UP *LATER* FOR A--

TERRY, DON'T BE *SILLY.*

NO, *REALLY,* IF YOU WANT TO HOOK UP *LATER* FOR DINNER AND SOME DANCING--

I'M SURE I'D BE MUCH NICER COMPANY--

PING

IF I DIDN'T *KNOW* BETTER, MR. STETSON, I'D SAY YOU WERE TRYING TO DUST ME OFF.

IS THAT WHAT'S HAPPENING, TERRY?

NOW DON'T BE SILLY. I'M JUST-- I JUST NEED SOME *TIME* TO GET MYSELF TOGETHER IS ALL.

NIGHT?

I DON'T MIND WAITING, IN FACT I'D *LOVE* TO JUST SIT AND TALK TO YOU WHILE YOU GET READY FOR OUR NIGHT TOGETHER.

OH YES. I FEEL I'VE *REALLY* COME TO KNOW YOU, THESE PAST FEW DAYS *ESPECIALLY.*

I HAVE A *VERY* SPECIAL NIGHT PLANNED.

NOW, CASSIE--

YOU KNOW, I'VE NEVER NOTICED THAT BOLO TIE BEFORE. WHAT AN *INTERESTING* DESIGN. HAVE YOU WORN IT TO *WORK?*

THIS?

UH...NO--

OR DO YOU ONLY WEAR IT TO KILL PEOPLE? OPEN THE *DOOR.*

13

AH GEEZ, LIEUTENANT, I'M JUST TRYIN' T' HELP HERE. YOU LOOK *REALLY* SICK--

YOU KNOW, LIEUTENANT, I DON'T THINK YOU LOOK TOO GOOD. ARE YOU SURE YOU WOULDN'T RATHER I TOOK YOU HOME?

OF COURSE I LOOK LIKE HELL. I'VE BEEN WHIPPED, POISONED, GASSED, AND SHOT FULL OF GOD KNOWS *WHAT* TONIGHT.

FUNNY THING, KEMP. I REMEMBER CALLING FOR A CAR. I DON'T REMEMBER CALLING FOR A GOD-DAMN WET NURSE.

YOU, ON THE OTHER HAND, PROBABLY HAD YOUR BIGGEST TROUBLE T'DAY WHEN THE LUNCH ROOM RAN OUTTA THEM SAUSAGE ROLLS--THAT--THA--

HURRAFFF

I'M TELLIN' YA, SIR--

I'M TELLIN' *YOU* TO SHUT UP AND *DRIVE*. WE GOTTA GET TO STETSON'S PLACE QUICK. AND I'M BETTIN' WE'RE GONNA FIND HIM THERE PATCHIN' UP A NASTY FLESH WOUND.

ROSS O'DONALD. YEAH?... YEAH, SULLIVAN, SHOOT... UH HUH...YEAH, UH...WE'VE GOT HIM AT 334 EAST 75TH STREET...

...RIGHT... YEAH, I'LL GET BACK-UP IN THERE *PRONTO*.

14

THAT WAS SULLIVAN. SAYS BURKE JUST TOOK OUT OF THE HOTEL ON A JAG.

DID HE COME UP WITH SOMETHING CONCRETE?

CAN'T SAY, FOR SURE, BUT HE THINKS IT'S ONE OF THE YOUNGER GUYS AT THE COMPANY...TERRY STETSON.

I THOUGHT THEY SAID BURKE HAD BEEN *HURT* IN THE SCUFFLE?

YEAH, BUT YOU KNOW BURKE. SATAN HIMSELF COULDN'T HOLD *THAT* MAN DOWN AGAINST HIS WILL.

STILL, I DON'T THINK BURKE SHOULD CONFRONT THIS FELLA *ALONE*.

MILLER!

YEAH, SARGE?

GET ME THREE CARS FULL AND MEET ME AT 334 EAST 75TH.

WE GOT A POSSIBLE MAKE ON THIS SCORPION, SO MAKE SURE WE'VE GOT THE FIREPOWER TO NAIL 'IM IF WE'RE RIGHT. HE'S A *TRICKY* BASTARD.

YOU *GOT* IT, SARGE.

CASSANDRA--

-- I DON'T KNOW WHAT YOU'RE *TALKING* ABOUT.

YOU'RE A *TALKER*, TERRY. I'VE KNOWN THAT ABOUT YOU SINCE DAY ONE, BUT IT'S *NOT* GOING TO WORK FOR YOU THIS TIME, SO CAN IT.

15

ALL RIGHT THEN, LITTLE LADY, SINCE *YOU'RE* THE ONE WITH THE *POWER* HERE, WHY DON'T YOU DO THE TALKING AN' TELL ME WHAT YOU *WANT*?

I WANT TO KNOW *WHY*. WHY DID YOU KILL THOSE MEN? I THOUGHT YOU LIKED ME, AND YOU TRIED TO KILL MY OWN FATHER. WHY?

BECAUSE HE HAD IT COMIN'. THEY *ALL* DID.

HAD IT COMING? MY FATHER TREATED YOU LIKE A SON.

YEAH? WELL, THAT'S MIGHTY IRONIC SINCE IT WAS YOUR FATHER AND HIS BUDDIES THAT DROVE MY PA TO AN EARLY GRAVE. THEY CRUSHED HIM. *BROKE* HIM.

WHERE *I* COME FROM, YOU DON'T THROW PEOPLE'S LIVES AWAY OVER NOTHING. THEY'RE JUST GETTIN' WHAT'S COMIN' TO 'EM.

THAT STORY I TOLD YOU ABOUT MY FATHER, AND THE RAILROAD? BULLSHIT. MY FATHER WAS A *FARMER* IN TEXAS.

AND WE WERE PERFECT- LY HAPPY UNTIL YOUR FATHER'S COMPANY SENT ITS GODDAMN OIL SURVEYORS AROUND. HE --

UNNH...

CLAC

YOU STEP AWAY FROM THAT CASE THIS *INSTANT*.

NOW, CASSANDRA, I'M NOT DOING ANYTHING WITH *THAT*. I'M JUST STEADYING MYSELF. I'VE BEEN...*HURT*.

LET ME GET THIS COAT OFF AND I'LL *SHOW* YOU.

16

206

SLOWLY, TERRY. I'M WARNING YOU--

I AIN'T FOOLIN.' HERE... LOOK.

OH MY GOD, YOU'RE BLEEDING. IT LOOKS LIKE YOU'VE BEEN SHO--

--AAAAAH! STOP IT! WHAT ARE YOU--

YOU'RE PRETTY, CASSIE--

YOU STAY AWAY FROM ME, OR I'LL SHOOT YOU--

--BUT YOU'RE STILL ONE OF THEM.

I SWEAR I'LL--

AIN'T POLITE T'SWEAR.

BLAM

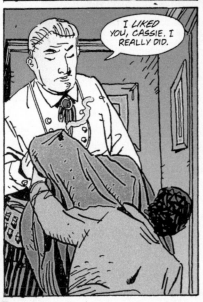

I LIKED YOU, CASSIE. I REALLY DID.

BUT WHEN YOU GET RIGHT DOWN TO IT--

--YOU'RE REALLY JUST POISON. LIKE THE REST OF 'EM. LIKE ALL OF 'EM.

17

NO, NO NEED TO WAIT. THANKS.

--YEAH, WELL, NO WHIP MARKS ON *THIS* DAME. LOOKS LIKE HE JUST *SHOT* HER--

EXCUSE ME. SORRY!

CASSANDRA?

NOT ANY MORE.

MIND TELLIN' ME JUST WHAT IN THE HELL *YOU'RE* DOIN' HERE, MISS BELMONT.

I KNEW HER, AND-- OH-- I WAS *SNOOPING*, I ADMIT IT. I WAS IN THE PRECINCT WITH DADDY AND OVERHEARD THE CRIME REPORT. ROSS O'DONALD SAID YOU WERE HEADED TO THIS ADDRESS.

LIEUTENANT, I THINK THE SANDMAN STAGED THIS EVENING'S EVENTS IN ORDER TO DRAW THE SCORPION OUT.

WE GOT A TIP-OFF ON THAT MEETING.

WHY WOULD A GUY BLOW HIS OWN SETUP?

MAYBE THE TIP WAS *CASSANDRA'S* DOING. SHE ACTED AS IF SHE KNEW MORE THAN SHE WAS LETTING ON WHEN I SPOKE WITH HER YESTERDAY. PERHAPS SHE UNCOVERED HIS VENDETTA.

HIS... SAY, IF HE ISN'T *HERE*, THAT PROBABLY MEANS HE'S GONE AFTER LANE.

I GOTTA GET *OVER* THERE.

I'LL GO *WITH* YOU.

THE *HELL* YOU WILL.

LIEUTENANT, YOU CAN'T LEAVE THIS SCENE UNATTENDED, YOUR BACKUP HASN'T ARRIVED--

--AND YET YOU CLEARLY ARE IN NO CONDITION TO DRIVE YOURSELF.

NOT A CHANCE IN HELL, SWEETHEART.

18

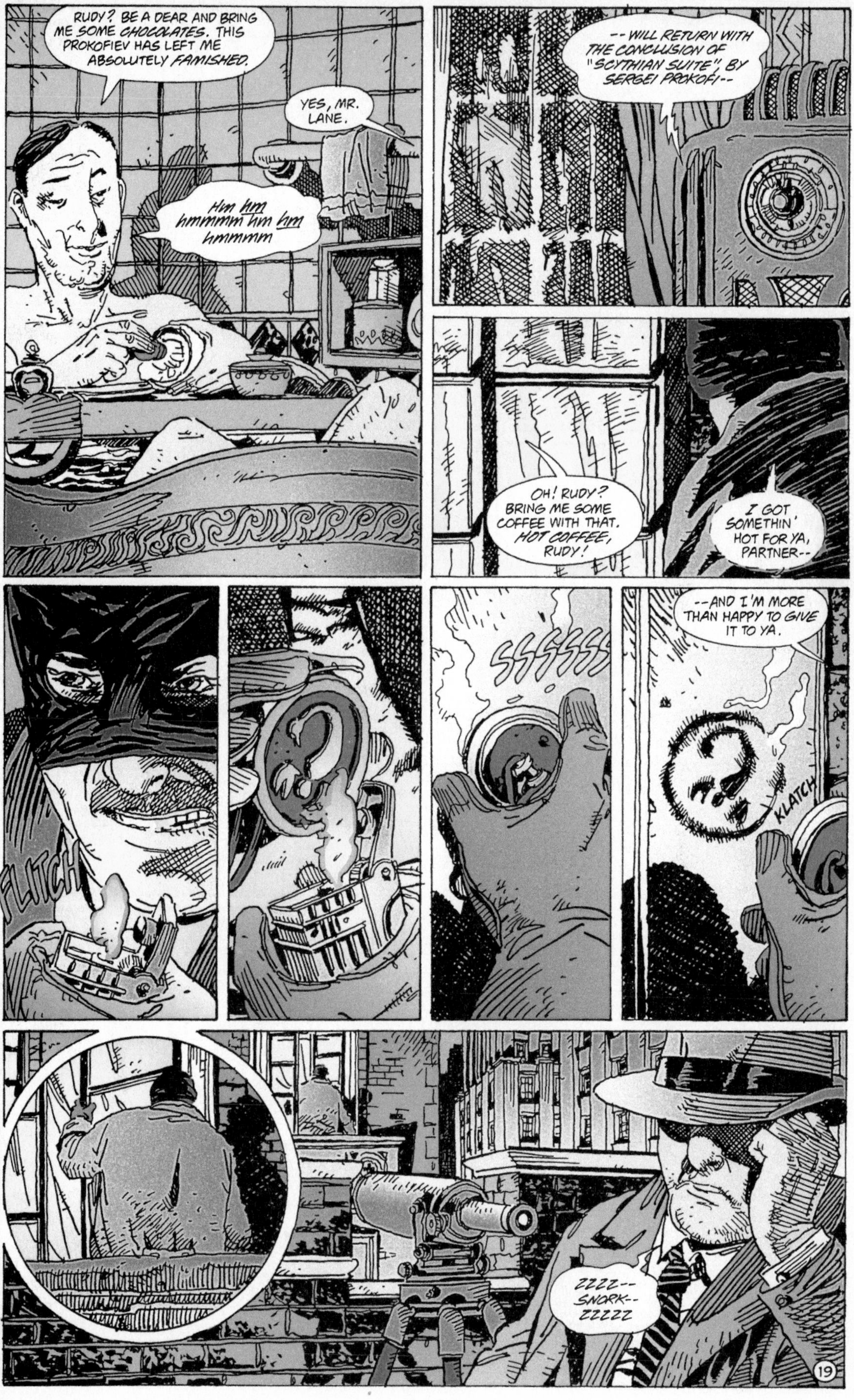
RUDY? BE A DEAR AND BRING ME SOME CHOCOLATES. THIS PROKOFIEV HAS LEFT ME ABSOLUTELY FAMISHED.
YES, MR. LANE.
Hm hm hmmmm hm hm hmmmm
--WILL RETURN WITH THE CONCLUSION OF "SCYTHIAN SUITE", BY SERGEI PROKOFI--
OH! RUDY? BRING ME SOME COFFEE WITH THAT. HOT COFFEE, RUDY!
I GOT SOMETHIN' HOT FOR YA, PARTNER--
FLITCH
SSSSSS
--AND I'M MORE THAN HAPPY TO GIVE IT TO YA.
KLATCH
ZZZZ-- SNORK-- ZZZZZ
19

--TOMORROW NIGHT, JAZZ MUSIC WITH LESTER "SAWTOOTH" HAWKINS AND THE EMPIRE CITY--

JAZZ?

THAT VULGAR MUSIC HAS *NO* PLACE IN THIS CULTURE.

AN' YOU'RE JUST THE ONE TO DECIDE, WHAT BELONGS AN' WHAT *DON'T*, AIN'T YA, LANE?

WHO--?

YOU! YOU'D BETTER STAY AWAY FROM ME! MY VALET IS ON HIS WAY BACK AND--

AND HE'S AS LIKELY TO RUN IN HERE AND *SUCK* ME AS THROW ME OUT.

HOW DO-- HOW *DARE* YOU!

HOW DARE I *WHAT?* POINT OUT THE TRUTH? EVERYONE AT THE OFFICE KNOWS ALL ABOUT YOU AND YOUR HOUSEBOYS, LANE.

THE OFFICE? YOU--?

YEAH, OLD MAN. WE KNOW EACH OTHER. AN' *LONGER* THAN YOU *THINK*.

PLEASE--

I'M SURE THAT WHATEVER THIS IS ABOUT, WE CAN WORK IT OUT. I CAN PAY YOU ANYTHING YOU--

20

210

YOU CAN *PAY* ME? I *DOUBT* IT. HOW MUCH IS A MAN'S LIFE WORTH? TWO THOUSAND? *TEN* THOUSAND?

HOW MUCH WAS MY *FATHER'S* LIFE WORTH? HUH? *NOTHING?* 'CAUSE THAT'S ALL IT AMOUNTED TO.

TERRY? I-- BUT I DIDN'T *KNOW* YOUR FATHER-- I-- I DON'T KNOW ANY OTHER STETSONS--

STETSON'S A HAT. MY REAL NAME IS *PRITCHARD!* TERRY *PRITCHARD.*

NOW YOU REMEMBER, DON'T YA? TWELVE YEARS AGO YOU TALKED MY FATHER INTO SELLING OFF OUR LANDS IN TEXAS SO YOU COULD PUMP THE LIFE OUTTA IT. OUTTA *US!*

NO! NO, NO... WE PAID A FAIR PRICE... A *GOOD* PRICE FOR THE LAND. PRITCHARD BECAME A WEALTHY MAN, HE--

YOU GAVE HIM *MONEY*, ALL RIGHT, AND AFTER YOU WINED AND DINED HIM, YOU TREATED HIM LIKE AN OUTCAST. HE WANTED A BETTER LIFE. TO BE SOMEBODY *OUTSIDE* OF TEXAS TOO, BUT YOU REFUSED HIM THAT.

YOUR MONEY RUINED HIS LIFE! HE PISSED IT AWAY GAMBLING UNTIL HE FINALLY COULDN'T SETTLE UP ONE HOT AUGUST AFTERNOON.

MA JUST DRANK HERSELF INTO THE GRAVE.

AND-- MY SISTER--

--EMMALINE... EMMALINE WENT TO... *HOLLYWOOD!*

SWEET JESUS.

NO, YOU DIDN'T DO ANY OF THAT, LANE--

--YOUR *MONEY* DID.

SAME DIFFERENCE.

21

THE PATH OF YOUR POISONOUS HATRED STOPS HERE, SCORPION.

YOU AGAIN? I'LL--

SLEEP AND DREAM OF THE EVIL YOU HAVE CRUELLY WROUGHT.

FOOOOSH

HUKK-- YOU AIN'T GONNA TAKE *ME* DOWN, LITTLE MAN.

YOU HIDE BEHIND THAT MASK LIKE THESE BASTARDS HIDE BEHIND THEIR WEALTH!

THUD

BUT WITHOUT THAT PROTECTION--

YOU'RE JUST AN-- *HUKK*-- ORDINARY MAN--

22

--NO DIFFERENT-- HUKFF--

--JUST A-- HUKK--

THUD

NNNH--

--JUST A MAN...

...JUST A NORMAL MAN WITH A DOLLAR IN HIS HAND HE...

...HE WANTED TO BUY A PONY..., A LITTLE PONY... BUT HIS DADDY...

...HIS DADDY MADE HIM... EARN IT...

MR. LANE?

...MADE HIM EARN IT DOING THINGS... HE...

...HE CAME INTO HIS ROOM WITH... A HANDFUL OF DOLLARS...

MR. LANE, IT'S ALL RIGHT NOW.

...AND HE SAID... GIVE YOU A DOLLAR IF YOU'LL KISS MY NECK...

...GIVE YOU ANOTHER DOLLAR IF YOU'LL... KISS MY SHOULDER...

OH DEAR, MR. LANE. WE'LL GET YOU SOME HELP.

23

IS MR. STETSON STILL ALIVE?

MAKE IT A DOUBLE.

DEPENDS ON YOUR DEFINITION. LOOKS LIKE HE'S HAD A STROKE OR SOMETHIN'.

WHAT ON EARTH DO YOU THINK HAPPENED? MR. LANE DOESN'T LOOK CAPABLE OF HARMING A MAN OF MR. STETSON'S SIZE.

NAH. THIS'S GOT SANDMAN WRITTEN ALL OVER IT.

YOU CAN STILL SMELL SOME OF THAT PUTRID SLEEPING GAS HE USES. ACCOUNTS FOR LANE'S MAN-SERVANT PASSED OUT DOWNSTAIRS TOO.

UH-HUH. HERE YA GO. THIS SEALS THE GODDAMN DEAL ALTOGETHER.

WHAT IS IT?

HE LOVES TO LEAVE THESE CUTESY LITTLE NOTES AT THE SCENE, STUPID LITTLE POEMS FOLDED UP LIKE ANIMALS. FORGET WHAT THEY'RE CALLED--

"THROUGH CURRENCY OF HUMAN SOULS--"

I HAVE DECIDED. I WILL TELL HER.

DIAN IS THE MOST PRECIOUS THING IN MY HEART, AND I CAN NO LONGER KEEP ANY PIECE OF MY LIFE CLOSED TO HER.

ORIGAMI. IT'S CALLED ORIGAMI.

T H E · E N D

SANDMAN MYSTERY THEATRE

ANNUAL

matt
WAGNER

steven t
SEAGLE

john
BOLTON

guy
DAVIS

stefano
GAUDIANO

david
LLOYD

dean
ORMSTON

george
PRATT

alex
ROSS

peter
SNEJBJERG

SANDMAN MYSTERY THEATRE Annual

I SOMETIMES WONDER IF CENTRAL PARK ISN'T THE TRUE HEART OF NEW YORK CITY.

WES!

Chapter 1
THE EYEWITNESS

THOUGH IT DOESN'T HAVE THE FLASH OF TIMES SQUARE, THE MYSTIQUE OF THE GREAT WHITE WAY OR THE TANGIBLE ENERGY OF THE FINANCIAL DISTRICT--

IT STILL SEEMS TO PULL EVERYONE INTO IT WITH SOME DEGREE OF REGULARITY.

WAIT RIGHT THERE, DIAN. I'LL COME ACROSS.

AND ONCE *WITHIN* ITS BOUNDARIES A PERSON CAN'T HELP BUT FEEL SOMEWHAT--

CAN YOU BELIEVE THIS TRAFFIC? IT'S INCREDIBLE, AND ON A *SUNDAY* AS WELL.

--INSIGNIFICANT.

I KNOW, IT'S ABSOLUTELY MANIC.

THANKS FOR MEETING ME. I KNOW HOW HARD IT IS FOR YOU TO PULL AWAY FROM THE OLD GRINDSTONE--

QUITE THE *CONTRARY*, DIAN. IT'S HARD FOR ME TO PULL AWAY FROM *YOU* TO DO MY *WORK*.

ALTHOUGH I MUST SAY, A DAY AS TERRIFIC AS THIS IS *JUST* THE THING TO *KEEP* ME OUT OF DOORS.

DID I SAY THE *TRAFFIC* WAS MANIC?

GUILTY AS CHARGED!

I DO FEEL QUITE LIBERATED. I'D BE AFRAID THAT I MIGHT WAKE FROM THIS DREAM--

--BUT MY DREAMS ARE *NOTHING* LIKE THIS.

WES? DO WE HAVE TO GO DOWN THIS *PATH?* THESE STATUES GIVE ME THE *WILLIES.* I ALWAYS FEEL LIKE I'M BEING *WATCHED* BY STRANGERS.

THESE FINE *GENTS?* DIAN, THE LITERARY WALK IS A REPRESENTATION OF SOME OF THE GREATEST MINDS EVER TO PUT PEN TO PAPER.

"AND NE'ER DID GRECIAN CHISEL TRACE / A NYMPH, A NAIAD, OR A GRACE / OF FINER FORM, OR LOVELIER FACE!" *SIR WALTER SCOTT,...*

"ALL THE WORLD'S A STAGE AND THE MEN AND WOMEN MERELY PLAYERS: THEY HAVE THEIR EXITS AND THEIR ENTRANCES;"

"AND ONE MAN IN HIS TIME PLAYS *MANY* PARTS," *WILLIAM SHAKESPEARE...*

"SLEEP I CAN GET NANE / FOR THINKING ON MY DEARIE," *ROBERT BURNS...*

DUH DUH DUH *DAAAAAA!...* LUDWIG VAN BEETHOVEN. HA HA!

PARDON ME, MA'AM. A *ROSE* FOR THE LADY--

TEN CENTS, SIR. THANK YOU VERY KINDLY.

A ROSE FOR *ME,* KIND SIR? IS THIS A *REWARD* FOR MY MUSICAL PERFORMANCE?

ACTUALLY, I WAS HOPING I COULD CONVINCE YOU TO HOLD IT IN YOUR *TEETH.*

OH? IS THAT TO MAKE ME MORE EXOTIC?

NO...THAT'S TO KEEP YOU FROM SINGING ANY *MORE.*

CAD!

GUILTY AS CHARGED AGAIN.

DIAN IS REALLY A FIND. NOT MANY WOMEN I'VE MET IN THIS CITY HAVE TAKEN MY SARCASM AS A PLAYFUL GESTURE.

BUT DIAN SEEMS TO KNOW *EXACTLY* WHAT I INTEND. LIKE SHE'S IN STEP WITH MY VERY THOUGHTS.

AND YET--SHE CLAIMS HER NIGHTS ARE PEACEFUL, UNTROUBLED BY DREAMS.

I'M ABSOLUTELY WINDED. SHALL WE TAKE A SEAT BY THE FOUNTAIN?

YOU KNOW, DIAN, FOR A MOMENT I WAS A BIT CONFUSED.

CONFUSED? WHATEVER BY?

WELL...THIS STATUE IS CALLED, "ANGEL OF THE WATERS," BUT--

I COULD SWEAR THE ANGEL *HERE* IS ON *MY* ARM.

TALK LIKE *THAT,* MR. DODDS--

WILL GET YOU *EVERY-WHERE.*

FOR THE FIRST TIME IN WHAT SEEMS LIKE MONTHS I AM COMPLETELY AT PEACE.

DIAN AND I LOSE OUR-SELVES IN EACH OTHER AND THE TRANQUILITY OF THE SURROUNDINGS.

AND THE TIME SLIPS BY UNNOTICED.

BUT INEXPLICABLY, MY EYES ARE SUDDENLY DRAWN TO A PATCH OF DARKNESS ACROSS THE LAKE--

--A FIGURE IN THE BRUSH LOOMING OVER UNSUSPECTING LOVERS--

--A DISTANCE TOO FAR FOR ME TO COVER--

--A CRIME I CANNOT PREVENT--

--AND SO I *WATCH.*

I WATCH A FORM AS MENACING AS ANY I HAVE EVER SEEN IN MY DREAMS --

--AND YET *MORE* TROUBLING *BECAUSE I* HAVE HAD NO VISION OF THIS FIGURE.

HAVE MY VISIONS LEFT ME?

HAVE THESE FEELINGS OF LOVE SILENCED MY INSIGHTS AND PURPOSE?

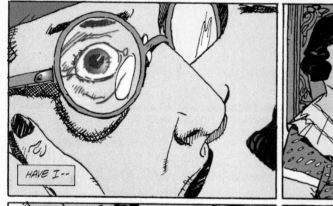

HAVE I--

WES? WHAT IS IT? YOU'VE SUDDENLY GONE ALL CLAMMY. IS SOMETHING THE MATTER?

WHAT? NO, NOTHING... JUST THE--WEATHER. WE SHOULD BE GOING. IT'S GETTING QUITE DARK.

IT HAS GOTTEN A BIT MORE *CHILLY* SUDDENLY, IF *THAT'S* WHAT YOU MEAN.

YES, EXACTLY. SHALL WE?

DINNER?

DINNER ...SURE.

IF I DO BELIEVE THAT THE PARK IS THE TRUE HEART OF THE CITY... I LEAVE KNOWING THAT EVEN THE TRUEST HEART...HAS ITS DARKEST CORNERS.

Chapter 2
THE BUTLER

I HAVE *ALWAYS* FELT THE DESIRE TO SERVE. I BELIEVE THAT SOME MEN ARE MEANT TO ASPIRE TO GREATNESS--

ASTONISHING, ISN'T IT, HUMPHRIES? SO MUCH POWER IN ONE SINGLE CREATURE.

QUITE, SIR.

A SHAME TO SEE IT IMPRISONED SO.

--AND THAT *OTHERS* ARE BETTER SUITED TO AID IN THE ASCENSION OF THESE GREAT MEN, RATHER THAN TO ASCEND THEMSELVES.

I THINK IT'S JUST ABOUT TIME, LET'S MOVE ON.

--ONE SUCH MAN IS MY CURRENT EMPLOYER, MR. WESLEY DODDS--

CERTAINLY, SIR.

I SUPPOSE THE TRUE TASK IN SUCH SERVICE--

--IS IN THE ABILITY TO RECOGNIZE THE POTENTIAL FOR SUCH GREATNESS--

--EARLY ON.

...FOUR YEARS IN THE HAMPTONS? THAT MUST HAVE BEEN A DIFFICULT POSITION TO LEAVE.

INDEED, SIR, BUT THE COUNTESS, WHO LOVED TO SUMMER IN THE STATES, PASSED ON AND THE ESTATE WAS PUT OUT--

CONSEQUENTLY, SO WAS I.

I SEE FROM YOUR REFERENCES THAT YOU HAVE NO CONTACT FOR YOUR LAST POSITION.

FURTHER, THE DATES YOU'VE TRANSCRIBED INDICATE A RATHER BRIEF STAY. WHY DID YOU LEAVE?

I WAS NOT *SUITED* FOR THE RESIDENCE.

MR. HUMPHRIES... GIVEN YOUR QUALIFICATIONS, I SIMPLY DO *NOT* BELIEVE THAT TO BE THE CASE. IF YOU PLEASE?

VERY WELL, SIR...

THE MASTER OF THAT PARTICULAR RESIDENCE WAS *NOT* AN AMIABLE GENTLEMAN.

"IN FACT, TO BE PERFECTLY *HONEST*, HE WAS DOWNRIGHT LECHEROUS AND MADE UNWANTED ADVANCES ON MARCELLA, THE CHAMBERMAID I HAD BROUGHT ON.

"RATHER *COMPROMISING* ADVANCES.

"I WAS *THEN* TOLD THAT IF I VALUED MY POSITION I WOULD TAKE MARCELLA TO HAVE THE RESULTS OF HIS ANIMAL URGINGS UN-DONE. I DID AS I WAS TOLD.

"AFTERWARDS, HOWEVER, I FELT QUITE ASHAMED OF MY COMPLICITY AND HELPED MARCELLA TO OBTAIN A POSITION IN A DIFFERENT HOUSEHOLD TO KEEP HER FROM ANY FURTHER TRAGEDIES.

"UPON FINDING THIS OUT, MY EMPLOYER THREATENED ME, *PHYSICALLY*, AN ACTION HE QUICKLY REGRETTED.

"I FELT I *HAD* TO LEAVE AT THIS TIME, AND I DID SO.

THIS MAN SOUNDS LIKE AN ABSOLUTE BEAST. WHAT WAS HIS NAME?

THOUGH I *TOO* FIND HIS BEHAVIOR BEYOND ACCOUNTING FOR--

--HE WAS NONE-THELESS MY EMPLOYER FOR A TIME AND I MUST RESPECT HIS PRIVACY.

MR. HUMPHRIES? YOU'RE HIRED. WELCOME TO MY HOME.

AT FIRST I FEARED THAT MR. DODDS HAD HIRED ME BECAUSE HE THOUGHT THAT I WOULD NOT DIVULGE *HIS* UNACCEPTABLE BEHAVIORS--

--BUT IN TIME I CAME TO REALIZE THAT IT WAS SIMPLY MY RESPECT FOR DISCRETION HE HAD TAKEN A LIKING TO.

I THOUGHT IT ALL A LITTLE *UNREMARKABLE.* IT IS *ALWAYS* A BUTLER'S DUTY TO MAINTAIN A HIGH LEVEL OF DISCRETION IN REGARD TO HIS MASTER'S AFFAIRS--

IT WAS JUST AROUND HERE THAT J. SAW THE MUGGER, HUMPHRIES...

HE MUST BE ABLE TO THINK OF HIS BUTLER AS A SECOND PERSON TO HIMSELF--

HM.

HE MUST KNOW THAT THE BUTLER IS ALWAYS THERE WHEN *NEEDED*--

HOW STRANGE...

--BUT NEVER IN NEED *HIM-SELF.*

CLOSE, AND YET ALWAYS DISTANT.

BUT AS I LEARNED DURING MY INITIAL NIGHTS IN THE HOUSE, THIS ASSURANCE WAS STILL NOT ENOUGH TO ALLOW MR. DODDS TO REST SOUNDLY.

AAAH!

...EH--?

MR. DODDS?

NO! N--N-- AAAHH!

MR. DODDS!

AAAAAAAAAH--!

MR. DODDS! WHAT IS--?

WAKE UP, SIR, YOU'RE HAVING A BAD--

--DREAM! DREAM-- HE... HE WAS--SO-- GLASSES! WHERE ARE MY--CAN'T SEE-- MY FATH--

I HAVE THEM HERE, SIR.

OH, HUMPHRIES... IT'S YOU. I THOUGHT--

ARE YOU ALL RIGHT, SIR? YOU WERE CALLING OUT QUITE LOUDLY IN YOUR--

NO, I'M FINE. PERFECTLY FINE. JUST A TROUBLING DREAM.

NOTHING TO BE CONCERNED OVER. THANK YOU, HUMPHRIES.

YES, SIR. I TRUST YOU WILL CALL ME IF YOU NEED ANYTHING? GOOD REST, SIR?

MOST NIGHTS I HAVE FOUND TO BE LITTLE DIFFERENT FROM THAT FIRST.

ALTHOUGH I AM NOW FAR LESS LIKELY TO TRESPASS INTO MASTER WESLEY'S NIGHTMARES.

HUMPHRIES?

YES, SIR?

I BELIEVE THIS IS THE PATH I SAW HIM TAKE. I'M GOING TO GO HAVE A LOOK. WOULD YOU PLEASE--

CONSIDER YOUR BACK WATCHED, SIR.

THANKS.

I MUST ADMIT THAT IT TOOK SOME TIME TO ADJUST TO MASTER DODDS' NIGHTLY RITUAL, BUT ONE LEARNS TO IGNORE CERTAIN SOUNDS--

THANKS, HUMPHRIES. THAT SMELLS TERRIFIC, AND I'M STARVING. I WAS UP ALL NIGHT.

WERE YOU? I HAD NO IDEA.

SCRAPE RUFFLE SHUFFLE

--THOUGH NOT ALL NOISES.

THERE WAS ONE CLASS OF SOUNDS I COULD NOT PLACE. VERMIN IN THE WALLS, I INITIALLY THOUGHT.

225

NOPE, NOTHIN' HERE, MR. HUMPHRIES, THERE'D BE DROPPINGS IF THERE WERE MICE.

I USUALLY DO NOT REQUIRE A SECOND OPINION ON MATTERS OF INFESTATION, HOWEVER--

--I WAS *NOT* CONVINCED. I AWAITED THEIR RETURN THAT VERY NIGHT.

WHILE THIS HOUSE WAS NOT WITHOUT ITS *NOISES*, I WAS UNABLE TO FIND THE *SOURCE*.

THOUGH SLIGHTLY HUMILIATED, I FELT I HAD TO TROUBLE MASTER DODDS WITH MY INADEQUACY.

--NOISES, EH? NO, I CAN'T SAY AS THOUGH I'VE HEARD ANYTHING OUT OF THE ORDINARY.

I'D JUST *IGNORE* IT, HUMPHRIES. IT'S AN OLD HOUSE AND THE RECENT WEATHER'S PROBABLY TO BLAME FOR SOME SETTLING FLOORBOARDS.

INCIDENTALLY, YOU MAY RETIRE *EARLY* IF YOU'D LIKE. I'LL BE OUT QUITE LATE.

YES, SIR. THANK YOU, SIR.

THERE WAS TO BE NO RETIRING FOR ME, HOWEVER--

CRESSH

BRAAAAAA

--AS A TREMENDOUS NOISE--SEEMINGLY FROM *BELOW* THE HOUSE--CALLED TO ME.

THOUGH I FEARED INTRUDERS--

--THE HOUSE AND I WERE QUITE ALONE TOGETHER.

THE NOISE WAS PERSISTENT, HOWEVER--

--AND I FOLLOWED IT TO ITS LOUDEST POINT, WHICH WAS, STRANGELY, A DEAD END.

PERHAPS IF I HAD *NOT* FELT THE NIGHT AIR CREEPING THROUGH THE STUDY WALL--

I WOULD NOT HAVE OVERSTEPPED MY PLACE.

BUT DESCENDING THE STAIRS I DISCOVERED--

BLAAAAAAAA

THAT MASTER DODDS HELD A SECRET FAR MORE COMPLICATED THAN A DESIRE FOR CHAMBERMAIDS.

227

I THOUGHT FOR A MOMENT OF RETURNING TO MY ROOM AND PRETENDING I HAD DISCOVERED NOTHING.

AT THIS CLOSE RANGE, IT WAS APPARENT, THOUGH, THAT THE NOISE WAS A CAR HORN AND THAT MASTER DODDS MIGHT BE HARMED, AND SO I CONTINUED.

THOUGH HIS APPEARANCE WAS *QUITE* UNUSUAL--

I KNEW THAT WHAT HE NEEDED WAS SLIGHT MEDICAL ATTENTION--

--AND ABOVE ALL ELSE... *PRIVACY.*

OKAY, HUMPHRIES, I'VE SEEN ENOUGH.

LET'S GO.

YES, SIR.

WHICH I WAS ONLY TOO HAPPY TO GIVE HIM, FOR WHAT *CAN* A MAN CALL HIS OWN IN THE NIGHT--

--IF NOT THE SANCTITY OF HIS THOUGHTS--

--AND THE SOLITARY PLACE IN WHICH HE THINKS THEM .

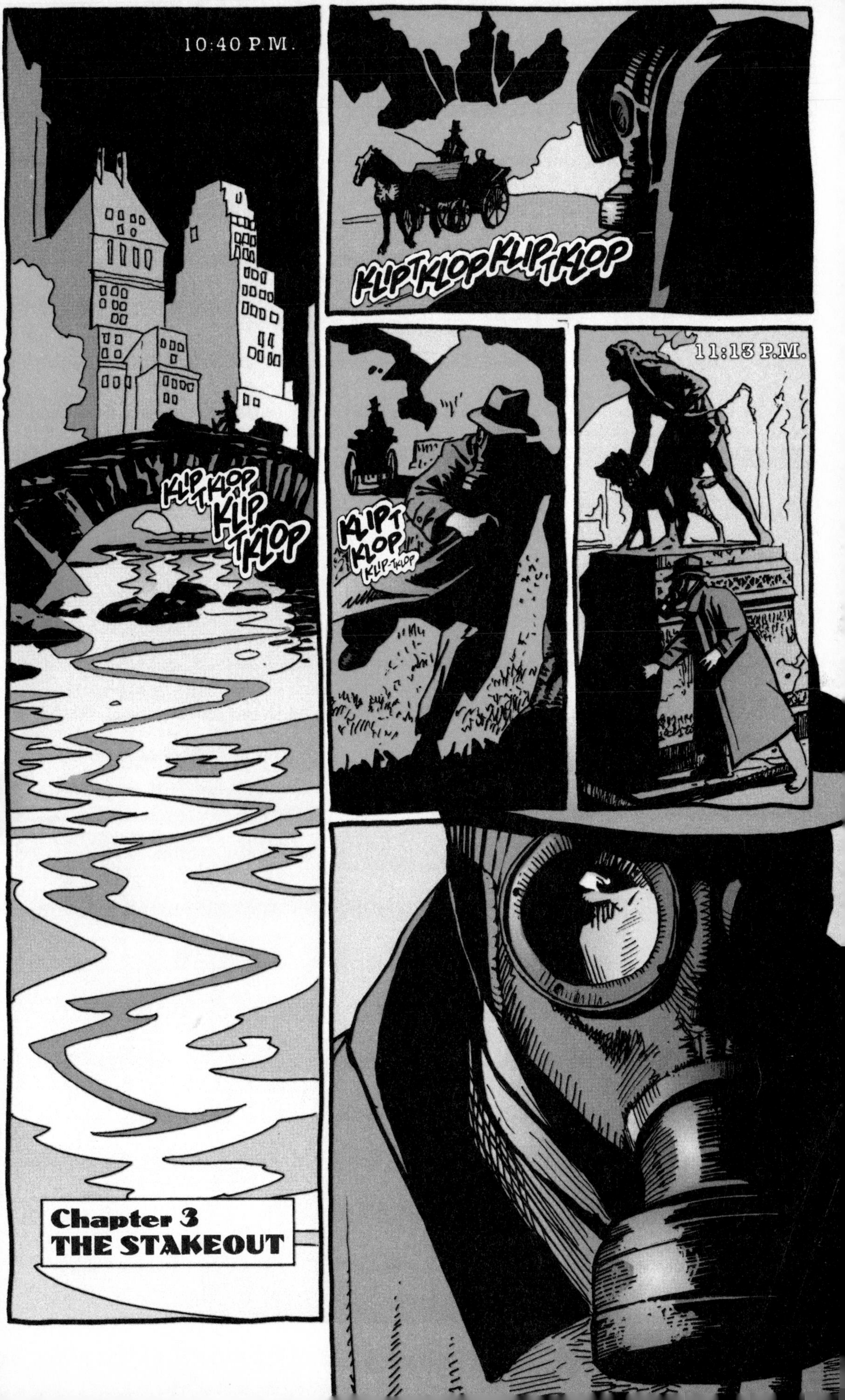
10:40 P.M.
KLIP T KLOP KLIP T KLOP
Chapter 3
THE STAKEOUT
KLIP T KLOP KLIP T KLOP
KLIP T KLOP KLIP-TKLOP
11:13 P.M.

11:20 P.M.

...JUST LIKE TALLULAH BANKHEAD.

≳GIGGLE≲

NO, REALLY-- NO DAMN CLOTHES AT ALL.

≳GIGGLE≲ OH, HAR-RY...

MIDNIGHT

1:21 A.M.

--NO ONE AROUND--

--I CAN DO WHATEVER I WANT TO YOU--

KL-CHK

SWISSH...

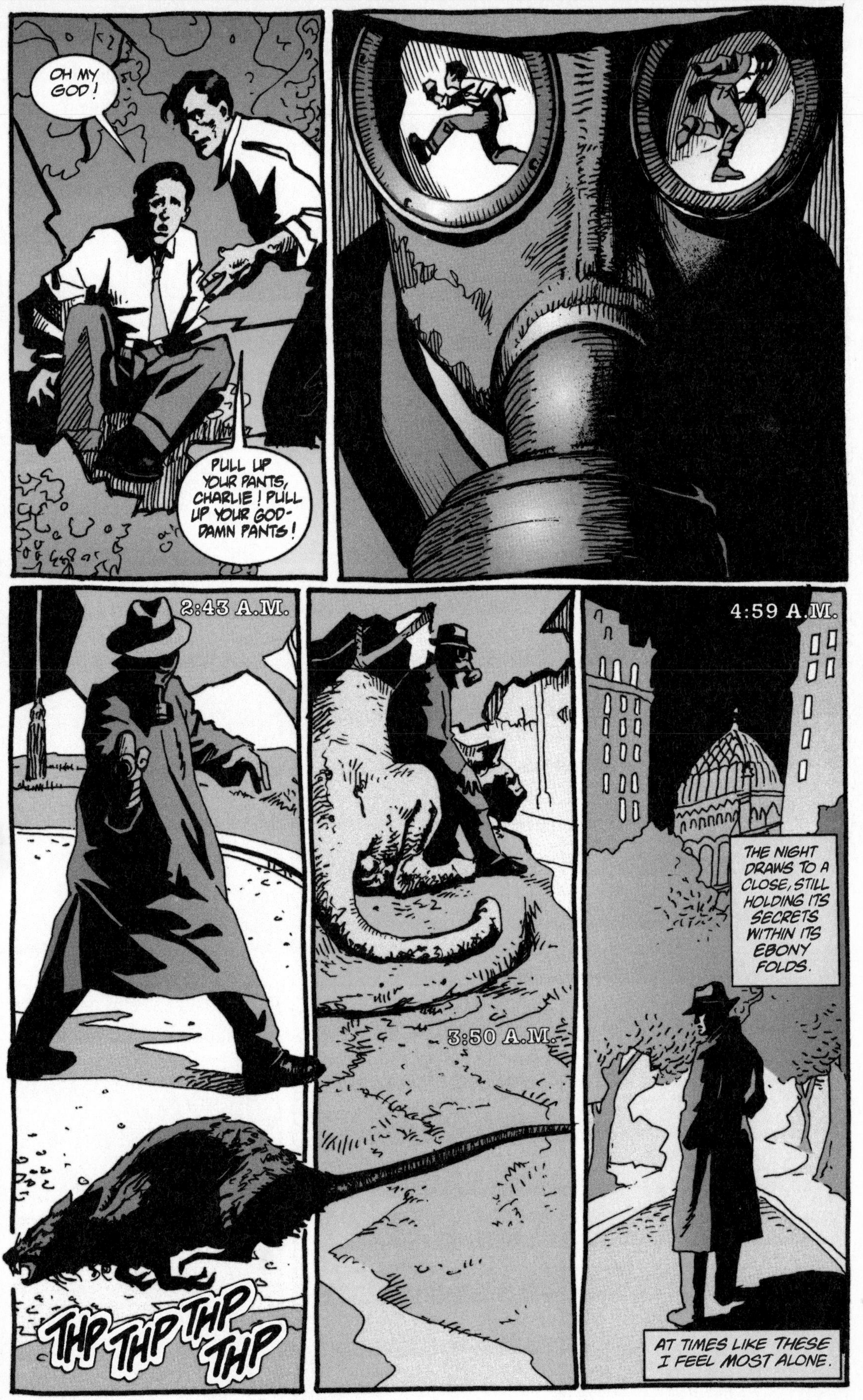
OH MY GOD!
PULL UP YOUR PANTS, CHARLIE! PULL UP YOUR GOD-DAMN PANTS!
2:43 A.M.
THP THP THP THP
3:50 A.M.
4:59 A.M.
THE NIGHT DRAWS TO A CLOSE, STILL HOLDING ITS SECRETS WITHIN ITS EBONY FOLDS.
AT TIMES LIKE THESE I FEEL MOST ALONE.

SEE EVERY ONE A' THESE PEOPLE?

USED TA BE I'D LOOK A' THEM AN' SEE NOTHIN' BUT TARGETS, YOU KNOW?

WHERE AM I?

OVER TO TH' RIGHT.

UH-HUH, NOW DOWN AND BACK, BY TH' TREES, SEE?

BEEN HERE ABOUT TWO YEARS.

DON'T LIKE IT ONE BIT.

HOW'D I GET HERE? THASSA STORY, NO?

YOU WAN' THE STORY?

WHY NOT? GOT PLENNY A' TIME.

SEE, I WAS HAVIN' A SMOKE WITH MY BUDDY, MARIO--

--JUS' HANGIN' IN TH' PARK. GETTIN' OUTTA THE SUMMER HEAT.

EH, MARIO, *YOU SEE WHAT I SEE?*

SURE DO, SALVATORE. CROWS IN LOVE.

"...AN' I SAY, "RIGHT ON TOP OF IT!"

MAKE YOU FEEL LIKE *LOVE,* MARIO?

MAKES ME FEEL WARM ALL OVER.

MAKES ME FEEL LIKE GETTIN' SOME GOOSE MYSELF.

...SO *FUNNY*...

YOU KNOW WHAT THEY SAY ABOUT GOOSE, HUH?

...BETTER GET YOU *HOME.*

THEY STAYED. WE STAYED. IT GOT LATE.

ME AN' MARIO, WE GO WAY BACK.

HIS POP'S FROM ROME, MINE, TOO.

WE GOT IN OUR FIRST FIGHT TOGETHER--

--HAD OUR FIRST GIRL TOGETHER--MARIO'S COUSIN, CELESTE--

--ROLLED OUR FIRST CROWS TOGETHER--

--RIGHT HERE IN HARLEM.

DAI! DAI! DAI!

WE DON'T LIKE THE CROWS. POPPY SAID THEY TOOK HIS JOB AT THE GARMENT FACTORY AWAY.

NUN CE LA FA!

AN' I AIN'T HAD AN EXTRA DIME SINCE I WAS SIX. THAT WAS ENOUGH FOR ME.

EH, BUCK. GOTTA LIGHT?

LEAVE US ALONE. WE DON'T WANT NO TROUBLE.

TROUBLE? JUS' ASKIN' FOR A LIGHT HERE, MAN. YA GOT ONE?

uh...SURE MAN, SURE, SORRY. HERE...

SO NOW AN' THEN, ME AND MARIO, WE'D ROLL ONE JUS' T' SHOW 'EM WHAT'S WHAT--

MARIO!

HEY! WHAT'RE YOU--?

--AN' CAUSE WE FELT LIKE IT.

STOP IT-- AAAGH!

SHUT YER FACE, BLACKIE!

YEAH, OR WE GIVE YOU SOMETHING TO CRY ABOUT.

LEAVE HIM ALONE! OH MY GOD--!

GOES FOR YOU TOO, GIRL!

KEEP A TIGHT HOLD ON 'IM, MARIO. I WANT HIM T' SEE THIS.

MMNNN! LNN MNN GUHH!

SEE, I NEVER THOUGHT OF IT AS WRONG.

NOT ONCE.

JUST DID WHAT I WANTED.

ONLY CROWS, AFTER ALL.

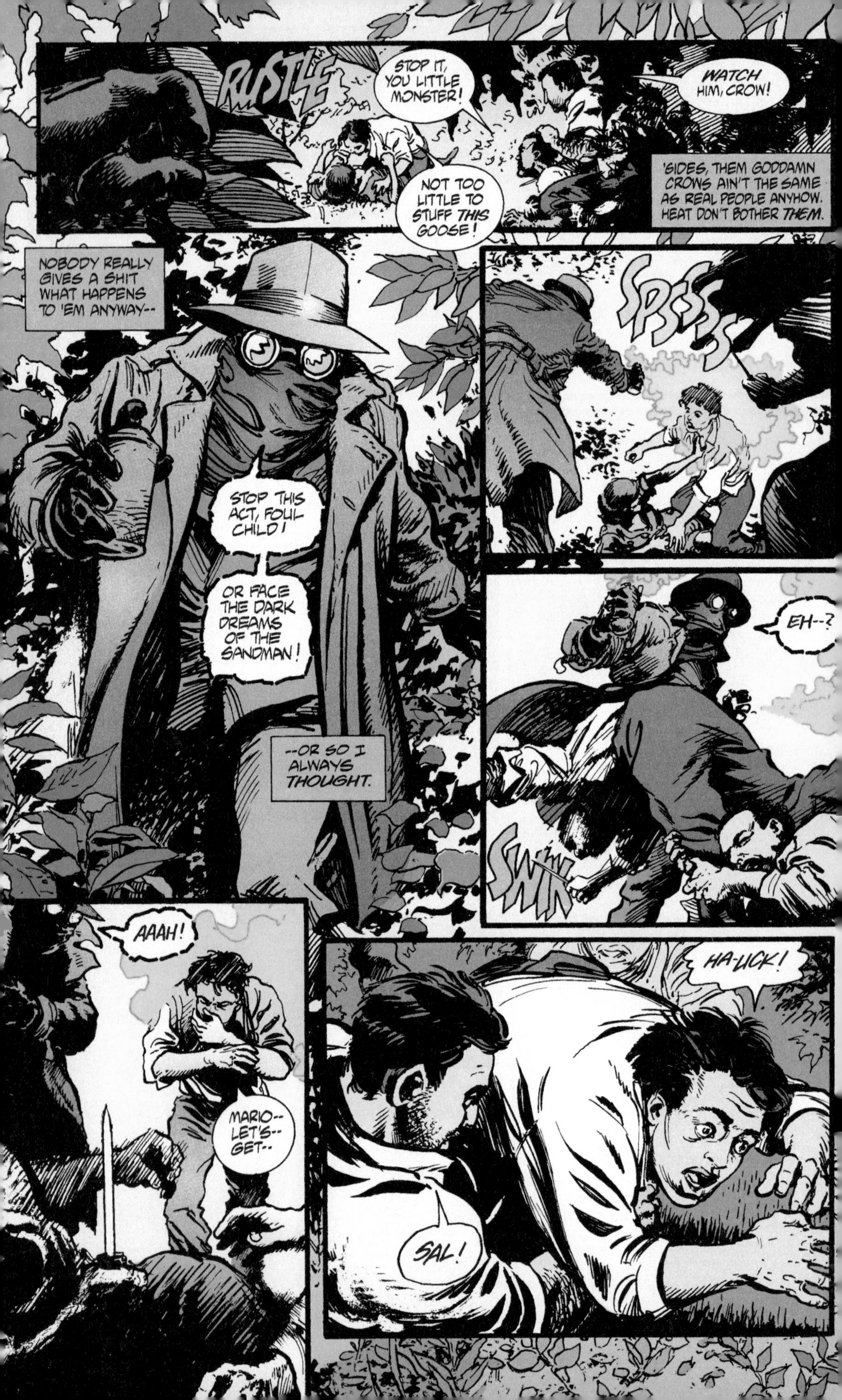
RUSTLE
STOP IT, YOU LITTLE MONSTER!
NOT TOO LITTLE TO STUFF THIS GOOSE!
WATCH HIM, CROW!
'SIDES, THEM GODDAMN CROWS AIN'T THE SAME AS REAL PEOPLE ANYHOW. HEAT DON'T BOTHER THEM.
NOBODY REALLY GIVES A SHIT WHAT HAPPENS TO 'EM ANYWAY--
STOP THIS ACT, FOUL CHILD!
OR FACE THE DARK DREAMS OF THE SANDMAN!
--OR SO I ALWAYS THOUGHT.
SPSSS
EH--?
SNIK
AAAH!
MARIO-- LET'S-- GET--
HA-LICK!
SAL!

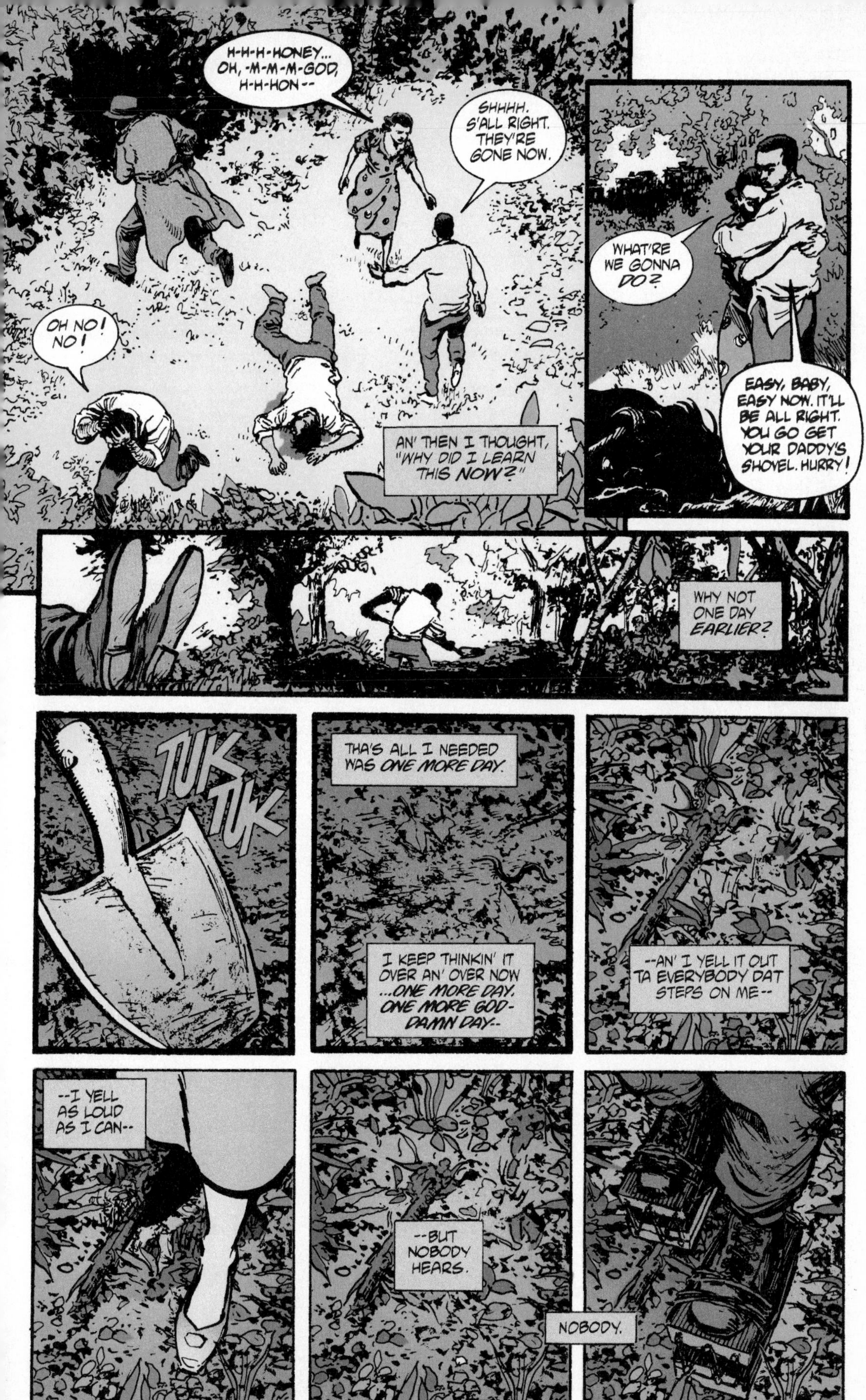
H-H-H-HONEY... OH, -M-M-M-GOD, H-H-HON--
SHHHH. S'ALL RIGHT. THEY'RE GONE NOW.
OH NO! NO!
AN' THEN I THOUGHT, "WHY DID I LEARN THIS NOW?"
WHAT'RE WE GONNA DO?
EASY, BABY, EASY NOW. IT'LL BE ALL RIGHT. YOU GO GET YOUR DADDY'S SHOVEL. HURRY!
WHY NOT ONE DAY EARLIER?
TUK TUK
THA'S ALL I NEEDED WAS ONE MORE DAY.
I KEEP THINKIN' IT OVER AN' OVER NOW ...ONE MORE DAY. ONE MORE GOD-DAMN DAY--
--AN' I YELL IT OUT TA EVERYBODY DAT STEPS ON ME--
--I YELL AS LOUD AS I CAN--
--BUT NOBODY HEARS.
NOBODY.

I'M A POLICEMAN. I WALK THE BEAT IN CENTRAL PARK EVERY DAY. IT'S HARD WORK, BUT I GET THROUGH IT KNOWIN' THAT AT THE END OF THE DAY--

--I'M GOIN' HOME TO MY WIFE, SARAH.

CENTRAL PARK PRECINCT

SO YESTERDAY, I GET HOME, AND I GUESS I'M COMPLAININ' ABOUT THE DAY WHEN SARAH, SHE SAYS T'ME--

"OH, THE PARK'S NOT SO BAD. IT'S A LOVELY AREA TO WALK IN."

JUS' LIKE *THAT*. SHE THINKS ALL I HAVE T'DO IS WALK AN' LOOK AT TH' *FLOWERS* ALL DAY.

SHEESH! IF *THAT* WAS ALL THERE WAS TO IT, A FELLA WOULDN'T BE *ABLE* T'GET A PARK BEAT.

Chapter 5
THE COP

KAUFMAN?

YEAH, SARGE?

YOU THINKIN' OF HEADIN' OUT SOMETIME TONIGHT?

SURE, SARGE, I WAS JUST WAITIN' FOR FLANNERY.

YEAH, WELL, FLANNERY JUST CALLED IN SICK. *YOU* TAKE THE LOOP BY YOURSELF.

HEY... LOOK AT THIS! KAUFMAN'S ACTUALLY GOIN' TA DO SOME WORK! SAY "HI" TO *THE MUGGER* FOR ME.

VERY FUNNY, HIRSCH. I KEEP TELLIN' YA, THERE *AIN'T* NO MUGGER. JUST MAKE SURE YOU KEEP THOSE CARDS WARM UNTIL I GET BACK.

I TRY T'TELL SARAH THAT THINGS *DO* HAPPEN IN TH' PARK

--THAT A PUBLIC SERVANT SUCH AS *MYSELF* HAS T'BE READY TO JUMP AT A MOMENT'S NOTICE.

OF COURSE USUALLY IT'S KIDS CAUGHT IN TREES, YOUNG TOUGHS FIGHTIN', DRIFTERS STEALIN' HOT DOGS. THAT KIND O' STUFF.

BUT NOT MUCH THAT REALLY CATCHES A JOE OFF-GUARD. NOT *USUALLY*--

HEY, FLATFOOT.

HUH?

FEEGEE.

SPIRIT AND THE FLESH. LOOK, WHAT'S THE WORD ON THIS MYSTERY MUGGER LOOSE IN THE PARK, KAUFMAN?

FEEGEE'S A PHOTOGRAPHER. MAKES HIS LIVING SNAPPIN' PHOTOS OF WHAT WE SEE EVERY DAY.

I CAN'T GET NO ONE ELSE AROUND THIS DUMP T'TALK T'ME ABOUT HIM.

THAT'S OFFICIAL POLICE BUSINESS, FEEGEE, NONE O' *YOURS*. BUT OFF THE RECORD? IT'S A LOTTA *TALK*, OKAY? WE HAVEN'T HAD A HOLD-UP IN WEEKS.

THIS HEAT'S GOT PEOPLE'S *IMAGINATIONS* IN AN UPROAR.

I GOTTA HIT MY BEAT. YOU HAVE A NICE NIGHT.

DON'T *KID* YOUR-SELF, KAUFMAN. I GOTTA *FEELIN'* 'BOUT THIS GUY. HE'S OUT THERE. YOU BETTER KEEP YOUR HAT LOW.

SAVE IT FOR YOUR EDITORS, FEEGEE. MAYBE *THEY'LL* CARE.

"HE'S OUT THERE," he says.

WHY DOES EVERYONE THINK *THEY* KNOW POLICE BUSINESS BETTER THAN THE POLICE?

SARAH'S ALWAYS GIVING ME ADVICE TOO. BUGS ME.

SOME THINGS ARE ONLY KNOWN BY THE PEOPLE BEHIND 'EM.

'COURSE, IF THERE *IS* A MYSTERY MUGGER...THERE'LL PROB'LY BE A PROMOTION FOR WHOEVER BRINGS 'IM IN...

SO WHY *NOT* KEEP AN OPEN EYE WHILE I'M WALKIN' THE PARK?

LONG AS I'M STILL AVAILABLE FOR THE OCCASIONAL CALL FOR HELP--

♪

--NO REASON I CAN'T SPEND A *LITTLE* TIME LOOKIN' FOR A DANGEROUS CRIMINAL.

WHAT'S THIS--?

ALL RIGHT, MR. MUGGER! COME OUT WITH YOUR HANDS--

...UP?

GETTING SO'S A MAN CAN'T GET NO SLEEP ANYWHERE IN THIS CITY...

WAIT. OVER THERE. SHADOWS--

DANNY... DANNY...

I KNOW, IRENE, I FEEL IT TOO--

NO, IT'S--

AH-HEM!

SORRY, SIR. WE'RE GOIN', WE'RE GOIN'.

TAP TAP TAP TAP

AH, WHAT'M I THINKIN'?

THIS'S CENTRAL PARK. THERE AIN'T NO MYSTERIES HERE--

--uh-oh.

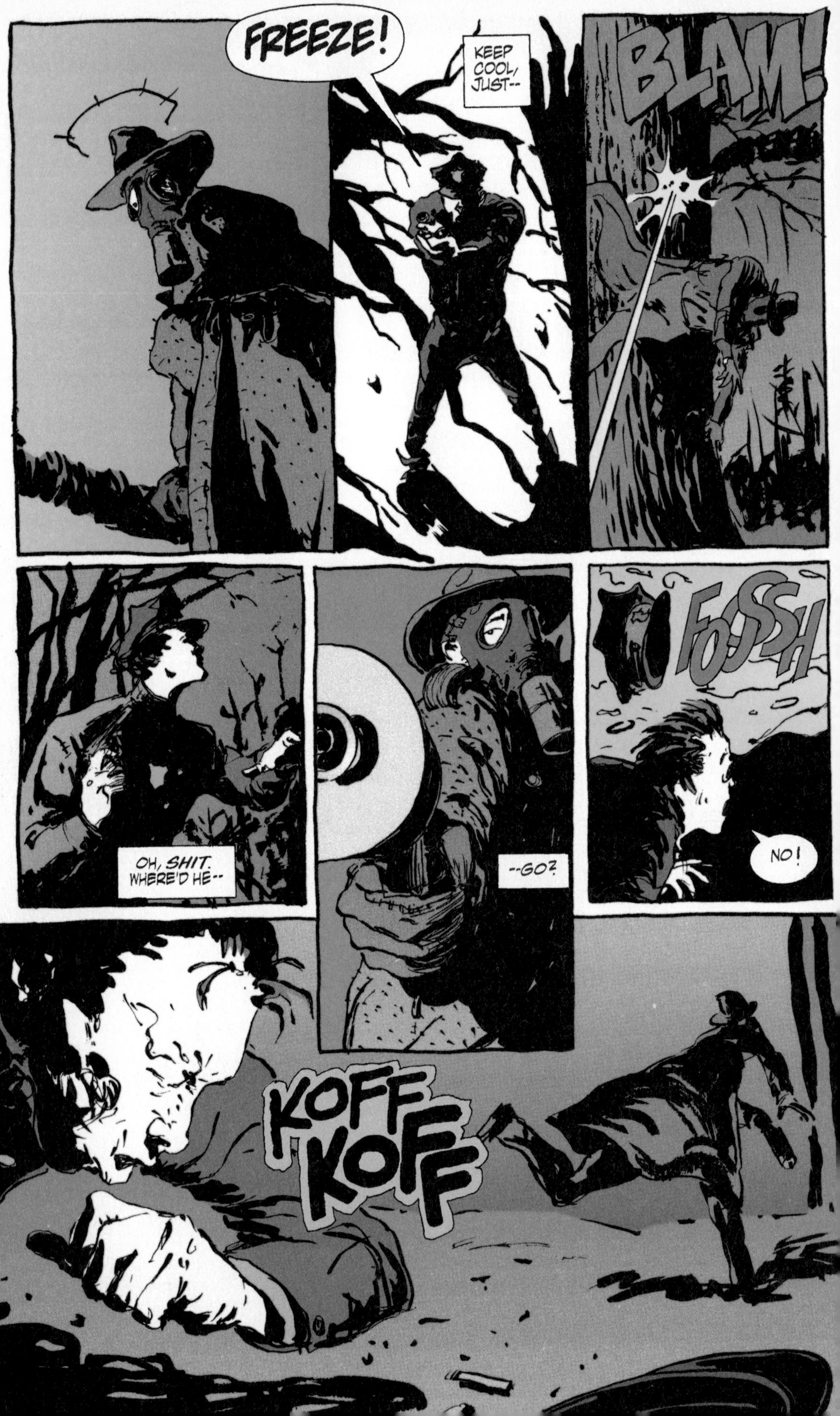
FREEZE!
KEEP COOL, JUST--
BLAM!
OH, SHIT. WHERE'D HE--
--GO?
FOOSSH
NO!
KOFF KOFF

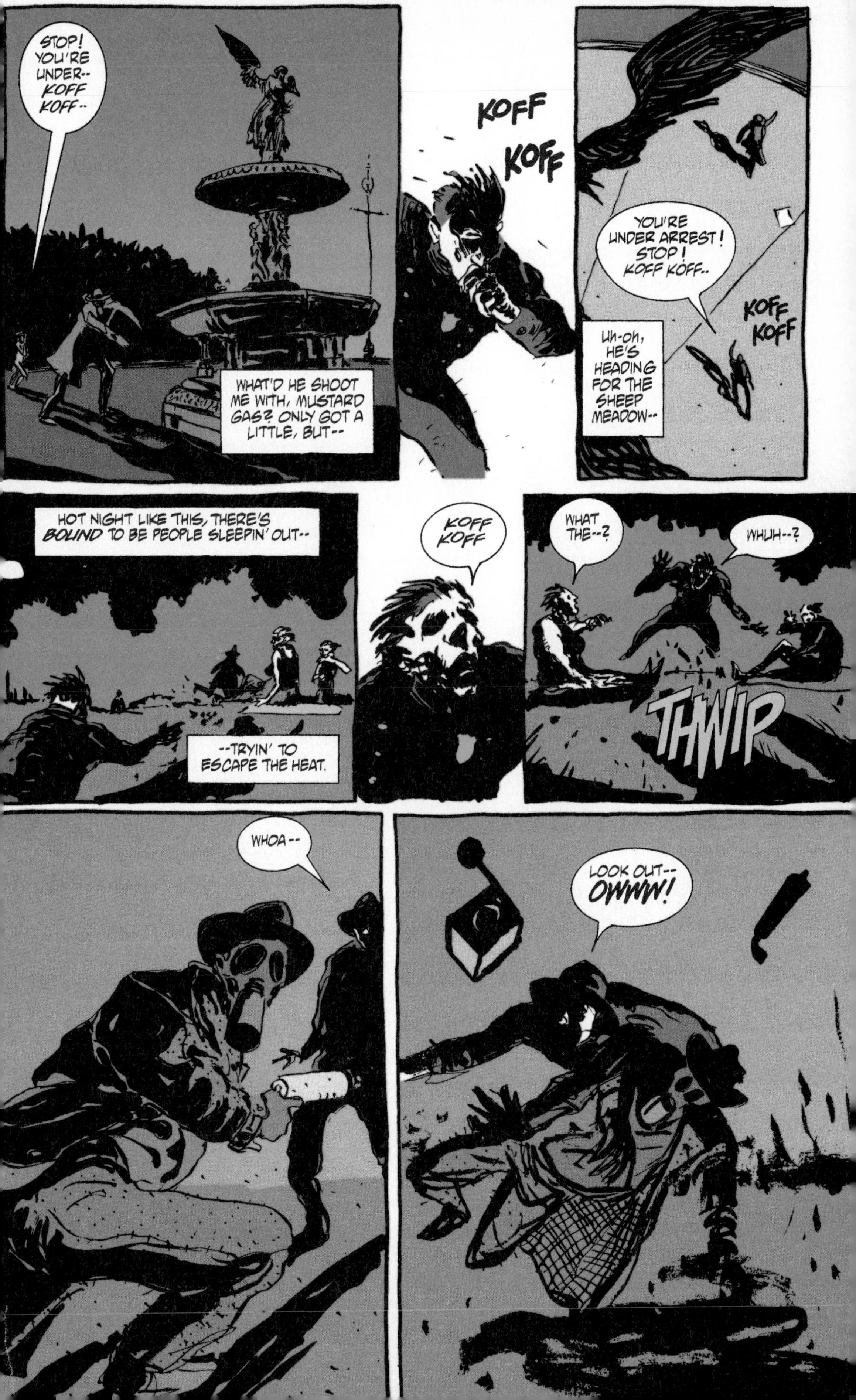
STOP! YOU'RE UNDER-- KOFF KOFF--
WHAT'D HE SHOOT ME WITH, MUSTARD GAS? ONLY GOT A LITTLE, BUT--
KOFF
KOFF
YOU'RE UNDER ARREST! STOP! KOFF KOFF..
KOFF KOFF
UH-OH, HE'S HEADING FOR THE SHEEP MEADOW--
HOT NIGHT LIKE THIS, THERE'S BOUND TO BE PEOPLE SLEEPIN' OUT--
--TRYIN' TO ESCAPE THE HEAT.
KOFF KOFF
WHAT THE--?
WHUH--?
THWIP
WHOA--
LOOK OUT-- OWWW!

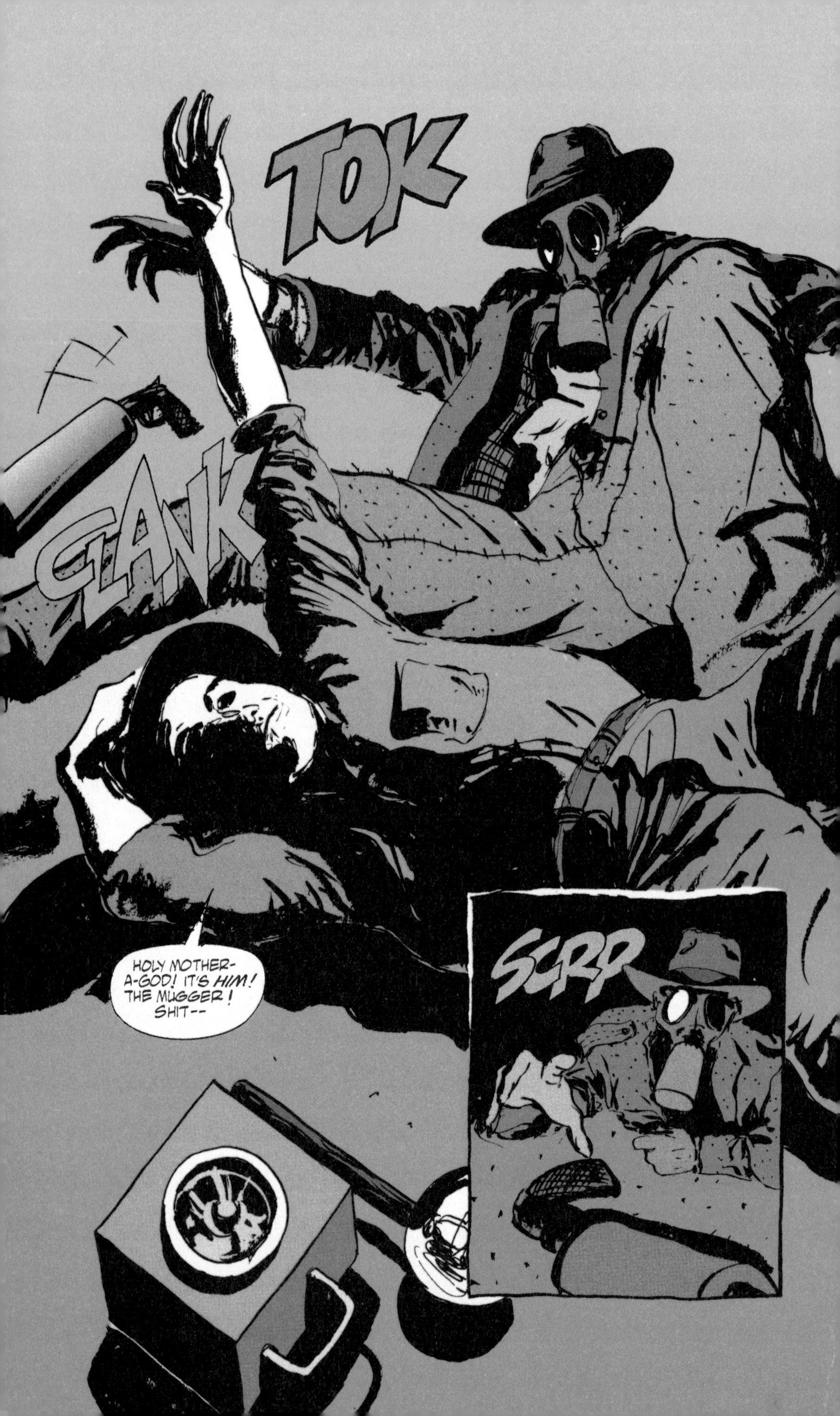
TOK
CLANK
HOLY MOTHER-A-GOD! IT'S *HIM*! THE MUGGER! SHIT--
SCRP

FLASH

FOOSH

RUN AS FAST AS YA WANT-- KOFF --BUT I GOT YA, YA BASTARD!

KOFF KOFF

WHERE IS--KOFF --HE?

TOO LATE, FLAT FOOT --KOFF--GOT AWAY

UHHH...

GUESS YOU WERE RIGHT. AH WELL, THERE GOES MY PROMOTION.

BUT MAYBE THAT SHOT WILL GET YOU YOURS, FEEGEE.

Central Park Mugger - 1st encounter - 6/23/38

WHAT WOULD I DO WITHOUT THE PARK?

PROBABLY GO *NUTS* IS WHAT.

Chapter 6 THE D. A.

THE LIFE OF A DISTRICT ATTORNEY CAN GET PRETTY FRANTIC, BUT IT'S ALWAYS GOOD TO KNOW I HAVE THE PARK FOR MY LUNCH HOUR--

AN' HOW'S IT GOIN' T'DAY, MISTUH B.

SAME AS USUAL, MORRIS.

SORRY T'HEAR THAT!

--OR LUNCH *HALF* HOUR AS IS THE CASE LATELY.

YEAH, ME TOO! *TWO*...WITH THE WORKS.

CASES COMING TO TRIAL LATELY ARE ALL SO...ODD. LIKE THE ELDRIDGE BENSON AFFAIR. WHAT KIND OF MAN TRIES TO START A RACE WAR?

AND THE MORE COMPLEX THE *CASE*, THE LESS TIME I HAVE TO *MYSELF.*

WHICH DOESN'T BOTHER ME *SO* MUCH, EXCEPT--

--THAT OUTSIDE OF THE BUSTER CALHOUN SHOW I'VE SPENT ALMOST *NO* TIME WITH DIAN LATELY--

DADDY!

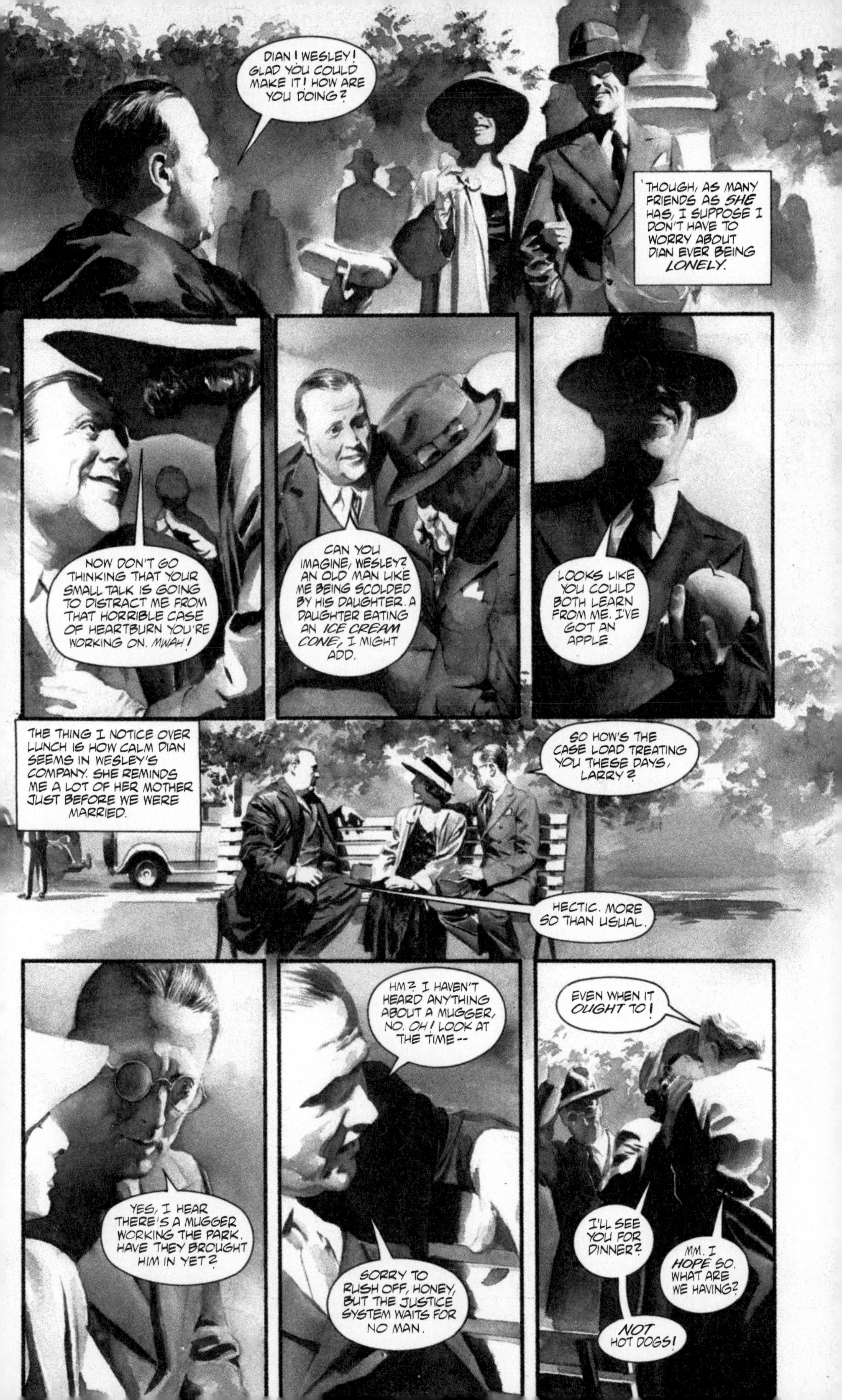
DIAN! WESLEY! GLAD YOU COULD MAKE IT! HOW ARE YOU DOING?
THOUGH, AS MANY FRIENDS AS SHE HAS, I SUPPOSE I DON'T HAVE TO WORRY ABOUT DIAN EVER BEING LONELY.
NOW DON'T GO THINKING THAT YOUR SMALL TALK IS GOING TO DISTRACT ME FROM THAT HORRIBLE CASE OF HEARTBURN YOU'RE WORKING ON. MWAH!
CAN YOU IMAGINE, WESLEY? AN OLD MAN LIKE ME BEING SCOLDED BY HIS DAUGHTER. A DAUGHTER EATING AN ICE CREAM CONE, I MIGHT ADD.
LOOKS LIKE YOU COULD BOTH LEARN FROM ME. I'VE GOT AN APPLE.
THE THING I NOTICE OVER LUNCH IS HOW CALM DIAN SEEMS IN WESLEY'S COMPANY. SHE REMINDS ME A LOT OF HER MOTHER JUST BEFORE WE WERE MARRIED.
SO HOW'S THE CASE LOAD TREATING YOU THESE DAYS, LARRY?
HECTIC. MORE SO THAN USUAL.
YES, I HEAR THERE'S A MUGGER WORKING THE PARK. HAVE THEY BROUGHT HIM IN YET?
HM? I HAVEN'T HEARD ANYTHING ABOUT A MUGGER, NO. OH! LOOK AT THE TIME--
SORRY TO RUSH OFF, HONEY, BUT THE JUSTICE SYSTEM WAITS FOR NO MAN.
EVEN WHEN IT OUGHT TO!
I'LL SEE YOU FOR DINNER?
MM. I HOPE SO. WHAT ARE WE HAVING?
NOT HOT DOGS!

...I'M NOT SAYING THAT WE *ARE* GOING TO PUSH FOR AN EXTENDED SENTENCE, BUT...uh-huh--

THE CASE FILES YOU REQUESTED, MR. BELMONT.

BILL? I'M GOING TO HAVE TO CALL YOU BACK ON THIS LATER ...uh-huh...BYE.

THANKS, HELEN.

CHK

MIRIAM GOLDMAN...WHAT A MIXED-UP WOMAN SHE TURNED OUT TO BE. STILL, I GOT HER SENT UP FOR LIFE. CAN'T HELP BUT THINK SHE DESERVED IT.

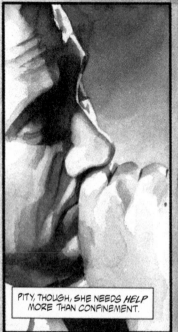

PITY, THOUGH, SHE NEEDS *HELP* MORE THAN CONFINEMENT.

COME ON NOW, LARRY. CAN'T BE GOING SOFT--

THEY'LL EAT YOU ALIVE IF YOU'RE *SOFT.*

THEY CATCH YA SLUGGIN' DOWN THE HOOTCH ON THE JOB LIKE THAT, THEY'RE LIKELY T'BRING BACK PROHIBITION!

HELLO, BURKE. HAVE A TASTE?

DON'T MIND IF I DO.

WHAT BRINGS YOU TO THIS LONELY CORNER OF CITY HALL?

WE GOT US SOME WEIRDNESS GOIN' DOWN IN THE PARK. I'D HEARD A COUPLE OF RUMORS, BUT NOTHIN' WORTH ACTIN' ON--

--'TIL NOW. PATROLMAN BY THE NAME OF KAUFMAN SAYS HE RAN INTO THIS CHARACTER THE OTHER NIGHT. LOOK LIKE ANYBODY YOU KNOW?

MY LORD! THIS LOOKS JUST LIKE--

YOU GOT IT--

--EITHER THE SANDMAN IS OUR MUGGER OR HE'S ALREADY LOOKIN' FOR THIS GOON, TOO.

WHAT ARE YOU DOING TO--

WE'VE TRIPLED OUR PATROLS AND PUT OUT A FEW MORE HORSEMEN.

WHO KNOWS? MAYBE WE'LL GET LUCKY AND BAG BOTH THESE BIRDS WITH ONE STONE. JUST THOUGHT YOU OUGHTA KNOW. BE SEEIN' YA, LARRY.

NO LOVE LOST BETWEEN BURKE AND THE SANDMAN.

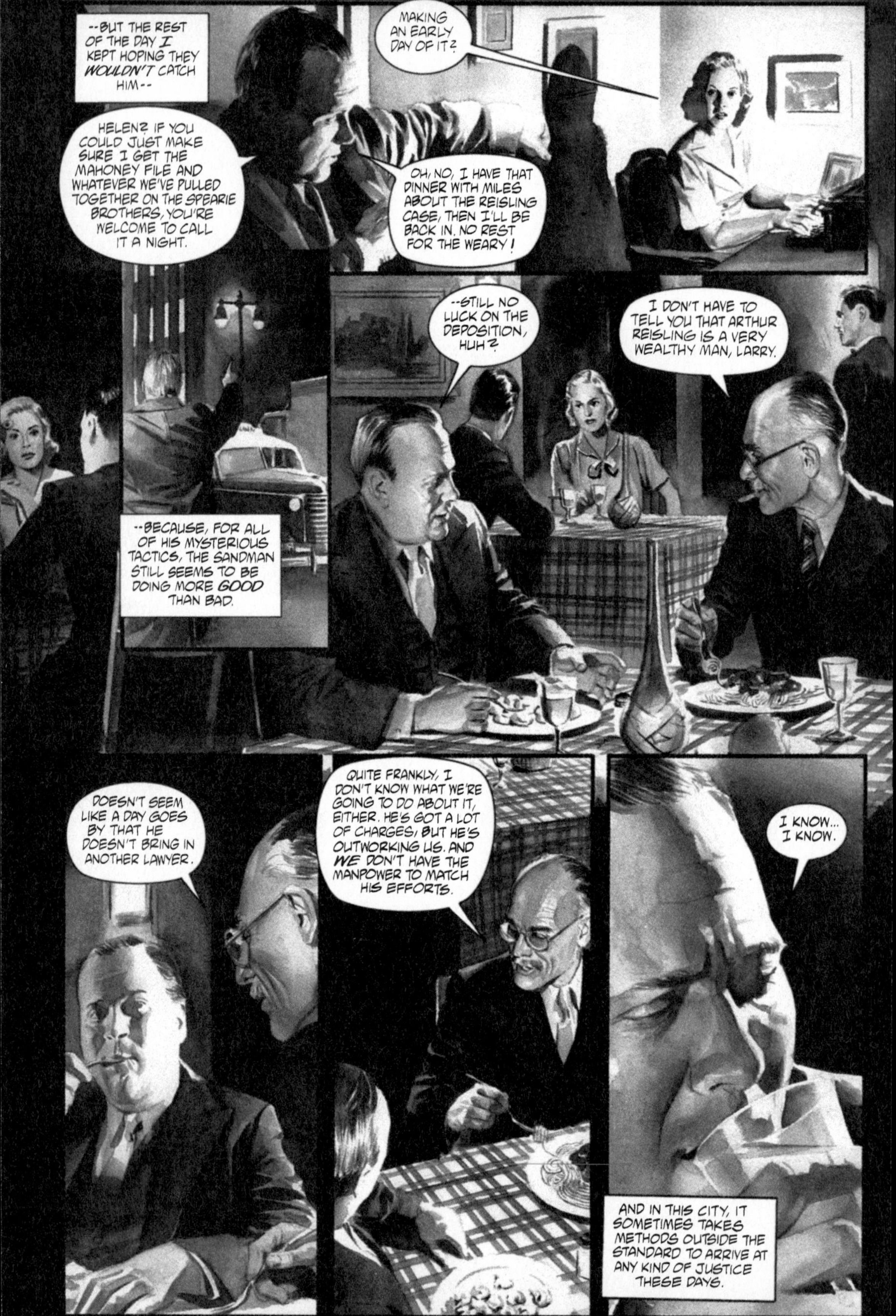
--BUT THE REST OF THE DAY I KEPT HOPING THEY WOULDN'T CATCH HIM--
MAKING AN EARLY DAY OF IT?
HELEN? IF YOU COULD JUST MAKE SURE I GET THE MAHONEY FILE AND WHATEVER WE'VE PULLED TOGETHER ON THE SPEARIE BROTHERS, YOU'RE WELCOME TO CALL IT A NIGHT.
OH, NO, I HAVE THAT DINNER WITH MILES ABOUT THE REISLING CASE, THEN I'LL BE BACK IN. NO REST FOR THE WEARY!
--BECAUSE, FOR ALL OF HIS MYSTERIOUS TACTICS, THE SANDMAN STILL SEEMS TO BE DOING MORE GOOD THAN BAD.
--STILL NO LUCK ON THE DEPOSITION, HUH?
I DON'T HAVE TO TELL YOU THAT ARTHUR REISLING IS A VERY WEALTHY MAN, LARRY.
DOESN'T SEEM LIKE A DAY GOES BY THAT HE DOESN'T BRING IN ANOTHER LAWYER.
QUITE FRANKLY, I DON'T KNOW WHAT WE'RE GOING TO DO ABOUT IT, EITHER. HE'S GOT A LOT OF CHARGES, BUT HE'S OUTWORKING US. AND WE DON'T HAVE THE MANPOWER TO MATCH HIS EFFORTS.
I KNOW... I KNOW.
AND IN THIS CITY, IT SOMETIMES TAKES METHODS OUTSIDE THE STANDARD TO ARRIVE AT ANY KIND OF JUSTICE THESE DAYS.

WHO WOULD HAVE THOUGHT THAT THE DISTRICT ATTORNEY WOULD FIND HIMSELF ROOTING FOR SOME VIGILANTE MYSTERY MAN.

WHAT'S THE MATTER WITH THE LIGHTS?

CHK CHK CHK CHK

TLK

LAWRENCE BELMONT--

OH! I DIDN'T-- DIDN'T *SEE* YOU THERE. WHAT-- WHAT--WHY ARE YOU HERE?

I COME SEEKING INFORMATION. WHAT DO YOU KNOW OF THE CENTRAL PARK MUGGER?

NOT *MUCH,* I'M AFRAID. I'VE ONLY JUST RECEIVED WORD THAT THERE *IS* ONE.

IN FACT, THERE'S SOME TALK THAT IT'S *YOU.* A POLICEMAN DESCRIBED YOU AS HIS SUSPECT.

MY ENCOUNTER WITH THE PATROLMAN WAS IN *PURSUIT* OF THE MUGGER.

OH, WELL, *GOOD.* I ACTUALLY SUSPECTED AS MUCH.

I AM NOT THE ONE THEY SEEK.

INCIDENTALLY, YOU'RE GOING TO HAVE TO BE CAREFUL.

MR. BELMONT, SIR? SAW YOUR LIGHT WAS ON AND JUST WANTED TO CHECK --

LIEUTENANT BURKE HAS PUT MORE MEN IN THE PARK AND THE DESCRIPTION THEY'RE RUNNING DOWN--

--IS *YOURS.* BY THE WAY, WHAT *IS*--

OFFICER ROSENE! DON'T--

HOLY SHIT!

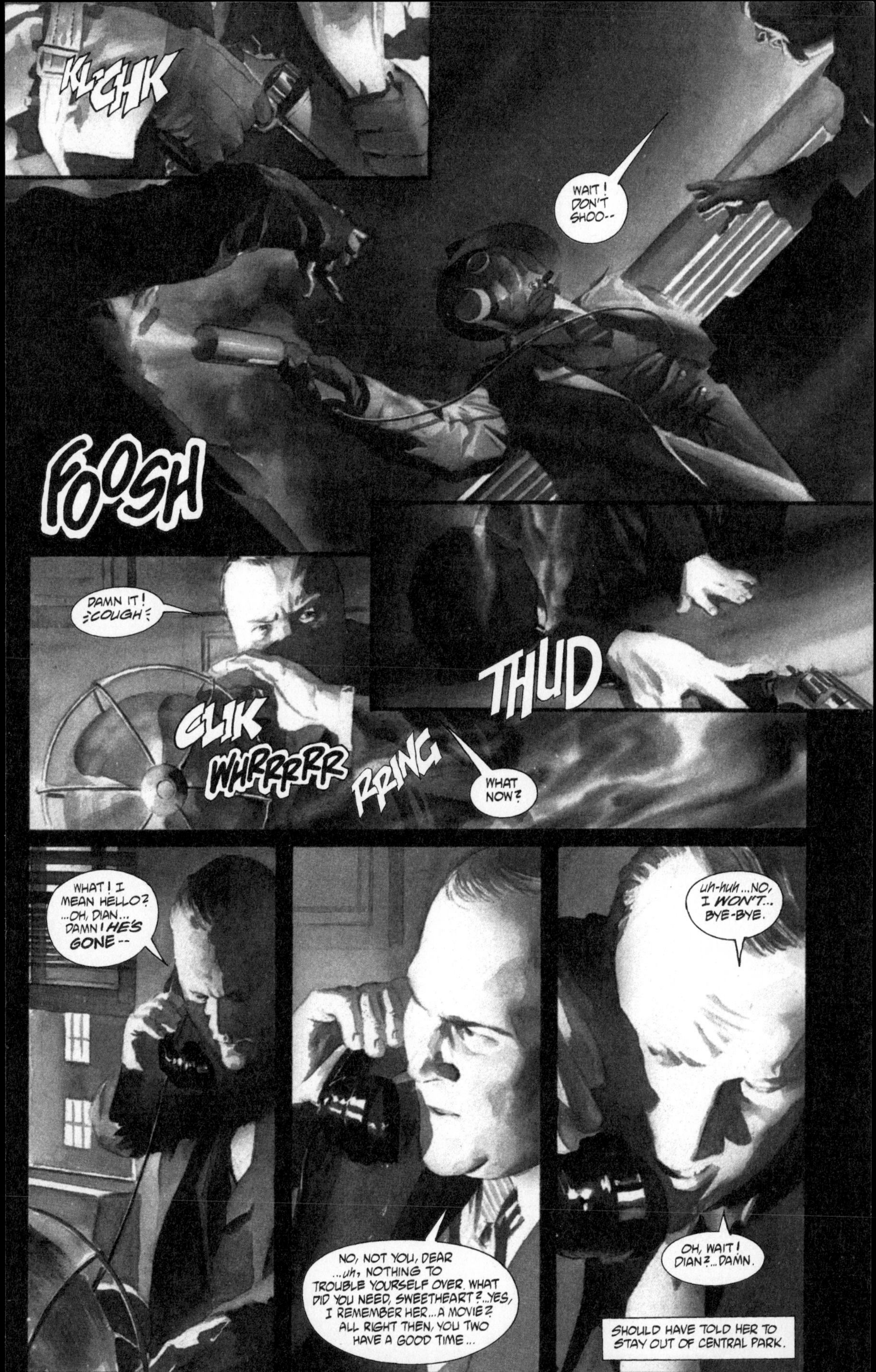
KL-CHK
WAIT! DON'T SHOO--
FOOSH
DAMN IT! COUGH
THUD
CLIK
WHRRRRR
RRING
WHAT NOW?
WHAT! I MEAN HELLO? ...OH, DIAN... DAMN! HE'S GONE--
NO, NOT YOU, DEAR ...uh, NOTHING TO TROUBLE YOURSELF OVER. WHAT DID YOU NEED, SWEETHEART? ...YES, I REMEMBER HER...A MOVIE? ALL RIGHT THEN, YOU TWO HAVE A GOOD TIME...
uh-huh...NO, I WON'T... BYE-BYE.
OH, WAIT! DIAN?...DAMN.
SHOULD HAVE TOLD HER TO STAY OUT OF CENTRAL PARK.

GLOBE

FRANK CAPRA'S
YOU CAN'T TAKE
IT WITH YOU

OH, DIAN,
THAT WAS SO
FUNNY. COULD YOU
BELIEVE THEM MAKING
FIREWORKS IN THE
BASEMENT?

FUNNY? I
SUPPOSE, BUT I
FOUND IT RATHER
ROMANTIC.

YOU FIND EVERYTHING
ROMANTIC THESE DAYS.
WHAT ABOUT FUN?

COME ON, LET'S CATCH
A CAB UP TO HARLEM. DUKE
ELLINGTON'S AT THE COTTON
CLUB.

OH...NO THANKS,
I'M POOPED! I THINK
I'LL JUST CUT HOME
THROUGH THE PARK.
YOU HAVE FUN THOUGH,
LILY.

BETTER
BELIEVE IT,
SWEETIE!
THAT'S
WHAT I DO!
G'NIGHT.

NIGHT.

Lily used to be such a doll,
but lately something about
her has changed.

Chapter 7
THE MUGGER

I can't quite put my finger on
what it is, but we just don't
seem to fit together as well
as we used to.

It's almost as
if she's suddenly
become--

--a stranger.

How unnerving it
was to be in the
company of some-
one so unfamiliar.

I wonder what causes a person to change like that?

Has she had some troubling event in her life?

Or is it life itself that scares her so?

Perhaps I should have asked.

If she *is* scared-- hiding inside the flash of good times.

She seems very...alone.

EVENIN', MISS.

GOOD EVENING.

Then again, what if I did ask her about it all--

"Lily, darling, you *obviously* have something deeply troubling you. Care to *tell* me about it?"

--And what if she just *stared* at me? Then what would I do?

What if she isn't even *aware* that she has changed?

Maybe only the people around her can notice it--

--because it's too *close* for her--

COMING THROUGH!

SORRY! SHE'S GOT A SPOOK!

THAT'S ALL RIGHT.

--to even *SEE*.

KLOPPITY KLOPPITY

I suppose I shouldn't take this all so personally.

KLOPPITA KLOPPITA

HRM.

After all...if people *weren't* capable of change--

--the world would be a *very* dark place.

256

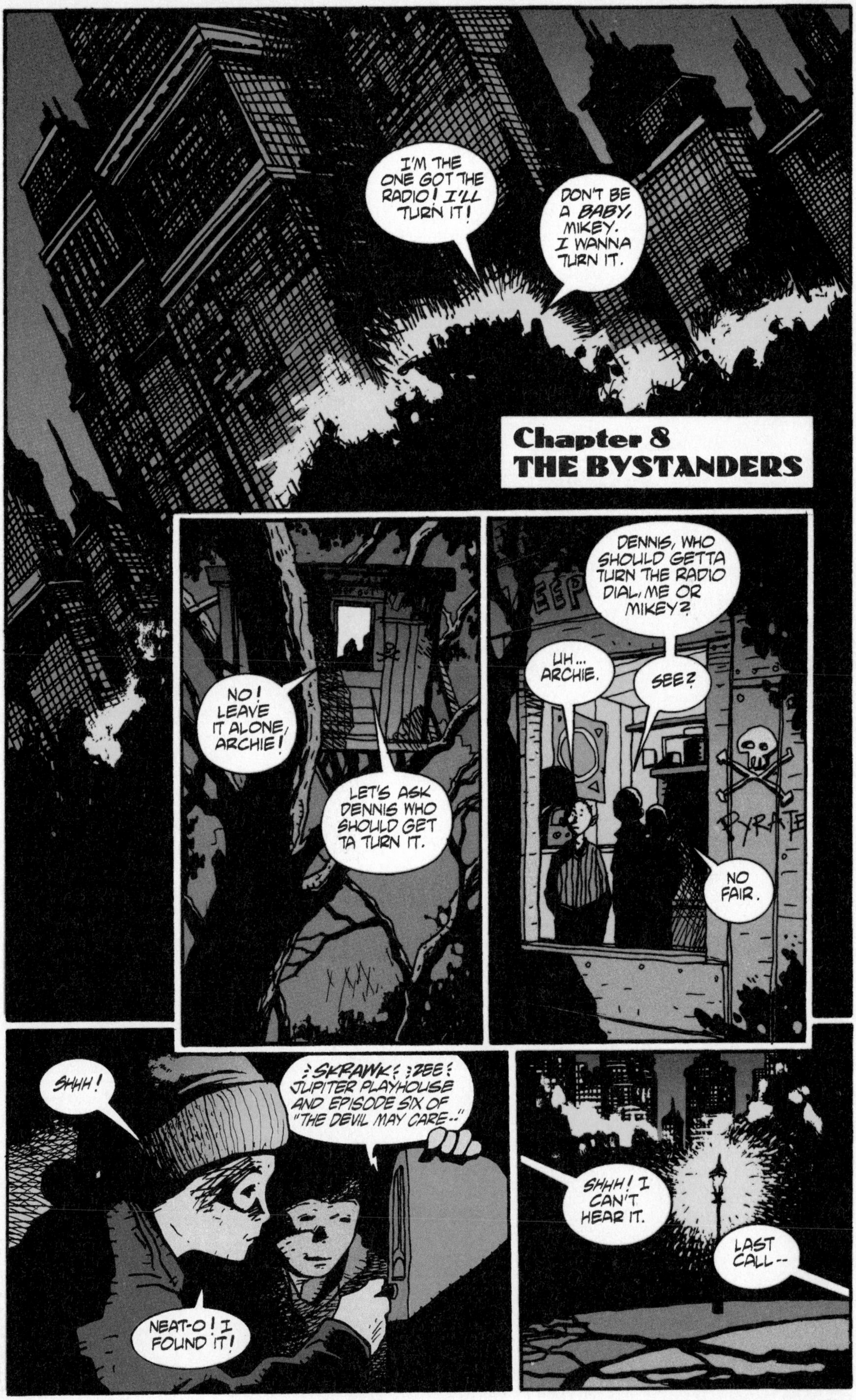

I'M THE ONE GOT THE RADIO! I'LL TURN IT!
DON'T BE A BABY, MIKEY. I WANNA TURN IT.
Chapter 8
THE BYSTANDERS
NO! LEAVE IT ALONE, ARCHIE!
LET'S ASK DENNIS WHO SHOULD GET TA TURN IT.
DENNIS, WHO SHOULD GETTA TURN THE RADIO DIAL, ME OR MIKEY?
UH... ARCHIE.
SEE?
NO FAIR.
PYRATE
SHHH!
SKRAWK! ZEE! JUPITER PLAYHOUSE AND EPISODE SIX OF "THE DEVIL MAY CARE--"
NEAT-O! I FOUND IT!
SHHH! I CAN'T HEAR IT.
LAST CALL--

LAST CALL FOR ESKI--MO PIES, GETCH'ER ESKI-MO--SHIT.

FORGET IT. FACE IT, MORTY, NOBODY WANTS ICE CREAM AT THIS TIME A' THE NIGHT.

NOT ONE DAMN SALE. NOT ONE.

SO WHAT, LUKE? YOU'RE AN ARTIST, AREN'T YA? YOU SHOULDN'T NEED MONEY TO DRAW, SO DRAW--

JUST DRAW SOME-THING.

PORTRAIT $1

YOU MIGHT AS WELL, LUKE, YOU SURE DON'T HAVE ANY MONEY TO BUY ANY FOOD TONIGHT--

MISTER? YA WANT ANY ESKI-MO PIES? MAYBE A BEEF PASTY?

SORRY, I'M BUST.

BUST--CRIPES, PATHETIC. AH WELL, HUNGER'S GOOD FOR THE SOUL, HUH, LUKE? JUST DRAW SOME-THING.

KLIPPITY KLOP

258

NEIGHH

I KNOW, GIRL, NOT MUCH LONGER TONIGHT--

KLIPITY KLOP

--I PROMISE.

KLOP KLOP

ED! WALT! WHAT YOU GUYS DOING?

BROKEN PIPE MESSIN' UP THE PRESSURE ON THE UPPER EAST SIDE, AND YOU KNOW HOW THOSE UPPERS ARE--

UPPITY! HA! HOW'S BUSINESS TONIGHT?

WHAT BUSINESS? THINK I'LL PACK IT. SEE YA!

YEAH, SURE, SEE YOU AROUND, NEIL.

DRIVER!

KLIPITY KLOP

WHERE TO, SIR?

JUST STAY IN THE PARK--

OTHER THAN THAT WE DON'T CARE.

hee heeheehee

YUH. I GETCHA, SIR.

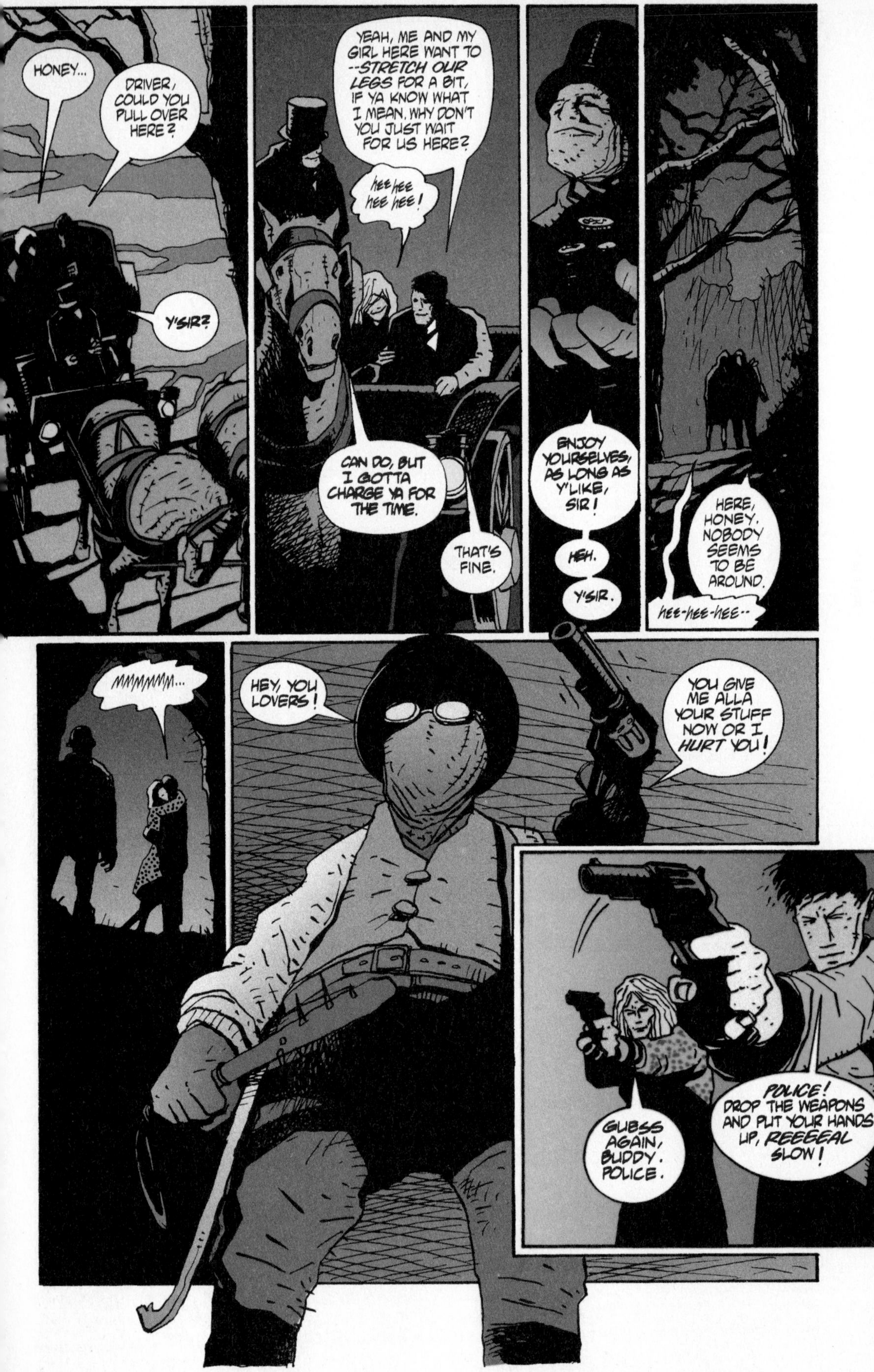
HONEY...
DRIVER, COULD YOU PULL OVER HERE?
Y'SIR?
YEAH, ME AND MY GIRL HERE WANT TO --STRETCH OUR LEGS FOR A BIT, IF YA KNOW WHAT I MEAN. WHY DON'T YOU JUST WAIT FOR US HERE?
hee hee hee hee!
CAN DO, BUT I GOTTA CHARGE YA FOR THE TIME.
THAT'S FINE.
ENJOY YOURSELVES, AS LONG AS Y'LIKE, SIR!
HEH.
Y'SIR.
HERE, HONEY. NOBODY SEEMS TO BE AROUND.
hee-hee-hee--
MMMMMM...
HEY, YOU LOVERS!
YOU GIVE ME ALLA YOUR STUFF NOW OR I HURT YOU!
GUESS AGAIN, BUDDY. POLICE.
POLICE! DROP THE WEAPONS AND PUT YOUR HANDS UP, REEEEAL SLOW!

THWUK

NUH-UH!

AHH! JESUS! MY HAND!

FREEZE, BASTARD!

LOOK OUT, JOHNSON!

KLOP KLOP

DAMMIT! YOU FOULED MY SHOT!

BLAM

KLOP KLOP

WHAT THE--?

COME ON, GIRL! HOLD ON THERE!

NEIGGH!

KLOP KLOP

261

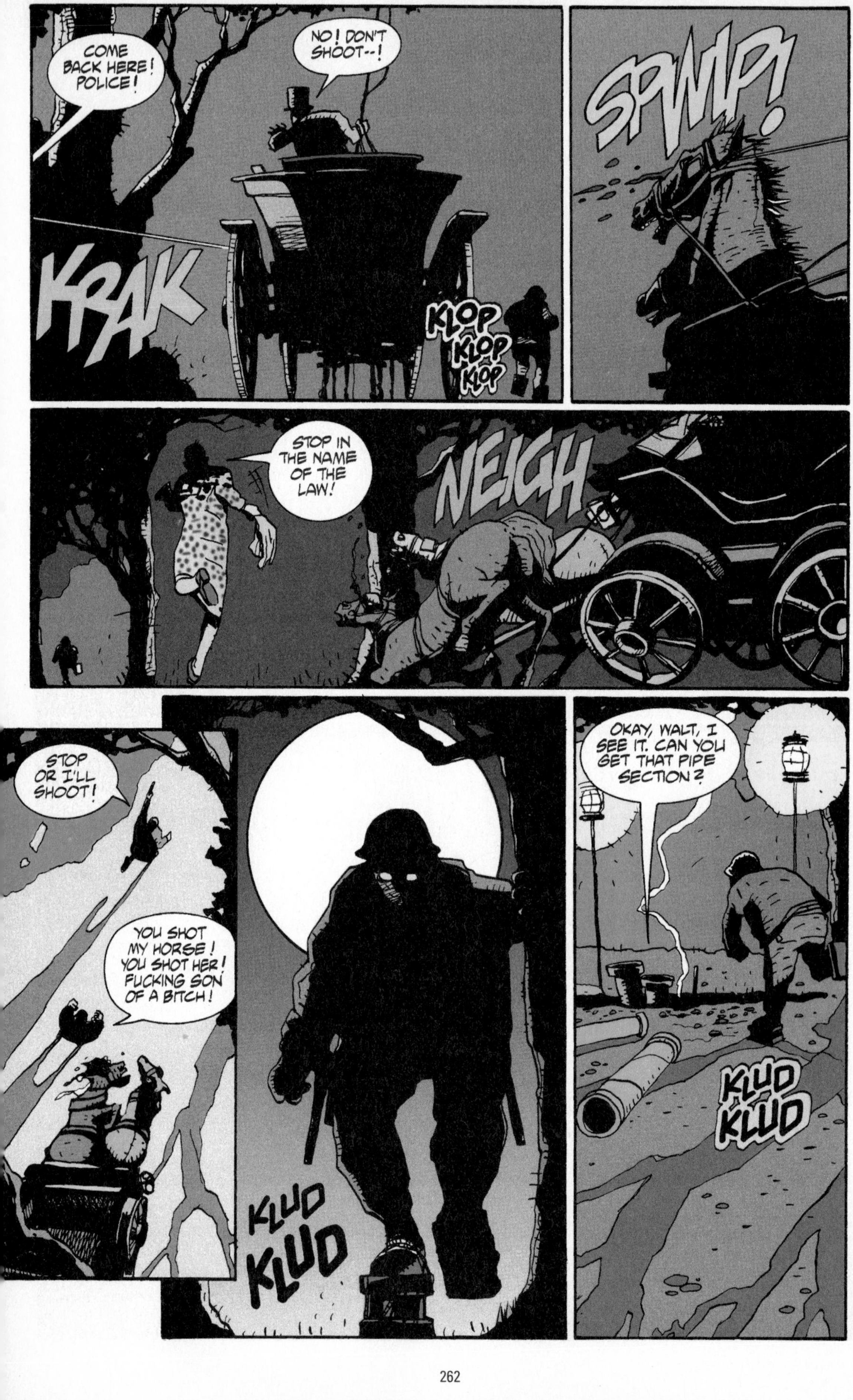

COME BACK HERE! POLICE!
NO! DON'T SHOOT--!
KRAK
KLOP KLOP KLOP
SPWAP!
STOP IN THE NAME OF THE LAW!
NEIGH
STOP OR I'LL SHOOT!
YOU SHOT MY HORSE! YOU SHOT HER! FUCKING SON OF A BITCH!
KLUD KLUD
OKAY, WALT, I SEE IT. CAN YOU GET THAT PIPE SECTION?
KLUD KLUD

KLUD

SURE THING, ED.

...WALT?

CITYSCAPE. ANOTHER CITYSCAPE, LUKE. IT'S LIFELESS! IT NEEDS--

LIFE--? HEY!

KLOP KLOP KLOP

STOP-- ?HUFF?--RIGHT --?HUFF?--THERE --?HUFF?--

BASTARD!

HOOOO-BOY! YOU'VE GOTTA START EATIN' REGULARLY, LUKE.

ARCHIE? M-MIKEY?

SHUT UP, DENNIS!

--SHE DID NOT SEE THE DARK FIGURE LOOOMING BEHIND HER--

ARCHIE? M-MIKEY?

WHAT D'YOU *WANT*, DENNI--

--HIS EYES BLACK AS DEATH--

--BUT AS SHE TURNED--

¿GASP¿ PANT PANT¿

CLIK

EEEEE!

EEEE!

EEEE!

...SHIT...

...NAH, I LOST 'IM.

Y'LOOK GREAT IN A DRESS, DELVECCHIO!

UP *YOURS*, KENNEDY--

LET'S SPLIT UP AND--

--MYSTERY THEATRE MAGAZINE? ARE WE *BOTH* GONNA BE GLAD YOU GUYS WORK LATE. I'VE GOT SOMETHING HERE YOU'RE GONNA *LOVE*...

PORTRAITS $1

CENTRAL PARK IS ACTUALLY A PERFECT SYMBOL FOR THE CITY AS A WHOLE.

IN THE MIDST OF A MASS OF IMPURITY--

Chapter 9
THE SOLUTION

--ONE SPOT OF TRUE BEAUTY--

--A REMINDER TO US ALL OF WHAT THE ENTIRE CITY ONCE WAS.

WHICH MADE THIS MUGGER IN THE PARK ALL THE MORE TROUBLING TO ME.

STOP!

OKAY! GIVE ME YOU THINGS!

OH!

WE WILL, WE WILL. PLEASE DON'T HURT US!

I AIN'T HURT YOU, JUST GIVE ME YOU THINGS!

ALSO TROUBLING WAS THAT I STILL HAD NO VISIONS OF HIM IN MY DREAMS, EVEN NOW--

--HE EXISTED ONLY IN THE REAL WORLD.

NO! NOT BOXES. PURSE AND WALLET. PURSE AND WALLET!

HERE, PLEASE, WE--

YOU NOT FOLLOW ME!

ALL RIGHT, HUMPHRIES, I THINK HE'S GONE. QUICKLY--

--MY MASK.

THANKS FOR YOUR HELP. I HAD A FEELING THIS WOULD WORK. SORRY ABOUT THE MUSTACHE, BUT IT WILL GROW BACK.

YES, I KNOW, SIR. IT'S THE HAIR ON MY LEGS I'M WORRIED ABOUT.

RUSTLE

HIS METHODS AND WEAPONS WERE SO CRUDE--

--HIS MOTIVATIONS SO BASE--

--THAT I KNEW HE WAS NOT A MAN OF EVIL MOTIVES--

--BUT OF DESPERATE ONES.

LAY DOWN YOUR ARMS OR FACE THE DARKEST NIGHT YOU'LL EVER KNOW.

EH?

KLIK KLIK KLIK KLIK

NO!

FURTHERMORE, WHAT SORT OF *CRIMINAL* ATTACKS WITH AN *UNLOADED WEAPON?* A PROP. PART OF THE CHARADE.

STAY WHERE YOU ARE OR--

AAH!

PANG

267

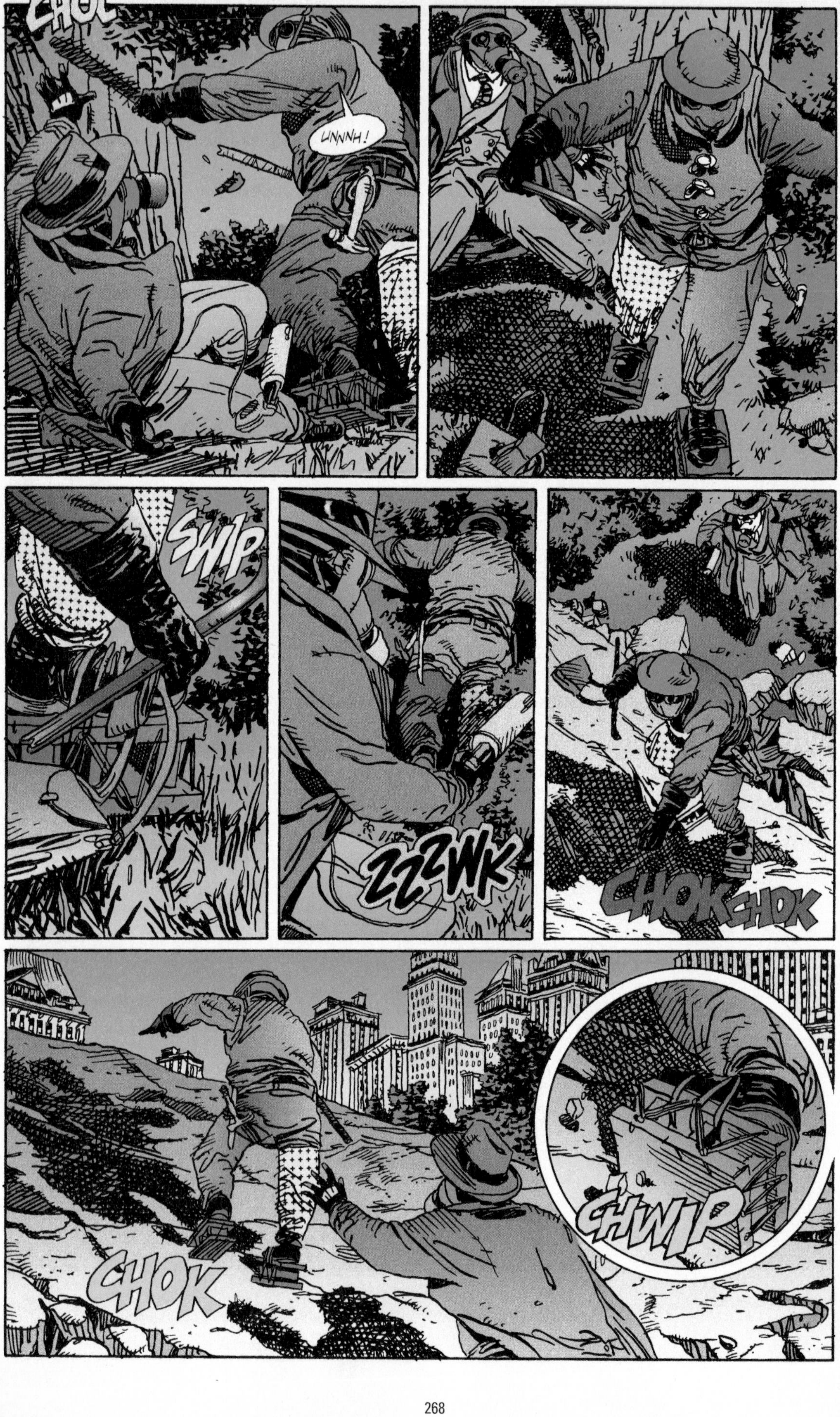

CHOC
UNNNH!
SWIP
ZZZWK
CHOKCHOK
CHOK
CHWIP

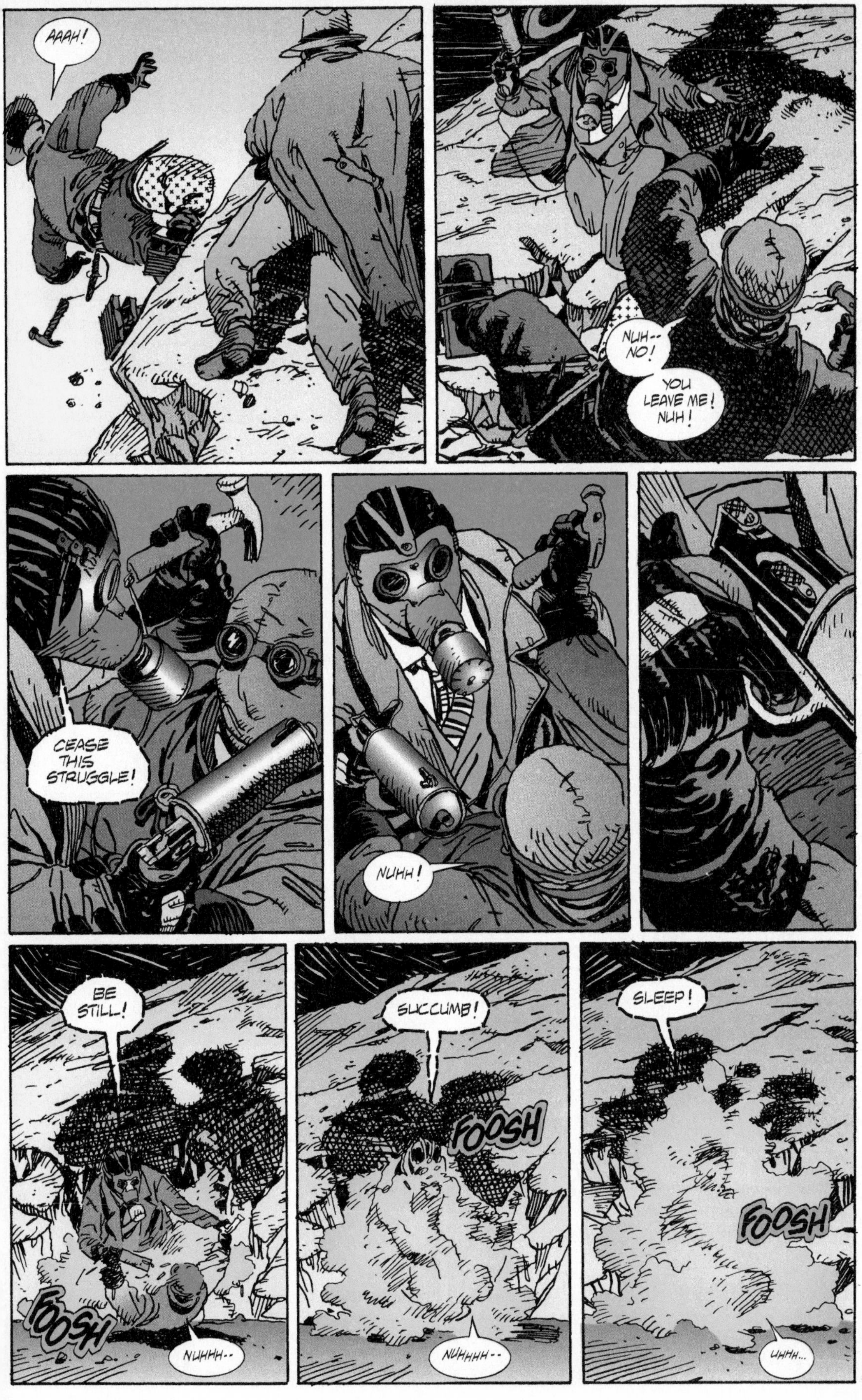
AAAH!
NUH-- NO!
YOU LEAVE ME! NUH!
CEASE THIS STRUGGLE!
NUHH!
BE STILL!
FOOSH
NUHHH--
SUCCUMB!
FOOSH
NUHHHH--
SLEEP!
FOOSH
UHHH...

--THE MYSTERY REMAINS--

--WHO IS THE MUGGER?

AND SO, IF NOT A FIGURE FROM MY DREAMS--

HIS TEETH--HIS CLOTHING. I SEE THE TENEMENTS RIDING HARD ON THIS MAN.

AWAKEN, PROWLER OF THE PARK! AND TELL ME YOUR PURPOSE HERE.

NAME'S-- STANISLAUS EMRICOVIK --THEY SHUT MY FACT'RY DOWN--TOOK MY JOB--MY WIFE HAVE NEXT BABY LAS' WEEK--

FIVE TO FEED--ALL HUNGRY--I NEVER HURT *NO ONE*--NOT EVEN NO BULLETS IN GUN--JUS' TRY TO SCARE PEOPLE --EXCEPT COP--

HIT HIM--DIDN' WAN' TO-- SCARED ME--DON' KNOW WHAT ELSE TO DO--AMERICA NOT KIN' TO ME--NOT--WORKING--

HIS WORDS ARE SO POORLY CHOSEN, AND YET SO UTTERLY MOVING ...UNFETTERED BY TRUE GREED OR HATE.

HUSH NOW, STANISLAUS EMRICOVIK TELL ME WHERE YOU LIVE AND THEN SLEEP.

EIGHT AVENUE ...AND 55TH STREET...THIRD... FLOOR...

THEY MAKE ME THINK THAT PERHAPS THE PARK CAN BE SAVED THIS TIME--

--PERHAPS A NEW BLOOM CAN BE SALVAGED FROM THIS DYING BUD--

--NOT BY JUSTICE--

...NUHHH?

--BUT THIS TIME--

EH?

Look under the pillow and you will find
A solution in part to your state
But treat others as you would be treated in kind
Or suffer a terrible fate

The Sandman

OH! OH!

--WAS A DREAM! IRINA! IRINA, LOOK! AN ANGEL COME TO ME FROM A DREAM!

--BY COMPASSION.

HEY, FLATFOOT! GOT YER MESSAGE FROM MY EDITOR, WHAT'S THE LOWDOWN?

AH, MR. FEEGEE. THOUGHT YOU MIGHT BE INTERESTED IN THIS.

271

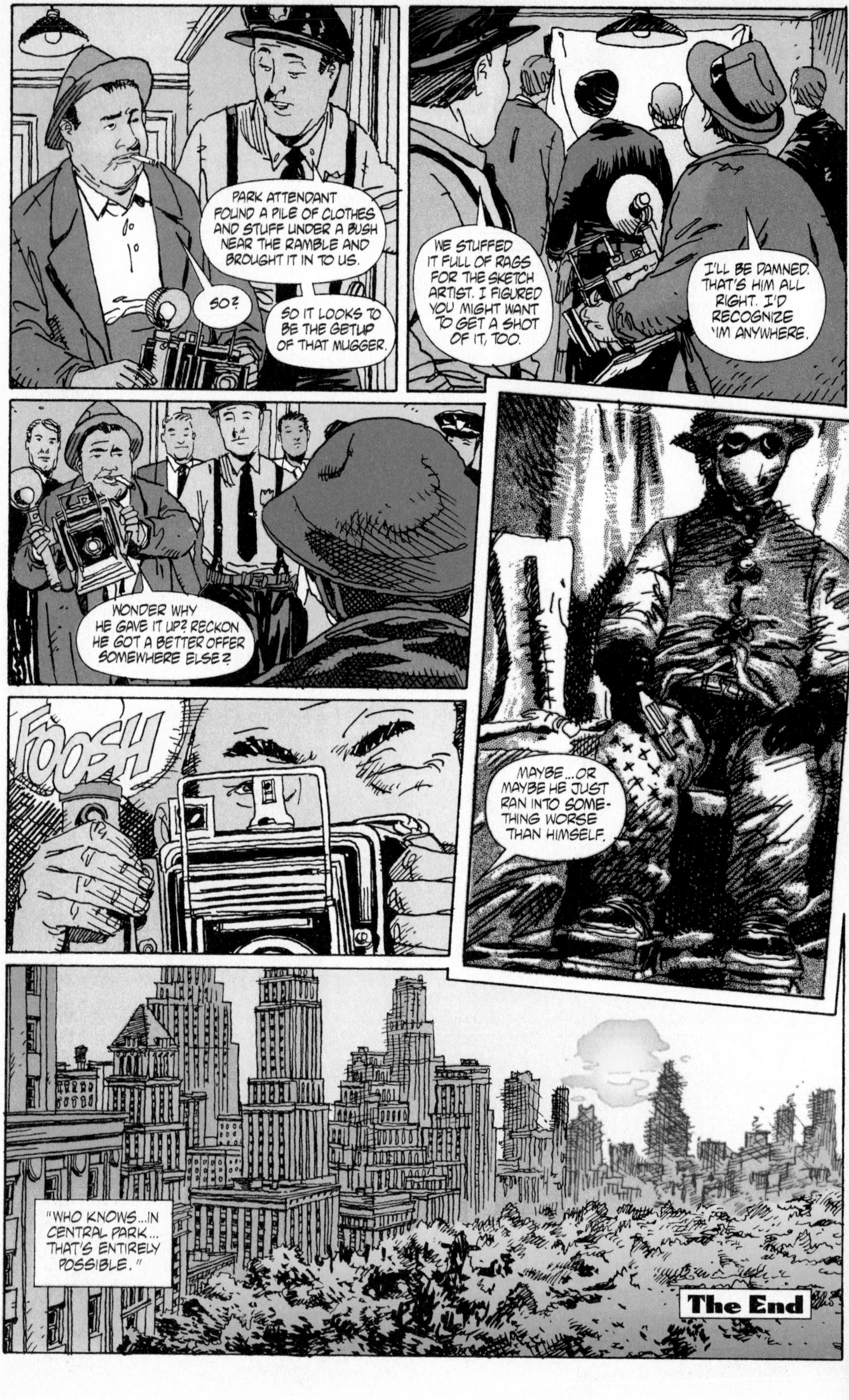
PARK ATTENDANT FOUND A PILE OF CLOTHES AND STUFF UNDER A BUSH NEAR THE RAMBLE AND BROUGHT IT IN TO US.
SO?
SO IT LOOKS TO BE THE GETUP OF THAT MUGGER.
WE STUFFED IT FULL OF RAGS FOR THE SKETCH ARTIST. I FIGURED YOU MIGHT WANT TO GET A SHOT OF IT, TOO.
I'LL BE DAMNED. THAT'S HIM ALL RIGHT. I'D RECOGNIZE 'IM ANYWHERE.
WONDER WHY HE GAVE IT UP? RECKON HE GOT A BETTER OFFER SOMEWHERE ELSE?
FOOSH
MAYBE...OR MAYBE HE JUST RAN INTO SOME-THING WORSE THAN HIMSELF.
"WHO KNOWS...IN CENTRAL PARK... THAT'S ENTIRELY POSSIBLE."
The End

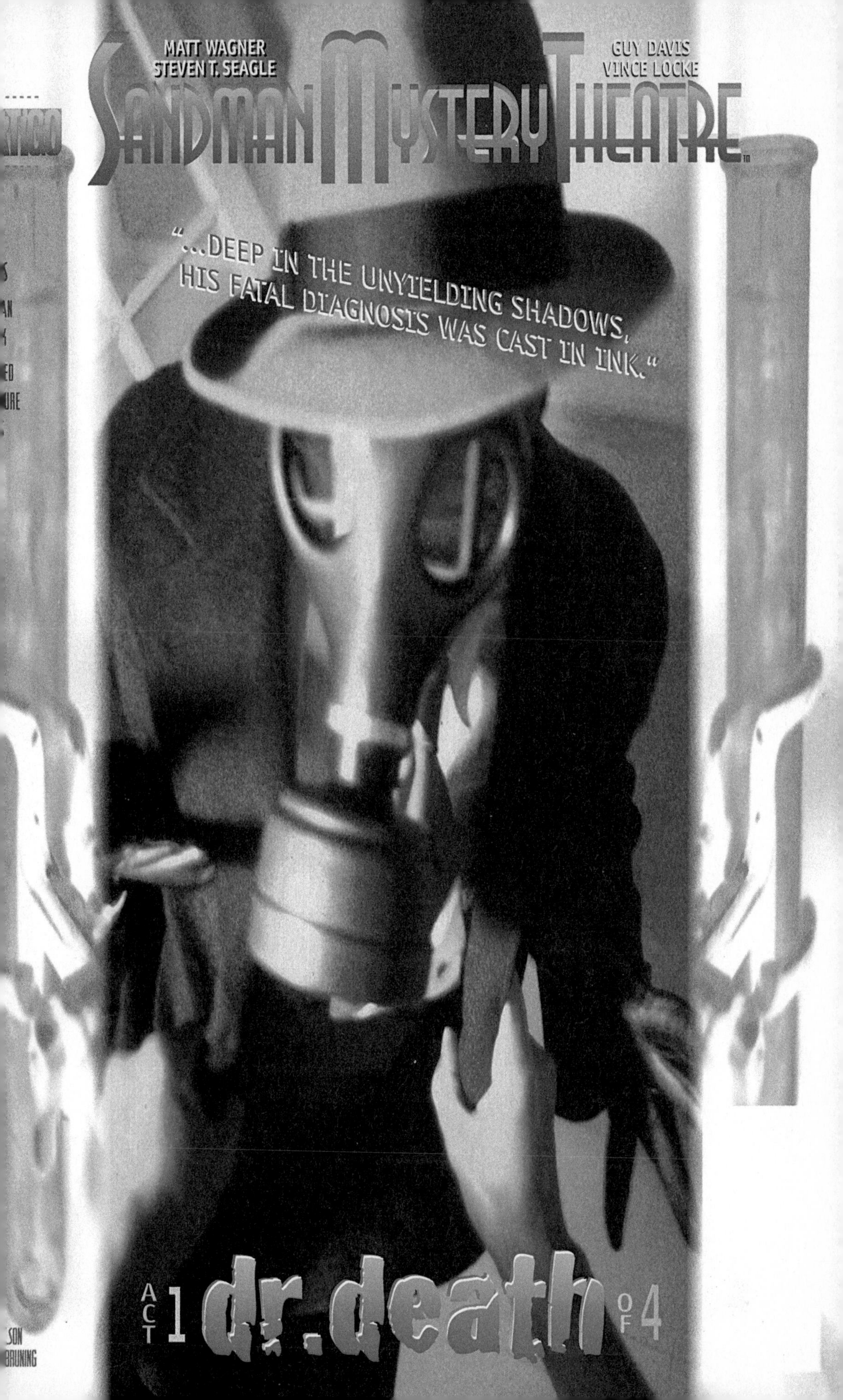
MATT WAGNER
STEVEN T. SEAGLE
GUY DAVIS
VINCE LOCKE
SANDMAN MYSTERY THEATRE
"...DEEP IN THE UNYIELDING SHADOWS, HIS FATAL DIAGNOSIS WAS CAST IN INK."
ACT 1 dr. death OF 4

"Just when
you're certain
that your life is
as bad as can be,
you're shown
a glimpse of
how much worse
things could go."

DR.
DEATH

There are, of course, two ways to look at this.

On one hand, Wesley is trying to protect me from harm--

--After all, the Sandman does get involved in some awfully frightful endeavors.

On the other hand, Wesley is intentionally lying to me.

Which would mean that despite what he says or does--

--He actually cares little about me.

Of course this isn't exactly the sort of thing one can just bring up over drinks at Rooker's.

"Yes, Wesley... I agree. Busby Berkeley is a genius. Oh, and by the way... you are the Sandman, aren't you?"

Even so, this can't hang like a specter between us. I'm going to have to do something.

DIAN? THAT IS YOU, ISN'T IT?

LUCY? HELLO.

MY GOODNESS BUT YOU'RE LOOKING WELL. HOW IS UNCLE BILL?

OH, FATHER'S WELL, THOUGH I'M **SURE** HE WISHES HIS FAVORITE NIECE WOULD DROP BY MORE OFTEN.

YOU'RE RIGHT, I **SHOULD** MAKE TIME FOR A VISIT, BUT I'VE JUST BEEN **FRANTIC**. ARE YOU STILL IN THE COUNTRY?

WELL...MY **BELONGINGS** ARE STILL ON THE FARM, BUT **I'VE** BEEN SPENDING MOST OF MY TIME IN THE CITY THESE DAYS.

I'M...**SEEING** SOMEONE SPECIAL, AND I JUST CAN'T STAY AWAY FOR MORE THAN A DAY OR TWO.

THIS MYSTERY MAN SOUNDS LIKE HE'S GOT MY COUSIN'S HEART WRAPPED ROUND HIS INDEX FINGER.

UGH! I FEEL ABSOLUTELY **ANCIENT**.

I COULD HAVE **SWORN** THAT THE LAST TIME I SAW YOU WE WERE STILL PLAYING WITH DOLLS AND TIN HORSES.

I **STILL** LIKE HORSES. ONLY NOW INSTEAD OF TIN, I HAVE A **REAL** ONE. FATHER'S BEEN BREEDING THEM LATELY AS SHOW HORSES.

REALLY? THAT SOUNDS FASCINATING.

OH, IT IS. YOU REALLY SHOULD COME OUT TO THE RANCH SOME TIME AND WE'LL TAKE AN AFTERNOON RIDE. THEY'RE GREAT FOR CLEARING THE HEAD.

YOU KNOW...THAT SOUNDS LIKE THE **EXACT** TREATMENT I NEED FOR MY CURRENT STATE OF MIND. MAYBE I **WILL** COME OUT.

LISTEN, I **HAVE** TO RUN, BUT I'LL PHONE YOU SOON.

OKAY, AND DO COME VISIT. WE NEED TO CATCH UP MORE **FULLY**. I'VE MISSED TALKING TO YOU, DIAN.

SAME HERE, LUCY. YOU TAKE CARE AND I'LL BE IN TOUCH.

Isn't that how it's supposed to be?

2

A woman meets a man--

They fall madly in love.

They speak each other's unspoken thoughts--

--Love swells within them--

--And they're together.

It seems to be that simple for all of my friends, so why is it turning out to be so complicated for me?

IT IS MISS BELMONT RETURNING YOUR CALL, SIR. DO YOU CARE TO TAKE IT HERE?

SURE. WOULD YOU PLEASE EXCUSE US, THOUGH?

CERTAINLY. I BELIEVE I SMELL THE BRISKET BURNING ANYHOW.

HELLO, WESLEY. SORRY TO TAKE SO LONG TO RETURN YOUR CALL, BUT I JUST GOT BACK FROM THE YWCA. LISTEN, I WAS WONDERING IF YOU'D LIKE TO HAVE DINNER TOGETHER THIS EVENING.

FROM THE SOUNDS COMING FROM THE KITCHEN, I THINK THAT WOULD BE BOTH ENJOYABLE AND PRAGMATIC.

I'LL BE BY FOR YOU AROUND SIX? GOOD... I'LL SEE YOU THEN.

"I'll see you then."

Not, "I'll see you then, sweetheart," or "I can't wait to see you."

What is wrong with me that you keep your distance in so many ways, Wesley?

What does it take to fully scale the walls that surround your heart?

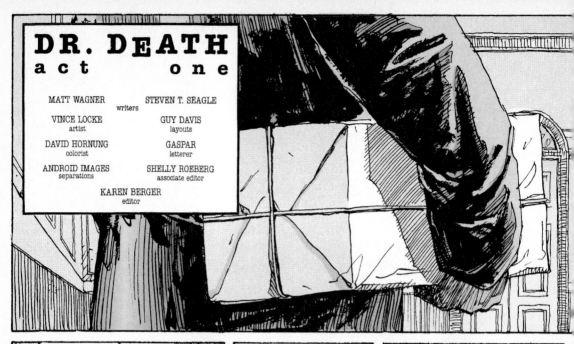

DR. DEATH
act one

MATT WAGNER   STEVEN T. SEAGLE
writers

VINCE LOCKE   GUY DAVIS
artist   layouts

DAVID HORNUNG   GASPAR
colorist   letterer

ANDROID IMAGES   SHELLY ROEBERG
separations   associate editor

KAREN BERGER
editor

SORRY T' INTERRUPT YOUR READIN'. GOT A PACKAGE FOR SUITE 34.

...JUST A MINNIT... JUST...GOTTA...FINISH... PARAGRAPH--

--OKAY. *DELIVERY* YOU SAY? YOU CAN JUST LEAVE IT HERE AN' I'LL TAKE IT UP IN A FEW.

CAN'T *DO* THAT. THIS'S GOTTA BE DELIVERED IN PERSON. MEDICAL SUPPLIES. YOU KNOW.

WELL THEN... GO AHEAD, I GUESS. JUST DON'T TOUCH NOTHIN' UP THERE, HUH?

SURE.

HEY!

SERVICE STAIRS'RE AROUND *BACK*, BUCK.

SURE. NO PROBLEM. SORRY.

4

--I'LL BE DAMNED--!

...JESUS, WHAT A CLIMB...

PHEW! WISH THEY HAD SOME WATER COOLERS 'ROUND HERE.

DELIVERY!

COME IN...

TAP TAP TAP

DR.

GOT A SPECIAL DELIVERY FOR YOU, DOCTOR. HAD T' BRING IT UP PERSONAL. GUESS YOU KNOW WHY.

I UNDERSTAND. PLEASE, COME IN.

5

YOU LOOK TIRED. ARE YOU FEELING WELL?

IT'S THE CLIMB, DOC. HAD T' TAKE THE SERVICE STAIRS. 'S LEFT ME WINDED.

YES I CAN SEE THAT.

RATHER UNFORGIVABLE IN THIS MODERN AGE, ISN'T IT?

'SCUSE ME?

UNFORGIVABLE. THAT WE'D BUILD ELEVATORS AND THEN FORCE SOME OF THE HARD-WORKING MEN OF THE CITY TO BYPASS THEM SIMPLY BECAUSE OF THEIR... STATION.

OH, IT'S NOT THAT BAD. USED T' BE I COULD TAKE IT IN STRIDE. I THINK IT'S JUS' THE YEARS CATCHIN' UP WITH ME FINALLY.

YES... WELL, THEY DO CATCH UP WITH US. ALL OF US. SOMETIMES MUCH SOONER THAN WE MIGHT EXPECT.

AIN'T THAT THE TRUTH, SIR. WELL, I'D BETTER BE GETTIN' BACK--

ALL IN GOOD TIME, MY FRIEND. I'M WORRIED ABOUT YOUR WELL-BEING. PLEASE, HAVE A SEAT.

UH... WELL, I DON'T REALLY HAVE ANY MONEY FOR A--

YOU INSULT ME. PART OF MY OATH AS A DOCTOR IS TO GIVE MY SERVICES WHERE NEEDED REGARD-LESS OF THE BINDING CIRCUMSTANCES. HELP YOURSELF TO A BRANDY?

6

I--THANKS--uh... THANK YOU.

YOU KNOW, YOU HAVE A VERY FAMILIAR FACE.

PEOPLE ARE ALWAYS TELLIN' ME THAT.

YES. LITTLE *OLDER* NOW, BUT I *DO* RECOGNIZE THE FEATURES.

CORRECT ME IF I'M MISTAKEN, BUT AREN'T YOU EDDIE ROBINSON? *EDDIE THE ENGINE?*

WELL NOW AIN'T *YOU* TH' EAGLE EYE? I DON'T GET RECOGNIZED MUCH THESE DAYS, NO SIR.

YEAH...BOXING. THOSE WERE THE DAYS ALL RIGHT. IF I HADN'T THROWN OUT MY BACK, I MIGHT'A GONE FAR... WHO KNOWS?

AND INSTEAD YOU'RE NOW JUST A JUNK RUNNER FOR THE MOB.

WELL NOW, I--I MEAN, I--

IT'S ALL RIGHT, EDDIE. WE ALL HAVE OUR LITTLE MALADIES.

BUT I'M GOING TO GIVE YOU A PRESCRIPTION THAT, ONCE FILLED, OUGHT TO SOLVE *ALL* OF YOUR PROBLEMS, INCLUDING THIS CAREER SLUMP YOU'RE IN.

HERE.

YOU KNOW, DOC. YOU ALL RIGHT.

I MUS' DELIVER EIGHTY PACKAGES A DAY, BUT AIN'T *NOBODY* TREATS ME THE WAY YOU DO.

mm. *COUNT* ON IT.

7

It's strange how knowledge can come between people.

Familiarity should bring people closer together--

--But the fact that I know something Wes hasn't told me only drives us farther apart.

I'M SORRY, I MUST HAVE BEEN DAYDREAMING. WHAT DID YOU SAY?

WELL... ACTUALLY I SAID YOU LOOK A MILLION MILES AWAY. AT LEAST I KNOW MY INTUITION IS STILL INTACT.

YES. THAT'S TRUE.

And yet, if I were to come right out with what I know to be true--

--It could sever our bonds completely.

DIAN? I GET THE FEELING I'VE OFFENDED YOU SOMEHOW.

I'M NOT EXACTLY SURE WHAT I'VE DONE, BUT I WANTED TO GO OUT WITH YOU TO MAKE YOU FEEL GOOD.

WHY DON'T I PROMISE TO NEVER DO IT AGAIN IF YOU PROMISE TO TELL ME WHAT IT IS I'VE DONE?

OH, WESLEY, IT'S NOT THAT. NOT THAT EXACTLY. I JUST FEEL... I FEEL LIKE YOU DON'T REALLY FEEL... COMFORTABLE WITH ME.

DIAN, I FEEL MORE COMFORTABLE WITH YOU THAN I'VE EVER FELT WITH ANYONE IN MY LIFE.

HONESTLY.

YOU KNOW, I THINK I'M JUST MOPEY. LET'S ENJOY THE REST OF OUR MEAL AND WE'LL TALK... OR WHATEVER... LATER.

8

--SO HERE'S THE RUB, VELIKOVSKY IS ONLY PLAYING ONE SHOW IN NEW YORK, AND IT'S A *PRIVATE* SHOW.

OH, THAT'S HORRIBLE.

VERY.

HUMPHRIES? I THINK WE'LL BE HEADING BACK TO THE HOUSE FOR A NIGHTCAP.

VERY GOOD, SIR.

ANYTHING YOU'D LIKE TO TELL ME, HANDSOME?

ONLY THAT I THINK THIS MAY BE THE LONGEST RIDE HOME I'LL EVER HAVE TO LIVE THROUGH.

...WESLEY...

WESLEY...

IS SOMETHING WRONG?

I FEEL...FUNNY. I JUST-- I DON'T THINK THIS IS THE TIME. I'M SORRY, I--

DIAN, THERE'S NOTHING TO BE SORRY ABOUT. THESE THINGS *TAKE* TIME, AND THE MORE TIME THEY TAKE, THE MORE THEY CAN BE SAVORED.

HUMPHRIES? CHANGE IN PLANS. WE'LL BE GOING BY MISS BELMONT'S RESIDENCE.

YES, SIR.

I don't know why this trepidation has such a hold on me.

9

Wesley is so understanding that I'm sure he wouldn't be evasive if I confronted him about his dual life.

But still, if I mattered to him--

--If I truly mattered--

GOOD NIGHT.

GOOD NIGHT, DIAN.

He would tell me of his own volition

Wouldn't he?

I DIDN'T EXPECT YOU BACK SO SOON.

YES, WELL, LIFE'S FULL OF LITTLE SURPRISES LIKE THAT, ISN'T IT?

DIAN? ARE YOU ALL RIGHT? IT'S NOT LIKE YOU TO SNAP.

YOU'RE RIGHT, DADDY. I'M SORRY. IT'S JUST ME, I THINK. I'LL FIGURE IT OUT.

IF YOU NEED ANY HELP, HONEY, I'M ALWAYS HERE.

THANKS, DADDY.

BY THE WAY, I RAN INTO LUCY THIS AFTERNOON. I THINK I MIGHT GO VISIT HER AND HER FAMILY THIS WEEKEND.

DO YOU THINK YOU MIGHT COME ALONG?

OH... I DON'T THINK THAT'S SUCH A GOOD IDEA.

I HAVEN'T REALLY GOTTEN ON WITH BILL SINCE YOUR MOTHER--

--WELL, ANYWAY, YOU ENJOY YOURSELF AND TELL THEM I SAID HELLO, WOULD YOU?

GOODNIGHT, DIAN.

10

HOW'S *THIS* MR. KLEIN?

YEAH...THAT'S FINE, FELLAS.

WHAT'S THE WRITE-UP ON THIS ONE?

SOMEONE FOUND HIM CURLED UP IN AN ALLEY DOWN-TOWN.

ONE TOO MANY SHOTS IN THE ARM, I'D GUESS.

WE'LL SEE. IN FORENSIC PATHOLOGY, IT'S ALWAYS BEST NOT TO GET TOO TIED TO ANY PARTICULAR THEORY.

THERE'S ALWAYS THE POSSIBILITY THAT WHAT LOOKS LIKE ONE THING--

--MIGHT TURN OUT TO BE SOMETHING *ELSE* ALTOGETHER.

CHARLES, GO AHEAD AND GET HIM UNDRESSED.

I'VE ALREADY PULLED HIS PERSONALS, MR. KLEIN.

OH, WELL, LET'S HAVE A LOOK. MMM HM. PRETTY COMMON.

WHAT'S *THIS?*

IT APPEARS TO BE A PRE-SCRIPTION--

--FOR, "AN ETERNITY OF REST..."

11

285

NNAHH!

OH, GOOD LORD...

THAT SETTLES IT...

...NO MORE CHOCOLATE PHOSPHATES BEFORE BED.

EXCUSE ME, SIR? I HEARD YOUR CALL. I'M SORRY TO SEE THAT THE DREAMS HAVE RETURNED.

YOU'RE NOT ALONE.

ACTUALLY, SIR, NEITHER ARE YOU. YOU HAD SCHEDULED A LUNCH WITH JUDGE SCHAEFFER WHO IS, IN FACT, ALREADY HERE.

DAMN. UH...SEE IF YOU CAN KEEP THE JUDGE ENTERTAINED, HUMPHRIES. I'LL BE DOWN AS SOON AS POSSIBLE.

SORRY TO HAVE KEPT YOU WAITING SO LONG. SOMETIMES MY MORNING ABLUTIONS STRETCH RIGHT INTO THE AFTERNOON.

YOU KNOW WHAT THEY SAY...

"LATE TO BED, LATE TO RISE, MEANS A LOOK OF LOVE IN THE EYES."

IF ONLY.

YOU'RE LOOKING WELL, WES. DIAN MUST BE JUST WHAT YOU NEEDED.

UH, I DIDN'T KNOW YOU--SHALL WE WALK SOMEWHERE FOR LUNCH?

FINE. IT'S A TERRIFIC DAY OUT.

12

SO HOW LONG HAVE YOU AND LARRY'S ONE-AND-ONLY BEEN DATING, WES?

OH, A WHILE NOW. IT'S REALLY BEEN WORKING OUT QUITE WELL... UNTIL LAST NIGHT.

GET A LITTLE TOO FORWARD, DID YOU?

NO, NOT THAT. I'M NOT SURE *WHAT* IT WAS. DIAN JUST SEEMED IRRITABLE, DETACHED.

WOMEN GET LIKE THAT, YOU KNOW. DAMNEDEST THING. CATHY GOES OFF ON ME LIKE THAT ALMOST EVERY MONTH, IT SEEMS. WON'T PUT OUT *OR* SHUT UP.

CATHY? I THOUGHT YOUR WIFE'S NAME WAS *ELLEN.*

WELL YEAH, HER *TOO,* NOW THAT YOU MENTION IT.

TAKE MY WORD FOR IT, WES, IF ONE WOMAN IN YOUR LIFE'S TROUBLE, TWO IS ABSOLUTE DAMNATION. DON'T EVER DO IT. OR MAYBE *THAT'S* THE TROUBLE YOU'RE HAVING--?

NO, NO. NOTHING LIKE THAT.

IT'S JUST THAT... WELL, ACTUALLY, I THINK I'M JUST UPSET OVER A NIGHTMARE I HAD LAST EVENING. I JUST CAN'T GET IT OUT OF MY HEAD.

WHY DON'T YOU JUST TELL GOOD OLD "DR." SCHAEFFER ABOUT IT? IT HELPS TO TALK THOSE BUGGERS OUT, YOU KNOW.

WELL, I CERTAINLY APPRECIATE THE *OFFER,* BUT I DON'T LIKE TALKING ABOUT MY DREAMS.

WITH *ANYONE.*

13

Idyllic.

Visions of places like this make me stop and wonder why I have any dealings with the city.

--COME ON GIRL, SHOW ME YOUR TEETH--

--ABSOLUTELY BEAUTIFUL HERE.

ISN'T IT THOUGH? I TRULY HAVE THE BEST OF BOTH WORLDS WHEN YOU THINK ABOUT IT.

--Or the people in it, for that matter.

WELL NOW--

--IF IT ISN'T THE FINEST BREEDING STOCK I'VE EVER LAID EYES ON!

BREEDING STOCK? I DON'T KNOW IF I'M READY FOR THAT QUITE YET.

YOU'LL HAVE TO PARDON FATHER, DIAN, HE DOESN'T GET OFF THE FARM MUCH.

HOW'RE YOU DOING, LITTLE LADY? LOOKING MORE LIKE YOUR MOM THAN EVER.

I'M FINE, UNCLE BILL. THANKS!

LISTEN, I DON'T WANT TO JUST UP AND RUN OFF, BUT I'VE GOT A MARE THAT HAS TO BE PUT DOWN. BROKE HER LEG. MEET YOU BACK AT THE HOUSE AFTER A WHILE?

THAT'S FINE, FATHER. WE'LL SEE YOU THERE.

OH!

GUESS WHO LOVES YOU LIKE NOBODY ELSE?

WHA--?

RAY! YOU RASCAL! I THOUGHT YOU WERE STAYING IN THE CITY FOR THE WEEKEND.

YEP. RIGHT UP TO THE MOMENT I REALIZED THAT WOULD MEAN I WOULDN'T BE SEEING YOU!

14

DIAN? THIS IS MY MAN, RAYMOND KESSLER.

SO I GATHERED. A PLEASURE TO MEET YOU, RAY.

YOU'RE LUCY'S COUSIN, DIAN?

YES, I--

OF *COURSE* SHE IS, SILLY. I *TOLD* YOU THAT. I TOLD HIM *THAT*, DIAN.

NOW, LUCY, YOU'VE *GONE* AND MESSED UP MY SMALL TALK. WHATEVER WILL I DO?

AM I BLUSHING?

YOU SILLY BOY!

Look at them.

So in love.

So perfectly, easily in love.

UH... WHERE DID THE TWO OF YOU MEET?

WELL, ACTUALLY I SAW LUCY AT A--

RAYMOND'S BEEN STABLING HIS MOUNT HERE. I ASKED HIM IF HIS HORSE NEEDED A BRUSH DOWN, ONE THING LED TO ANOTHER, AND, WELL... ONE THING LED TO ANOTHER.

RAY'S REALLY BROADENED MY HORIZONS. I EVEN LISTEN TO CLASSICAL MUSIC NOW. TOMORROW WE'RE GOING TO HEAR VLATA-- UH--VALA--

VLADIMIR VELIKOVSKY, YOU MINX.

HE'S PLAYING AT THE AMERICAN MEDICAL ASSOCIATION DINNER.

OH, *MY*... BOYFRIEND WAS JUST TALKING ABOUT HIM. SAID THAT HE'S A BRILLIANT PIANIST--

JOIN US. IT'S A PRIVATE AFFAIR, BUT I'M ENTITLED TO GUESTS. AND GOD KNOWS *MY* SON WON'T ATTEND. JUST TELL HIM TO DRESS LIKE A PHYSICIAN.

KRAK

LUCY? I'LL SEE YOU LATER, NO?

OF *COURSE* YOU WILL, RAY.

I don't know if I should be saddest or envious.

15

--ALL I'M SAYIN', HUBERT, IS YA FOUND THE GUY SMELLIN' LIKE A FRIGGIN' BREWERY. LET'S JUST CHALK IT UP TO BEIN' A DRUNK AN' CALL IT A DAY.

BUT LIEUTENANT, YOU HAVEN'T LET ME TELL YOU ABOUT THE PRESCRIPTION YET.

HE WAS CARRYING A WRITTEN PRESCRIPTION WITH HIM THAT READ, "AN ETERNITY OF REST..." WHAT KIND OF DOCTOR WOULD WRITE SUCH A THING?

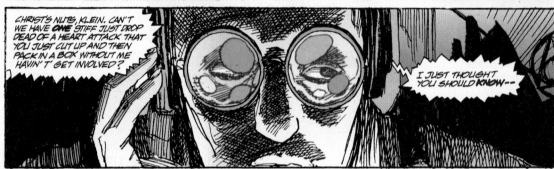

CHRIST'S NUTS, KLEIN. CAN'T WE HAVE **ONE** STIFF JUST DROP DEAD OF A HEART ATTACK THAT YOU JUST CUT UP AND THEN PACK IN A BOX WITHOUT ME HAVIN' T' GET INVOLVED?

I JUST THOUGHT YOU SHOULD **KNOW**--

MASTER DODDS?

SORRY TO INTERRUPT, BUT MISS BELMONT IS ON THE LINE. I THOUGHT YOU MIGHT WANT TO--

YES, HUMPHRIES, I'LL TAKE IT. THANK YOU.

HELLO, DIAN?... REALLY? THAT'S FANTASTIC! I'D **LOVE** TO.

...SHOULD BE OUTSTANDING...

...HOPE THEY'RE NOT SERVING FISH...

...RUSSIAN, THOUGH...

TONIGHT WELCOME AMA ANNUAL BANQUET featuring VLADIMIR VELIKOVSKY

PARAMOU

16

"...SERIOUSLY LODGED IN THE COLON...."

DON'T THINK YOU COULD EVER KEEP THEM ALIVE LONG ENOUGH TO MAKE THE SWITCH...

"...NO, DON'T EAT THAT FISH, IT'LL *KILL* YOU...

"...WHEN'S THIS GOING TO *START*, ANYWAY...

WELL *THERE* YOU ARE. I WAS JUST TELLING RAY THAT I THOUGHT YOU MIGHT HAVE DECIDED NOT TO COME.

AND MISS THE LEGENDARY VELIKOVSKY? *NEVER*.

LUCY, RAY? THIS IS MY BOYFRIEND, WESLEY DODDS.

HI, WESLEY. AREN'T *YOU* A CUTIE. THIS IS *MY* BEAU, DR. RAYMOND KESSLER.

PLEASURE TO MEET YOU, WESLEY.

LIKEWISE, RAYMOND. NNN. QUITE A *GRIP* YOU'VE GOT THERE.

I GET A LOT OF PRACTICE AT THESE SORTS OF FUNCTIONS.

DID I HEAR YOU CALL VELIKOVSKY "LEGENDARY"? YOU OBVIOUSLY HAVEN'T HEARD HIM PLAY *LATELY*.

WELL, ACTUALLY, I'VE NEVER HEARD HIM PLAY LIVE AT *ALL*. BUT I DOUBT THAT A MAN OF HIS STATURE COULD *EVER* FALL APPRECIABLY.

17

DON'T PAY TOO MUCH ATTENTION TO DR. TURNER, WESLEY. HE'S BEEN GRUMPY ABOUT *EVERYTHING* SINCE HIS HANDS GAVE OUT.

THAT'S ALL RIGHT, RAYMOND. I LIKE A GOOD SPAR NOW AND AGAIN.

OH, THERE GO THE LIGHTS. WE SHOULD GET OURSELVES IN FOR THE PERFORMANCE.

YOU KNOW, VELIKOVSKY'S HAD A WHOLE *SECOND LIFE* SINCE COMING TO THE STATES.

I'M *REALLY* EXCITED, DIAN. THANKS AGAIN FOR ARRANGING THIS.

YOU CAN THANK ME *LATER*.

Though it would make me happier to have you tell me about your second life.

THANK YOU.

CLAP CLAP CLAP CLAP

To explain why a man as cultured as yourself--

--As secure as yourself--

--Would feel the need to dress up at night in that outrageous getup.

Why do you live behind that mask of yours, Wesley?

18

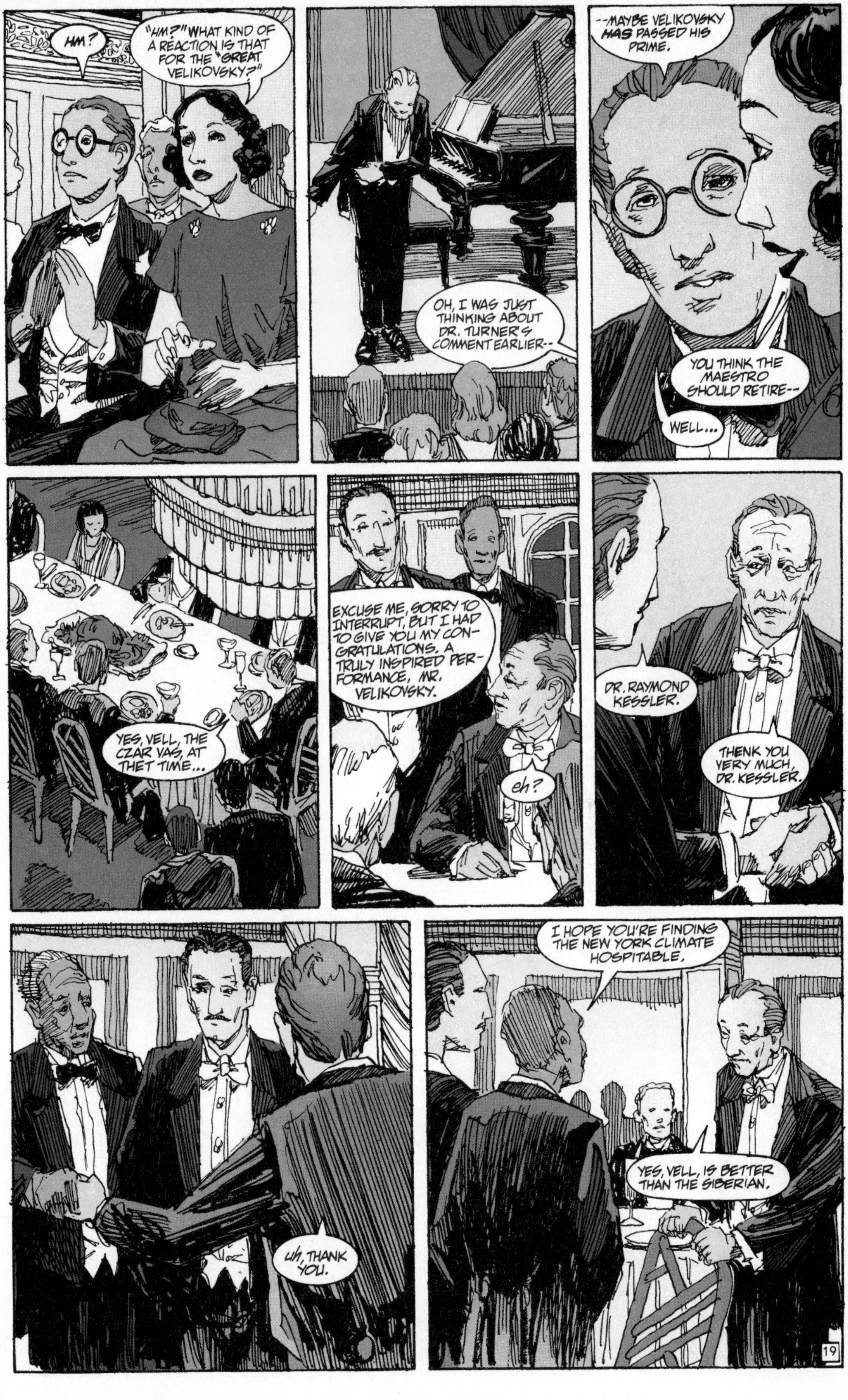
HM?
"HM?" WHAT KIND OF A REACTION IS THAT FOR THE "GREAT VELIKOVSKY?"
OH, I WAS JUST THINKING ABOUT DR. TURNER'S COMMENT EARLIER--
--MAYBE VELIKOVSKY HAS PASSED HIS PRIME.
YOU THINK THE MAESTRO SHOULD RETIRE--
WELL...
YES, VELL, THE CZAR VAS, AT THET TIME...
EXCUSE ME, SORRY TO INTERRUPT, BUT I HAD TO GIVE YOU MY CONGRATULATIONS. A TRULY INSPIRED PERFORMANCE, MR. VELIKOVSKY.
eh?
DR. RAYMOND KESSLER.
THENK YOU VERY MUCH, DR. KESSLER.
uh, THANK YOU.
I HOPE YOU'RE FINDING THE NEW YORK CLIMATE HOSPITABLE.
YES, VELL, IS BETTER THAN THE SIBERIAN.
19

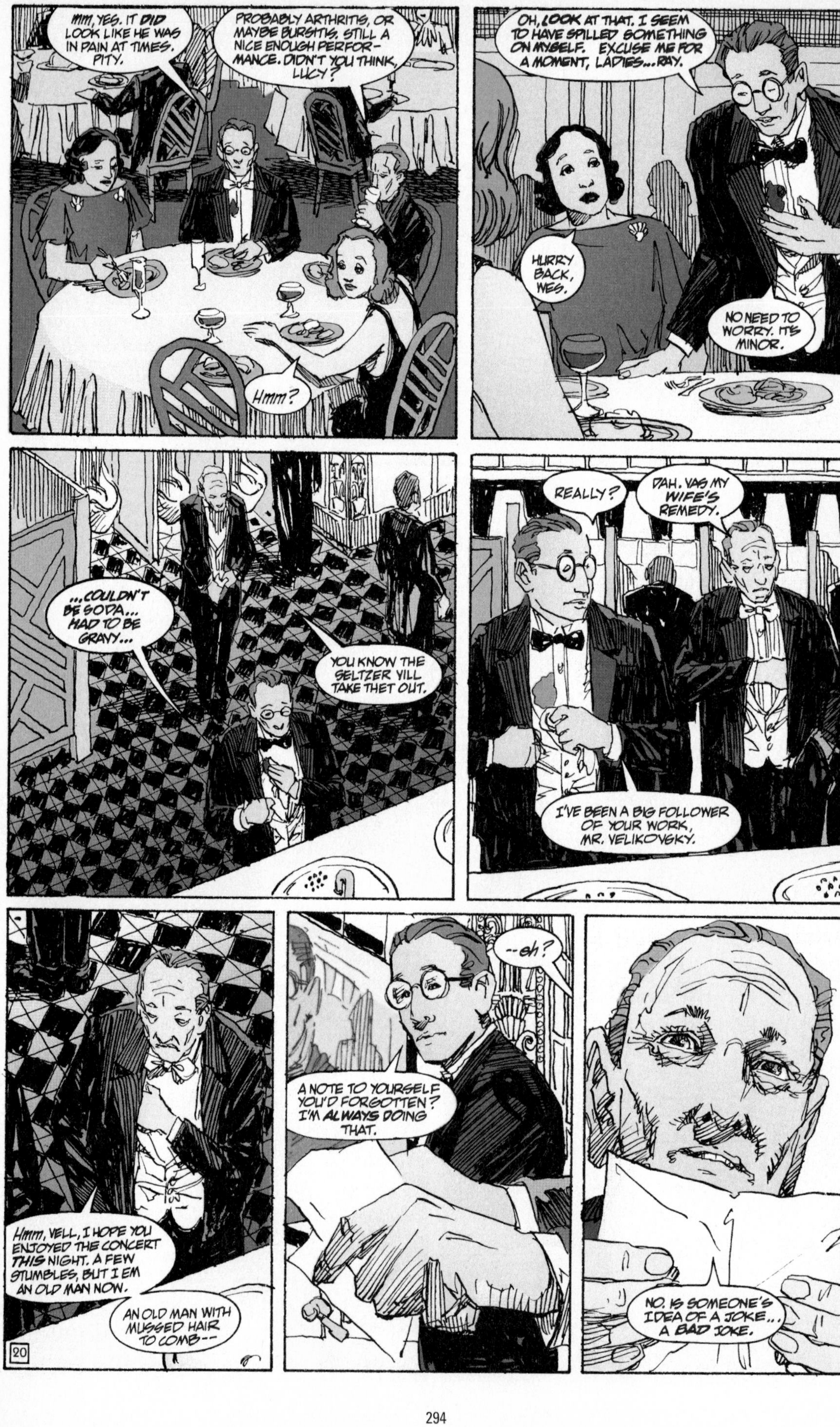

MM, YES. IT DID LOOK LIKE HE WAS IN PAIN AT TIMES. PITY.
PROBABLY ARTHRITIS, OR MAYBE BURSITIS. STILL A NICE ENOUGH PERFORMANCE. DIDN'T YOU THINK, LUCY?
Hmm?
OH, LOOK AT THAT. I SEEM TO HAVE SPILLED SOMETHING ON MYSELF. EXCUSE ME FOR A MOMENT, LADIES... RAY.
HURRY BACK, WES.
NO NEED TO WORRY. IT'S MINOR.
...COULDN'T BE SODA... HAD TO BE GRAVY...
YOU KNOW THE SELTZER VILL TAKE THET OUT.
REALLY?
DAH. VAS MY WIFE'S REMEDY.
I'VE BEEN A BIG FOLLOWER OF YOUR WORK, MR. VELIKOVSKY.
Hmm, VELL, I HOPE YOU ENJOYED THE CONCERT THIS NIGHT. A FEW STUMBLES, BUT I EM AN OLD MAN NOW.
AN OLD MAN WITH MUSSED HAIR TO COMB--
20
--eh?
A NOTE TO YOURSELF YOU'D FORGOTTEN? I'M ALWAYS DOING THAT.
NO, IS SOMEONE'S IDEA OF A JOKE... A BAD JOKE.

EXCUSE ME.

Permanent Retirement

--AND GOOD SEEING *YOU* AGAIN, RAY. YOU TAKE CARE OF MY COUSIN, NOW!

NO NEED TO WORRY ABOUT *THAT*, DIAN. GOODNIGHT.

GOODNIGHT. COME ON, RAY, LET'S GO!

WELL THAT WAS SPIRITED, BUT I'M GLAD TO FINALLY BE *ALONE* WITH YOU. I WAS HOPING WE--

ACTUALLY, DIAN, THOUGH I HATE TO DO IT, I'M AFRAID I'M GOING TO HAVE TO CALL IT A NIGHT.

IT'S ANOTHER EARLY MORNING FOR ME TOMORROW, BUT LET'S *DO* GET TOGETHER IN THE EVENING AND FINISH THIS DISCUSSION.

WESLEY--

NO, DON'T WORRY ABOUT ME, I'LL JUST CATCH A CAB. GOODNIGHT!

An early morning or a late night?

21

295

UNHH! CHRIST!

NOT NOW, *PLEASE* MY FRIENDS, NOT AGAIN TONIGHT--

RACHMANINOFF SUITS YOU, VLADIMIR VELIKOVSKY. IT IS DARK AND BROODING... LIKE THE NIGHT.

WHAT? GOOD LORD! HAVE YOU COME TO KILL ME?

22

I AM HERE NEITHER FOR YOUR LIFE NOR YOUR MUSIC, BUT ONLY TO INQUIRE ABOUT YOUR PERFORMANCE AT THE AMERICAN MEDICAL ASSOCIATION DINNER.

THERE IS NOT MUCH MUSIC LEFT IN THESE HANDS, I AM AFRAID. ARTHRITIS. THE BRANDY HELPS, BUT LESS SO EACH DAY.

PLEASE.... ASK YOUR QUESTIONS.

I HAVE REASON TO BELIEVE THAT YOU RECEIVED A PRESCRIPTION NOTICE BEFORE YOU PLAYED. IS THIS SO?

THAT WAS FROM YOU? I THOUGHT IT A JOKE. "PERMANENT RETIREMENT." A BIT *DRAMATIC* DON'T YOU THINK?

THE NOTE WAS NOT OF MY DEVISING. I SEEK ITS PRACTITIONER--

OH! CHRIST! UNNH--!

VELIKOVSKY! YOUR FATE IS UPON YOU--

UNHHH! AAAAH! HURRF!

--QUICKLY, YOU MUST TELL ME WHO GAVE YOU THE PRESCRIPTION WHAT DID HE LOOK LIKE?

BLACK--

HE WAS NEGRO?

--AND WHITE... ALWAYS...BLACK AND WHI--

23

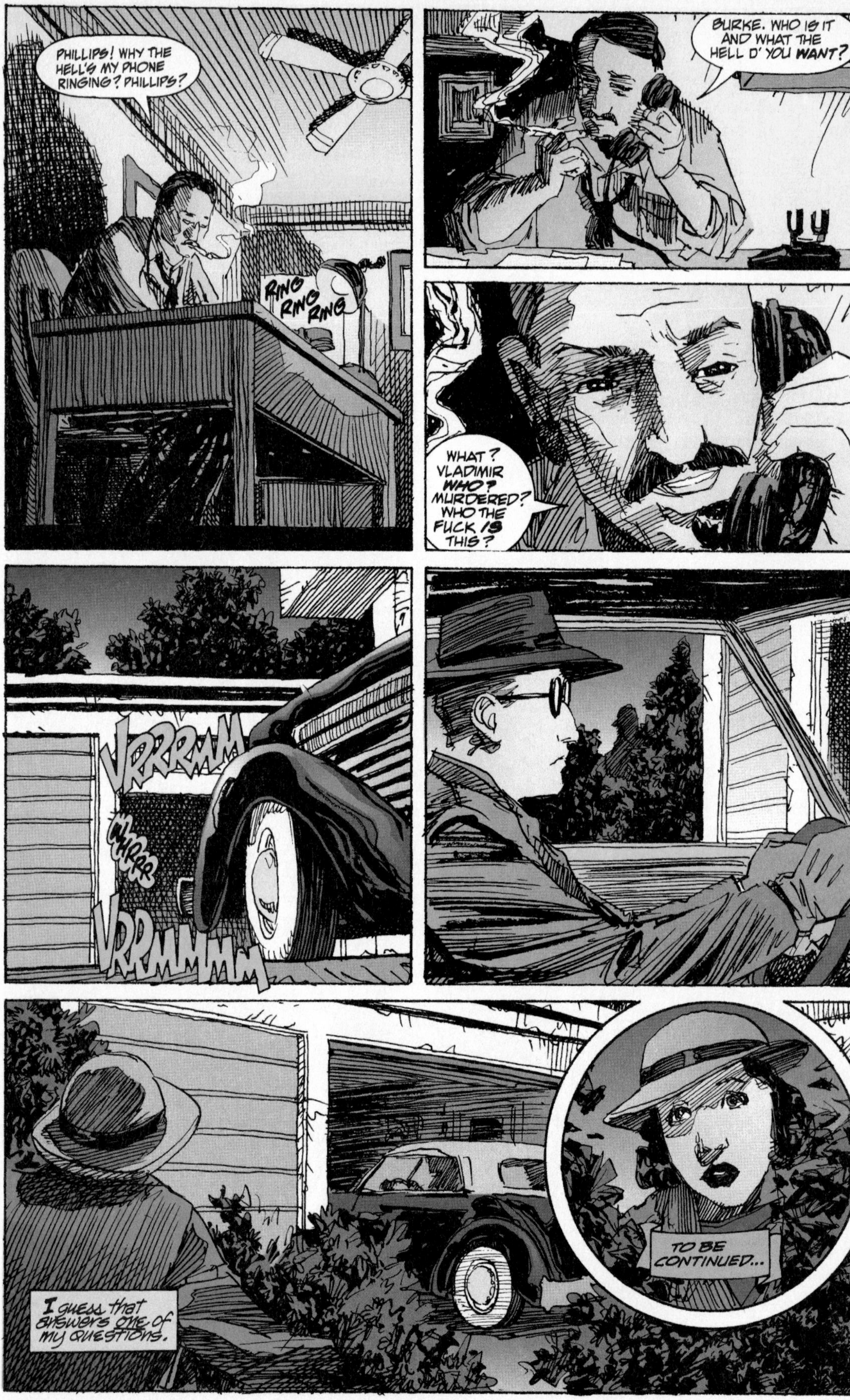
PHILLIPS! WHY THE HELL'S MY PHONE RINGING? PHILLIPS?
RING RING RING
BURKE. WHO IS IT AND WHAT THE HELL D' YOU WANT?
WHAT? VLADIMIR WHO? MURDERED? WHO THE FUCK IS THIS?
VRRRAM
VRRMMMM
I guess that answers one of my questions.
TO BE CONTINUED...

MATT WAGNER
STEVEN T. SEAGLE

GUY DAVIS
VINCE LOCKE

SANDMAN MYSTERY THEATRE

"...THE SONATA CUT SHORT BY AN UNEXPECTED NOTE."

ACT 2 dr.death OF 4

GAVIN WILSON
RICHARD BRUNING

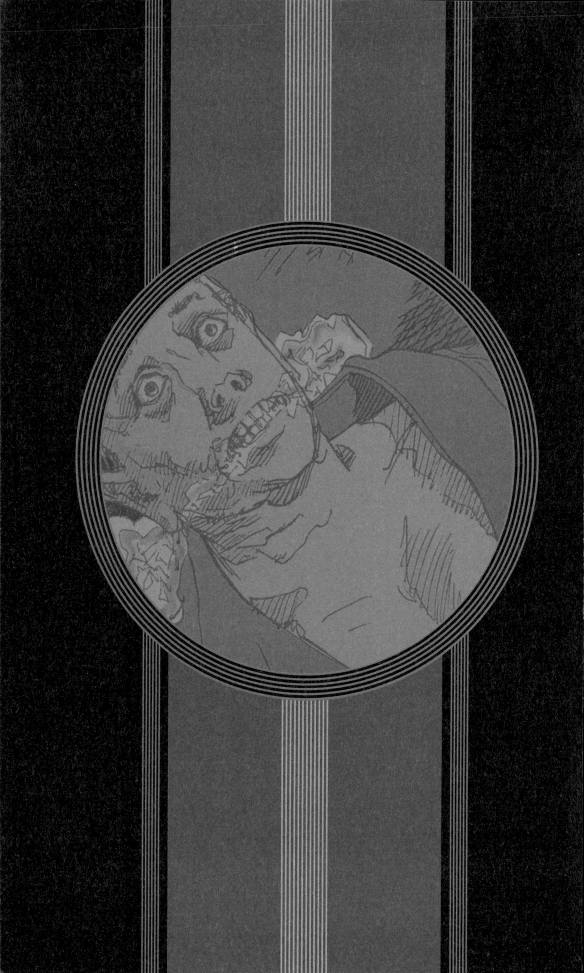

THAT'S IT, BABY...

C'MON, LITTLE GIRL--

OH! RAY... OH--OHHH--

FFLTCH

RAY?

HOW YOU HOLDIN' UP, BABY?

JESUS, I *HOPE* SO.

THAT WAS *SO* GOOD. I REALLY FELT YOU IN ME.

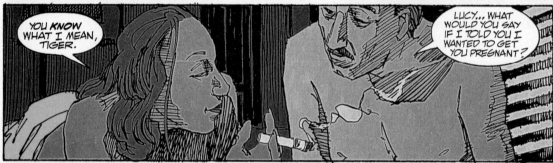

YOU *KNOW* WHAT I MEAN, TIGER.

LUCY... WHAT WOULD YOU SAY IF I TOLD YOU I WANTED TO GET YOU PREGNANT?

IS THAT A PROPOSAL OR A PROPOSITION?

WHAT IF IT'S *BOTH*? COME HERE, BABY.

AGAIN? AL*READY*? RAY, YOU--

THAT'S RIGHT, I *AM*.

WELL, OKAY... I MEAN, YES, DARL--

OH RAY! P-PLEASE, RAY... OHHH... YES, RAY...

NNNNNNNH...

2

What happens when you get what you want?

I've convinced myself more than ever that Wesley is secretly the Sandman, but NOW what?

Do I try to understand Wesley's evasiveness?

Do I confront him?

Do I leave him altogether? That would probably be the safest thing.

Maybe I should just go to sleep.

But what good would that do? I just know I won't be able to rest tonight.

I'll be up and awake. Wondering.

Wondering and worrying about you, Wes...

Afraid that you might be hurt...

Or worse...

Afraid that I may never see you again...

...Afraid that I will.

3

Why is this so difficult?

...AND WHAT DOES THIS MEAN...?

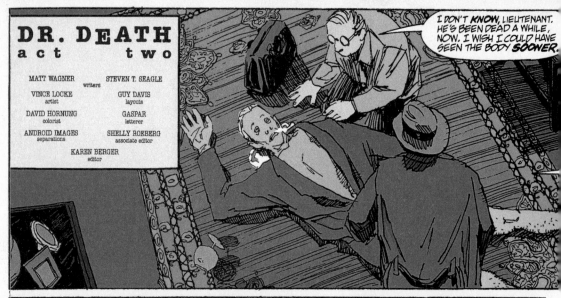

DR. DEATH
act two

MATT WAGNER
STEVEN T. SEAGLE
writers

VINCE LOCKE
artist

GUY DAVIS
layouts

DAVID HORNUNG
colorist

GASPAR
letterer

ANDROID IMAGES
separations

SHELLY ROEBERG
associate editor

KAREN BERGER
editor

I DON'T **KNOW**, LIEUTENANT. HE'S BEEN DEAD A WHILE, NOW. I WISH I COULD HAVE SEEN THE BODY **SOONER**.

WELL, **HOWEVER** YOU GOT THE TIP, IT'S NEARLY NOON--

--AND I'D SAY THIS MAN HAS BEEN DEAD SINCE LATE LAST NIGHT.

WE'VE ALREADY LOST AN AWFUL LOT OF VALUABLE INFORMATION. I'M NOT EVEN SURE IF I'LL BE ABLE TO--

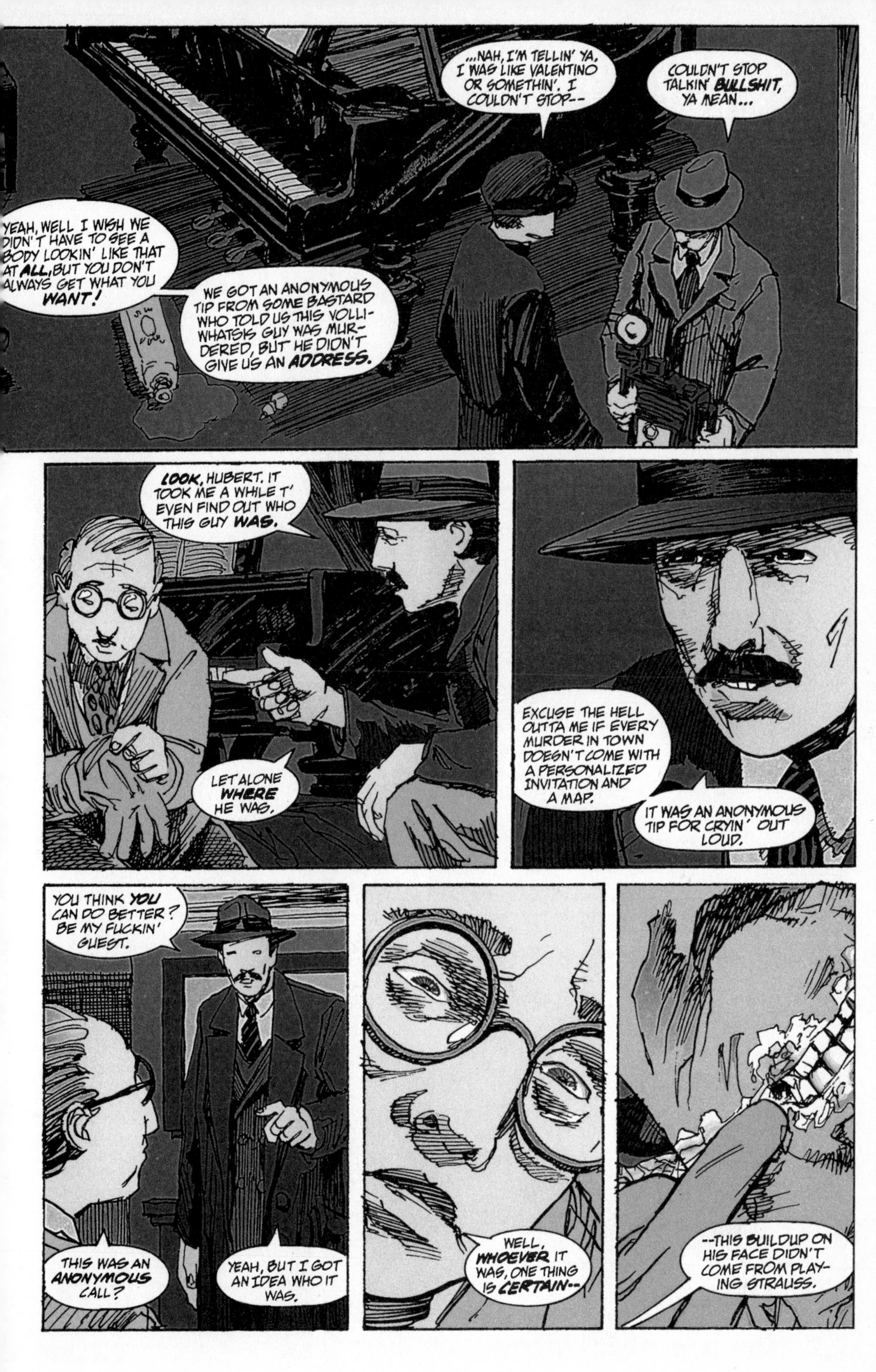
YEAH, WELL I WISH WE DIDN'T HAVE TO SEE A BODY LOOKIN' LIKE THAT AT ALL, BUT YOU DON'T ALWAYS GET WHAT YOU WANT!
WE GOT AN ANONYMOUS TIP FROM SOME BASTARD WHO TOLD US THIS VOLLI-WHATSIS GUY WAS MUR-DERED, BUT HE DIDN'T GIVE US AN ADDRESS.
...NAH, I'M TELLIN' YA, I WAS LIKE VALENTINO OR SOMETHIN'. I COULDN'T STOP--
COULDN'T STOP TALKIN' BULLSHIT, YA MEAN...
LOOK, HUBERT. IT TOOK ME A WHILE T' EVEN FIND OUT WHO THIS GUY WAS.
LET ALONE WHERE HE WAS.
EXCUSE THE HELL OUTTA ME IF EVERY MURDER IN TOWN DOESN'T COME WITH A PERSONALIZED INVITATION AND A MAP.
IT WAS AN ANONYMOUS TIP FOR CRYIN' OUT LOUD.
YOU THINK YOU CAN DO BETTER? BE MY FUCKIN' GUEST.
THIS WAS AN ANONYMOUS CALL?
YEAH, BUT I GOT AN IDEA WHO IT WAS.
WELL, WHOEVER IT WAS, ONE THING IS CERTAIN--
--THIS BUILDUP ON HIS FACE DIDN'T COME FROM PLAY-ING STRAUSS.

BING BONG

I'M COMING!

FOR CRYING OUT LOUD... STOP **RING-ING** ALREADY...

BING BONG

LUCY? WHAT **TIME** IS IT?

OH, I'M SURE IT'S **EARLY**, DIAN, BUT I JUST **HAD** TO STOP BY. I AM HAVING THE **BEST** MORNING. I'M **SO** ENERGETIC FOR SOME REASON.

DID YOU STOP BY FURROWS FOR COFFEE? SAY...TWENTY OR THIRTY CUPS?

NO, SILLY. I'M IN LOVE. I...I THINK RAY IS GOING TO ASK ME TO MARRY HIM! CAN YOU **BELIEVE** IT?

OH, LISTEN TO ME. BABBLING ON AND ON. WHERE ARE MY MANNERS? HOW ARE **YOU** DOING THIS MORNING? YOU LOOK A LITTLE, A LITTLE—

TIRED? THAT'S PROBABLY BECAUSE I DIDN'T SLEEP ONE WINK LAST NIGHT, I—

OH, I JUST CAN'T **STAND** IT. CAN YOU IMAGINE ME **MARRIED? ME?** OF ALL PEOPLE?

WELL ACTUALLY...

LET'S HAVE LUNCH. MY TREAT. I WON'T TAKE "NO" FOR AN ANSWER SO GO MAKE YOURSELF PRESENTABLE, COUSIN.

PRESENTABLE? GEE, I HOPE YOU HAVE AN **HOUR OR TWO**—

POSH. DON'T BE SO **HARD** ON YOURSELF, DIAN. I DIDN'T MEAN IT IN **THAT** WAY.

OF COURSE you didn't.

6

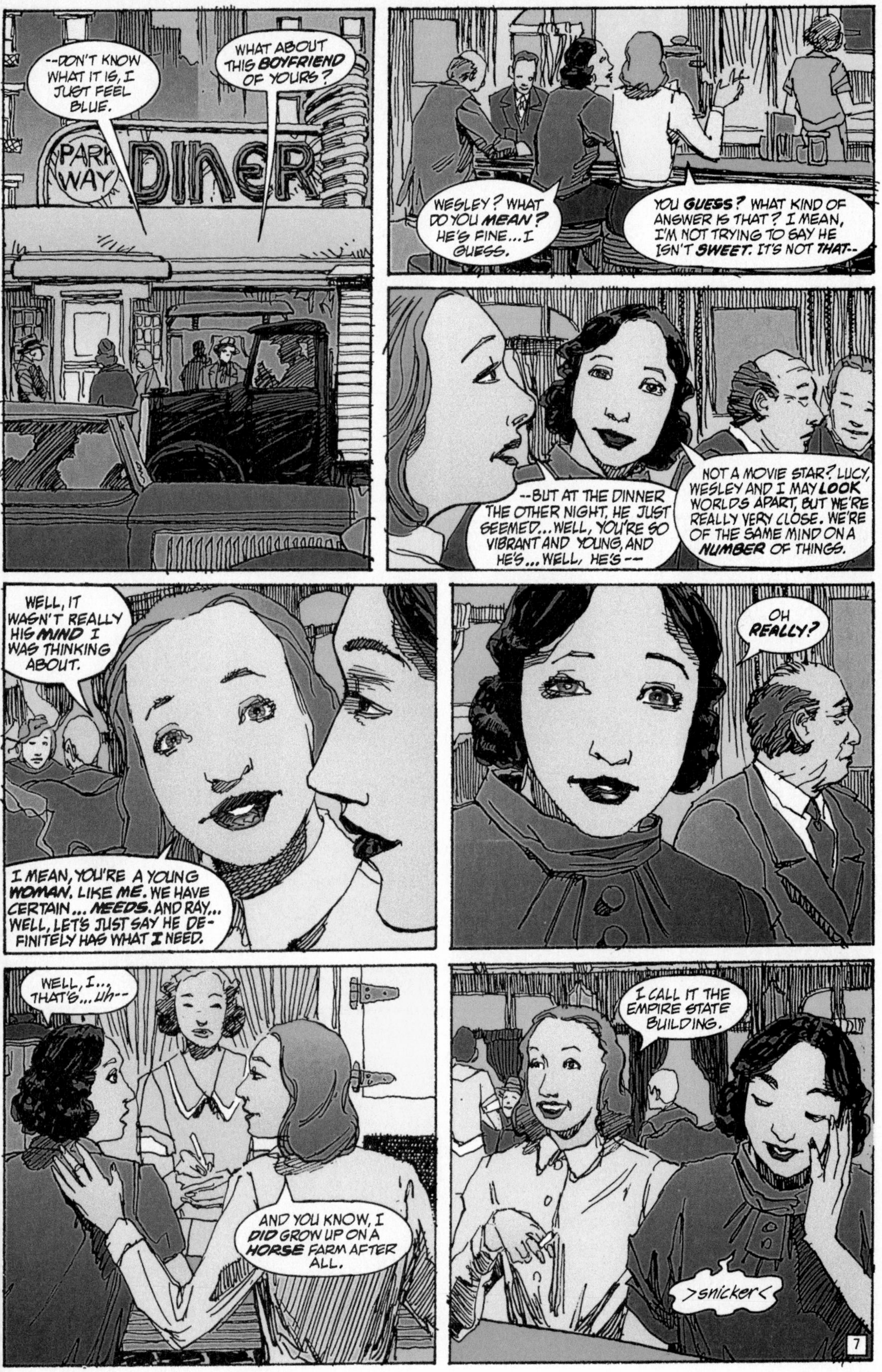
--DON'T KNOW WHAT IT IS, I JUST FEEL BLUE.
WHAT ABOUT THIS BOYFRIEND OF YOURS?
PARK WAY DINER
WESLEY? WHAT DO YOU MEAN? HE'S FINE... I GUESS.
YOU GUESS? WHAT KIND OF ANSWER IS THAT? I MEAN, I'M NOT TRYING TO SAY HE ISN'T SWEET. IT'S NOT THAT--
--BUT AT THE DINNER THE OTHER NIGHT, HE JUST SEEMED... WELL, YOU'RE SO VIBRANT AND YOUNG, AND HE'S... WELL, HE'S--
NOT A MOVIE STAR? LUCY, WESLEY AND I MAY LOOK WORLDS APART, BUT WE'RE REALLY VERY CLOSE. WE'RE OF THE SAME MIND ON A NUMBER OF THINGS.
WELL, IT WASN'T REALLY HIS MIND I WAS THINKING ABOUT.
I MEAN, YOU'RE A YOUNG WOMAN. LIKE ME. WE HAVE CERTAIN... NEEDS. AND RAY... WELL, LET'S JUST SAY HE DEFINITELY HAS WHAT I NEED.
OH REALLY?
WELL, I... THAT'S... uh--
AND YOU KNOW, I DID GROW UP ON A HORSE FARM AFTER ALL.
I CALL IT THE EMPIRE STATE BUILDING.
>snicker<
7

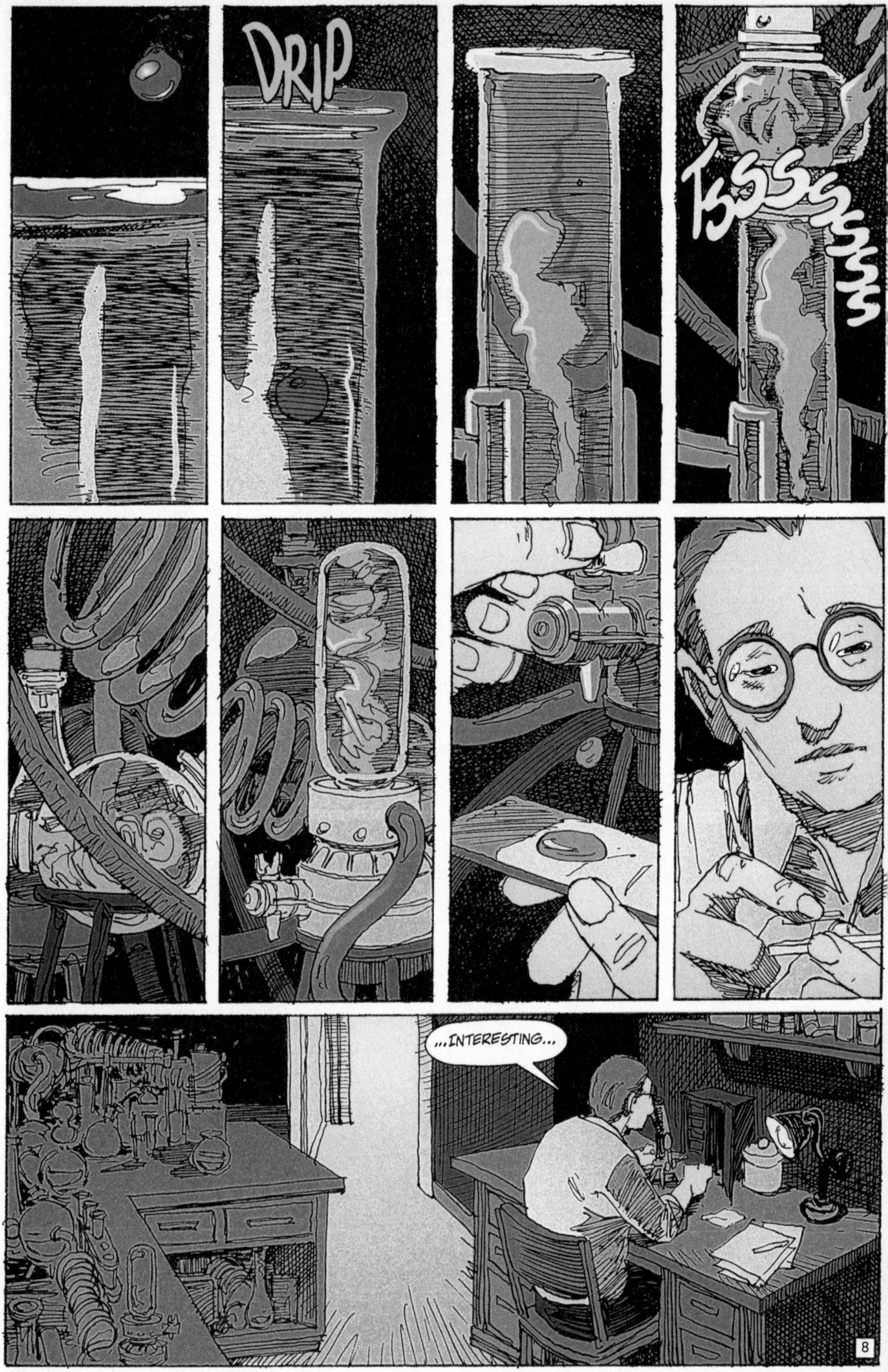
DRIP
TSSSSSSS
...INTERESTING...
8

--INTERESTING.

WHAT IN THE WORLD ARE YOU DOING WITH *THAT* IN YOUR STOMACH, VLADIMIR?

ACID-BASE REACTIONS AREN'T VERY PLEASURABLE GASTRO-INTESTINAL *COCKTAILS.*

HERE WE ARE...*uh-huh*... GOODNESS ME.

SORRY TO HAVE TO TELL YOU THIS--

--BUT THE INTENSITY OF THE DOINGS IN YOUR GUT INDICATE THAT YOU HAD TO SOMEHOW CONSUME HUGE AMOUNTS OF THE BASE FOLLOWED BY THE ACID.

THAT MEANS I'M GOING TO NEED YOUR *LIVER* TOO, MY FRIEND.

BUT IF YOU'LL PARDON THE INDISCRETION--

--WE *MAY* JUST GET TO THE BOTTOM OF THIS.

9

Lucy is quite the bundle of surprises.

Not only is she dating an older man...

--But she's apparently deeply involved with him sexually as well.

And I thought Wesley and *I* were adventurous.

But that's our relationship all over, isn't it, Wesley?

Committed, but not terribly advanced.

HELLO, WES?

DIAN! HELLO. IT'S GOOD TO HEAR YOUR VOICE. I WAS STARTING TO GO A LITTLE STIR CRAZY SITTING HERE AT MY DESK.

WELL THAT'S JUST ACES, BECAUSE I WAS ABOUT TO INVITE YOU OUT FOR AN EARLY DINNER...IF YOU'RE INTERESTED--?

INTERESTED, BUT UNAVAILABLE. I'VE BEEN UP WORKING ALL NIGHT AND I'M STILL NOT QUITE DONE WITH--

WES!

YOU-- YOU'RE ALWAYS BUSY. WHAT ABOUT FINDING TIME FOR ME? FOR US?

I--I'M SORRY, DIAN. I THOUGHT YOU UNDER-STOOD.

MY WORK DEMANDS A LOT OF TIME. I'M SURE YOU'LL SEE HOW HARD IT IS TO MANAGE THINGS WHEN YOU'RE NO LONGER LIVING WITH YOUR FATHER. IT'S--

AND JUST WHAT THE--WHAT THE *HELL* IS *THAT* SUPPOSED TO MEAN?

YOU THINK I'M JUST SOME IDLE *DEBUTANTE.* IS *THAT* IT?

I--NO, DIAN. OF COURSE NOT. THAT'S NOT WHAT I MEANT TO SAY AT ALL, I JUST--

10

I THINK IT'S *EXACTLY* WHAT YOU MEANT TO SAY--

--BUT AS FAR AS *I'M* CONCERNED, YOU CAN JUST TELL IT TO YOUR *WORK!* GOOD BYE!

DUMB, WESLEY... VERY DUMB.

--NO THANK YOU, DRIVER. I DON'T WANT MY BOYFRIEND TO KNOW HOW I GOT HERE, HE ISN'T EXPECTING ME.

THANKS ANYHOW! THE EXTRA QUARTER IS FOR YOU!

VRRRNM

-- THE *FUCK* YOU WILL!

...RAY--?

YOU ARE THE MOST *UNGRATEFUL* BASTARD TO EVER SET FOOT ON THIS EARTH, YOU KNOW THAT?

LIKE FATHER LIKE SON, *eh*, RAYMOND?

THAT'S IT--!

OH DEAR.

BING BONG

11

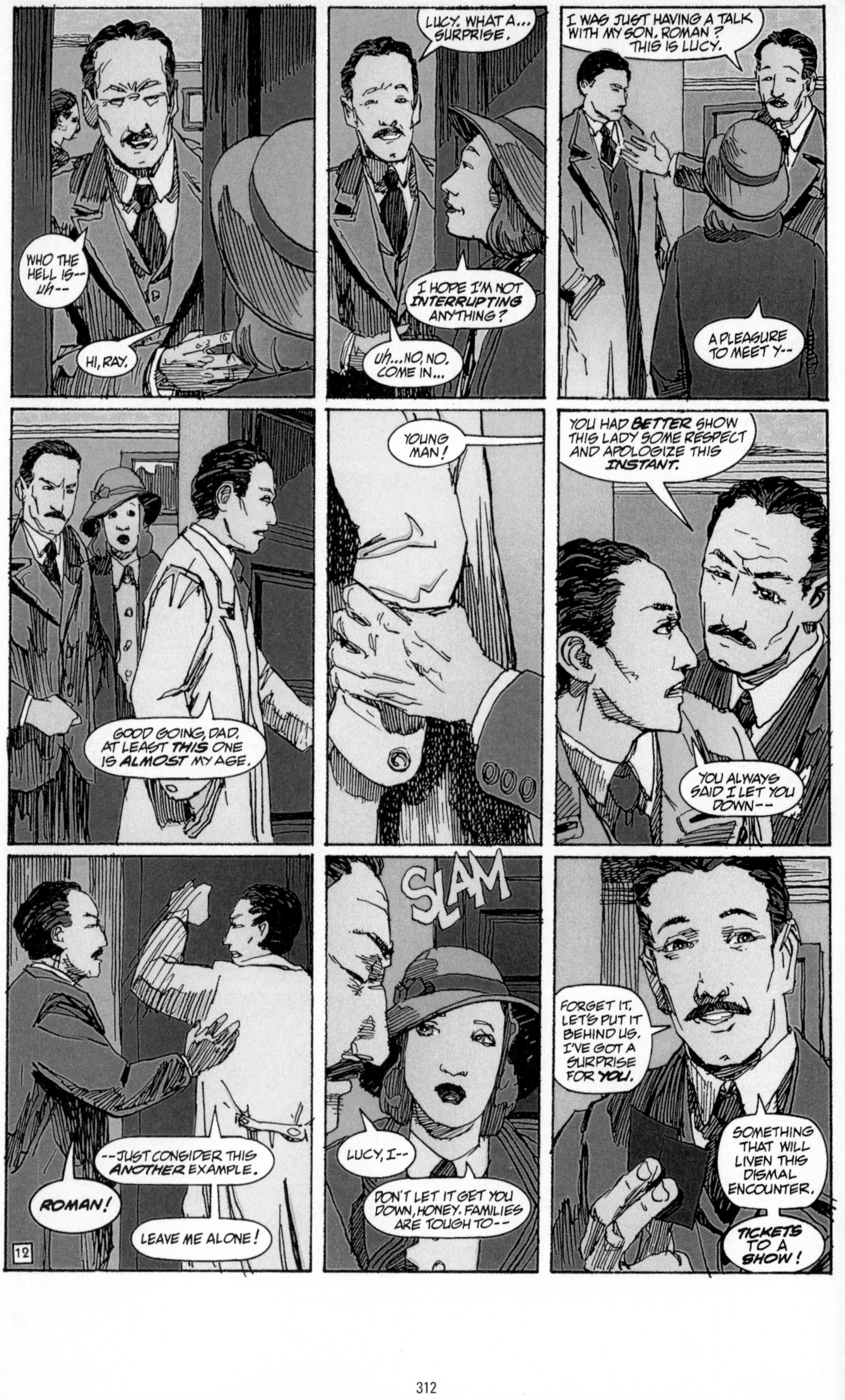
WHO THE HELL IS-- uh--
HI, RAY.
LUCY. WHAT A... SURPRISE.
I HOPE I'M NOT INTERRUPTING ANYTHING?
uh...NO, NO. COME IN...
I WAS JUST HAVING A TALK WITH MY SON. ROMAN? THIS IS LUCY.
A PLEASURE TO MEET Y--
GOOD GOING, DAD. AT LEAST THIS ONE IS ALMOST MY AGE.
YOUNG MAN!
YOU HAD BETTER SHOW THIS LADY SOME RESPECT AND APOLOGIZE THIS INSTANT.
YOU ALWAYS SAID I LET YOU DOWN--
--JUST CONSIDER THIS ANOTHER EXAMPLE.
ROMAN!
LEAVE ME ALONE!
12
SLAM
LUCY, I--
DON'T LET IT GET YOU DOWN, HONEY. FAMILIES ARE TOUGH TO--
FORGET IT. LET'S PUT IT BEHIND US. I'VE GOT A SURPRISE FOR YOU.
SOMETHING THAT WILL LIVEN THIS DISMAL ENCOUNTER.
TICKETS TO A SHOW!

KLEIN?

KLEIN!

--eh?

OH! IT'S *YOU*. PLEASE, DON'T SHOOT ME! REMEMBER MY ALLER--

SHOOT YA? WHAT TH' HELL'RE YOU TALKIN' ABOUT?

OH... BURKE, I'M SORRY, I THOUGHT YOU WERE... SOMEONE *ELSE*.

YEAH, WELL, I'M NOT. WHAT YA GOT FOR ME ON THAT STIFFED RUSSKIE?

OH, VELIKOVSKY... YES. STRANGE CASE.

FROM WHAT I CAN GATHER, HE DIED FROM AN ACUTE ACID-BASE REACTION IN HIS STOMACH.

SHOULD I BRING MY OWN GODDAMN TRANSLATOR OR YOU GOT ONE HIDDEN IN THE BROOM CLOSET?

SORRY. ESSENTIALLY, VELIKOVSKY ATE OR DRANK TWO THINGS WHICH WHEN MIXED, BOILED HIS STOMACH AND SUFFOCATED HIM BY BLISTERING HIS ESOPHAGUS.

EVEN MORE STRANGE IS THAT I BELIEVE THIS TO BE THE *SAME* CAUSE OF DEATH FOR EDDIE THE ENGINE ROBINSON.

SAME CAUSE? NAH. NO LINK WHATSOEVER BETWEEN THE DEFECTOR AND THE COON, KLEIN.

GUESS THAT'S WHY *I'M* THE DETECTIVE AND YOU'RE THE GRAVE ROBBER. KEEP WORKING, I'LL CHECK BACK WITH YOU LATER.

13

SLAM

COONS, HUH? WHAT DO YOU THINK OF JEWS?

HUBERT KLEIN--

BURKE HAS GONE. I LISTENED AS YOU SPOKE TO HIM. I *TOO* BELIEVE THESE KILLINGS TO BE CONNECTED.

YOU?!

THIS IS A NOTE GIVEN TO ONE OF THE MEN BEFORE HIS DEATH.

I'LL BET I KNOW WHAT THIS SAYS.

EDDIE ROBINSON HAD ONE, TOO.

HMM, ISN'T *THAT* STRANGE? SAME M.O. BUT A DIFFERENT MESSAGE. AND THIS WEIRD SYMBOL...

LOOKS TO BE *STAMPED* RATHER THAN PRINTED.

THE REACTION THAT KILLED VELIKOVSKY WOULD SUGGEST A *CHEMIST?*

UM...POSSIBLY, BUT CHEMISTS DON'T ISSUE *PRESCRIPTIONS.* MORE LIKELY A PHYSICIAN.

A *LEFT-HANDED* PHYSICIAN FROM THE SLANT OF BOTH WRITINGS.

YOU ARE A MAN OF KEEN SENSES, HUBERT KLEIN.

SHOULD YOU NEED TO CONTACT ME AGAIN, USE THE PERSONAL COLUMNS OF THE *TIMES.*

14

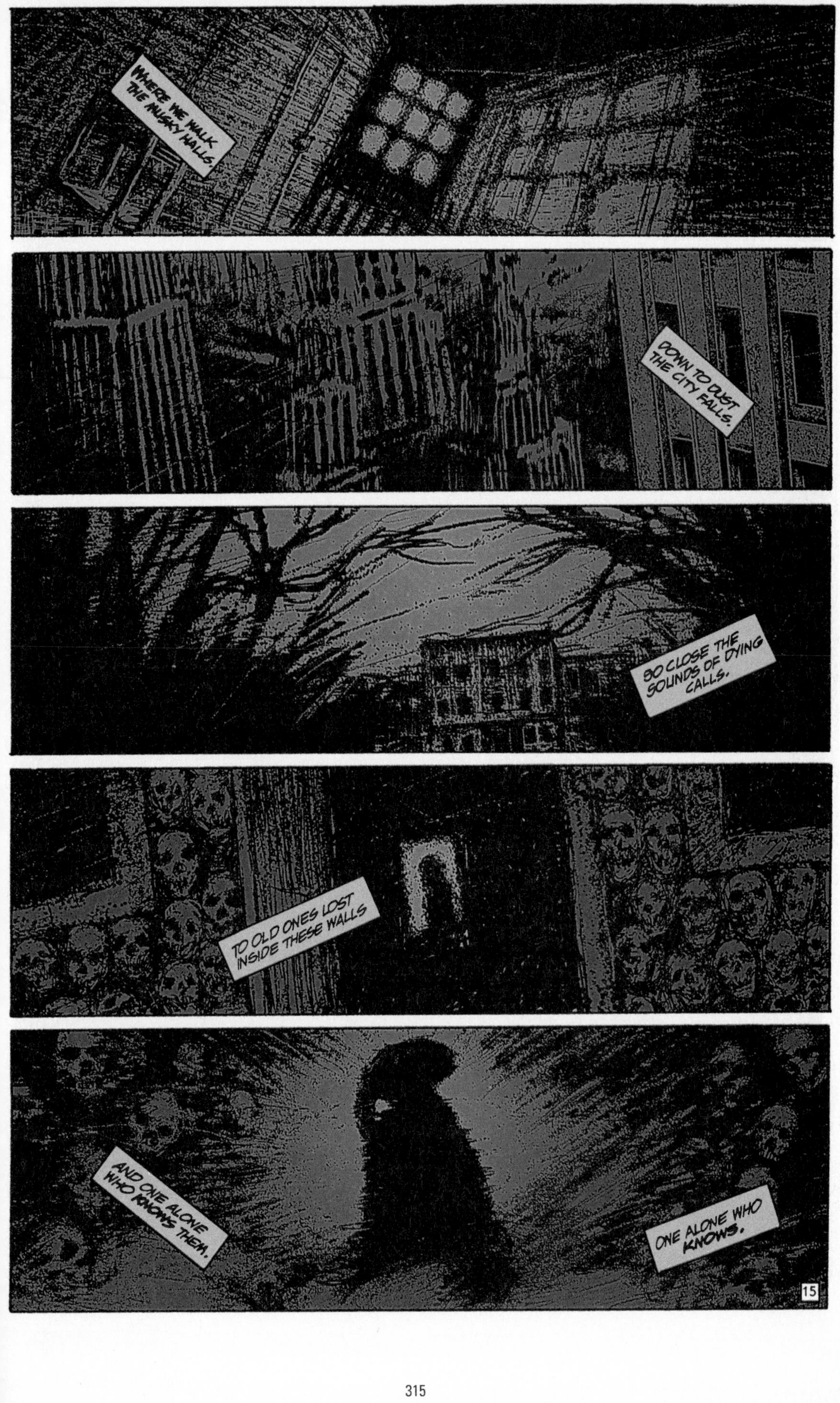
WHERE WE WALK THE MUSKY HALLS.
DOWN TO DUST THE CITY FALLS.
SO CLOSE THE SOUNDS OF DYING CALLS.
TO OLD ONES LOST INSIDE THESE WALLS
AND ONE ALONE WHO KNOWS THEM.
ONE ALONE WHO KNOWS.
15

OH...OH MY **GOODNESS.**

I haven't felt this... *scared* since my mother passed away.

I never have dreams like that. What could have caused such **horrible** visions?

Minnie's mother is a spiritualist. Maybe I should call *her* and ask her what it all *means.*

WEGLEY--?

What an *awful* dream.

Oh, get a grip on yourself, Dian.

You just had a bad day and a bad night was *sure* to follow.

The only thing you need is to clear up all of those oppressive thoughts swirling around in your head.

--SO HE TELLS THE DANCER, "NO, BUT THOSE AREN'T MY **TOES!"** Heh heh!

TONIGHT ONLY **CLACKIE BROWN**

HEH...GET IT? **TOES...**?

ALL RIGHT, WELL...DID I TELL YOU THE ONE ABOUT THE **WAITER?** GOOD!

16

316

SO, THIS WAITER IS CALLED OVER BY THIS GENTLEMAN--

--AND THE GENTLEMAN SAYS, "WAITER, THERE'S A FLY IN MY SOUP!"

AND THE WAITER SAYS--GET *THIS* HE SAYS--

"THAT MUST BE THE ONE THE BROOKLYN *DODGERS* ARE LOOKING FOR!" HEH HEH!

THAT'S ALL FOR NOW, LADIES AND GERMS! GOOOOOOOD NIGHT!

STOP RIGHT *THERE*, YOU LITTLE CREEP.

SOMETHING WRONG, MR. TROWER? YOU LOOK *ANGRY*--

AT LEAST I DON'T LOOK *BORED* LIKE THE AUDIENCE. YOU TOLD ME YOU HAD ALL NEW JOKES, YOU LITTLE SONUVABITCH, I WAS GIVIN' YOU A *BREAK* HERE.

WELL SURE, I *HAD* NEW MATERIAL, BUT THAT WAS A TOUGH CROWD... UH...I DECIDED THE *CLASSICS* WOULD FLY BETTER. YOU KNOW...

WHAT ABOUT ALL THEM SKINNY JOKES? HUH? AT LEAST *THOSE* USED T'GET LAUGHS.

AHHH...NOBODY *LIKES* THOSE JOKES ANYMORE. THEY WANNA THINK THE DEPRESSION'S OVER--

LOOK, CLACKIE. WE BOTH KNOW THE DEAL HERE. YOU JUST AIN'T GOT IT ANYMORE. WHAT THE SMACK DIDN'T *TEAR* OUTTA YOU, THE *BOOZE* PICKLED.

EITHER WAY, I CAN'T JUST SUPPORT YOUR PATHETIC PUSS NO MORE. THERE'S THE DOOR--

17

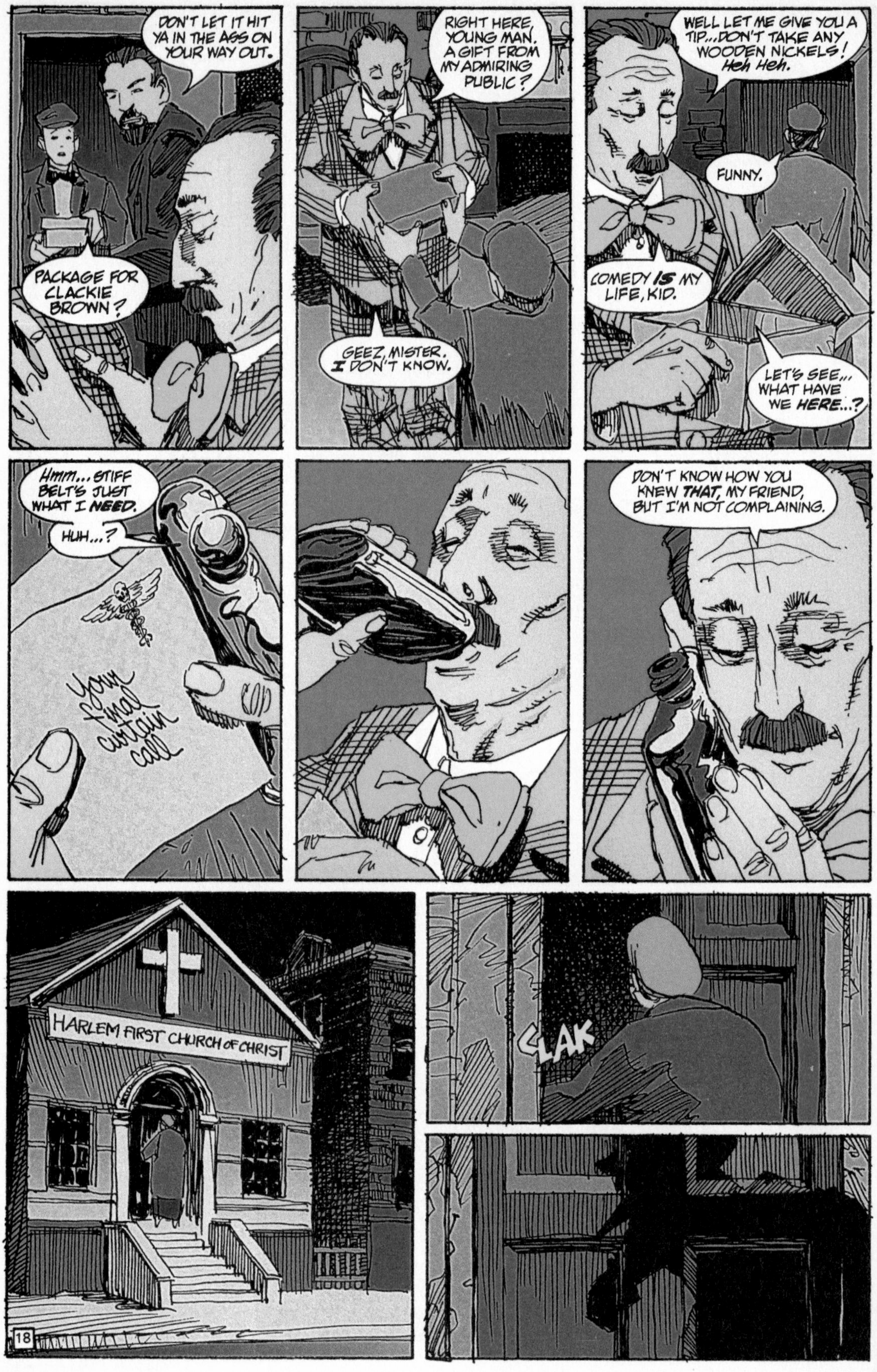
DON'T LET IT HIT YA IN THE ASS ON YOUR WAY OUT.
PACKAGE FOR CLACKIE BROWN?
RIGHT HERE, YOUNG MAN. A GIFT FROM MY ADMIRING PUBLIC?
GEEZ, MISTER, I DON'T KNOW.
WELL LET ME GIVE YOU A TIP...DON'T TAKE ANY WOODEN NICKELS! Heh Heh.
FUNNY.
COMEDY IS MY LIFE, KID.
LET'S SEE... WHAT HAVE WE HERE...?
Hmm... STIFF BELT'S JUST WHAT I NEED.
HUH...?
your final curtain call
DON'T KNOW HOW YOU KNEW THAT, MY FRIEND, BUT I'M NOT COMPLAINING.
HARLEM FIRST CHURCH of CHRIST
18
CLAK

JESUS DONE TOL' ME-- ♪ HE'S COMIN' HOME-- ♪

--JESUS DONE TOL' ME-- ♪ HE'S COMIN' HOME-- ♪

MIRANDA ROBINSON?

--JESUS--!

YOU STAY RIGHT THERE OR I'M GONNA LAY YOU OUT.

I AM NOT HERE TO *HURT* YOU. I HAVE COME FOR INFORMATION REGARDING YOUR BROTHER, EDDIE.

WELL... I DONE *TALKED* TO THE POLICE AN' I AIN'T GOT NOTHIN' MORE TO TELL NO SPOOK WORKIN' WITH 'EM!

I AM NOT WITH THE POLICE. BUT, I DO INTEND TO SEE YOUR BROTHERS KILLER BROUGHT TO JUSTICE.

MISTER, I *LOVED* EDDIE. I *DID*. BUT HE DID STUFF TO HISSELF THAT HE GONNA HAVE TO EXPLAIN TO THE LORD ALMIGHTY JESUS HIS-SELF. DIDN'T NOBODY KILL EDDIE BUT EDDIE.

MISS ROBINSON... YOUR BROTHER WAS MURDERED. I CAN ASSURE YOU OF THAT.

MURDERED? EDDIE?

YES.

OH, EDDIE. I'M *SORRY*. I DIDN'T MEAN YOU NO DISRESPECT.

BUT THEM DRUGS YOU GOT FOR DELIVERIN' THEM PACKAGES...

... I *TOL'* YOU THAT WEREN'T GONNA COME TO NO GOOD.

MAY THE LORD JESUS CHRIST HAVE MERCY ON YOUR SOUL, EDDIE--

AN' MERCY ON MINE TOO.

19

319

GETTA LOAD A **THIS** PLACE. *SHEESH!* SOME PEOPLE GOT IT ROUGH.

MAY I **HELP** YOU?

SURE, BUB. GOTA PIANO HERE FOR A.... "WESLY DOBBS?"

A PIANO? THERE MUST BE SOME **MISTAKE.**

NOPE. LOOK RIGHT THERE. THAT'S YOUR ADDRESS AIN'T IT?

WELL YES, IT IS. BUT I CAN **ASSURE** YOU THAT MASTER DODDS HAS **NOT** ORDERED A PIANO--

MUSTA DID. I'M LOOKIN' AT IT RIGHT THERE--

NOW SEE **HERE.** YOU CAN'T JUST LEAVE A PIANO--

I suppose I should feel guilty...a little bit.

ISN'T THERE SOMEONE I COULD **PHONE** TO TALK TO ABOUT THIS--?

But then again, this is what you yourself do, isn't it, Wes?

Behave in a bold fashion to arrive at the answers you need.

*Well, what's good for the **gander**...*

20

Besides, what other choice do I have?

I remember once, when I was in Catholic school--

--I brought my mother's ring for show and tell.

At the end of the day, it was missing from my desk.

Someone told me that Ruda, who was my best friend in the whole world, had taken it.

I was crestfallen, but I asked her if she had it.

She looked me straight in the eye and said, "Of course not, Dian. We're best friends. How could you think that?"

Two weeks later I found the ring in her jewelry box.

I took it and I never spoke to her again. We both knew why.

How much better it would have been if she had just told me the truth when I asked--

SLAM

SHOOT!

CH-CHOK

RRRING

DODDS RESIDENCE... HELLO? IS ANY-ONE THERE?

--and not forced me to find it on my own.

21

ROBERT LI! N.Y.U. MUST BE TREATING ITS STATISTICS PROFESSORS *VERY* WELL THESE DAYS.

WESLEY! YOU'RE LOOKING FIT!

ME? YOU STILL LOOK THE SAME AS YOU DID THE DAY I MET YOU AT THE NATIONAL HONOR SOCIETY MEETING.

IT IS THE CHINESE IN ME. IT KEEPS ME *YOUTHFUL*.

I WAS IN THE NEIGHBORHOOD AND WONDERED IF YOU STILL HAUNT THE EDISON AT LUNCH.

STATISTICALLY SOLID, MY FRIEND.

I'D HEARD YOU MOVED BACK TO TOWN. HOW'S IT FEEL TO BE BACK IN THE *BIG APPLE*?

NOSTALGIC. SPEAKING OF WHICH... *MENTAL CHALLENGE.*

HA! YOU REMEMBER.

I CHALLENGE YOU, SOCIETY BROTHER, TO COMPILE A LIST OF ALL THE... UH... *LEFT-HANDED PHYSICIANS* ON MANHATTAN ISLAND.

SIMPLICITY ITSELF. I CHALLENGE *YOU*, SOCIETY BROTHER, TO... *MEMORIZE* TWO COMPLETE PAGES OF THE *NEW YORK TIMES*.

I MAY HAVE CHOSEN THE WRONG DAY TO *CHALLENGE* YOU, ROBERT! THAT'S A *TOUGH* ONE.

WE'LL MEET AGAIN, SAY THE DAY AFTER TOMORROW? WINNER BUYS NOT *ONLY* DRINKS AND DINNER, BUT TWO TICKETS TO THE *OPERA* AS WELL.

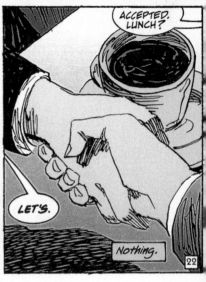

ACCEPTED. LUNCH?

LET'S.

Nothing.

22

322

I don't believe that there was no trace of... of anything.

I can't be imagining all this... can I?

There are such things as coincidences after all—

YOU LOOK LIKE YOU'RE ON ANOTHER WORLD.

LUCY?

IN THE FLESH. I JUST DROPPED BY TO INTRODUCE RAY TO UNCLE LARRY. YOU KNOW... MEET THE *FAMILY* AND ALL.

OF COURSE. I'M SORRY, I JUST DIDN'T *SEE* YOU THERE, I'VE BEEN A BIT PREOCCUPIED TODAY.

WELL I HOPE HE'S TALL, DARK AND HANDSOME! >giggle<

NOW, LUCY. DON'T TEASE. WESLEY IS A CHARMING CHAP... IN HIS OWN WAY.

Uh, LISTEN, WHY DON'T I JUST GO AND SEE WHAT'S KEEPING DADDY?

WE'LL BE RIGHT HERE WAITING.

SURE THING.

DADDY?

23

--NO, NO. I'LL COME DOWN TO THE *STATION.* I'M TRYING TO KEEP THESE THINGS AWAY FROM THE HOUSE... *YOU* KNOW...

...NO, NOTHING LIKE *THAT,* IT'S JUST THAT SHE GOT A LITTLE TOO CLOSE TO THE LAST SITUATION AND--

EXACTLY...EXACTLY... SHE *IS* MY LITTLE GIRL--

"*Daddy's little girl.*"

--RA-AAAY! STOP IT! >giggle<

WHAT IF DIAN COMES BACK?

WE'LL HEAR HER.

How many fathers really know what their little girls are up to?

YOU'RE SOOOOO BAD.

Or would really want to know what lurks inside their... I guess I should say "hearts."

Then again...maybe Lucy's right.

Perhaps there is only one way to really know the man you love.

324

MATT WAGNER
STEVEN T. SEAGLE

GUY DAVIS
VINCE LOCKE

SANDMAN MYSTERY THEATRE

"...SKIN ON SKIN, THEIR SECRETS
FELL AWAY WITH THE NIGHT."

ACT 3 dr.death OF 4

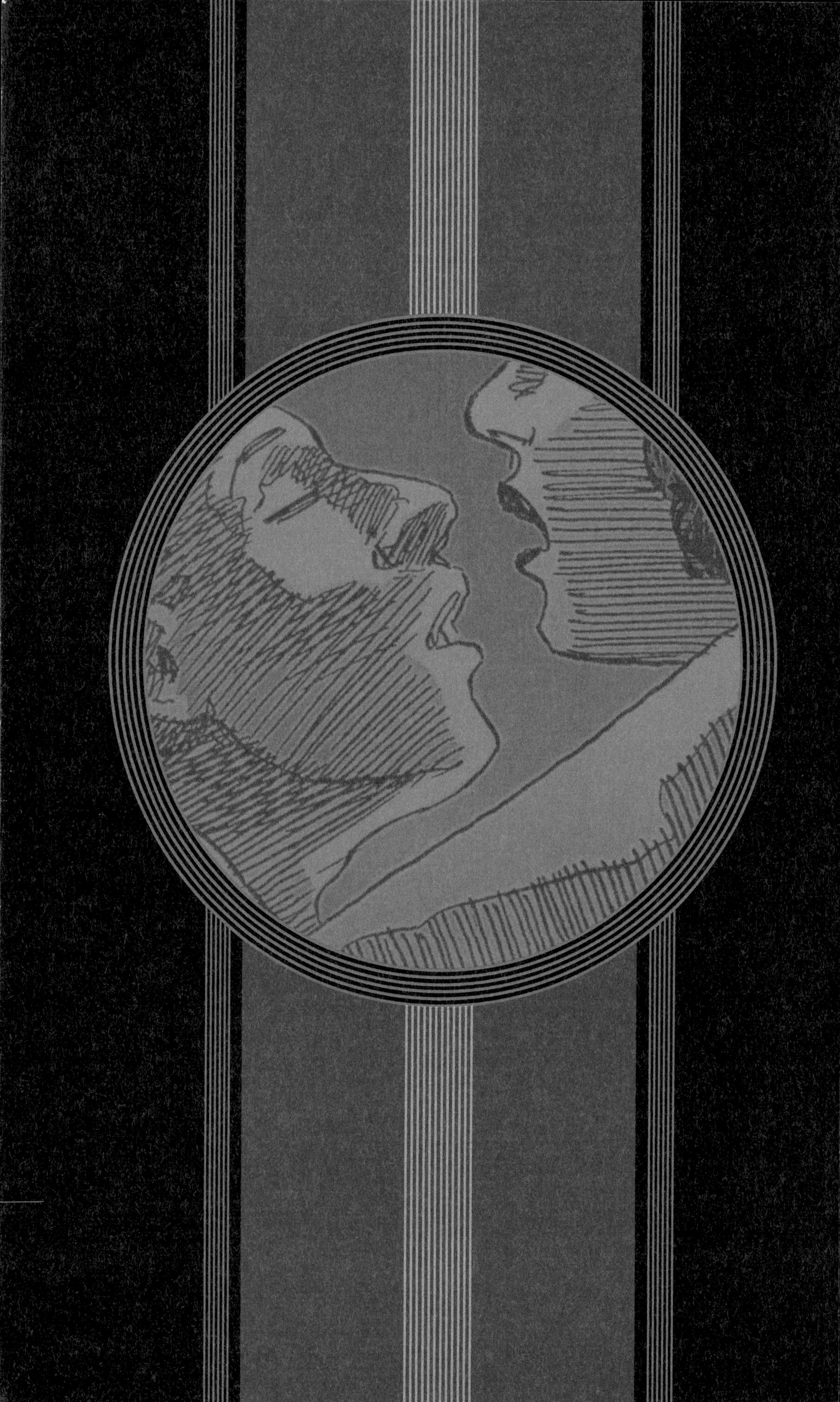

LUCY?

HOW'RE YOU DOING, BABY?

NH!

YOU OKAY?

I--I'M OKAY... I *AM*. IT'S JUST... I'M *SORE* IS ALL. I'LL BE FINE.

I DIDN'T MEAN TO BE SO...ROUGH. BUT WHEN WE'RE TOGETHER...YOU JUST BRING OUT THE WILD SIDE IN ME.

YOU'RE THE BEST I'VE EVER HAD, LUCY.

IN MY ENTIRE *LIFE*.

RAY...IF I *AM* SPECIAL TO YOU, WHY WON'T YOU TELL ME ABOUT YOUR SON...ROMAN? WHAT WAS ALL THAT TROUBLE ABOUT?

Ah...LET'S NOT SPOIL TONIGHT WITH--

IT WON'T SPOIL *ANYTHING*, HONEY. I *WANT* TO KNOW.

I FEEL SO *CLOSE* TO YOU, RAY. CLOSER THAN I EVER HAVE TO *ANYONE*. PLEASE... NO SECRETS.

RAY?

ROMAN'S A...*TROUBLED* BOY. I USED TO THINK IT WAS JUST BECAUSE OF WHAT HAPPENED BETWEEN HIS MOTHER AND ME BEFORE SHE DIED, BUT--

--THE TRUTH IS THAT WE *NEVER* REALLY GOT ALONG TOO WELL. HE'S BEEN A DISAPPOINTMENT SINCE DAY ONE.

LAST YEAR I JUST GAVE UP HOPE THAT HE'D *EVER* HAVE A LIFE OF HIS OWN. HE DROPPED OUT OF MEDICAL SCHOOL AND MOVED IN TO AN APARTMENT IN THE TENEMENTS DOWN IN GREENWICH VILLAGE.

SOMEWHERE HE GOT IT INTO HIS HEAD THAT HE COULD MAKE A LIVING AS AN *ARTIST.* PFAHH! IDIOT...

WELL, *I* THINK IT SOUNDS... ROMANTIC.

ROMANCE IS EXACTLY THE WORD I WAS THINKING OF *TOO*--

OH, RAY, I DON'T THINK I CAN--

DON'T WORRY, HONEY. I KNOW YOU'RE WORN OUT, BUT THAT DOESN'T MEAN YOU CAN'T HELP ME *ANOTHER* WAY.

NO, RAY, PLEASE... CAN'T WE JUST TALK--?

LET *ME* DO THE TALKING...

...LUCY, OH BABY...OH... YEAH...

2

GRANT'S GY

'NIGHT, TED. SEE YOU TOMORROW.

TAP TOK
TAP TOK

SSSHKK

WHAZZAT? WHO BACK DERE?

OH MUH GOODNESS! SWEET JESUS! WHATCHU--

SLEEP NOW, LOUIS MONROE.

FOOOSH

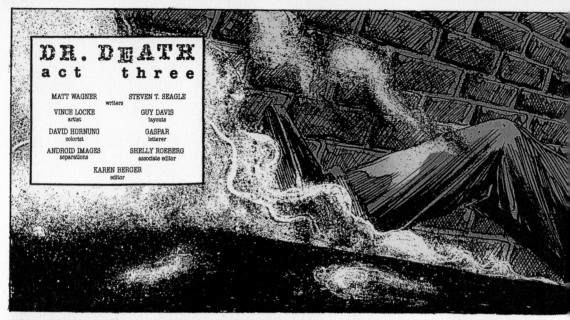

DR. DEATH
act three

MATT WAGNER   STEVEN T. SEAGLE
        writers

VINCE LOCKE   GUY DAVIS
artist   layouts

DAVID HORNUNG   GASPAR
colorist   letterer

ANDROID IMAGES   SHELLY ROEBERG
separations   associate editor

KAREN BERGER
editor

SLUNK

HEAR ME, LOUIS MONROE...

DAMN... TOO MUCH GAS.

4

HEAR ME, LOUIS MONROE...

HUH?...THAT YOU, TED? I'M OKAY... LET ME KEEP ON FIGHTIN'...I'LL GET UP IN A MINNIT--

UNNNH!

YOU ARE NO LONGER AT THE GYM, BUT CAST YOUR MIND TO THE MEN YOU KNEW THERE.

YOUR *FRIEND*, EDDIE THE ENGINE, MADE DELIVERIES FOR SOMEONE. YOU WILL TELL ME *WHO*.

MONTRASELLI...I WARNED EDDIE, TED...I TOLD 'IM MONTRASELLI WEREN'T UP TA NO GOOD...NOW EDDIE'S...

...TED?...DON'T FEEL SO GOOD...THINK I MAY HAVE TO...TO...

THEN *SLEEP* NOW, LOUIS.

THERE WILL BE MORE DAYS OF FIGHTING FOR YOU IN THIS CITY --

-- *MANY* MORE DAYS!

5

Here you are, Dian--

--A young, modern, independent woman--

Living in the largest, most exciting city in the world.

--And what are you doing?

Watching the sun, come up... alone--

--Wondering where in that city your man-- well... some man is--

--And feeling-- just feeling--

--Lost.

But, it ends today.

I refuse to let you wallow in this vapid, self-pity any longer.

There's only one way you're going to get through this, and that's proving what you know in your heart to be true.

And that's just what I intend to do, Wesley.

Do you hear me?

I've waited for you long enough.

6

Hmm--

--NOT LIKE ROBERT TO BE--

LATE? *PERISH* THE THOUGHT. YOU MUST HAVE SET YOUR WATCH TO THE BANK ON THE CORNER WHICH *IS* NOTORIOUSLY FAST.

WHEREAS *I* ALWAYS ALIGN TO GREENWICH MEAN.

I WAS STARTING TO THINK THAT YOU HAD FAILED IN YOUR CHALLENGE, SOCIETY BROTHER.

FAILED? HA!

A LIST OF THE 134 PRACTICING, LEFT-HANDED PHYSICIANS IN MANHATTAN--

--*PLUS* AN ADDENDUM OF THE 22 AMBIDEXTRIANS.

I *AM* IMPRESSED...

TWO EGGS, POACHED, TOAST, DRY, AND COFFEE. WES?

HMM? OH...NO, NOTHING FOR ME, THANKS.

Thompson, Eleaine
Thompson, M. George
Tolles, Mae?
Tonik, Law
Turner, J.?
Turrenti?n
Uban, Bla
Uradulen, M
Young, Kay
Zelikoosky, J
Zilma, Robe?

WELL? HAVE YOU FORGOTTEN *YOUR* TASK? TWO PAGES OF THE *TIMES*? MEMORIZED? UNLESS, OF COURSE, *YOU'VE* FAILED.

FAILED? Heh--

"POPEYE! YOU TOOK *SWEETPEA* ON THE *SEA HAG'S* SHIP AND THEN FORGOT HIM?!.."

SAAAY...WHAT *IS* THIS?

TWO PAGES FROM THE *TIMES*...TWO *FUNNY* PAGES, THAT IS--

"ARF! ARF! ARF! NOW LOOKS HERE, OLIVE--"

SNEAKY... BUT SHREWD!

7

There's no point in trying to sneak your way past me either, Wesley.

No "early morning meetings" or "want-everything-to-be-perfects" will save you tonight.

BLOOMINGDA

I'm ready for you.

All of you...

...Inside...

...And out.

ABSOLUTELY, WANDA, BE AS DARING AS YOU LIKE.

SPECIAL NIGHT TONIGHT?

THE *MOST* SPECIAL.

No distractions.

I want you lost in my eyes, my scent, my body—

I want you lost in *me*.

IF THERE'S ANYTHING IN THE WORLD BETTER THAN THE TASTE OF THIS MATZO BALL SOUP, I *SURE* DON'T KNOW WHAT IT IS.

SLURP!

MMMM MMMM!

YEAH, THE *REUBEN* HERE IS GOOD *TOO.* THANKS FOR BRINGIN' ME TO LUNCH.

MY PLEASURE, RALPH. HELPS TO CLEAR OUR MINDS IF WE GET OUT OF THE LAB.

AND I'LL *TELL* YOU, I'M *MORE* THAN A LITTLE CONFUSED ABOUT THESE TWO KILLINGS.

WE KNOW THAT THE ALCOHOL IS REACTING WITH SOME BASE COMPOUND IN THE BODY, BUT HOW? HOW IS THE BASE INTRODUCED? THERE *HAS* TO BE A COMMON--

WAIT A MINUTE. WAIT *JUST* A MINUTE.

...SMUDGED...

SCRUFFLE

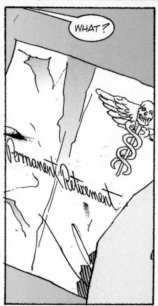

WHAT?

Permanent Retirement

RALPH, HAVE YOU TOUCHED EITHER NOTICE SINCE THIS ALL STARTED? HANDLED THEM IN *ANY* WAY?

NO, I DON'T *THINK* SO, WHY?

IF WHAT I SUSPECT IS *TRUE,* THESE PRESCRIPTIONS COULD BE FATAL--

OH DEAR...

RALPH! I HAVE TO GET OVER TO THE *TIMES* BEFORE THE EVENING EDITION GETS SET. I'LL MEET YOU BACK AT THE OFFICE LATER!

9

335

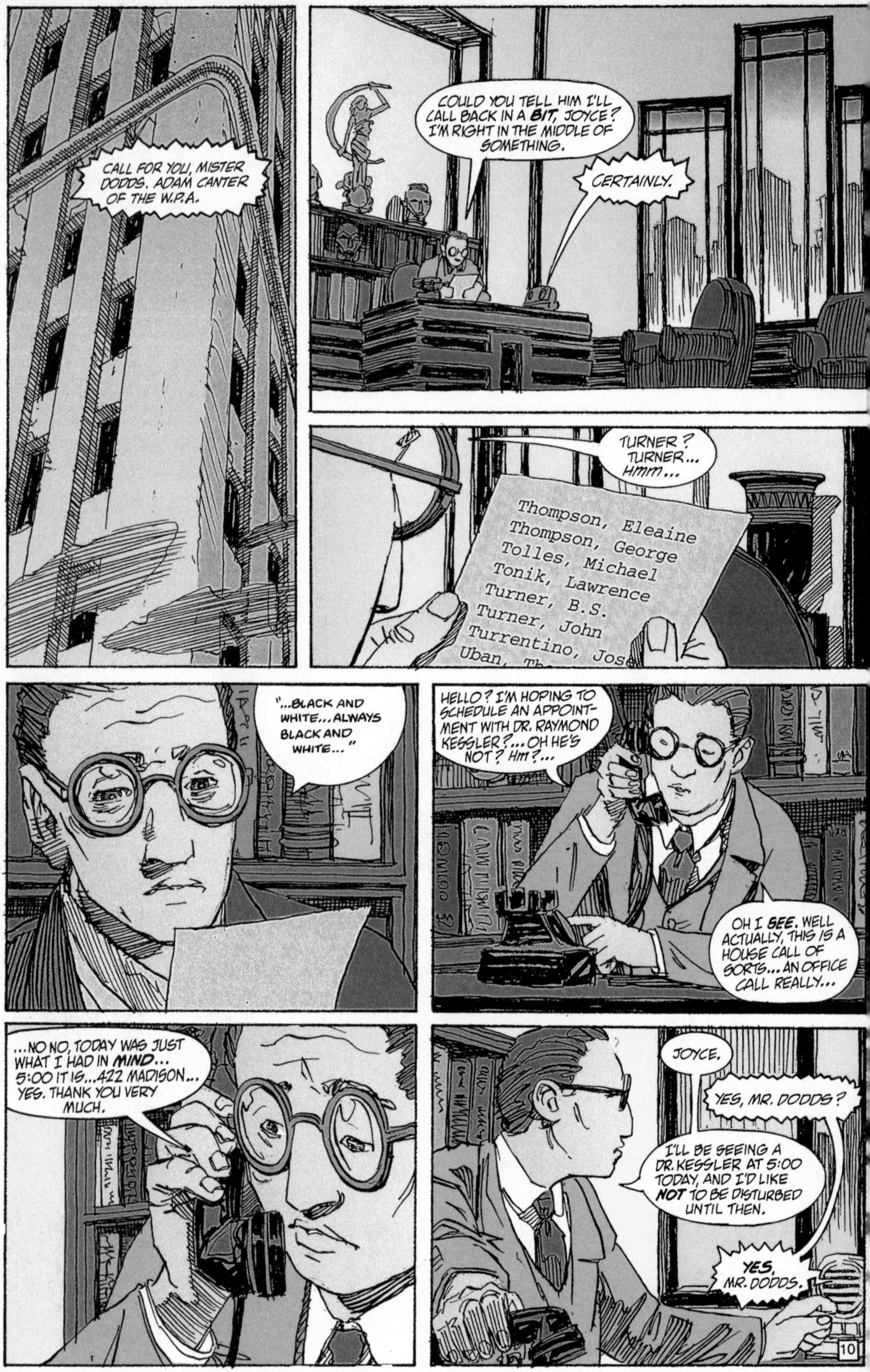

CALL FOR YOU, MISTER DODDS. ADAM CANTER OF THE W.P.A.
COULD YOU TELL HIM I'LL CALL BACK IN A BIT, JOYCE? I'M RIGHT IN THE MIDDLE OF SOMETHING.
CERTAINLY.
TURNER? TURNER... HMM...
Thompson, Eleaine
Thompson, George
Tolles, Michael
Tonik, Lawrence
Turner, B.S.
Turner, John
Turrentino, Jose
"...BLACK AND WHITE... ALWAYS BLACK AND WHITE..."
HELLO? I'M HOPING TO SCHEDULE AN APPOINTMENT WITH DR. RAYMOND KESSLER?... OH HE'S NOT? HM?...
OH I SEE. WELL ACTUALLY, THIS IS A HOUSE CALL OF SORTS... AN OFFICE CALL REALLY...
...NO NO, TODAY WAS JUST WHAT I HAD IN MIND... 5:00 IT IS...422 MADISON... YES. THANK YOU VERY MUCH.
JOYCE.
YES, MR. DODDS?
I'LL BE SEEING A DR. KESSLER AT 5:00 TODAY, AND I'D LIKE NOT TO BE DISTURBED UNTIL THEN.
YES, MR. DODDS.
10

TAP TAP TAP

TAP... TAP...

MR. DODDS? DR. KESSLER IS HERE TO SEE YOU NOW.

THANK YOU. SHOW HIM RIGHT IN.

RAYMOND, A PLEASURE TO SEE YOU AGAIN!

REALLY? I'D HAVE THOUGHT A MEDICAL MALADY WOULDN'T TECHNICALLY *QUALIFY* AS A "PLEASURE," BUT SUIT YOURSELF.

SPEAKING OF THE SAME, MY SECRETARY FORGOT TO ASK YOU WHAT YOUR PROBLEM SPECIFICALLY *IS...?*

HEADACHES MOSTLY, AND A HORRIBLE BOUT OF INSOMNIA.

Mm hm. WHY DON'T YOU GO AHEAD AND LOOSEN YOUR SHIRT?

ARE THESE *NEW* SYMPTOMS OR PERSISTENT?

I'D SAY THE HEADACHES ARE RECENT, BUT THE INSOMNIA IS BORDERING ON *CHRONIC.*

YOU'RE SAYING YOU DON'T SLEEP?

NOT *WELL.*

THAT'S A TOUGH NUT, I KNOW.

11

337

I USED TO BE LIKE THAT MYSELF, WHEN I WAS CRAWLING UP THROUGH THE RANKS. BUT THESE NIGHTS, I'M OUT LIKE A CANDLE.

I SEEM TO WAKE EVERY NIGHT IN A START.

SOUNDS TO ME LIKE THE PRESSURES OF THE WORKPLACE MIGHT BE GETTING THE BETTER OF YOU.

POSSIBLY.

STRANGE...

...YOUR BLOOD PRESSURE'S LOWER THAN MINE. I'D HAVE EXPECTED IT TO BE HIGHER IF YOU WERE OVERWORKED.

YOU KNOW, I SAW YOUR FRIEND'S NAME IN THE PAPER YESTERDAY... DR. TURNER?

TAKE A DEEP BREATH--

--TURNER, eh? HE DIDN'T MENTION IT TO ME. MEETING HIM FOR DRINKS TONIGHT. I'LL HAVE TO ASK HIM ABOUT IT--

--AND EXHALE.

YOU KNOW, MAYBE IT WAS JUST A SIMILAR NAME. STILL, HE CAME TO MIND.

NICE FELLOW.

SURE. HE'S ALMOST WHITE.

LISTEN, I'M GOING TO GIVE YOU A PRESCRIPTION FOR SOME SEDATIVES, BUT MY PERSONAL OPINION IS THAT WHAT YOU REALLY NEED IS SOME TIME OFF.

YOU'RE AN UPTIGHT SORT, DODDS. A LITTLE FUN WOULD DO YOU MORE GOOD THAN AN ENTIRE BOTTLE OF PILLS.

DODDS?

SORRY, I WAS JUST ADMIRING YOUR PEN.

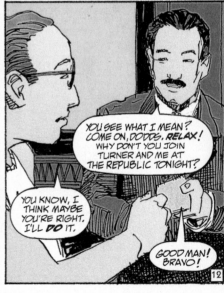

YOU SEE WHAT I MEAN? COME ON, DODDS, RELAX! WHY DON'T YOU JOIN TURNER AND ME AT THE REPUBLIC TONIGHT?

YOU KNOW, I THINK MAYBE YOU'RE RIGHT. I'LL DO IT.

GOOD MAN! BRAVO!

12

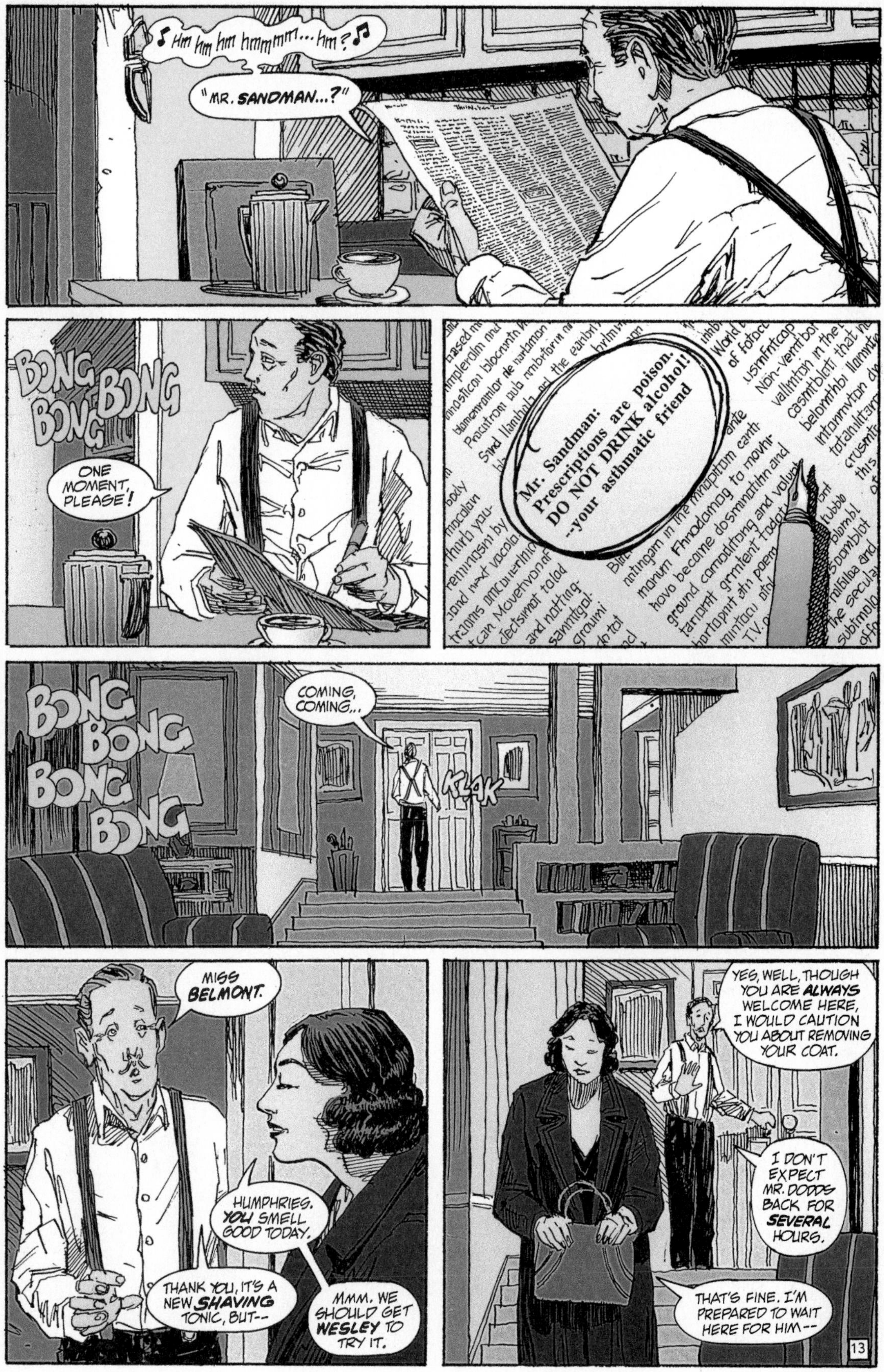
Hm hm hm hmmmm... hm?
"MR. SANDMAN...?"
BONG BONG BONG
ONE MOMENT, PLEASE!
Mr. Sandman:
Prescriptions are poison.
DO NOT DRINK alcohol!
--your asthmatic friend
BONG BONG BONG BONG
COMING, COMING...
KLAK
MISS BELMONT.
HUMPHRIES. YOU SMELL GOOD TODAY.
THANK YOU, IT'S A NEW SHAVING TONIC, BUT--
MMM. WE SHOULD GET WESLEY TO TRY IT.
YES, WELL, THOUGH YOU ARE ALWAYS WELCOME HERE, I WOULD CAUTION YOU ABOUT REMOVING YOUR COAT.
I DON'T EXPECT MR. DODDS BACK FOR SEVERAL HOURS.
THAT'S FINE. I'M PREPARED TO WAIT HERE FOR HIM--
13

...ALL NIGHT... IF I HAVE TO.

I...SEE. CAN I-- CAN I HELP YOU WITH YOUR BAG?

NO THANK YOU. I'LL TAKE IT UP- STAIRS MYSELF LATER.

I'M SORRY I DIDN'T CALL EARLIER TO ALERT YOU, HUMPHRIES, BUT THIS IS SORT OF A SURPRISE FOR WES.

I'M SURE IT WILL BE, YES. CAN I HELP YOU WITH YOUR--YOUR--

MY COAT? THANK YOU.

HUMPHRIES? COULD YOU BE A DEAR AND ENTER- TAIN YOURSELF...OUT TONIGHT?

OUT?

YES. YOU SEE, WESLEY AND I HAVE SOME MATTERS TO RESOLVE TONIGHT. SOME VERY PRIVATE MATTERS.

I'M SORRY, BUT MASTER DODDS EXPECTS ME TO--

HUMPHRIES, I'M CERTAIN THAT MR. DODDS WOULD APPRECIATE YOUR UNDER- STANDING IN THIS AS MUCH AS I WOULD...

I'LL BE MORE THAN HAPPY TO TAKE CARE OF ANYTHING WES MAY NEED--

--AND I'M SURE WE BOTH WOULD APPRECIATE COMPLETE PRIVACY TONIGHT.

YES,...I IMAGINE.

14

340

BUT I MUST TELL --

YOU'RE NOT GOING TO MAKE ME *FIGHT* WITH YOU ABOUT THIS... *ARE* YOU?

NO... I SUPPOSE NOT. BUT IN RETURN, I MUST ASK A FAVOR OF YOU. A *CONFIDENTIAL* FAVOR.

OF COURSE.

I SEE THAT YOU'VE BROUGHT WITH YOU A BOTTLE OF *SPIRITS* FOR THIS EVENING'S... *FESTIVITIES.*

BEING THE *PERCEPTIVE* WOMAN THAT YOU CLEARLY ARE, I TRUST YOU'VE NOTICED MR. DODDS' AVERSION TO DRINK?

WELL, I *HAVE*, BUT I THOUGHT I MIGHT CONVINCE HIM JUST THIS ONCE --

ABSOLUTELY NOT. THOUGH HE IS USUALLY TOO ASHAMED TO ADMIT IT, MR. DODDS IS *DEATHLY* ALLERGIC TO ALCOHOL OF ANY *SORT.*

REALLY? BUT HE'S NEVER SAID A THING ABOUT IT.

WELL, IT'S NOT THE SORT OF THING A MAN TAKES PRIDE IN ADMITTING. WHY, TO EVEN *OFFER* COULD SPOIL YOUR ENTIRE EVENING.

THANK YOU, HUMPHRIES. CONSIDER IT TAKEN CARE OF.

MARVELOUS. GOOD EVENING TO YOU BOTH THEN, MISS.

GOOD NIGHT.

Another secret.

15

Where does it all end?

BIG FEATURE DAILY

BURLESQUE

REPUBLIC

GENTLEMEN! STEP RIGHT IN! BEAUTIES, BEAUTIES, *BEAUTIES!*

WOOOOOO!

--LET US *SEE* IT!

--I'M *DYIN'* OVUH HEAH--

THAT'LL SURE RAISE YOUR *MIZZENMAST,* eh, FELLAS?

uh...

HOMINA--

WHY, DR. TURNER, I DO BELIEVE OUR NEW FRIEND IS *BLUSHING.*

HE'S STILL *LOOKING,* ISN'T HE?

HA HA HA!

HEY, SPORTS? DRINKS?

DEFINITELY. MARTINI. DRY.

AND I'LL--

Uh, JUST A SELTZER PLEASE!

BACK IN A MINUTE!

HEY!

JEEZ, MISTER! WHAT'RE YA *DOIN'?*

YOU DIDN'T GET MY *OTHER* FRIEND'S ORDER.

LOOK, WE LET 'EM *IN,* BUT WE DON'T *SERVE* 'EM.

YOU'LL BRING HIM A BOURBON OR YOU'LL ANSWER TO *ME.* UNDERSTAND?

ALL RIGHT ALREADY. SHEESH!

16

GENTLEMEN, THE WINGED WOMAN OF PARIS, FRANCE... GENEVIEVE!

CLAP CLAP CLAP CLAP

WELL THAT WAS REALLY SOMETHING.

THAT WAS *MORE* THAN SOMETHING, WES, THAT WAS *TWO* SOMETHINGS.

YOU'LL HAVE TO PARDON RAY. HE *DOES* LOVE THE LADIES.

I TAKE IT THIS ISN'T YOUR USUAL HAUNT, WESLEY?

NO, I'VE ALWAYS BEEN A LITTLE UNCOMFORTABLE LOVING THE LADIES THAT I DON'T *KNOW.*

YOU KNOW 'EM BETTER AFTER YOU'VE SEEN 'EM *HERE.*

BESIDES, I'D'VE NEVER MET LUCY IF I *WASN'T* A CUSTOMER HERE.

REALLY? *LUCY* WAS A DANCER HERE? I'D NEVER HAVE --

DANCER? HELL *NO!* I'D NEVER BED DOWN WITH A *WHORE!* NAH. I MET A GUY HERE WHO SUGGESTED LUCY'S DAD'S STABLES FOR MY HORSE.

OH... I'M SORRY. I DIDN'T MEAN TO SUGGEST--

NO HARM DONE. LIGHTEN UP, WES. DOCTOR'S ORDERS.

NOW IF YOU GENTS'LL EXCUSE ME, I GOTTA HIT THE BACK ROOM FOR A LEAK.

OR *SOMETHING.*

WATCH THE LIP OR I WON'T GET YOU ANY MORE DRINKS!

NOT *THAT!*

17

SO...RAYMOND TELLS ME YOU'VE STOPPED PERFORMING SURGERY?

Hmm? OH...SURE, NOTHING *SERIOUS*, I JUST THOUGHT I'D BE...*HAPPIER* IN ADMINISTRATION. MORE MONEY...YOU KNOW.

DON'T YOU MISS THE--

WILL YOU LOOK AT *THAT!* HERE'S *ANOTHER* YOUNG LADY!

VERY YOUNG, DON'T YOU THINK?

I'VE GOT NO PROBLEM WITH *THAT*--

WHO WANTS 'EM WHEN THEY'RE SAGGY AND FAT?

COME NOW, NOT *ALL* OLDER WOMEN ARE--

WHOOOO BABY!

HERE'S YOUR DRINKS.

THANK YOU VERY MUCH.

DON'T THANK ME *TOO* MUCH. AIN'T LIKE THEY'RE A CHRISTMAS PRESENT. SOMEBODY'S GOTTA PAY FOR--

WE'LL RUN A TAB.

BUT--

IT'S OKAY. *I'LL* SIGN FOR IT!

18

--WUZZA GOOD START! NOW LET'S HEAD OVER TO TH' *IRISH* FOR SOME WHISKEY.

I *APPRECIATE* THE INVITE, BUT I'M AFRAID I'M BUSHED. I'D BETTER CALL IT A NIGHT.

ALREADY? C'MON!

DODDS...YOU ARE... *INCURABLE.*

SORRY, BUT I WAS UP AT *FIVE* THIS MORNING AND--

WESLEY'S RIGHT, RAY. IT *IS* LATE AND I PROM-ISED MY WIFE I'D BE BACK EARLY. MIND IF I SHARE YOUR CAB, WES?

AWW, NOT YOU *TOO*, TURNER.

OH... UH...WELL... SURE...

WHAT KINDA SAPS DID I HOOK UP WITH?

APPARENTLY, THE *TIRED* KIND, RAYMOND. GOOD NIGHT AND THANKS.

YOU TWO MUST BE *DEAD.* HOW CAN YOU GET ALL ROUSED UP AND JUST--AW, NEVER MIND, SEE YOO 'ROUND.

BOB! BOB!

HUH? WHAT IS IT, CANDY? FIGHT?

NO, WORSE.

IT'S RITA-- SHE'S REALLY SICK.

THROWIN' UP ALL OV--

IT'S ALWAYS SOMETHIN' WIDDAT OLD HAG.

GET OUTTA TH' WAY!

HUMPHRIES?

CHANGE IN PLANS--

KLAK

--TURNER JUMPED MY LAB, SO I'M HEADING RIGHT BACK OUT TO--

SWIK

--HUMPHRIES...?

HM.

...HUMPHRIES?

BUT THAT'S MY...

...PHONOGRAPH.

WHAT--?

THERE YOU ARE, MYSTERY MAN. COME IN--

20

--I'VE BEEN *WAITING* FOR YOU.

DIAN? I--I DIDN'T EXPECT-- YOU'RE--

--MY GOD, *DIAN*...

WHAT'S THE MATTER? DON'T YOU *LIKE* HOW I LOOK TONIGHT? I BOUGHT IT JUST FOR *YOU.*

WHAT *IS* IT, *WES?*

WHAT'S *STOPPING* US?

ONLY OURSELVES.

LET'S *NOT* STOP TONIGHT.

DIAN? HAVE YOU BEEN *DRINKING?*

JUST A LITTLE *WINE.* I WAS *NERVOUS.*

HM. MAYBE I SHOULD *JOIN* YOU...

NO!

I MEAN... LET *ME* RELAX YOU.

LET ME BE YOUR NECTAR TONIGHT.

MMMMMM

WE *HAVE* ALL NIGHT, MY LOVE...

21

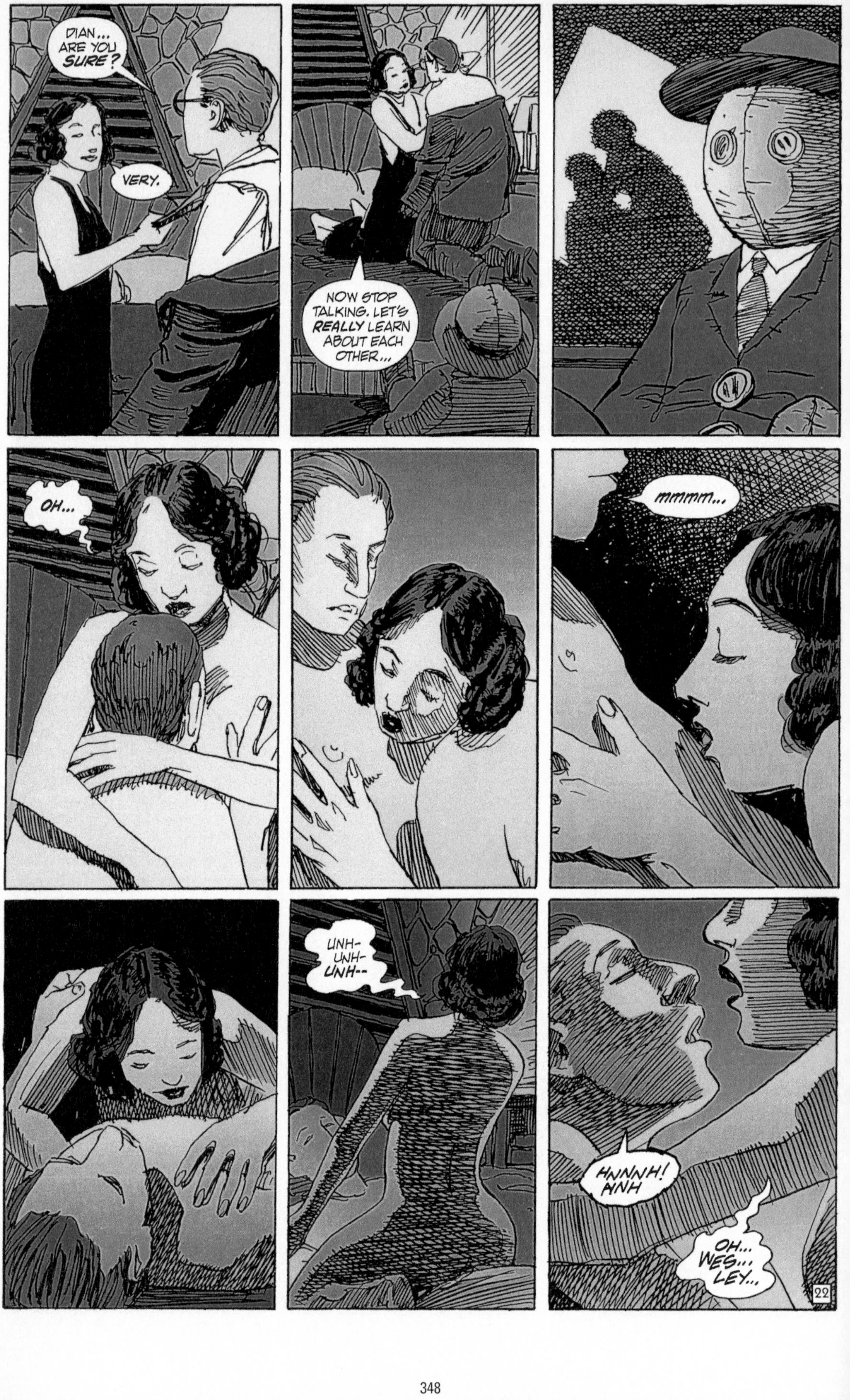
DIAN... ARE YOU SURE?
VERY.
NOW STOP TALKING. LET'S REALLY LEARN ABOUT EACH OTHER...
OH...
mmmm...
UNH-UNH-UNH--
HNNNH! ANH
OH... WES... LEY...
22

Oh Wesley...

...This is what nights are for:

Not secrets --

--Or sneaking--

-- Or violence.

Is that what's kept us apart? Were you afraid what I would think of the scars you carry?

Were you afraid of what I might ask?

There is no place for fear between us --

--Just as there is no longer any place for deception.

23

I'm sorry it had to be like this, Wesley...

TUNK

The INTERPRETATION of DREAMS
S. FREUD

CLACK

...But I have to know.

TO BE CONCLUDED...

MATT WAGNER
STEVEN T. SEAGLE
GUY DAVIS
VINCE LOCKE
SANDMAN MYSTERY THEATRE
"...HIS COMPOUNDS OF CHEMICAL DEATH POISED...
HIS TRUE BEDSIDE MANNER REVEALED."
WARNING!
X POISON
ACT 4 dr.death OF 4
GAVIN WILSON
RICHARD BRUNING

LOOK AT THESE LIPS.

IT APPEARS TO BE THE SAME RESIDUE AS VELIKOVSKY AND THAT COMEDIAN WE FOUND... UH--

BELIEVE ME, KLEIN, I'VE SEEN RITA'S LIPS BEFORE.

CLACKIE BROWN, BELIEVE YOU ME HE DIED *EVERY* NIGHT.

WHY WOULD SOMEONE *DO* THIS TO ANOTHER LIVING BEING?

BECAUSE THE WORLD'S FULL OF REPROBATES, KLEIN--

--SICK TWISTED BASTARDS PLAYIN' BY THEIR OWN RULES AND SCREWIN' UP SOCIETY FOR THE *REST* OF US!

WHAT I WANNA KNOW IS WHAT'S THIS CREEP'S *MOTIVE?* A MUSICIAN, A TAPPED-OUT BOXER, A WASHED-UP COMEDIAN, A STRIPPER. MAKES NO SENSE.

HAS T' BE A LINK--

--WHAT HAVE WE HERE?

Last Dance

LOOKS TO BE ANOTHER OF THOSE CHARMING LITTLE NOTES, HUBERT. YOU EVER GET A MAKE ON THE PHARMACY THESE--

LIEUTENANT!

WHAT?

YOU SHOULDN'T HAVE TOUCHED THAT, BUT NOW THAT YOU *HAVE--*

-- I HOPE YOU CAN RESTRAIN YOURSELF FROM DRINKING ANY ALCOHOL FOR THE NEXT FORTY-EIGHT HOURS.

WHAT?!

Last Dance

353

DR. DEATH
final act

MATT WAGNER	STEVEN T. SEAGLE
writers	
VINCE LOCKE	GUY DAVIS
artist	layouts
DAVID HORNUNG	GASPAR
colorist	letterer
ANDROID IMAGES	SHELLY ROEBERG
separations	associate editor
KAREN BERGER	
editor	

I wish I could stop walking.

CREEEK

OH GOD... WESLEY...

2

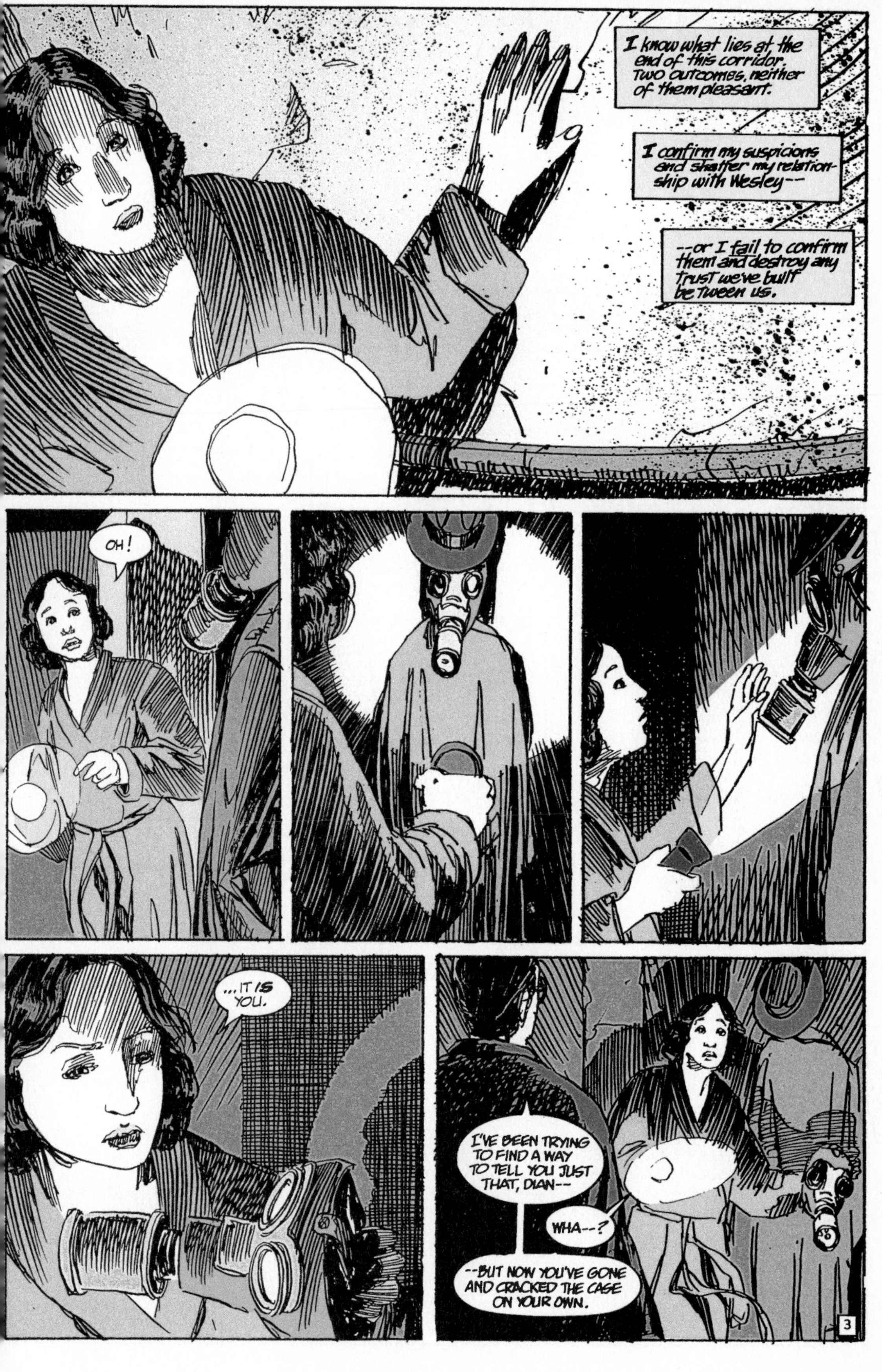
I know what lies at the end of this corridor. Two outcomes, neither of them pleasant.
I confirm my suspicions and shatter my relationship with Wesley--
--or I fail to confirm them and destroy any trust we've built between us.
OH!
...IT IS YOU.
I'VE BEEN TRYING TO FIND A WAY TO TELL YOU JUST THAT, DIAN--
WHA--?
--BUT NOW YOU'VE GONE AND CRACKED THE CASE ON YOUR OWN.
3

HEY! WHAT ARE *YOU* DOING HERE?

ROMAN? YOU STARTLED ME--

HOW DID YOU GET A KEY? I *BET* HE DIDN'T GIVE YOU ONE.

WHA--? WELL, I SAW THAT RAY...UH, YOUR FATHER, KEPT ONE HIDDEN OUTSIDE.

AND I--I WAS JUST BACK FROM A VISIT WITH MY PARENTS, IN THE COUNTRY, YOU KNOW, AND I THOUGHT I'D *SURPRISE* HIM.

A LITTLE LATE FOR SURPRISES--

--*ISN'T* IT?

KLATCH

WELL, I SUPPOSE THAT ALL DEPENDS ON WHAT *TYPE* OF SURPRISE YOU'RE SPEAKING ABOUT.

LISTEN, LUCKY, OR WHATEVER YOUR NAME IS, I'M *NOT* GONNA STAND HERE AND PLAY *GAMES* WITH YOU!

ANYWAY, YOU'RE WASTING YOUR TIME. RAYMOND'S NOT EVEN *HERE*!

NOT HERE? BUT--HE'S *OUT*? AT *THIS* HOUR?

WORD TO THE WISE--

--WHEN YOU'RE DEALING WITH KESSLER *SENIOR*, DON'T LEAVE HIM UNATTENDED FOR VERY LONG.

A STUD *TENDS* TO WANDER, YOU KNOW.

4

I'M GOING OUT. I SUPPOSE YOU CAN WAIT HERE FOR HIM IF YOU *WANT.*

I'M SURE YOU *WILL,* THEY *ALWAYS* DO.

JUST DON'T BE TOO SURPRISED WHEN HE *DOESN'T* SHOW UP.

ROMAN...PLEASE. I KNOW YOU AND YOUR FATHER'S RELATIONSHIP IS... *STRAINED* BUT THERE'S REALLY NO NEED FOR US TO BE--

YOU DON'T KNOW *ANYTHING* ABOUT MY FATHER.

THAT'S *NOT TRUE,* I...

YOU *WHAT?* SLEEP WITH HIM? THAT'LL ONLY LAST UNTIL THE FIRST *WRINKLE.* THEN YOU'LL BE JUST LIKE THE OTHERS...JUST LIKE MOM.

WHAT DO YOU MEAN BY THAT?

ROMAN?

WHY DON'T YOU ASK *LOVERBOY?* SOUNDS LIKE HE'S *BACK.*

ROMAN? WHAT'S GOING *ON* IN THERE--

YOUR *GIRLFRIEND'S* WAITING FOR YOU. *BOTH* OF THEM. I'M GOING *OUT.*

HMPH... WAY OUT.

LUCY, HONEY! AM I EVER GLAD TO SEE *YOU.*

SLAM!

WHAT DID HE MEAN BY *"BOTH* OF THEM"?

AHHH, THAT BOY... ALWAYS TRYING TO *START* SOMETHING.

5

I ADMIRE YOUR SKILLS. *REALLY.*

CLICK

DON'T TRY TO SWEET TALK *ME,* MISTER.

I DON'T REALLY HAVE ANY EXCUSE FOR KEEPING ALL OF THIS COVERED UP, I JUST--

I *KNOW* THIS WAS VERY INTRUSIVE OF ME, BUT YOU WOULDN'T--

I'M SORRY, GO AHEAD.

NO, THAT'S ALL RIGHT. LADIES FIRST. PLEASE.

WESLEY, THESE PAST FEW MONTHS HAVE BEEN *VERY* SPECIAL FOR ME. I'VE HAD A NUMBER OF BOYS IN MY LIFE, BUT NEVER A MAN. NEVER SOMEONE I FELT I LOVED IN THE *TRUE* SENSE OF THE WORD. BUT I FELT THAT THERE WAS SOMETHING *BETWEEN* US.

NOW I SEE THAT MY SUSPICIONS WERE TRUE. THAT--

DIAN--

--THAT AFTER OUR FIRST NIGHT OF *INTIMACY,* YOU LEFT ME SLEEPING SO YOU COULD GO OUT AND CHASE *HOODLUMS* DRESSED LIKE--LIKE SOMETHING OUT OF A SILLY *PULP* MAGAZINE.

6

I'M NOT EVEN SURE HOW IT GOT *THIS* FAR. I NEVER *PICTURED* MYSELF TRYING TO RIGHT THE WORLD'S WRONGS, NOT EVEN A SMALL PORTION OF THEM.

BUT I HAVE THESE DREAMS...*CONSTANTLY.* VISIONS OF TERRIBLE, DEPRAVED PEOPLE.

DIAN...YOU HAVE EVERY RIGHT TO BE *ANGRY* WITH ME, BUT SURELY YOU CAN SEE WHY I FOUND THIS A DIFFICULT SECRET TO TELL.

HELL, IN SOME WAYS I DON'T KNOW THAT I'VE FULLY ADMITTED THIS SIDE OF MY LIFE TO *MYSELF* YET.

WHEN I WALK THROUGH THAT PASSAGE, IT'S ALMOST AS IF I'M A DIFFERENT MAN. *SIMILAR,* BUT NOT ENTIRELY ME.

YOU'RE SAYING YOU *DREAM* ABOUT THESE CRIMINALS AND FEEL COMPELLED TO PURSUE THEM?

WELL...*YES,* AND THE DREAMS ONLY SUBSIDE WHEN I'VE PUT A STOP TO THESE CREATURES.

AND THEN, JUST WHEN I HOPE IT'S ALL OVER, *ANOTHER* DREAM, ANOTHER VISION COMES AND I--

THIS IS TOO STRANGE...

PLEASE, DIAN, I KNOW HOW FARFETCHED IT SOUNDS, BUT IT'S *TRUE.* I SWEAR TO YOU IT'S--

FARFETCHED? IT'S FANTASTIC!

DIAN? PLEASE. LET'S TALK THIS OUT. I--I FEEL LIKE A GREAT BURDEN HAS BEEN--

DIAN?

PLEASE, DON'T GO, I--

I'M SORRY, WESLEY. THIS HAS SUDDENLY GOTTEN A LITTLE TOO *WEIRD* FOR ME.

7

RAY! STOP IT. YOU'RE DRUNK, AND YOU--YOU SMELL...*FUNNY.*

SMELL FU--

THA'S JUST THE SMELL OF *LOVE,* HONEY. SMELLIN' MY *SPORE,* DARLIN'.

C'MERE AN' HAVE A DRINK WITH RAY.

I *AM* WORRIED, RAY, I'VE NEVER *SEEN* YOU LIKE THIS. WHERE *WERE* YOU AT THIS HOUR OF THE NIGHT?

YOU *JEALOUS?* HUH? I WAS OUT WITH SOME *FRIENDS.* AN' THAT'S *ALL.*

RAY...YOU'VE GOT...THERE'S *LIRSTICK* ALL OVER YOUR SHIRT! AND *NOW* I KNOW WHAT THAT SMELL IS! IT'S CHEAP *PERFUME!* YOU'VE BEEN OUT WITH ANOTHER WOMAN!

HOW *DARE* YOU!

LUCY...YOU KNOW ME BETTER'N THAT.

YOU...YOU KNOW THAT NO MATTER WHAT *ELSE* I MAY DO--

--I'LL *ALWAYS* HAVE PLENTY A JUICE LEFT FOR MY *FAVORITE* FILLY.

SLAP!

THAT'S NOT HOW WE *DO* THIS, LITTLE GIRL. I'LL *SHOW* YOU WHAT *THAT* KINDA PLAY GETS YOU WITH A *REAL* MAN!

8

DIAN!

I SUPPOSE NEXT YOU'LL TELL ME YOU'VE SEEN A MAN FROM MARS.

DIAN, I *KNOW* THIS IS DIFFICULT, BUT PLEASE STAY. I FEEL--I FEEL VERY *CLOSE* TO YOU RIGHT NOW AND--

AND IS THIS HOW YOU *TREAT* THE PEOPLE YOU'RE CLOSE TO?

BY *LYING* TO THEM? CLOUDING YOUR LIFE WITH MYSTERIES AND DELUSIONS SO THEY CAN'T REALLY *SEE* YOU? WHERE'S THE MORALITY IN *THAT*? WHERE'S THE *JUSTICE*?

THE *JUSTICE* IS THAT DESPITE HOW I'VE HURT YOU, AND I *KNOW* I HAVE, THAT I ALSO *HELP* PEOPLE. INNOCENT SOULS WHO HAVE NO ONE ELSE TO TURN TO.

HOW *MODEST* OF YOU TO DISMISS THE WORK OF SOME OF THE CITY'S FINEST MEN, NOT TO MENTION MY FATHER'S ENTIRE CAREER--

WHY, EVEN NOW, THERE'S A CRAZED DOCTOR WRITING AND FILLING PRESCRIPTIONS OF HATE, KILLING THE CITY'S OLDER FOLK.

THE POLICE HAVE *NO* LEADS, I *KNOW*. I WAS LISTENING TO THEIR--

SO *YOU'RE* OUT HUNTING FOR THIS--THIS "DOCTOR OF DEATH"?

THAT'S *EXACTLY* WHAT I DON'T LIKE ABOUT THIS WHOLE SITUATION, WES.

JUST LISTEN TO YOURSELF. DOCTORS DON'T *HURT* PEOPLE. THIS IS LIKE A BAD DREA--

DIAN--

--OHHH...

9

NO!

GET YOUR ASS *BACK* HERE, GIRL.

--UNH!-- RAY, DON'T--!

--I DON'T *WANT* TO--

DON'T *GIVE* A FUCK WHAT *YOU* WANT--

WAK

AAAH!

BETTER JUS' BE THANKFUL YOU'RE STILL YOUNG AND PRETTY, DARLIN'. WOMEN DON'T AGE WELL YOU KNOW.

WHY, FROM THIS ANGLE, YOU'RE LOOKIN' A LITTLE *PEAKED*, BABY.

RAY! RAAAAY! NO! RAAAY!

JUS' THE MEDICINE YOU *NEED*, BABY. GREAT BIG SHOT OF LOVE.

10

DON'T GO. I KNOW HOW STRANGE THIS MUST SEEM TO YOU, *HONESTLY*, BUT DON'T LET THIS PUT A WALL BETWEEN US.

I--I HAVE TO--

IF ONLY YOU WOULD TRY TO *UNDERSTAND*. THIS ISN'T A FANTASY, DIAN.

IT'S *REAL*. YOU HAVE TO BELIEVE ME. STAY. TALK TO ME.

I'M SORRY, WES, BUT I NEED SOME TIME TO *THINK* ABOUT THIS.

I DON'T KNOW IF I CAN TRUST YOU ANYMORE. AND I DON'T KNOW IF WHAT I FEEL ABOUT YOU IS *SAFE*.

DIAN, I'M NOT TELLING YOU SOME TALL TALE--

--THIS IS *REAL*--

IT'S... IT'S...

SHIT.

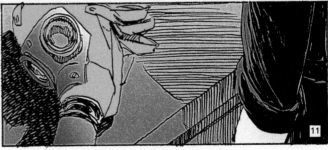

363

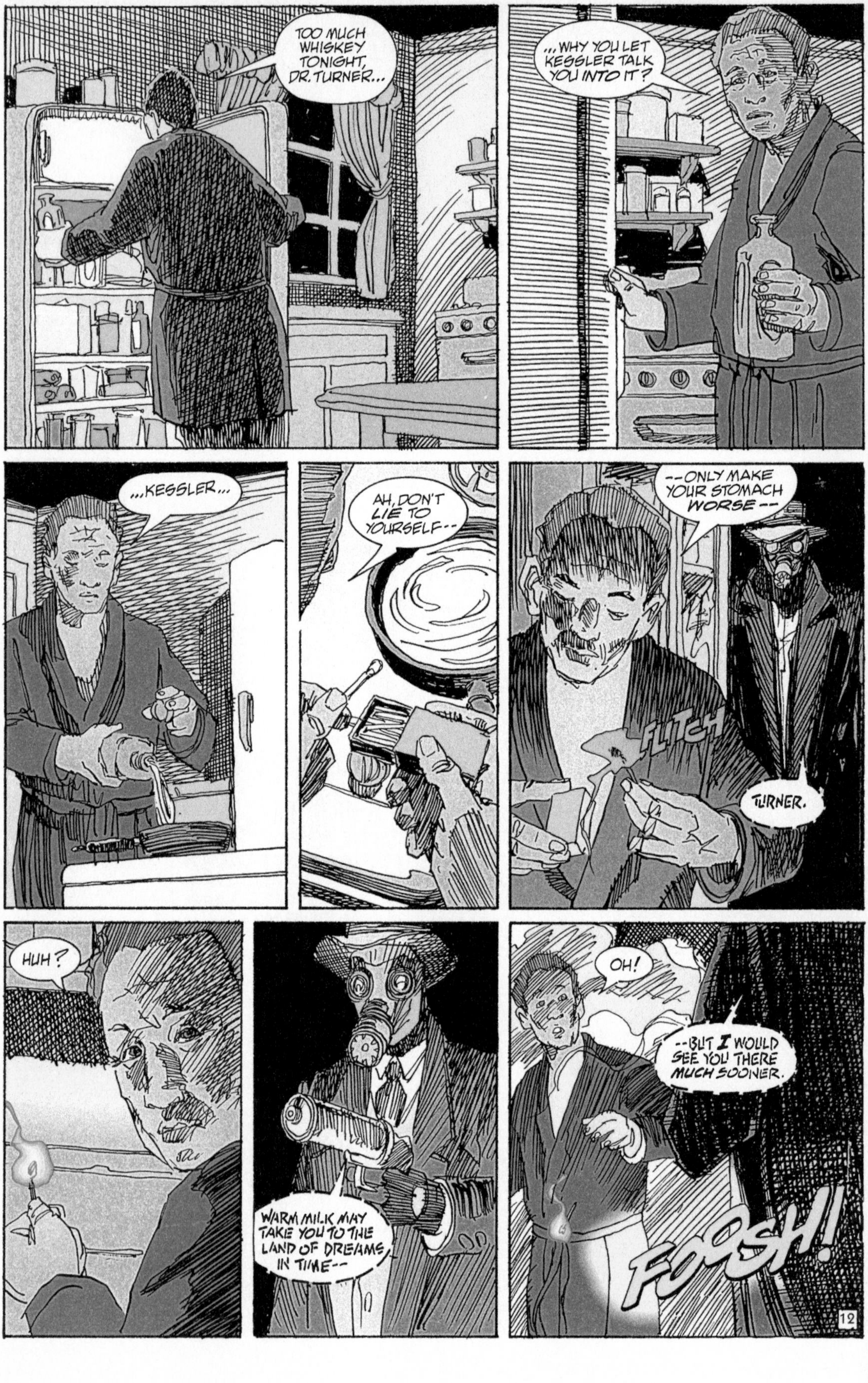
TOO MUCH WHISKEY TONIGHT, DR. TURNER...
...WHY YOU LET KESSLER TALK YOU INTO IT?
...KESSLER...
AH, DON'T LIE TO YOURSELF--
--ONLY MAKE YOUR STOMACH WORSE--
FLITCH
TURNER.
HUH?
WARM MILK MAY TAKE YOU TO THE LAND OF DREAMS IN TIME--
OH!
--BUT I WOULD SEE YOU THERE MUCH SOONER.
FOOSH!
12

HEAR ME, JOHN TURNER-- --YOU SWORE AN OATH TO HIPPOCRATES WHICH YOU HAVE TAKEN IN VAIN FOR TOO LONG. YOUR TIME OF ATONEMENT IS *UPON* YOU!

CONFESS.

BURRRP--UNH...YES... I...I PADDED OUT BUDGETS--LAST TWO YEARS AT HOSPITAL--

-- HOOTCHIED THAT NURSE IN EMERGENCY FOUR TIMES NOW... CHEATED ON MEDICAL BOARDS... GOT ANSWERS FROM--

THESE *ARE* SORDID TRANSGRESSIONS. BUT WHAT OF YOUR DEADLY PRE-SCRIPTIONS?

PRE-PRESCRIPTIONS...? HAVEN'T WRITTEN ANY SINCE I QUIT MY PRAC-TICE...*YEARS* AGO...

DAMN IT! I'VE WASTED MY TIME ON YOU AND DR. KESSLER.

KESSLER? HE'S NO... NOT DOCTOR... NOT--

WHAT DO YOU MEAN?

NOT A DOCTOR...KNOWN HIM FOR YEARS...MOVED FUNNY MONEY AND SMACK--CHICAGO... THEN MOVED HERE... SIX, EIGHT YEARS AN' SUDDENLY HE'S A *DOCTOR*...?

...GIMME A BREAK...

KLAK KLAK

JOHN? ARE YOU IN--

JOHN? WHAT IS IT? *TELL* ME!

...STILL LOVE YOU, HONEY... JUST NOT *ATTRACTED* TO YOU ANY-MORE...

WHAT!?

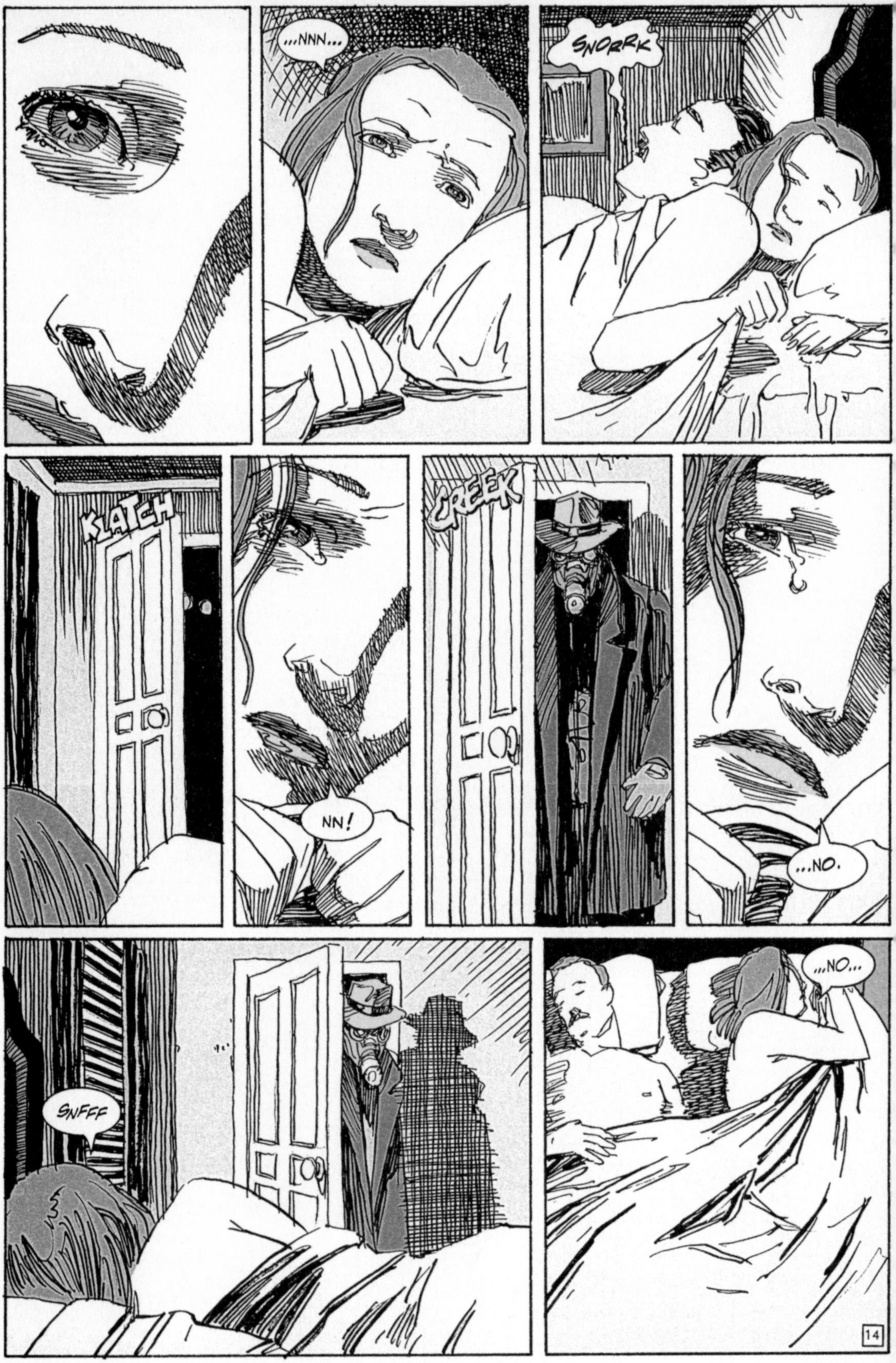
...NNN...
SNORRK
KLATCH
NN!
CREEK
...NO.
SNFFF
...NO...
14

DAMN IT.

YAAWWWN.

HUBERT KLEIN?. THE SANDMAN HAS NEED OF YOUR KNOWLEDGE.

THANK GOODNESS YOU'VE CALLED. DID YOU GET MY MESSAGE?

MESSAGE?

IN THE TIMES. IT WAS LATE BUT I HAVE A FRIEND THERE WHO GOT IT IN, ABOUT NOT DRINKING ALCOHOL?

THE PRESCRIPTION CARDS CONTAIN A STRANGE CHEMICAL BASE COMPOUND-- INCREDIBLY STRONG. I'VE NEVER SEEN ANYTHING LIKE IT. THE ACIDS IN ALCOHOL ARE THE CATALYST. IF YOU'VE TOUCHED ONE OF THOSE CARDS BARE-HANDED, YOU MUST STAY AWAY FROM ANY LIQUOR.

I DON'T... HAVEN'T HANDLED IT UNGLOVED. I NEED YOU TO CHECK A MEDICAL LICENSE FOR ME.

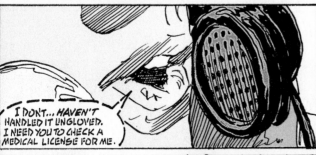

A SUSPECT?

A PRACTITIONER I HAVE REASON TO BELIEVE IS NOT A DOCTOR. HIS NAME IS RAYMOND KESSLER.

YES. CALL ME BACK TOMORROW. I'LL DO MY BEST.

THAT'S ALL YOU CAN DO, MY FRIEND.

15

IT'S ALL **ANY** OF US CAN DO.

SIGHHHH...

RRIING

...MM?

HELLO?

DIAN, THANK **GOD** YOU'RE THERE. I HAVE TO TALK TO SOMEONE, I--

LISTEN, LUCY, I'M NOT REALLY **AWAKE** YET. COULD I CALL YOU BACK--

HE **HURT** ME, DIAN.

WHAT? WHO HURT YOU?

RAY...AND I...WE... HAD SOME...TROUBLE LAST NIGHT. I DON'T KNOW IF I'M ALL RIGHT...

MY GOD, LUCY. WHERE **ARE** YOU?

AT RAY'S, HE... I JUST DIDN'T KNOW WHERE TO GO--

LUCY, I'M COMING **RIGHT** OVER THERE TO GET YOU.

DIAN...COULD YOU... B-BRING ME A DRESS AND SOME STOCKINGS?

OH DEAR GOD. I WILL. NOW GIVE ME THE ADDRESS--

There's always some sort of balance, isn't there?

Just when you're certain that your life is as bad as can be--

DIAN?

--you're shown a glimpse of how much worse things could go.

I'M *HERE*, HONEY! IT'S *OKAY!*

COME IN.

I APPRECIATE THIS, DIAN. AND I'M *SORRY* TO PULL YOU INTO IT. I-I REALLY THOUGHT RAY WAS A DIFFERENT MAN THAN HE IS!

BELIEVE ME, HONEY, I *KNOW* HOW THAT CAN BE.

BUT DON'T THINK A THING OF IT. WE'RE *FAMILY.* AND FAMILY *HELPS* FAMILY.

NOT RAY'S. HIS GODDAMN *SON* IS THE ONE WHO BROUGHT THIS ALL OUT OF HIM.

I GUESS I JUST GOT CAUGHT IN THE *MIDDLE* OF THEIR ANGER.

THAT BOY IS *NOTHING* BUT TROUBLE. DO YOU KNOW THAT LAST NIGHT WHEN I GOT HERE, HE EVEN HAD THE GALL TO *LOCK* THIS DOOR?

THE NERVE. AS IF I WOULD EVER *STEAL* SOMETHING FROM R-R-RAAAAY--

U-HUH-HUH OH, RAY... WHY...?

HERE, COME ON, LUCY. IT'S GOING TO BE ALL RIGHT.

LET'S GET YOU *OUT* OF HERE.

17

369

--THANK YOU, YOU'VE BEEN **SO** KIND, AND AFTER I SAID SUCH CATTY THINGS ABOUT YOUR WESLEY.

I MUST REALLY LOOK THE FOOL.

NO, NOT AT ALL. WESLEY HAS HIS SHORTCOMINGS AS WELL.

NOW TELL ME, WHAT BROUGHT ON THIS HORRIBLE BEHAVIOR OF RAY'S? YOU SAID IT WAS HIS **SON**?

OH, I DON'T KNOW. IT'S REALLY **MY** FAULT. I USED HIS KEY TO GET IN WHEN I SHOULDN'T HAVE, AND THEN, RAY WAS...**AMOROUS,** AND I TOLD HIM "NO."

I--I SHOULD HAVE JUST--

WELL, RAY **ALWAYS** GETS WHAT HE WANTS IN THE END--

YOU MEAN HE **RAPED** YOU, LUCY?

I--I DON'T KNOW THAT I'D CALL IT **THAT,** BUT...

OH, DIAN, THERE'S NO NEED TO GET RILED UP ON MY BEHALF.

AFTER ALL, I DE- SERVED IT.

IF I **REALLY** LOVED HIM, I'D BE MORE...UNDER- STANDING, **WOULDN'T** I?

LUCY, WHAT RAY DID WAS **WRONG.** I THINK YOU SHOULD--

I WILL, DIAN, **TOMORROW** I'LL APOLOGIZE.

APOLO--?! LUCY!

BUT FOR RIGHT NOW WOULD YOU MIND IF I HAD A **NAP?**

I STILL NEED TO RETURN THAT HOUSE KEY. I'M BUSHED.

DO YOU KNOW THAT LAST NIGHT I EVEN DREAMT THAT A MAN IN A **GAS MASK** CAME INTO OUR ROOM?

HAVE YOU EVER **HEARD** OF SUCH A THING?

A GAS MASK?

YEAH. CRAZY, HUH?

YOU REST AS LONG AS YOU LIKE, LUCY. I'LL WAKE YOU LATER.

Much later.

18

370

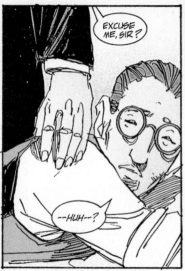

EXCUSE ME, SIR?

--HUH--?

IT'S PAST FIVE, SIR, I THOUGHT I SHOULD WAKE YOU.

PAST FIVE? GOOD HEAVENS, I'VE SLEPT ALL--

HUMPHRIES, COULD YOU FRY ME AN OMELET? I'M GOING TO MAKE A FEW CALLS, SHOWER, AND I'LL BE RIGHT DOWN.

CERTAINLY, SIR.

RWG RWG

THERE YOU ARE.

CORONER'S OFFICE, THIS IS HUBERT SPEAKING.

HUBERT KLEIN, THIS IS THE SANDMAN.

HAVE YOU DISCOVERED THE ANSWER TO MY QUERY?

THE LICENSE LOOKS SUSPICIOUS. I DID SOME DIGGING, THROUGH MY MEDICAL ASSOCIATES, ON THIS "DR." KESSLER. QUITE A QUACK, APPARENTLY.

DOES LITTLE MORE THAN DOLE OUT NERVE PILLS TO SOCIETY MATRONS. ONLY MAKES HOUSE CALLS. VERY SHADY.

TELL WHAT YOU HAVE LEARNED TO THE PROPER AUTHORITIES.

CONVINCE THEM TO SEARCH KESSLER'S OFFICES FOR RROOF AND THEN PROCEED TO HIS HOUSE.

I WILL ENSURE DR. DEATH WRITES NO MORE PRESCRIPTIONS.

19

Lucy's story did nothing to bring any new light to my confusion over Wesley—

HM...

—But it did plenty to convince me that there's something more to Ray's behavior than a troublesome son.

Heaven knows I give daddy no end of confusion—

—But he would never go so far as to attack anyone.

THERE YOU ARE.

There has to be some greater reason.

KI-CHAK

Extreme behavior has to have equally strong motivations behind it.

20

GOODNIGHT.

GOOD NIGHT? YOU TOLD ME WE WERE GOING *OUT* TONIGHT, RAY.

MAYBE WE *WILL.* I'LL GIVE YOU A CALL LATER IF MY EVENING OPENS UP.

YOUR EVENING MIGHT, BUT *I* SURE WON'T. GOOD *NIGHT*, MR. KESSLER.

THAT'S *DOCTOR* KESSLER, ARLENE.

WHATEVER YOU SAY... *DOCTOR.*

"MISTER."

BITCH.

People do what they're driven to do...

...what they must do.

Maybe that's what Wesley was trying to say...

WHAT--?

21

ROMAN? IS DAT YOU? MOMMA VUNTS--

ROMAN? NO? IS *RAYMOND*? HONEY, PLEASE GIFF MOMMA HER SHOT... *NOW*--

--PLEASE, HONEY, YOU *FORGOT* AGAIN--

MA'AM? I...I'M SORRY TO INTRUDE. I --

VUNT TO FEEL BETTER...NOT SO COLD UND STIFF--BITTE, MEIN KINDER, RAYMOND FORGOT... RAYMOND--

RAYMOND DID THIS TO YOU? HIS OWN *MOTHER*?

YOU'RE ... RAYMOND'S MOTHER?

WHO...? WHO IS DER? VAT DO YOU VUNT? PLEASE--I AM ONLY OLD WOMAN...

MA'AM, LISTEN TO ME. I'M SORRY, BUT I *CAN'T* GIVE YOU THAT SHOT. I *WILL* GO GET SOME HELP FOR YOU THOUGH. I--I *PROMISE.*

But in the greater balance of things, no matter how strong the motivation--

--there are some behaviors that simply CAN'T be justified.

OH!

WHAT IN THE FUCK WERE *YOU* DOING UP THERE?! WHAT ARE YOU DOING IN MY *HOUSE*?

I COULD ASK *YOU* THE SAME QUESTIONS. THAT WOMAN UPSTAIRS IS--IS-- IT'S LIKE A LIVING *DEATH*!

IT'S WORSE THAN DEATH, SWEETHEART. TO BE OLD AND IN PAIN...WEAK LIKE A BABY.

THAT'S NO WAY TO LIVE!

WHY, I'D PUT 'EM *ALL* DOWN IF I COULD.

AND YET YOUR MOTHER LINGERS IN DELIRIUM...

<gasp>

CLIK

KILL MY OWN MOTHER...?

YOU STUPID GODDAMN BITCH!

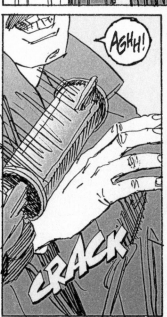

AGHH!

CRACK

YOUR CLINIC OF MURDER HAS BEEN *CLOSED*, DR. DEATH.

LICENSE *REVOKED*.

NO! I WAS DOING THEM A FAVOR! THEIR LIVES WERE MISERABLE--*POINTLESS*, THEY JUST SADDLED ME-- US WITH DEAD WEIGHT. I--

YOU ARE *SICK*, RAYMOND KESSLER--

--I PRESCRIBE AN UNHOLY DOSAGE OF NIGHTMARES.

ERK--

FOOOOSH!

23

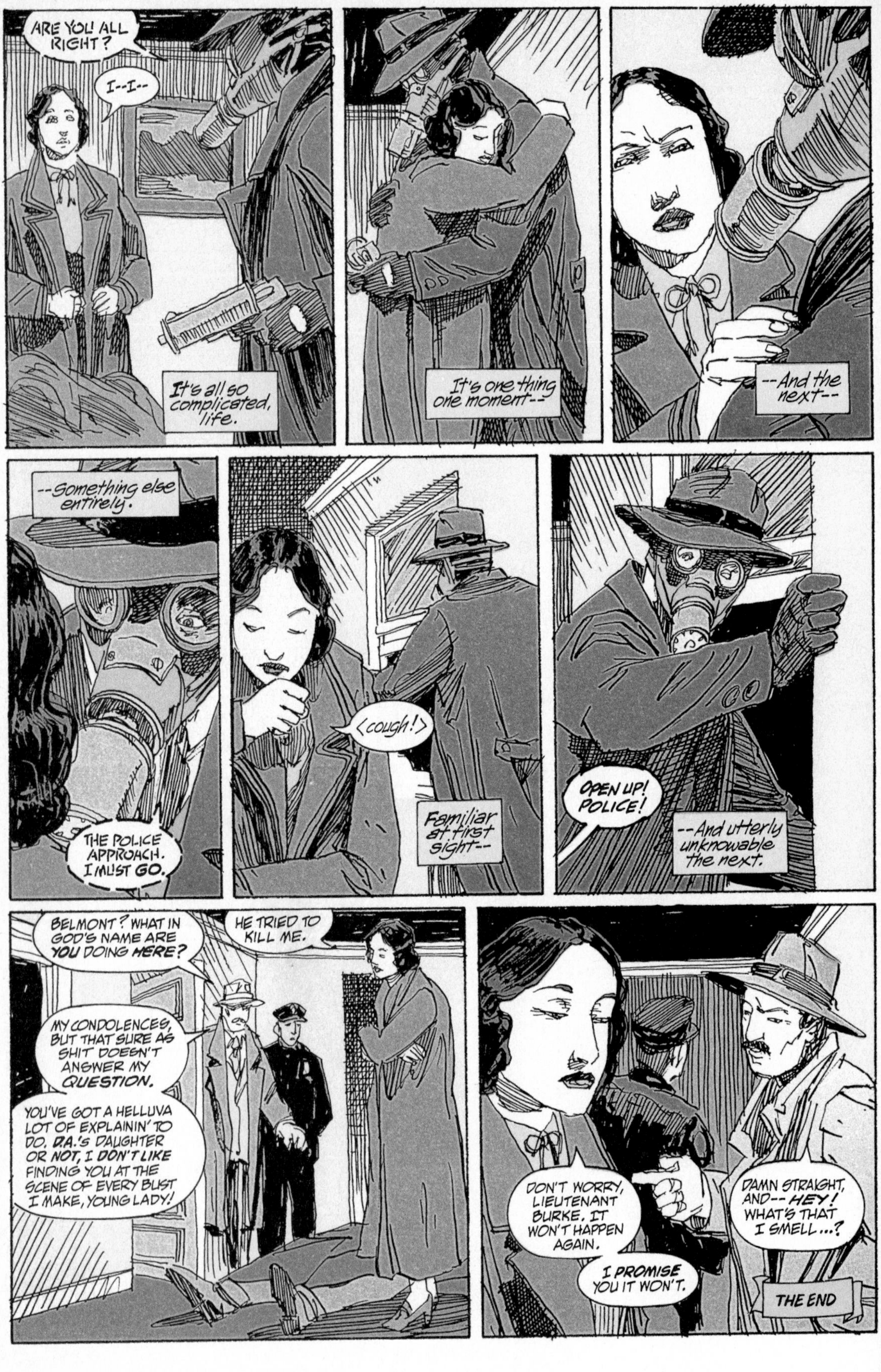
ARE YOU ALL RIGHT?
I--I--
It's all so complicated, life.
It's one thing one moment--
--And the next--
--Something else entirely.
THE POLICE APPROACH. I MUST GO.
<cough!>
Familiar at first sight--
OPEN UP! POLICE!
--And utterly unknowable the next.
BELMONT? WHAT IN GOD'S NAME ARE YOU DOING HERE?
HE TRIED TO KILL ME.
MY CONDOLENCES, BUT THAT SURE AS SHIT DOESN'T ANSWER MY QUESTION.
YOU'VE GOT A HELLUVA LOT OF EXPLAININ' TO DO. D.A.'s DAUGHTER OR NOT, I DON'T LIKE FINDING YOU AT THE SCENE OF EVERY BUST I MAKE, YOUNG LADY!
DON'T WORRY, LIEUTENANT BURKE. IT WON'T HAPPEN AGAIN.
I PROMISE YOU IT WON'T.
DAMN STRAIGHT, AND-- HEY! WHAT'S THAT I SMELL...?
THE END

BEHIND THE GAS MASK

*The original series proposal for SANDMAN MYSTERY THEATRE by **Matt Wagner**, with character designs and concept art by **Guy Davis**.*

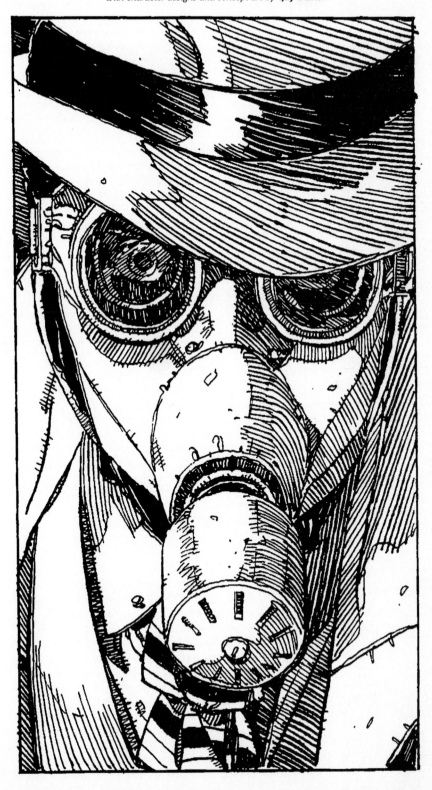

SANDMAN MYSTERY THEATRE

SANDMAN MYSTERY THEATRE would be a monthly new-format series designed to capitalize on the popularity of the current SANDMAN title utilizing the character of the Golden Age Sandman. I refer here to the earliest version of the Wesley Dodds character, and not the more superheroic one that Kirby later introduced. In the current title, Neil has already addressed the '70s Kirby incarnation of the Sandman and, in the first issue, briefly referred to Wesley Dodds himself. It seems Morpheus' years of magical imprisonment were a catalyst to Wes' donning of a gas mask and taking on the persona of the Sandman.

THE SERIES

So, here is a great opportunity to breathe new life into yet another character DC already owns.

The original Golden Age adventures of the Sandman are from an era of comics more closely related to pulp magazines than to superheroes. The stories are really quite strange—dark, crime-laden mysteries with a dreamy, surreal pacing that often turns absolutely nightmarish. Given a more serious fleshing out, this certainly stands to attract readers of the current title as well as drawing the attention of the superhero fans. Crime-noir is *extremely* popular these days, and a good comparison for how I intend to approach this series would be to the works of such writers as Jim Thompson, Raymond Chandler, James Ellroy or Andrew Vachss. Or even—what would've made a great comic book if it hadn't crashed so quickly—the first season of *Twin Peaks*.

THE STORIES

These tales would be grouped into four-chapter segments. Each story would usually but not always bear the name of the pulpy mystery villain that the Sandman would currently be trying to thwart. Thus, the first story is called "The Tarantula," the second "The Face," "The Mist," "The Phantom of the Fair," etc.

The setting is New York of the late '30s. The class system is one of extremes as the nation tries to recover from nearly a decade of economic depression. Thus, most of our characters will be either mobsters or socialites. Prohibition had been repealed nearly four years ago and now the populace seems only concerned with drowning itself in a good time and ignoring the threat of impending war in the air. The crimes depicted will be dark, twisted—the product of a time of moral decay. I plan on incorporating some real characters of the era as well as various authentic locales. Babe Ruth, E.B. White, Dorothy Parker and Orson Welles will all make appearances in the course of the series.

THE CHARACTERS

WESLEY DODDS

A wealthy inheritor of oil interests, Wes is one of the decidedly nouveau riche. As a result, he has never felt completely comfortable in the many high-society functions he is often obligated to attend. Wes is best described as a disaffected aesthete—a sensitive soul who has never had the chance to hide himself from the horrors of the world. We often see him jotting short bits of poetry in a small notebook. These, of course, eventually evolve into the cryptic messages he uses later as the Sandman. Plagued by nightmares from a young age, Wes has spent most of his youth abroad, dragged along in the wake of his father's business pursuits. Thus, he is both amazed and appalled by American life since returning to New York after his father's death in 1935. Wes is currently around 30 and, although he really has no desire to be any part of his father's business, he nonetheless has a strong sense of duty and responsibility. Thus, he fells obligated to assume his inherited place as president of the company in New York. Unfortunately, Wesley's nightmares have become progressively worse since his return to the States. Deeply troubled by the rampant poverty, apathy and cruelty he sees around him, he is finally haunted into a state of action.

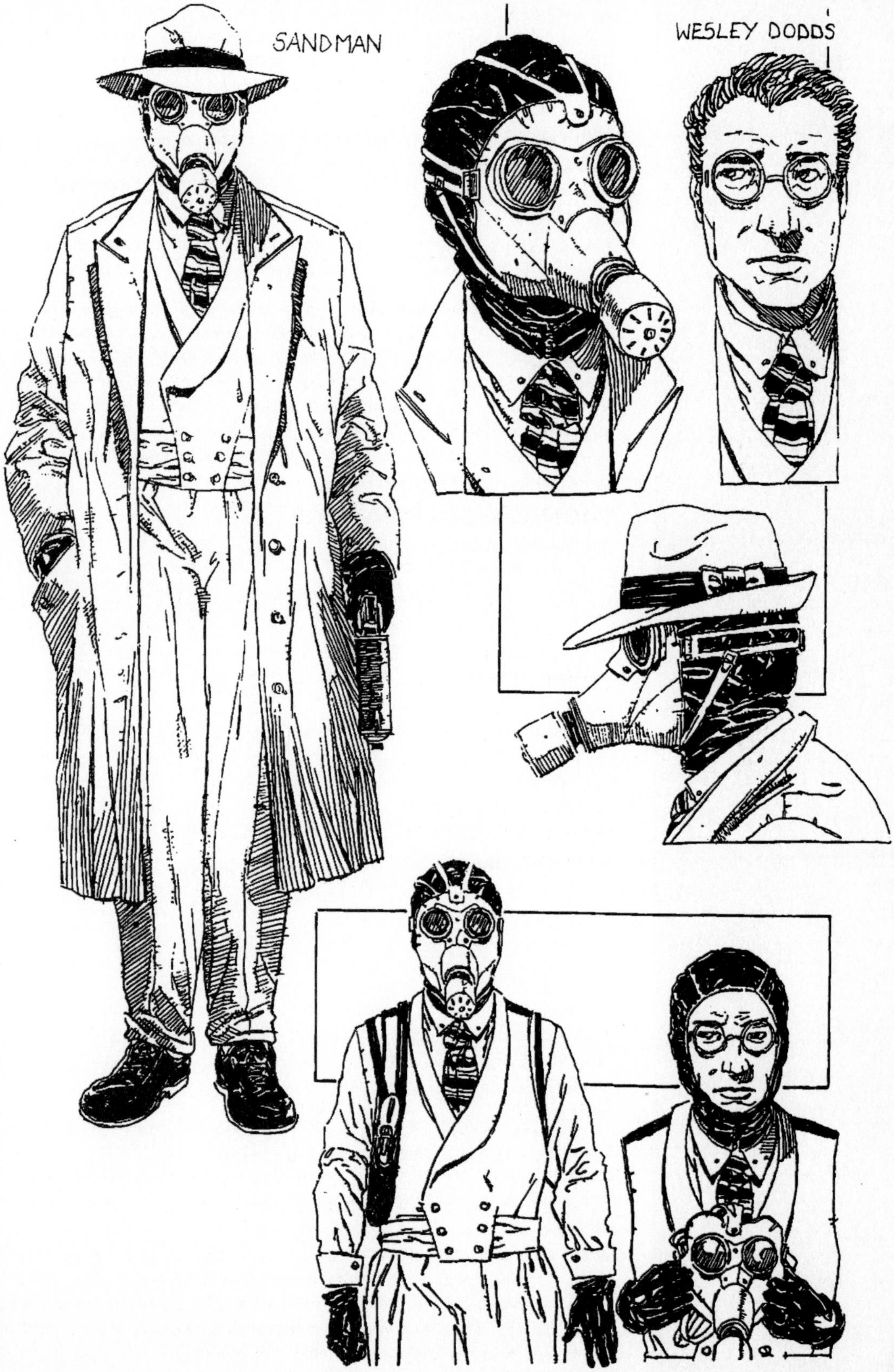
SANDMAN
WESLEY DODDS

DIAN BELMONT

Daughter of District Attorney Lawrence Belmont. A Vassar girl, Dian is quite headstrong and capable but at this point rather undirected. It has been over two years since she graduated and Dian has basically been killing time ever since. More than once she's caused her father public embarrassment with the kind of antics brought on by idle anxiety. Dian and her crowd of debutante good-timers often end their evenings at sunrise in one of the many Harlem jazz clubs her father so frowns upon. If Dian had any interest in marriage, he wouldn't worry very much about her lack of motivation, but Dian only sees men as playthings—subject to her whims and abject to her will.

It is at a party held by Mayor LaGuardia to raise money for the Metropolitan Library that Dian first meets Wesley Dodds—a distracted but sensitively handsome man who seems to take little notice of Dian and her seemingly invincible feminine charm.

LAWRENCE BELMONT

Dian's father. A man past his prime and past his effectiveness as a public servant. Larry Belmont started his career in law as a crusading public defender, but has since become too embroiled in the twisted economic system of the city—one hand stroking the other stabbing the other. Larry too often looks the other way when one of his high-society friends stands to benefit from any "minor" illegalities. Larry is a stodgy though benevolent father, even if he doesn't quite understand his daughter's strange attraction to that rather funny Wesley Dodds.

THOMAS STOCKTON-JONES

A retired judge and an old friend of Wesley's father, Tom has been one of Wes' only close acquaintances since he returned to New York. Tom is a firebrand even at 67. Brilliant and gruff, Tom is always complaining about the state of the criminal justice system in Manhattan and the political status of the world at large.

Tom believes in reform and the power of individual action. He now regrets his decision to retire as being premature, and as a result he feels hamstrung in his ability to affect any change for the city he both loves and abhors.

His opinion is mixed about Wesley. Tom has always felt deep disappointment over the fact that his oldest friend, Wesley's father, ended up following such a sadly money-driven lifestyle. And, although he quite enjoys Wesley's keen mind and verbal wit, it seems the son has inherited the lifestyle and social inactions of the father. Tom considers Wesley bright and interesting, but fragile as far as manhood is concerned.

THE SANDMAN

In fact, Wesley is tougher and more focused than anyone realizes. Although slight of build, he is wiry and strong, maintaining a daily regimen of the very unpopular practice of calisthenics (it used to be thought that too much exercise would give you "athlete's heart"). Additionally, spending most of his youth in the Orient has left Wesley with quite some skill in jiu-jitsu, a fighting style that left the Western world mystified around this time.

Another of his many Eastern influences is the practice of origami. We will often see Wesley at parties and such, just completing yet another tiny folding. This habit, of course, will translate into the folded poem-cards he leaves for the police.

Wesley is something of an academic prodigy as well. Even while depriving him of the security of a stable home life, Wesley's father always saw to it that his son had the best tutors his newfound fortune could buy. Wesley holds a master's degree in both business and political science as well as a bachelor's in literature with a minor in chemistry.

Wesley's mother had died when he was very young, and thus he remembers very little of her. Occasionally her sees a feminine figure, enshrouded in white, standing at the edge of his dreams, but she is always overshadowed by the presence of a man in black. This is, of course, Morpheus, whose bone-encrusted helmet is an image Wesley firmly retains deep in his subconscious.

THE PHANTOM OF THE WORLDS FAIR

DIAN BELMONT

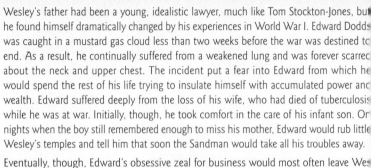

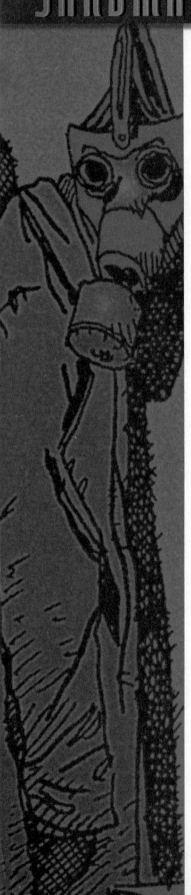

Wesley's father had been a young, idealistic lawyer, much like Tom Stockton-Jones, but he found himself dramatically changed by his experiences in World War I. Edward Dodds was caught in a mustard gas cloud less than two weeks before the war was destined to end. As a result, he continually suffered from a weakened lung and was forever scarred about the neck and upper chest. The incident put a fear into Edward from which he would spend the rest of his life trying to insulate himself with accumulated power and wealth. Edward suffered deeply from the loss of his wife, who had died of tuberculosis while he was at war. Initially, though, he took comfort in the care of his infant son. On nights when the boy still remembered enough to miss his mother, Edward would rub little Wesley's temples and tell him that soon the Sandman would take all his troubles away.

Eventually, though, Edward's obsessive zeal for business would most often leave Wes alone and in the care of household servants. Soon Wesley came to feel that he had lost both his parents even long before his father finally passed away as well.

Thus, we have several good reasons for Wesley's various M.O.s as a vigilante.

❖

I don't want there to be an "origin" issue, per se, in this series. Wesley is already operating as the Sandman when we first meet him via Dian, and (even though we, the readers, will surely know) his secret identity will not actually be stated as such until Dian herself accidentally discovers it, somewhere around issue #6 or #7. All the background info you have just read will be revealed in bits, so that the readers will gradually get to know the characters through the course of the series. This will be the unifying link between a progression of otherwise self-contained storylines.

Dian and Wesley will eventually develop a Lamont Cranston/Margo Lane, John Steed/ Emma Peel, Clark Kent/Lois Lane relationship—the twist on this cliché being that *Dian* will be the common-sensical brains of the duo. Far more socially powerful and efficient than her dreamer partner, Dian will often play a vital role in solving the central mystery of each adventure. Rather than being just a sounding board for the Sandman's brilliant deducing, Dian will be Wesley's anchor to reality.

But despite her pragmatic sense of things, Dian will continually find herself swept along into danger and intrigue time and time again at the side of the most mysteriously compelling man she has ever met.

That's the immediate core group of characters, but other semi-regulars will pop up as the series progresses.

THE TEAM

I'm willing to definitely commit to at least one year of this series; probably two, and possibly more.

As far as the artistic teams go, I would like to nail down three different artists to each do a four-issue story over the course of the first year. Hopefully they will also be able to commit to a second tour of duty during year two. This regular rotation would help strengthen reader identification and serve to make the series a special event all its own.

Guy Davis is slated to begin the run, and I'm *sure* his stuff is going to go over big. His initial developmental work for the characters is astounding, as is the promo piece he did for the recent distributors' catalog of upcoming DC projects for '93. Additionally, check out Guy's own book, *Baker Street* from Calibre Press, for further examples of his lovely work.

THE FIRST STORYLINE:

"THE TARANTULA"

The first story will introduce all of our major characters along with the first meeting of Wes and Dian. The mystery involves a series of kidnappings performed by an unknown abductor calling himself the Tarantula. The first victim is one of Dian's party friends, so she becomes involved in the mystery from the very beginning. At this point Wesley

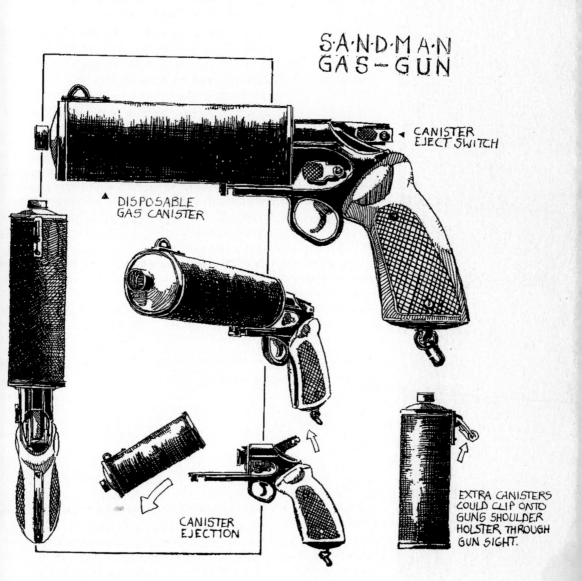

S·A·N·D·M·A·N GAS–GUN

CANISTER EJECT SWITCH

DISPOSABLE GAS CANISTER

CANISTER EJECTION

EXTRA CANISTERS COULD CLIP ONTO GUNS SHOULDER HOLSTER THROUGH GUN SIGHT.

has had three previous adventures as the Sandman, but as yet only the police are aware of his presence (and only slightly, at that). As the Sandman, Wes is currently investigating a racketeer named Albert Goldman when the kidnappings first begin.

Even before any response to the initial ransom demands can be delivered, the Tarantula unexpectedly strikes again! Suddenly the stakes are raised, as two hostages now give the abductor the luxury of killing one of his victims in order to put pressure on the survivor's family. This trend continues, with some killings as well as some releases, and with the Sandman and Dian both going through several adventurous scrapes along the way. Eventually Albert Goldman's daughter is kidnapped as well, and Wesley's dual investigations coalesce.

In the end, the Goldman family's private lives are revealed to be the source of both crimes. For years, Albert has been closer to his daughter, Celia, than his wife, Miriam. Both women are bitter and conniving, and their distaste for each other is a direct result of Celia's growing beauty alongside Miriam's fading glory. Celia fairly controls her father. In fact, several years ago Celia even succeeded in seducing Albert, and has held that fact over his head ever since. Thus, Albert has been laundering a lot of money into various hidden ventures that only Celia would know about and that only Celia would inherit.

Miriam Goldman knew of the incest in her household by way of her and Albert's only son, Bailey. Bailey is the shame of his father after losing a fortune in illegal gambling. While trying to cover the trail of his taxable losses, Bailey was nailed by the IRS for fraud. He narrowly escaped a jail sentence, but will almost certainly never own much of anything for the rest of his life. Albert is slowly paying off his son's many debts, but will barely speak to him even though Bailey, without a penny to his name, has been forced to live at home again.

Thus, Bailey was witness to what took place in Celia's bedroom that Sunday afternoon when Mother was out. Always a momma's boy, he reported what he saw to his mother at once. Miriam took the news of this betrayal with a calm, methodical hatred. She began to observe her husband's business dealings more minutely, searching for a way to strike back where she knew the wound would hurt the most. When she was finally sure of his financial jugglings on Celia's behalf, Miriam easily convinced Bailey to kidnap Albert's regular mistress in order to obtain information from her. This turns out to be Dian's friend Catherine Van Der Meer—the first victim. Abduction and torture are tasks the socially gelded Bailey readily takes to, and Miriam soon notices how her son seems suddenly more alive after so many months of the ennui that was surely in response to all the emotional abuse Albert had heaped upon the boy. The evil twosome soon decide to continue their kidnapping motif in order to throw off the scent from their true motives—and thus the Tarantula is born.

Eventually, though, Celia drags a confession about the truth of their actions out of her brother one evening, whereupon she secures his loyalty as she best seems to know how: she seduces him as well.

Upon discovering this, Miriam's hatred for her daughter comes to a head, and she orders Bailey to take Celia away and kill her.

The Sandman manages to save Celia even though the rest of the family is killed off in the climax. The story concludes with Dian still unaware of Wesley's secret, but now stirred and even obsessed to know more of the mystery man who had saved Catherine's life and whose folded calling card identifies him only as the Sandman.

Well, that's about it for now. The actual plot for the first issue should follow in a couple of days. Hope to hear from you soon.

—**Matt Wagner**
1992